OXFORD MEDICAL PUBLICATIONS

Commission of the European Communities
Health Services Research Series
No. 8

This book is one of a series concerned with health services research. It is an outcome of coordinated work by COMAC-HSR (Comité d'Action concertée) which reports to the CGC Medical and Health Research (Comité de Gestion et de Coordination) of the Commission of the European Communities, Directorate-General Science, Research and Development (DG XII).

The research is carried out by the 'concerted action' method. The Commission of the European Communities pays the costs of coordination and of bringing together researchers from various countries, while the actual research is paid for and executed by each country. The aim is to accelerate joint research activities by Member States in selected fields, such as health services research.

EQUITY IN THE FINANCE AND DELIVERY OF HEALTH CARE

An International Perspective

Edited by

EDDY VAN DOORSLAER
Lecturer in Health Economics
Department of Health Policy and Management
Erasmus University
Rotterdam

ADAM WAGSTAFF
Lecturer in Economics
School of Social Sciences
University of Sussex

and

FRANS RUTTEN
Professor of Health Economics
and Medical Technology Assessment
Department of Health Policy and Management
Erasmus University
Rotterdam

Oxford   New York   Tokyo
OXFORD UNIVERSITY PRESS
1993

Oxford University Press, Walton Street, Oxford OX2 6DP
Oxford New York Toronto
Delhi Bombay Calcutta Madras Karachi
Kuala Lumpur Singapore Hong Kong Tokyo
Nairobi Dar es Salaam Cape Town
Melbourne Auckland Madrid
and associated companies in
Berlin Ibadan

Oxford is a trade mark of Oxford University Press

Published in the United States
by Oxford University Press Inc., New York

© ECSC-EEC-EAEC Brussels-Luxembourg, 1993

Publication No. EUR 14655 EN of the
Commission of the European Communities,
Dissemination of Scientific and Technical Knowledge Unit,
Directorate-General Telecommunications, Information
Industries and Innovation,
Luxembourg

A catalogue record for this book is available from the British Library

Library of Congress Cataloging in Publication Data
Equity in the finance and delivery of health care: an international
perspective / edited by Eddy van Doorslaer, Adam Wagstaff, and Frans
Rutten.
(Oxford medical publications)
Includes bibliographical references and index.
1. Medical economics.   I. Doorslaer, Eddy K. A. van.
II. Wagstaff, Adam.   III. Rutten, F. F. H.   IV. Series.
[DNLM: 1. Delivery of Health Care–Europe.   2. Delivery of Health
Care–United States.   3. Financing, Organized. W 84 GA1 E6]
RA410.E64 1993   338.4'33621–dc20   92–19064
ISBN 0–19–262291–9
Typeset by Graphicraft Typesetters Ltd, Hong Kong
Printed in Great Britain

This volume is dedicated to the late Peter Elleman-Jensen who participated in the project until his sudden death on 9 June, 1990.

Foreword

Alan Maynard, Centre for Health Economics,
University of York, York, UK.

This volume presents the results of research which has been facilitated by funding from the European Community and it represents a significant contribution to knowledge about equity in the finance and delivery of health care in 10 countries. It compares the experiences of nine European countries and the US using a consistent methodology so as to draw out comparable results from 10 very different health care systems.

Such an approach facilitates not only a greater understanding of the performance of the health care systems of individual countries but also the identification of the lessons that can be learnt from international comparisons. It is surprising how reluctant researchers and policy-makers have been to learn from the successes and failures of foreign health care systems. Only in the last few years has there been a recognition that many health and health care problems are similar across many countries and their solution can be usefully informed by the abandonment both of isolation and belief that individual country problems are unique.

The development of systematic analyses of the attributes and performance of health care systems has been slow. The initial attempts to develop such work were descriptive (e.g., Maynard 1975; Maxwell 1981; McLachlan and Maynard 1982) and had a short 'shelf life' due to the continuous evolution of finance and delivery systems. Furthermore, ensuring comparability of definitions (a general practitioner in England and Italy may have very different functions), scope (spa treatment in Germany is a routine part of health care but it is not available in the UK–NHS), and measurement ('under-the-counter' payments in some countries are significant but unreported elements of health care expenditure) is not easy and, if not achieved efficiently can seriously bias the results of the comparative analysis of different systems.

The recognition of these problems in the more recent work of Poullier and Hurst at the OECD (e.g., OECD 1987) has produced more robust and comparable data whose analysis has provided useful insights into the characteristics of different health care systems.

The comparative approach to the analysis of the problems of health care systems and the subsequent advocacy of particular policy changes inevitably reflects the felt necessity of the time. During the 1980s, the focus of health care reform throughout the world was on the supply side: producing additional health gains from existing budgets. This was the product of the dominant ideology of the time, epitomized in the US by Reaganism and in the UK by Thatcherism, and the increasing recognition that health care systems, controlled for decades by the medical profession, were using resources inefficiently. It is often difficult to demonstrate inefficiencies in medical practice because of the paucity of data about inputs, processes of care, and outcomes. However, a consensus has emerged, generated by much assertion and some evidence, from both medical practitioners (e.g., Cochrane 1972, and Black 1986) and economists (e.g., Fuchs 1984), that a considerable portion, perhaps 20 per cent of the total, of health care expenditure has little impact on the health of patients.

This inefficiency is not surprising given the evidence which is available, both within and between countries, about existing variations in medical practice. For instance, the variation in the treatment of particular cancer conditions by radiotherapists in the UK is considerable (Priestman *et al.* 1989). Similar variation can be seen across countries also (e.g., Maher 1990) and reflects differences in supply, demand, morbidity, and clinical practice (Anderson and Mooney 1990). Perhaps the most significant of these explanatory factors is clinical practice. It seems there are few agreed 'best practices' and practitioners are 'experimenting on the job' to explore, often quite unsystematically and with inadequate controls and statistical power, the impact of different approaches to patient care.

The evolving consensus, across all health care systems, that the supply of care is inefficient provided a fertile ground for the dissemination of reform proposals, long advocated in the US and largely ignored there (Enthoven 1979), based on the assertion that competition and the separation of purchaser-provider roles would improve the efficiency of resource allocation. The impact of the international comparative approach adopted by Enthoven (1985) on the UK health care system was significant and similar ideas have influenced policy changes in countries such as the Netherlands and New Zealand.

Policy analysts and reformers in the US are increasingly concerned by the inadequacies of a health care system which leaves 37 million citizens uninsured for hospital care. The response of some of these people is to use international comparisons to advocate change based on the Canadian, the German, or some other model. The interest of policy-makers in the US in the experience of other countries has grown significantly (e.g., see Iglehart 1991, whose content covers the UK, Japan, the USSR, Canada, Germany, Australia, and Spain).

There can be little doubt that the comparative analysis of health care systems is potentially very useful. For instance, the policy instrument used to cap costs in the early 1980s in the US, the diagnostic related groups (DRG) system of prospective reimbursement for Medicare hospital patients, is now widely used in European health care systems. The problems it created in the US has produced a literature and lessons which can be learnt by policy-makers elsewhere in the world.

For instance, DRGs led to initial and significant reduction in the length of stay of patients in hospitals and the assertion that patient outcomes were adverse: the quicker-sicker syndrome! This assertion was shown to be inaccurate by a Rand Study (Kahn *et al.* 1990) whose methods, in terms of trial design and instrumentation as well as results (e.g., they showed that DRG systems may require more nursing inputs if outcome quality is to be maintained), can be adapted to evaluate European DRG systems.

Perhaps the most important area for future international comparison and collaboration is the measurement of outcomes. The 'guesstimation' of crude outcome measures, which combine survival duration with weights reflecting the quality of life into integrated measures, such as quality adjusted life years (QALYs), raises major methodological and policy issues which will be best explored by combining and contrasting international experience. Instruments, such as the quality of well-being scale (e.g., Kaplan *et al.* 1976), the SF36 of John Ware in the US (Wu *et al.* 1991), and that of the EuroQol group in Europe (EuroQol Group 1990) need to be validated and compared rather than developed in a compartmentalized way which ignores the lessons to be learnt from the triumphs and failures of foreign groups involved in developing measures of health status.

It is significant that the increasing volume of interest and practice in international comparison and collaboration has focused on the supply side. This volume will reduce this imbalance because it focuses on the demand side, in particular the distribution of financial burdens and morbidity between different socio-economic groups across 10 countries.

The public–private mix of finance, and taxes, social insurance contributions, private medical insurance contributions, and out-of-pocket payments, differs between the 10 nations examined here, and in 8 over 50 per cent of the cost of care is publicly financed. Although the finances of tax-based health care system (e.g., Denmark and the UK) are progressive in their incidence, social and private-based insurance systems are typically regressive (e.g., the Netherlands, France, and the US).

Morbidity is shown to be unequally distributed in all countries, and concentrated on the poor. With the exception of the US, a general conclusion is that high health care spenders tend to have a relatively low degree of inequality in morbidity. The issue of whether patients get 'equal treatment for equal need' is resolved by careful definition and measurement and the general conclusion is that the amount of health care received by people in equal need does appear to depend on their income. Thus, income does appear to determine access to and use of care, although whether, on balance, such inequity favours the rich or poor is unclear. Inevitably, as the authors emphasize, such conclusions have to be treated with care. The morbidity measures are limited and more research is needed to explore these issues.

As with all innovative research the results in this volume reflect the quality of the data and the care with which it is manipulated. The latter is high quality with alternative definitions and measurements of inequality being deployed carefully and productively. The former is limited in volume and quality but sufficient to provide significant new knowledge when analysed, as it is here, with care. This research sets a challenging benchmark for future work which will, no doubt, improve measurement techniques and, it is hoped, have access to better outcome data.

The group reporting their national experiences in this volume have made significant progress with very limited funds. The fourth Medical and Health Research (MHR) programme of the European Commission was funded parsimoniously and its funds allocated only to finance 'concerted actions', that is, the gathering together of researchers to agree common protocols for their activity. The managers of this concerted action, Rutten, Van Doorslaer, and Wagstaff, not only produced a common protocol, they also controlled its deployment to produce 10 similar country reports. This required a degree of dedication and single-mindedness which is truly admirable if somewhat Stalinist, like all good management!

The next MHR research programme of the European Commission (called Biomed I) will fund both concerned actions and substantive research. The contents of this volume demonstrate admirably that given to efficient research teams, such research funding can produce both significant new knowledge of direct relevance to the reform of health care systems world-wide and also collaborative, mutually informative work between Europeans and foreigners living outside a united Europe.

Contents

Part III. Reflections on equity in health care

Contributors

JUDY L. BAKER
United States

Judy L. Baker is a consultant in the Human Resources Technical Division of the Latin America Region at the World Bank, currently working on the targeting of social sector programmes. Previously, she has worked for the Welfare and Human Resources Division, concentrating on equity in the delivery and finance of health care services, and the 1991 *World Development Report*. She received her MA in Economic Geography from Boston University and her BA from the University of Michigan.

SAMUEL CALONGE
Spain

Samuel Calonge is a Lecturer in Applied Economics in the Department of Econometrics, Statistics, and Spanish Economy. He obtained an undergraduate degree in Econometrics at the University of La Laguna (Spain), and his Ph.D. at the University of Barcelona. Current research interests are focused on microeconometric models.

TERKEL CHRISTIANSEN
Denmark

Terkel Christiansen is Associate Professor of microeconomics at the University of Odense. He was attached to the Department of Economics in 1971; he is also a Senior Research Fellow at the Centre for Health and Social Policy. His main area of research is health economics. He is also a member of an advisory committee to the National Board of Health.

A.J. CULYER
United Kingdom

A.J. Culyer is a Professor of Economics at the University of York. He is Co-Editor of the *Journal of Health Economics* and is on the editorial boards of several other economic journals; a member of the council of the Royal Economic Society and a member of the Central Research and Development Committee for the National Health Service. He is currently working together with Adam Wagstaff on a series of papers concerning distributive justice in health and health care.

KAREN DAVIS
United States

Karen Davis Ph.D. is Chairperson of the Department of Health Policy and Management in the School of Hygiene and Public Health and has a Joint Appointment as Professor of Economics at The Johns Hopkins University. Dr Davis is Director of the Commonwealth Fund Commission on Elderly People Living Alone. She is a member of the Physician Payment Review Commission, the Institute of Medicine, and the National Academy of Sciences. She also sits on several boards and committees concerned with health policy issues. Dr Davis is the author of numerous books and articles on health economics and policy analysis including *Health care cost containment*; *Medicare policy: New directions for health and long-term care*; *Health and the war on poverty: A ten year appraisal*; *National health insurance: Benefits, costs and consequences*.

EDDY VAN DOORSLAER
The Netherlands

Eddy Van Doorslaer is a Lecturer in Health Economics in the Department of Health Policy and Management of the Erasmus University in Rotterdam. He is also a Senior Research Fellow at the Institute for Medical Technology Assessment of the same University. He obtained an undergraduate degree in Econometrics at the University of Antwerp, an M.Sc. in Health Economics at the University of York and his Ph.D. at the University of Maastricht.

JACQUES VAN DER GAAG
United States

After studying econometrics in Rotterdam, Jacques van der Gaag worked at Leyden University where he received his Ph.D. in 1978. He was subsequently invited to teach at the Economics Department of Wisconsin University at Madison and to do research at the Institute for Research on Poverty. He joined the World Bank in 1981. He was head of the Welfare and Human Resource Division, is co-author of the 1990 *World Development Report on Poverty*, and serves on the editorial board of the *World Bank Economic Review*. He has published extensively on issues of human development and poverty. His current position is Chief, Human Resources Division, Latin America and the Caribbean Region.

MICHAEL GERFIN
Switzerland

Michael Gerfin is a research and teaching assistant at the Economics Institute of the University of Bern. His current research focuses on labour supply in the presence of income taxes and hours restrictions, and on the relation between bad health, labour market participation, and low income.

PETER GOTTSCHALK
United States

Peter Gottschalk is Professor of Economics at Boston College and Research Associate at the Institute for Research on Poverty at the University of Wisconsin, Madison. His research has focused on the economics of poverty and inequality. He is currently writing a book (with Sheldon Danziger) on the growing inequality of family income in the US. In another project he is comparing the changes in inequality across seven countries.

RICHARD JANSSEN
The Netherlands

Richard Janssen is Lecturer in Health Economics in the Department of Health Economics of the University of Limburg in Maastricht. Currently, he is also head of this department. His Ph.D. thesis was about the effects of time prices on medical consumption. Current research interests are focused on equity in health care, international comparison of public policies of health care, and development of management instruments in health care organizations.

CLAIRE LACHAUD
France

Claire Lachaud is a Ph.D. student in health economics at the University of Lyon, and affiliated with the National Centre of Scientific Research.

JULIAN LE GRAND
United Kingdom

Julian Le Grand is Professor of Public Policy at, and Director of, the School for Advanced Urban Studies at the University of Bristol. He is also co-director of the Welfare State Programme at the Suntory–Toyota International Centre for Economics and Related Disciplines, London School of Economics. He was previously Lecturer in Economics at the

University of Sussex and at the London School of Economics. He has acted as a consultant to the OECD, the French Government and the World Bank.

ROBERT E. LEU
Switzerland

Robert E. Leu is professor of economics at the University of Bern and one of the directors of the Economics Institute. He is specializing in public finance, public choice, industrial organization and health economics. His major publications are in public finance, labour and health economics. Current research interests are mainly focused on questions of social policy (income distribution and redistribution, poverty) as well as on current health economics problems.

ALAN MAYNARD
United Kingdom

Alan Maynard is Professor of Economics and Director of the Centre for Health Economics at the University of York. He has been a consultant for the World Bank, the World Health Organization, and the European Commission. In addition to his continued work on international comparisons of health care systems, he is also working on the economics of primary care.

BRIAN NOLAN
Ireland

Brian Nolan is a Research Professor in the Economic and Social Research Institute, Dublin. He studied for his Ph.D. at the London School of Economics. He has been working for a number of years in the areas of income distribution, poverty, and health services utilization and financing. He is editor of *The Economic and Social Review*.

OWEN O'DONNELL
United Kingdom

Owen O'Donnell is a Research Fellow in the Centre for Health Economics at the University of York. In addition to his work on equity issues in health care, he is currently engaged in research into the employment and living standards consequences of disability.

PIERELLA PACI
United Kingdom

Pierella Paci is Lecturer in Economics in the Department of Social Sciences at the City University, London. She holds degrees from the

Universities of Rome, York, and Manchester and before taking up her present appointment, was Lecturer in Economics at the University of Sussex. Outside health economics her main research interests are in the field of labour economics, especially trade unions.

JOÃO PEREIRA
Spain

João Pereira is Lecturer in Health Economics at the National School of Public Health, Lisbon. He graduated from Warwick University and took an M.Sc. degree in Health Economics at the University of York, where he is currently also undertaking research. He has acted as a consultant to the World Health Organization and the World Bank.

CARLOS GOUVEIA PINTO
Portugal

Carlos Gouveia Pinto is assistant professor in Public Economics (graduate course in economics) and in Health Economics (master course in social economics and policy) in the Department of Economics of the Technical University of Lisbon. He is also a senior researcher and member of the Scientific Council of the Research Center on the Portuguese Economy of the same University. He obtained an undergraduate degree and his Ph.D. in economics at the Technical University of Lisbon. His current research interests focus on social policy evaluation.

CAROL PROPPER
United Kingdom

Carol Propper is Lecturer in Economics in the Department of Economics and in the School for Advanced Urban Studies, University of Bristol. She is a Research Associate of the Institute for Fiscal Studies, of the Welfare State Programme at the London School of Economics and of the Centre for Health Economics at York. In addition to work arising from the COMAC project, she is currently undertaking research on the impact of the NHS reform.

JOANA REÑÉ
Spain

Joana Reñé obtained a postgraduate Diploma in Health Economics at the University of Barcelona. She is a Research Fellow in SOIKOS SL (Centre for Studies in Health Economics and Health Policy) and Technical Secretary in the Master's Course in Health Economics and Health Care

Management at the University of Barcelona. She also teaches various courses in health economics.

LISE ROCHAIX
France

Lise Rochaix is a researcher in health economics at the CNRS (Centre National de la Recherche Scientific) in France, currently on secondment as health economics adviser at the forecasting division of the Treasury in Paris. She obtained her Ph.D. at the University of York, where she is now visiting Research Fellow at the Centre for Health Economics, and member of the editorial board of *Health Economics*. Research interests focus on supply side analysis and international comparison of health care systems.

MARISOL RODRÍGUEZ
Spain

Marisol Rodríguez is Associate Professor in Economics at the University of Barcelona. She is also the Director of the Master's Course in Health Economics and Health Care Management of the same University. She obtained an M.Sc. in Economics at the London School of Economics and a Diploma in Health Systems at the Johns Hopkins School of Hygiene and Public Health. Current interests are focused mainly on financing and demand studies and co-operation projects with Latin America.

FRANS RUTTEN
The Netherlands

Frans Rutten is Professor of Health Economics and Medical Technology Assessment in the Department of Health Policy and Management at the Erasmus University in Rotterdam and Director of the Institute for Medical Technology Assessment. He is Senior Editor for *Health Economics of Social Science and Medicine* and serves on the editorial boards of various other scientific journals. He advises the European Commission on medical research and initiated the concerted action research programme on equity reported in this volume.

RICHARD UPWARD
United Kingdom

Richard Upward worked as a Research Assistant at the School for Advanced Urban Studies, University of Bristol. He obtained an undergraduate degree in Economics from the University of Bristol, and is currently studying for a higher degree in economics at Oxford University.

ADAM WAGSTAFF
United Kingdom

Adam Wagstaff is Lecturer in Economics in the School of Social Sciences at the University of Sussex and Visiting Research Fellow at the Centre for Health Economics at the University of York. He has been a consultant for the World Health Organization and the World Bank and is an Associate Editor of the *Journal of Health Economics*. In addition to his work on the COMAC-HSR project, he is currently working together with A.J. Culyer on a series of papers on distributive justice in health and health care.

ALAN WILLIAMS
United Kingdom

Alan Williams is a Professor of Economics at the University of York. In the past he has been a member of the Royal Commission on the National Health Service, and of the Department of Health Chief Scientist's Research Committee. His research interests are concentrated on the development and application of better outcome measures for the evaluation of health care technologies.

BARBARA WOLFE
United States

Barbara Wolfe is a Professor in the Departments of Economics, Preventive Medicine and the La Follette Institute of Public Affairs, as well as a research affiliate of the Institute for Research on Poverty at the University of Wisconsin-Madison. She is currently on leave at the Russell Sage Foundation in New York City. She has written numerous articles on health, education, and income distribution. She has been the Co-Editor of several journals including the *Journal of Human Resources* and *Social Science and Medicine*.

Acknowledgements

The editors would like to thank a number of persons and organizations for their contributions to the preparation of this volume.

We gratefully acknowledge the financial support provided by the European Community's COMAC-Health Services Research Committee which funded the co-ordination of the international comparative research reported in this volume. We also have to thank the Rockefeller Foundation for its generous hospitality. This book represents the tangible outcome of a conference held in November 1990 at their Villa Serbelloni Study and Conference Center in Bellagio, Italy. Neither the conference, nor the book, however, would have been possible without the inputs of both the country teams involved in the project and the invited external experts. The interaction between the two types of participants proved to be immensely fruitful. In addition to the Bellagio conference, the project benefited from workshops in Brussels, Lisbon, and Lyon; we are grateful to João Pereira and Lise Rochaix for organizing the Lisbon and Lyon workshops so efficiently.

Co-ordination of cross-country comparative work proved to be difficult at times and all electronic and other modern means of communication have had to be used to keep one another informed about progress, protocol modifications, or data problems. We are grateful to all participants for bearing with us and our telephone, fax, modem, electronic mail and other messages for the last four years. In this co-ordination task, we were lucky to be able to count on the help of three people in particular: Brigitte Kerbusch, the project secretary at Maastricht for the first half of the project; Caroline Verboom, her successor at Rotterdam for the last half; and last but not least Jan van Emmerik, who made sure that we could benefit of the most recent developments in computing and electronic communication. Their skills proved to be indispensable in a venture such as this.

When we started off with this project in 1987 we were not really sure what 'concerted action' could involve. We know now that working in concert and harmony on a uniform protocol requires a fair amount of cross-cultural understanding, especially with a subject like equity. Although we appreciate that some of the participants may at some stage have felt involved in a 'coerced action', we believe that most of us have in the end regarded the exercise as very rewarding and we look forward to further concerted action in the future.

E.V.D.
A.W.
F.R.

1

Introduction

Adam Wagstaff, Eddy Van Doorslaer, and Frans Rutten

Health care reform looks set to stay high on the policy-making agenda during the 1990s. Some reforms that were planned during the 1980s have already begun to be implemented. These include the so-called *internal market* programme in the UK, the move from fee-for-service to capitation payments for general practitioners' low-income patients in Ireland, and the switch from social insurance to tax financing in Spain. Other reforms are likely to follow elsewhere. The current Secretary of State in the Netherlands seems determined to push for a gradual implementation of a diluted version of the 1988 'Dekker Plan' (see van de Ven 1990). The Swiss look set to vote in favour of a referendum proposing a large increase in the role of taxation in the financing of health care. In addition, reforms to the American health care system look increasingly likely, as health care costs and the number of uninsured continue to rise remorselessly.

Despite the widespread interest in health care reform, the debate so far has been somewhat parochial in character. As Peet (1991), in a recent survey in *The Economist*, put it:

Most countries are dealing with health care reform as if each was on Mars. Few have tried to learn from others. Many who are expert in the politics and economics of their own country's health systems know little about how things work next door.... This indifference to the international face of doctoring is a huge mistake. This is not because any one country has miraculously solved all its problems, or because (say) Britain would do better to scrap its beloved health service and replace it with (say) Germany's. It is just that there are lessons to be learnt from looking at different ways of paying for and delivering the goods. Instead of each country trying out its own experiments, they should be studying each other's for ideas and pitfalls. (p. 4)

Not all of this is entirely true. The early comparative studies of Maynard (1975) and Maxwell (1981), the recent work of the OECD (Hurst 1991 *a*; Schieber and Poullier 1989 *a*, *b*, 1991; Schieber *et al.* 1991) and the King's Fund Institute (Ham *et al.* 1990), have done much to increase awareness of international differences and similarities in health care financing and delivery systems. Britain's internal market programme owes much to the research undertaken by the American economist Alain Enthoven during his sabbatical at Oxford University in 1985. An international team of economists has been advising on possible reforms to the Swedish health care delivery system (cf. Culyer *et al.* 1991). Furthermore, experiments can be useful, particularly if set up and evaluated with the same rigour as the RAND Corporation's health insurance experiment (Newhouse *et al.* 1981). Nonetheless, the main thrust of Peet's argument is sound: more can be learnt from cross-country comparisons than has been learnt to date about the advantages and disadvantages associated with alternative methods of financing and delivering health care, and hence about the likely effects of health care reforms.

Of the two yardsticks used by economists to judge the performance of health care systems—equity and efficiency—the latter has dominated cross-country comparisons. Thus the debate has focused on issues such as the implications of alternative financing and delivery systems for aggregate expenditure levels (are some systems better than others at containing 'costs'?) and the effects of expenditures on health outcomes (to what extent are the high American expenditures reflected in better outcome data?). Although equity *has* been the subject of some cross-country comparisons, such studies are comparatively few in number. As a result, little is known about the equity characteristics of alternative health care financing and delivery systems, and about the likely equity implications of reforms to these systems. This is despite the apparent importance attached to equity as a policy objective in most OECD countries. Indeed, some (McLachlan and Maynard 1982; Mooney 1986) claim that the public attaches greater importance to equity than to efficiency in health care, although one suspects that this commitment itself varies across countries.

This project, which has been co-ordinated jointly by the authors of this Introduction and is one of several in the European Community's COMAC Health Services Research (HSR) programmes, seeks to go some way towards filling this gap in the literature. Its aim to date has been to generate evidence on the comparative performance—in terms of equity—of different health care financing and delivery systems. The 10 countries currently participating in the study—Denmark, France, Ireland, Italy, the Netherlands, Portugal, Spain, Switzerland, the UK, and the US—encompass the full spectrum of health care financing and delivery systems, ranging from the predominantly private American system, through the mixed public–private social insurance systems of countries like France and the Netherlands, to the almost 100 per cent public systems operating in the UK and Denmark.

Besides its focus on equity, three other features of the project distinguish it from previous cross-country comparisons. One is that, in contrast to previous empirical studies of a comparative nature, which have almost all been based on aggregate data, the present study employs *micro-level data*. This is line with the recommendation of Schieber and Poullier

(1991), who, in their latest OECD comparative study, urged that greater use be made of micro-level data in cross-country comparisons in the health care field. A second feature of the present study is that those participating have together developed and then applied a *common methodology*. There is, as a result, a high degree of comparability in the empirical results reported in the country reports in Part II of this book. Differences in results ought therefore to reflect genuine differences between countries rather than differences in methods. A third feature of the project is that the analysis for each of the 10 countries has been undertaken, for the most part, by *research teams from the country in question*. This contrasts with previous comparative studies in the health field where one or two researchers have invariably performed the analysis for all the countries in the study.

Parts I and II of this volume relate specifically to the COMAC-HSR project on equity in health care. Part I summarizes the methods and findings of the project, and Part II contains the 10 country reports. All of the latter have much the same format and adopt the methods set out in Part I, although many go on to explore additional issues of interest to the country in question.

Part III of the volume contains a selection of essays on equity in health care by economists with an international reputation in the field. The essays were commissioned especially for the conference at which the results of this first part of the project were presented, which was held at the Rockefeller Foundation's Bellagio Study and Conference Center in November 1990. Although these essays are intended primarily to complement the project (many authors address themselves specifically to the questions raised in the project), many papers, if not most, are likely to become important contributions to the equity debate in their own right. Alan Williams considers the role of ideology in health care, comparing various ideological viewpoints and examining their implications for equity objectives and for the finance and delivery of health care. He suggests that in most countries there is no one dominant ideology and, as a result, policies and health care systems reflect a blend of often incompatible ideologies. Culyer explores the motivation behind the present study and analyses diagrammatically the conflicts that can arise between equity and efficiency, and between different equity principles. Karen Davis examines the American experience *vis-à-vis* equity in health care. She notes that, following the retrenchment of the Reagan years, there has been a shift back to the concern with equity that marked the 1960s and 1970s and suggests that this shift is due in part to the growth in the number of uninsured (from 29 million in 1980 to 37 million in 1986). She goes on to analyse the 1990 plan for universal health insurance coverage of the bi-partisan Pepper Commission. In his overview of the British literature on equity in the delivery of health care, Le Grand sets out to solve a mystery: why is it that studies undertaken in the 1970s—including Le Grand's (1978) own influential study—concluded that the British National Health Service (NHS) appeared to favour the better-off (in the sense that they received a higher share of NHS expenditure than was warranted given their share of the community's illness), whereas more recent studies have concluded the opposite? Judy Baker and Jacques van der Gaag examine equity in the finance and delivery of health care in five developing countries—Bolivia, Ghana, the Ivory Coast, Jamaica, and Peru—using similar methods to those employed in the COMAC-HSR equity project and data from the World Bank's *Living Standards Measurement Study*. Their findings suggest that although the financing burden in these countries is distributed in a fairly progressive fashion, substantial inequities persist in the delivery of health care.

Part I

Equity in the finance and delivery of health care: an overview

2

Equity in the finance and delivery of health care: concepts and definitions

Adam Wagstaff and Eddy Van Doorslaer

INTRODUCTION

Equity, like efficiency, is a goal that is pursued by policy-makers in all types of health care system. But what is equity? How should it be defined? And how is it to be measured? Answers to these questions are far from self-evident but are clearly required if meaningful cross-country comparisons are to be performed. This chapter addresses the first two of these questions. The third is addressed in Chapters 3 and 4, which also summarizes the methods and results of the COMAC-HSR study.

WHAT IS EQUITY?

It is often claimed that academics and policy-makers agree much less over what they mean by equity than they do over what they mean by efficiency. McLachlan and Maynard (1982), for example, have suggested that '... equity, like beauty, is in the mind of the beholder...' (p. 520). As Le Grand (1987) notes, this view is not entirely justified. Of the various theories of social justice that might be brought to bear on the issue of equity in health care, it is generally agreed that some have a greater applicability and acceptability than others (Gillon 1986). Moreover, a comparison of policy statements on equity in several OECD countries suggests that policy-makers are in broad agreement over what they mean by equity, even if the precise details vary. Finally, in empirical work, researchers from countries with such different health care systems as Britain and the US have adopted much the same notions of equity in their analysis. In this section we consider each of these areas in turn.

Equity versus altruism

It is worth noting that distributional objectives in health care, and in social policy generally, can arise from two sources, of which equity (or social justice) is one. Such objectives may instead arise from feelings of altruism or caring. The concepts of equity and altruism are often confused. They are, however, as Culyer (1980) and Goodin and Le Grand (1987) emphasize, quite distinct and have quite different implications for health policy.

Caring and altruism are matters of *preference*. In the context of health care a caring individual might be one who derives utility—i.e., an external benefit—from seeing another person receiving health care (Culyer, Chapter 17). In this case, the caring individual *prefers* that the person in question receives health care and is prepared to sacrifice resources to ensure that the person actually obtains treatment. Quite how much he is prepared to sacrifice will depend on how much he cares (which will depend on *inter alia* his income) and on the cost of providing health care. Alternatively, a caring individual might be one that derives utility from the *act* of providing health care for others (Mooney 1986). Quite how much of his income the individual will be prepared to sacrifice to provide health care for others will depend on the utility he derives from the act of providing medical care (which again will depend on his income) and on the cost of providing health care. With caring preferences of either type, therefore, 'costs and benefits are balanced at the margin and . . . the level of provision is . . . determined by the wealth of the community' (Culyer 1980, p. 70). The language of caring is thus, as Culyer (Chapter 17) notes, the language of efficiency. Hence the term 'Pareto optimal redistribution' (Hochman and Rodgers 1969).

Social justice (or equity), on the other hand, is not a matter of preference. As Culyer (1980) puts it: '. . . the source of value for making judgements about equity lies outside, or is extrinsic to, preferences . . . The whole point of making a judgement about justice is so to frame it that it is (and can be seen to be) a judgement made independently of the interests of the individual making it' (p. 60). Social justice thus derives from a set of principles concerning what a person ought to have *as of right*. One ingenious device that has been used to ensure that principles of justice are genuinely impartial is the 'veil of ignorance' (Rawls 1971). This puts self-interested individuals in an 'original position' where they are ignorant about the positions they will occupy in society. The rules of justice agreed upon by individuals in these circumstances are argued to be genuinely impartial. The 'veil of ignorance' is not, however, the only means of arriving at a set of just rules.[1] Barry (1989) has argued that justice can more simply be construed as the set of rules that can be justified on an impartial basis.

The different motivations behind equity and caring have at least three important implications for health care policy. First, decisions regarding health care provision prompted by considerations of social justice ought not to be influenced by cost: justice requires that an equitable pattern of provision be ensured, irrespective of the sacrifice to the rest of society (Culyer 1980, pp. 69–70). Secondly, there is scope for conflict between efficiency and equity: an efficient redistributional programme prompted by caring preferences need not be equitable, and *vice versa* (Culyer 1980, p. 98). Thirdly, the distributional 'rules' derived from the two approaches are likely to be different. Indeed, differences emerge even *within* the two approaches, depending on the precise stance adopted. For example, different rules emerge in the caring approach, depending on whether caring is postulated to relate to a person's absolute level of medical care consumption (Culyer 1971), to the deviation of their consumption from the mean (Lindsay 1969), or to health itself (Culyer 1980).

Equity, social justice, and ideology

In a study of equity, one would like ideally to analyse equity objectives independently of distributional objectives that are motivated by altruism. The philosophy literature contains some useful pointers in this respect.

Gillon (1986) provides a helpful summary of the various theories of social justice and discusses their applicability to health care. Libertarians, he notes, emphasize a respect for natural rights, focusing in particular on two of Locke's natural rights—the rights to life (i.e., not to be unjustly killed) and to possessions. Providing people acquire and transfer their 'holdings' without violating others' rights, their holdings are regarded by libertarians as just. Hence Nozick's (1974) claim that taxation is warranted only to maintain a 'minimal state'. Utilitarians, by contrast, aim at maximizing the sum of individual utilities or welfare, although some utilitarian writers have incorporated a concern for individual autonomy into this maximand. Marxists emphasize 'needs'. Hence the principle of 'distribution according to need'. In Marxist writings, this principle is often coupled with the principle of 'from each according to his ability'. The latter in the present context is intepreted as 'ability to pay', suggesting, as Culyer (Chapter 17) notes, a concern about the distribution of income *after* payments for health care. Rawls (1971) proposes two principles of social justice, namely, that individuals should have the maximal liberty compatible with the same degree of liberty for everyone and that deliberate inequalities are unjust unless they work to the advantage of the least well-off. Yet another view of social justice is that justice should reward merit.

Which of these theories of justice appear to command the greatest support in the context of medical care? Gillon suggests that 'allocation of medical resources on the basis of non-medical merits is widely regarded as repugnant' (p. 97), but argues that the principle of 'distribution according to need' commands widespread support amongst physicians and others working in the medical field. He challenges the extreme libertarian position, pointing out that if Locke's right to health were to be included in the libertarian list of natural rights, writers like Nozick would be forced to accept the legitimacy of taxation to benefit the poor and sick. Gillon also notes that utilitarianism, with its emphasis on maximizing the sum of welfare, has much in common with the notion of efficiency as allocating resources according to the likelihood of medical success.

The two most frequently encountered theories of justice in the context of medical care are, in fact, the libertarian and the Marxist approaches (Donabedian 1971). As Gillon notes, however, the principle of 'distribution according to need' is not exclusively Marxist. Indeed, it is a key component of twentieth-century egalitarianism (Sugden 1983). In his chapter in this volume, Williams compares and contrasts the libertarian and egalitarian position.[2] He notes that in the egalitarian view, 'access to health care is every citizen's right (like access to the ballot box or to courts of justice), and this ought not to be influenced by income and wealth' (p. 291). In the libertarian view, by contrast, access to health care is viewed as 'part of society's reward system'. As Williams puts it, 'at the margin at least, people should be able to use their income and wealth to get more or better health care than their fellow citizens if they so wish' (p. 291).

Ideology, health care systems, and health care policies

The egalitarian and libertarian viewpoints point, as Williams notes, towards quite different health care systems. The egalitarian viewpoint suggests that a state sector of a similar type to the British National Health Service (NHS) should predominate, with health care being distributed according to 'need' and financed according to 'ability to pay'. The libertarian viewpoint, by contrast, points towards a mainly private health care sector, with health care being rationed primarily according to willingness and ability to pay. State involvement should be minimal and limited to providing a minimum standard of care for the poor. The two viewpoints also indicate different success criteria in evaluating distributional outcomes. Egalitarians would judge equity by assessing the extent to which health care is, in practice, distributed according to need, and is, in practice, financed according to ability to pay. Libertarians, by contrast, would focus on the extent to which people are free to purchase the health care they want, subject (perhaps) to the proviso that the poor and sick are adequately provided for. Libertarians who are concerned about distributional issues are thus concerned not with equality, but rather with minimum standards.

In practice, as Williams emphasizes, in most countries, health care is financed and delivered by a mixture of systems and there are traces of both ideologies in policy-making, with the emphasis often changing with changes of government. Broadly speaking, however, policy-makers in Europe give the impression of being much more inclined towards the egalitarian viewpoint in health care matters than the libertarian. This is apparent from Table 2.1, which reproduces from the country reports in Part II of this volume some key quotations on equity objectives. There appears to be less agreement amongst American policy-makers about equity objectives in the health care field.

As is clear from Table 2.1, there appears to be broad agreement amongst policy-makers in at least eight of the nine European countries that payments towards health care should be related to ability to pay rather than to use of medical facilities.[3] This is still apparently the case despite the growth of user charges in some countries in the 1980s. The health care financing reforms in the 1970s and 1980s in Denmark, Italy, Portugal, and Spain, for example, were all motivated largely by a desire to see payments towards health care become more closely related to ability to pay. It is also significant that proposals to reduce the emphasis on tax finance in the UK were never included in the 1991 reforms. The commitment to linking health care payments to ability to pay is much less in evidence in the US, although as is apparent from Davis (Chapter 18), much of the recent debate about health care reform in the US has focused on the link or lack of it. The bipartisan Pepper Commission, for example, in its *Blueprint for health care reform* (Rockefeller 1991), urged that progressive taxation be used to raise new revenues to finance the Commission's proposed reforms. Finally, in Switzerland, where until recently there has been no consensus on the issue, a referendum is to be held to determine whether the role of taxation in health care financing should be increased and the role of private expenditures reduced.

It is also evident from Table 2.1 that policy-makers in all European countries are committed to the notion that all citizens should have *access* to health care.[4] In many countries this is taken further, it being made clear that access to and receipt of health care should depend on need, rather than on ability to pay. The increases in public coverage in Italy, Portugal and Spain in the 1970s and 1980s suggest a continuing commitment to the notion that access to health care should be the same for all. The commitment to the notion of universal and equal access is less evident in the US. Tobin (1970) suggests that although Americans may, in principle, be concerned about inequality in access to medical care, in practice the American health care system aims at bringing the medical care received by the poor up to a minimum standard rather than at promoting equality of access. Despite this ambivalence, it is apparent from Davis (Chapter

Table 2.1.   Equity and health policy statements in 10 countries

Country	Finance of health care	Delivery of health care
Denmark	'Expenses are to be financed in the same way as expenses for other public services are financed, that is by means of taxes and duties which are adjusted to each individual's ability to pay.'	'Access to health care in the event of illness ought to be open automatically to the whole population . . . Equal and free (or almost free) access to the various health-related services for all irrespective of economic means and social status.'
France		'The nation guarantees to everyone, in particular to children, mothers and older workers, the protection of health . . . Hospitals are open to anyone whose health requires their services.'
Ireland	'. . . an equitable sharing of the cost of providing . . . services . . . individuals being asked to pay on the basis of their financial means.'	' . . . distribution of available services over the population on the basis of need.'
Italy	Talk of 'solidarity' in financing of health care.	'. . . maintaining and restoring the mental and physical health of all persons regardless of their individual circumstances.'
The Netherlands	Talk of 'solidarity' in financing of health care.	Constitution gives every citizen right to health care.
Portugal	Change to tax finance in late 1970s motivated by desire to promote equity in the burden of payments.	'. . . access to the NHS is guaranteed to all citizens, independently of their economic or social status . . . all citizens have access in equality of circumstances.'
Spain	Recent (1989) change to tax finance motivated by desire to promote equity in the burden of payments.	'Public health care will be extended to cover all the Spanish population. Access and services will be carried out in conditions of effective equality.'

Table 2.1. (*cont.*)

Country	Finance of health care	Delivery of health care
Switzerland	Referendum to be voted on proposing greater emphasis on tax financing.	Cantons require communes to guarantee everyone access to health care.
UK	Continuing commitment to linking payments towards health care to ability to pay via general taxation.	'The Government . . . wants to ensure that in future every man, woman and child can rely on getting . . . the best medical and other facilities available; that their getting them shall not depend on whether they can pay for them or any other factor irrelevant to real need.'

18), that much of the recent debate about reform has actually been motivated by a concern about growing inequalities in access. Hence the Pepper Commission's desire to 'guarantee all Americans, no matter what their income, employment status, or place of residence, access to affordable insurance protection' (Rockefeller 1991, p. 2509).

Quite what is meant by 'access' in these policy statements is unclear. Le Grand (1982) and Mooney (1983) make a distinction between *access* to treatment and *receipt* of treatment. The former refers to the opportunities open to people, which can usefully be thought of in terms of the costs that people incur in obtaining health care. These include not only money costs but also time costs. Where access is non-existent, these costs can be regarded as infinite. As Mooney emphasizes, access is but one of the factors influencing receipt of medical care. Other factors include the individual's perception of the benefits associated with the treatment and the incentives facing the physician—in short, anything affecting the *demand* for health care as opposed to its cost. Two people may thus enjoy the same access to health care and be in the same degree of 'need', and yet the treatment they receive may differ. A poorly educated person may, for example, perceive the health benefits to be lower than his well-educated peer, with the result that the poorly educated person does not contact a physician, whereas the well-educated person does. Conversely, access may differ across individuals and yet the amount of medical care received may be the same.

Although useful, Mooney's distinction between access and treatment is not widely appreciated, either by policy-makers or by academics.[5] One suspects that when the term 'access' is used, what is often meant—indeed perhaps what is *usually* meant—is 'receipt of treatment'. This is well illustrated by Tobin's (1970) remarks, where, after noting Americans' apparent concern with equality of access, suggests that equality in health care might be taken to mean that 'the *treatment* of an individual depends on his medical condition and symptoms, not on his ability or willingness to pay' (emphasis added).[6] Likewise, as Mooney and McGuire (1987) note, although the so-called Resource Allocation Working Party (RAWP) formula used to allocate resources to NHS regions claims to attempt to equalize *access*, in practice the focus is firmly on *expenditures*, or—more precisely—resources.

Ideology and the empirical literature on equity in health care

The empirical work to date on equity in health care reflects the apparently pro-egalitarian bias amongst policy-makers. Most studies of equity in the *delivery* of health care—in both Europe and the US—start from the premise that health care ought to be distributed according to need rather than willingness and ability to pay. Andersen (1975)—American—suggests that an equitable distribution of health care is one in which the amount of health care received correlates highly with indicators of need and is independent of variables such as income, which are irrelevant to need. This definition is adopted by L. Benham and A. Benham (1975) in their study of equity in the delivery of health care in the US before and after the introduction of Medicare and Medicaid. Le Grand (1978)—a Briton—also starts from the premise that receipt of health care should depend on need and not on socio-economic status. Several American and British studies[7] *claim* to examine the extent to which *access* to health care is linked to need, but actually interpret access in terms of treatment received—suggesting once again that the two concepts may not be so distinct as some would have us believe. Studies of equity in the *finance* of health care have been fewer in number, but have without exception taken as their starting point the premise that health care ought to be financed according to ability to pay.[8]

It should be noted that the empirical literature does contain two groups of studies which start from a premise other than the egalitarian. One explores the issue of inequalities in health.[9] The notion that equity might be defined in terms of 'equality of health' is not, in fact, inconsistent with egalitarianism. As Gillon (1986) notes, it is not self-evident why the principle of 'distribution according to need' commands such widespread support. More generally, as Culyer (Chapter 17) notes, it is not clear why one should be concerned with the distribution of health care in the first place. The obvious answer to this latter question, as Culyer notes, is that health care is thought to improve health, and it is this that is the ultimate source of concern. One possible justification of the principle of 'distribution according to need', then, is that distributing medical care according to need is likely to promote equality of health. It is, in fact, typically argued that the principles of equality and distribution according to need are intimately related (Miller 1976). Indeed, one assumes that it is for this reason that the Marxist distributional principle has come to be accepted by egalitarians. If this is the case, it clearly makes sense, as Williams (Chapter 16) notes, to address the issue of inequalities in health as well as (or perhaps instead of) the issue of 'distribution according to need'.

The second group of studies starting from an apparently non-egalitarian premise are those seeking to establish the extent of *income redistribution* associated with a particular mode of financing health care. Such studies have been undertaken in France, Germany, Italy, the Netherlands, Portugal, Switzerland, and the UK.[10] It appears that these studies start from a variant of the egalitarian viewpoint, where reducing inequality in 'final' incomes is regarded as the equity goal. The usefulness of these studies is, it has to be said, less than clear. There is, after all, very little evidence that equity objectives in the health field are couched in terms of income redistribution, although, clearly, in so far as the poor also tend to be the sick, such redistribution is implied by a commitment to financing health care according to ability to pay.

HOW SHOULD EQUITY BE DEFINED?

Contrary to what is sometimes claimed, then, there seems to be a broad measure of support for the notion that health care ought to be distributed according to need and financed according to ability to pay. Deciding on an ethical premise is one thing. Giving the premise empirical content is quite another.

Defining equity in the finance of health care

The requirement that health care be financed according to ability to pay can be interpreted in terms of both *vertical equity* (in this case the requirement that persons or families of unequal ability to pay make appropriately dissimilar payments for health care) and *horizontal equity* (the requirement that persons or families of the same ability to pay make the same contribution).

Both interpretations require a definition of 'ability to pay'. Should this be measured by pre-tax income? By pre-tax income plus imputed income from physical assets such as the individual's or family's house? While the latter is probably preferable, data limitations meant that the former had to be used in the empirical work in the present volume.

In addressing the issue of vertical equity, consideration has to be given to the precise form that the differential treatment of unequals should take. Should those with greater ability to pay be paying more in proportional terms? In other words ought the relationship between ability to pay and payments to be progressive?[11] Or should they merely be paying more in absolute terms? In other words can the relationship between ability to pay and payments be proportional or even regressive?[12] If the relationship is to be progressive, how progressive ought it to be? Typically, policy statements fail to address questions such as these. In the absence of a clear statement from policy-makers on just how much more the rich should pay towards health care than the poor, the present project focuses simply on the degree of progressivity. Do the rich pay a larger proportion of their income on health care than the poor? How progressive or regressive is the relationship between income and payments towards health care? Are some ways of raising revenues more progressive than others? How are these differences reflected in the progressivity characteristics of individual countries' financing systems?

The issue of horizontal equity in the finance of health care has received little attention in the health economics literature. The logic of the discussion above suggests that horizontal equity might be defined in terms of the extent to which those of equal ability to pay actually end up making equal payments, regardless of, for example, gender, marital status, trade union membership, place of residence, etc. Horizontal *inequity* might arise for a number of reasons. In a pure private insurance system high risk groups (e.g., the elderly) would pay higher premiums than lower risk persons of the same ability to pay. In a tax-funded system, such as the British NHS, horizontal inequity might arise through anomalies in the personal income tax system (e.g., certain tax reliefs). In a social insurance system, different occupational groups may be eligible for different health insurance schemes or may face different contribution schedules. Rutten and Janssen (1987), for example, note that in the Netherlands, single persons on an income of Dfl17 000 in 1981 could have ended up paying as little as 2 per cent of their income towards health care if they were over 65 but as much as 13 per cent if they were under 65 but self-employed. Although horizontal equity appears to be regarded by policy-makers in several countries as an important issue in the finance of health care (Hurst 1991 *a*, 1991 *b*), it is not investigated in the present volume.

Defining equity in the delivery of health care

The requirement that health care be distributed according to need can also be interpreted in terms of both *vertical equity* (in this case the requirement that persons in unequal need be treated in an appropriately dissimilar way) and *horizontal equity* (the requirement that persons in equal need be treated equally).

Definitions are again required before these interpretations of equity can be operationalized. How, for example, should need be defined? In common with previous empirical studies in this area, 'need' in this project is assessed in terms of ill-health. Being ill does not, of course, necessarily imply a need for medical care. As Culyer (1989) points out, someone cannot be said to need medical care if there is nothing that it can do for him. Moreover, persons who are not ill may still have a need for medical care, in the sense that preventive medical care can improve their future health over and above what it would otherwise be. The method employed in the empirical analysis in this volume does not fall into this trap: it does not assume that those who are especially ill (e.g., the chronically sick) necessarily need more medical care than those who are only marginally ill (e.g., the acutely sick). Indeed, the method takes into account that the latter group may actually need (and obtain) *more* medical care than the former group, in the sense that they have a greater 'capacity to benefit'.[13] What *is* assumed is that people in different degrees of ill-health have different medical needs, and that people in the same state of ill-health have the same need. Neither is, of course, necessarily the case.[14] It is, however, difficult to see how with the data available, anything more sophisticated could be done. Some definition of treatment is also clearly required. Ideally, as Culyer (Chapter 17) notes, treatment should embrace only those resources that result in improvements in people's health. Expenditures on lavish hotel services received during the course of in-patient treatment ought, for example, not to be classified as 'treatment'.

As before, the notion of vertical equity raises the question: what is the precise form that the differential treatment of unequals should take? Should the relationship between need and treatment be proportional? Or 'progressive'? With some exceptions (Cullis and West 1979), the issue of vertical equity in the delivery of health care rarely gets discussed in the health economics literature and is not addressed in the empirical work in the present volume.

The issue of horizontal equity has received much more attention in the literature and it is this that provides the focus of the present empirical work on equity in the delivery of health care. This principle requires that persons in equal need actually end up receiving equal treatment, irrespective of personal characteristics that are irrelevant to need, such as 'ability to pay', race, gender and place of residence. In common with previous studies in the field, the present study focuses on violations of the horizontal equity principle that are related to ability to pay. Thus, do persons in equal need of health care receive the same amount of treatment? Or do the better-off secure more than their 'fair' share? Do some countries come closer to achieving horizontal equity than others? If so, what features of health care systems seem to promote equity in the delivery of health care and which features seem to hinder its attainment?

CONCLUSIONS

In contrast to what has sometimes been claimed, then, there does appear to be a broad measure of agreement amongst both academics and policy-makers over what equity in health care means. Policy-makers in most countries appear to accept the egalitarian principle that payments for health care should be related primarily to ability to pay rather than to the amount of medical care received. Most also seem to accept that access to health care should be available to all persons in need of care, irrespective of their willingness and ability to pay. Rarely, however, is access to medical care distinguished from receipt of treatment, suggesting that there is broad acceptance too of the egalitarian principle that health care itself should be distributed according to need. The twin principles of 'finance according to ability to pay' and 'distribution according to need' have, in fact, been the points of departure of the majority of empirical studies in the field to date, both in Europe and the US. Because of the apparent widespread support that they command, these principles are also adopted as the point of departure in the present study. The next two chapters present a summary of the methods and results of the COMAC-HSR project, the first being concerned with the finance of health care, and the second with the delivery of health care.

NOTES

1. Indeed, there is some debate about precisely what would be agreed behind such a veil.
2. Cf. Culyer *et al.* (1981); Maynard and Williams (1984); and Williams (1988).
3. Hurst (1991 *a*) concludes the same in his comparison of the health care systems of Belgium, France, Germany, The Netherlands, Ireland, Spain, and the UK.
4. Again, the same conclusion has been reached by Hurst (1991 *a*) in his comparative study.

5. Hence the title of Mooney's article.
6. Cf. also Andersen (1975).
7. Cf. Aday and Andersen (1980), Collins and Klein (1980), and Puffer (1986).
8. See Hurst (1985), who compares the American, British and Canadian financing systems, and Gottshalk *et al.* (1989), who compare the American, British, and Dutch systems.
9. There is a huge literature on this topic. Seminal contributions to the British literature include: Illsley and Le Grand (1986); Le Grand and Rabin (1986); Pamuk (1985, 1988); Preston *et al.* (1981); Townsend and Davidson (1982); Wilkinson (1986). Fox (1990) contains many useful papers from other European countries.
10. For a comprehensive study (in English), see Leu and Frey (1985).
11. A finance system is progressive if the proportion of income paid out for health care rises as the level of income rises.
12. A finance system is proportional if the proportion of income paid out for health care is the same at all income levels and regressive if the proportion of income paid out falls as income rises.
13. Cf. Chapter 16 (Williams) and Chapter 17 (Culyer) in this volume.
14. Cf. Culyer (Chapter 17) and Culyer and Wagstaff (1991 *a*).

3

Equity in the finance of health care: methods and findings

Eddy Van Doorslaer and Adam Wagstaff

INTRODUCTION

For reasons indicated in the previous chapter, the analysis of equity in the finance of health care starts from the premise that payments for health care ought to be positively related to ability to pay, rather than to the receipt of care. This chapter summarizes the evidence on the progressivity of health care finance in 10 OECD countries. Evidence is presented on the progressivity of each country's financing system overall, as well as on the progressivity of each of its constituent parts. The chapter begins with a brief overview of the principal differences between the health care financing systems of the countries concerned. It then outlines the methods used to measure progressivity, as well as the data, variable definitions and incidence assumptions used in the empirical analysis. The chapter then goes on to discuss the principal findings of this part of the project. The final section contains a summary and discussion.

CROSS-COUNTRY DIFFERENCES IN HEALTH CARE FINANCING

Countries typically finance the bulk of their health care expenditures from two or more of four sources: (1) taxation; (2) social insurance contributions; (3) private insurance premia; and (4) out-of-pocket payments. There is, however, substantial variation across countries both in the way revenue is raised within each source and in the relative importance of each source. Both, as will be seen, are important determinants of the overall progressivity of any health care financing system.

Table 3.1 shows how revenue is raised from each source in each of the 10 countries in the present study. The year indicated is the year to which the data used in the empirical work in the country report in Part II of this volume refer. In only two cases—Spain and Portugal—has there been a major change in the health care financing system since the year indicated in Table 3.1.

A variety of taxes are used to finance health care. Sometimes they are earmarked, an obvious example being the 'tax expenditures' associated with tax deductibility of private health insurance. More often than not, however, they are simply general tax revenues. By contrast, social insurance revenues are frequently earmarked: this is true of countries like the Netherlands which still have a network of sickness funds, but also of countries like Italy where the state has taken over the role of the old sickness funds. Whatever the precise system, contributions to these funds are compulsory for almost all the population (opting out tends to be restricted to groups with high earnings) and linked to earnings (contributions are frequently split between employee and employer, and are often proportional to earnings up to a ceiling). The role of private insurance also varies across countries. In some countries (e.g., Ireland, the Netherlands, and the US), private insurance is geared to providing cover for persons without comprehensive public cover. In others (e.g., Italy, Portugal, Spain, and the UK), private insurance provides supplementary (i.e., double) cover to persons who already have comprehensive public cover, but in other countries (e.g., Denmark and France), private insurance provides cover against public sector copayments levied on prescription medicines, dental care, etc. Finally, the role of out-of-pocket payments varies somewhat across countries. In some (e.g., Denmark, France, Ireland, the Netherlands, the UK, and the US), they are predominantly copayments, with a third party picking up (usually) the major share of the bill. In others (e.g., Italy, Portugal, and Spain) there is extensive use of the private sector on a fee-paying basis.

The importance attached to each source of finance varies substantially across countries (see Appendix). One important distinction is between financing systems that are predominantly public and those that are predominantly private. Figure 3.1 shows the proportion of health care expenditures financed privately in each of the 10 countries. The US and Switzerland stand out as the only countries relying on out-of-pocket payments and private insurance premiums for the majority of their revenues.[1] In European countries other than Switzerland the picture is markedly different: private expenditures typically account for around one-quarter of health care expenditures. There is, however, some variation: in Britain only 13.5 per cent of expenditures are private of which 64 per cent are out-of-pocket, whereas in Portugal in 1981 almost 30 per cent was financed privately and virtually all was out-of-pocket. Moreover, according to Pereira and Pinto (Chapter 11) in 1987, this figure had grown to almost 40 per cent, making Portugal the country with the highest share of health care paid for out-of-pocket.

Figure 3.1 also shows the relative shares of private insurance and out-of-pocket payments in private expenditures in each of the other countries.

Table 3.1. Health care financing in 10 OECD countries

Country	Year	Taxation	Social insurance	Private insurance	Out-of-pocket payments
Denmark	1981	General central and local government tax revenues used to fund public health care.	None.	Usually provides cover only for public sector copayments.	Copayments for prescription drugs, dental care, physiotherapy.
France	1985	Some revenues from tax on car insurance used to cover social insurance fund deficit.	Three separate occupational health insurance funds covering 98% of population. Contributions related to earnings but vary across schemes. Compulsory in case of employees and split between employee and employer. Ceiling on contributions recently removed for *Régime Général*.	Supplementary insurance paid to mutuelles and private insurance companies. Premiums to *mutuelles* related to earnings and provide cover for *ticket modérateur*. Premiums to private insurees related to risk.	*Ticket modérateur* covers 25% of cost of GP visits and 30% of cost of medicines. Private and *mutuelle* policy-holders can obtain at least partial reimbursement except for some medicines. Some groups and some medicines exempt from *ticket modérateur*. Some small copayments for inpatient care.
Ireland	1987	General central government tax revenues used to fund public health care. Tax deductibility of private insurance.	Small health-specific social insurance contribution goes towards funding of public health care.	Mainly taken out by persons in middle and upper income groups whose public cover is limited. Private insurance tax deductible.	Middle income group liable for copayments for inpatient and outpatient treatment, and payment in full for GP visits and prescription medicines.

Italy	1987	General central government tax revenues paid into national health service fund in respect of fiscalization and under other headings. Taxes also used ex-post to cover health services fund defecit.	Compulsory earnings-related contributions to social health insurance fund. Some general social insurance contributions also used to fund public health care. In both cases, contribution schedules vary across professional groups.	Taken out as supplementary cover to health service cover. Includes compulsory scheme for managers.	Top income group liable for copayment for inpatient hotel facilities, and payment in full for consultant services, outpatient and primary care, and prescription medicines. *Ticket modérateur* payable for prescription drugs, with disabled, etc., exempt. Direct payments to private sector by persons with and without private insurance.
Netherlands	1987	General central government tax revenues used to subsidize sick funds and to finance preventive care.	Compulsory contributions payable by all to AWBZ scheme for catastrophic expenses. Additional insurance contributions payable to sickness funds by	Taken out by persons with income in excess of Dfl49 150 to cover non-catastrophic expenses.	Copayments and deductibles paid by persons with private insurance. Direct payments by persons without insurance cover for non-catastrophic

Table 3.1. (*cont.*)

Country	Year	Taxation	Social insurance	Private insurance	Out-of-pocket payments
			persons with income less than Dfl49 150 for non-catastrophic expenses. In both cases contributions proportional to earnings but subject to ceiling.		expenses. Copayments by sickness fund-insured.
Portugal	1981	General central government tax revenues used to fund public health care and subsidize occupational health insurance schemes operating in public sector.	Some compulsory occupational schemes providing double cover to public sector employees. Contributions related to earnings.	Taken out as supplementary cover to public sector cover.	Copayments to public sector for consultations, diagnostic tests, and medicines. Direct payments to private sector by those with and without private/occupational insurance.
Spain	1980	General central government tax revenues used to cover social insurance deficit and to fund some public care.	Compulsory contributions to social health insurance fund. Contributions proportional to earnings but subject to ceiling which varies across professional groups.	Taken out by persons without public cover and as supplementary cover by persons with public cover.	40% *ticket modérateur* for prescription medicines, but pensioners exempt. Payments to private sector for some services available in public sector and for other services.

Country	Year				
Switzerland	1981	General federal, cantonal, and communal government tax revenues used to subsidize basic cover provided by sickness funds and to fund public hospitals.	Compulsory contributions to the national accident and disability insurance.	Non-compulsory health insurance premiums paid to sickness funds. Premiums not related to earnings, but vary according to age at time of entry into sickness fund, gender, and (mainly) comfort of inpatient care. Sickness funds are private but subsidized and regulated by the federal government.	Persons with basic sickness fund cover face 10% co-insurance for ambulatory care and deductible for first GP visit of episode. 95% of dental care paid for out-of-pocket.
UK	1985	General central government tax revenues used to fund NHS.	Some general social insurance contributions used to fund NHS.	Taken out as supplementary cover to NHS cover.	Charges for prescribed medicines, dental care, and opthalmic care.
US	1981	Federal and state general revenues used to fund Medicaid and some Medicare, and general assistance. Some state and local revenues used to support public hospitals.	Some social insurance contributions go towards funding of Medicare.	Provided mostly as fringe benefit to employees. Participants in Medicare also purchase supplementary cover.	Copayments for inpatient and primary care payable by the privately insured and Medicare enrollees.

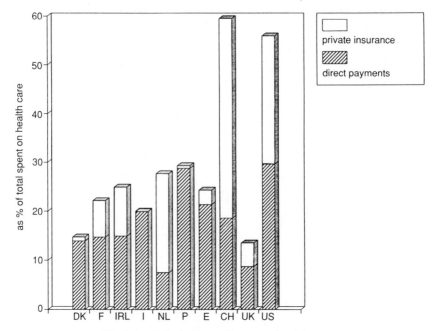

Fig. 3.1.   Private expenditures on health care.

In most countries, out-of-pocket payments account for the majority of private expenditures, the exceptions being the Netherlands and Switzerland. Again, however, there is substantial variation: in Denmark and the three southern European countries almost all private expenditures are out-of-pocket, whereas in the US, private expenditures are almost equally divided between private insurance premiums and out-of-pocket payments.

Another important distinction is between social insurance-based public systems and tax-based public systems (see Fig. 3.2). In the years indicated in Table 3.1, France, the Netherlands, and Spain all financed the bulk of their public expenditures out of earmarked social insurance contributions. At the other extreme are Denmark, Ireland, Portugal, Switzerland, and the UK, where the majority of public expenditures are financed out of general taxation. Public health care expenditures in Italy and the US are financed more or less equally from social insurance and general tax revenues, although Italy is unlike the US in that most social insurance contributions used to finance health care are earmarked.

The overall differences between countries in health care financing are illustrated in the 'health care financing triangle' in Fig. 3.3. The closer a country is to the bottom left-hand corner, the closer it is to being 100 per cent private. Of the 10 countries in the study, Switzerland and the US are the most private. By contrast, the closer a country is to the hypotenuse,

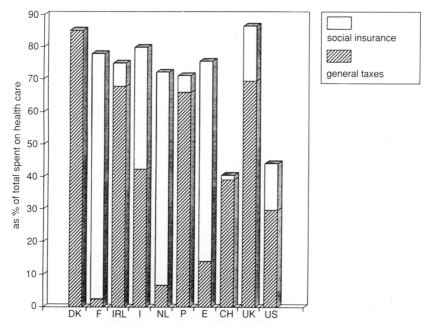

Fig. 3.2. Public expenditures on health care.

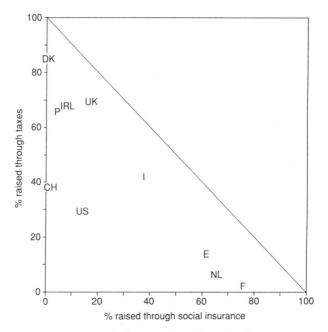

Fig. 3.3. Health care financing triangle.

the closer it is to being 100 per cent public. Of the countries in the present study, the UK and Denmark are the most public. Amongst the pre-dominantly public systems one can distinguish between those that are predominantly tax-financed and those that are predominantly social insurance-financed. The former, which lie at the top left-hand corner, include Denmark, Ireland, Portugal, and the UK. The latter, which lie at the bottom right-hand corner, include France, the Netherlands, and Spain (as of 1980). Only Italy fails to fall into one of the three groups, despite the stated intent of the Italian government to move firmly towards a tax-financed public health care system.

During the 1980s only two of the 10 countries have significantly changed their location in the health care financing triangle: Spain and Portugal. As the authors of the Spanish report point out, the share of taxes grew rapidly in Spain during the 1980s as an act of policy, and is now larger than the social insurance share. Spain has thus moved towards the top left-hand corner in Fig. 3.3. Portugal, by contrast, has seen a rapid rise in the share of health care expenditures financed privately during the 1980s, with the result that Portugal is now roughly midway between the tax-financed bloc of countries in the top left-hand corner and the predominantly privately financed bloc of countries towards the bottom lefthand corner.

MEASUREMENT OF PROGRESSIVITY

The progressivity of a health care financing system refers to the extent to which payments for health care rise or fall as a proportion of a person's income as his or her income rises. A *progressive* system is one in which health care payments rise as a proportion of income as income rises, whereas a *regressive* system is one in which payments fall as a proportion of income as income rises. A *proportional* system is one in which health care payments account for the same proportion of income for everyone, irrespective of their income.

Previous work on progressivity in the finance of health care has been based on tabulations of health care payments by income group. In his comparison of the UK, Canada and the US, Hurst (1985), for example, presents tables indicating average payments for health care by income group for each country. Payments were, however, presented in absolute terms rather than as a proportion of income, so that it is impossible to assess from the tables the degree of progressivity of each country's financing system.[2] Cantor's (1988) results for the United States—reported in Fig. 18.13 in Chapter 18—are easier to interpet. They show that the proportion of income spent on health care in the US falls continuously

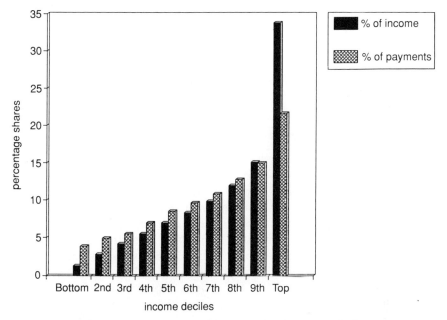

Fig. 3.4.   Distribution of US financing burden across deciles.

as one moves up the income distribution, implying that the American financing system is regressive.

An implication of a progressive financing system is that the share of the total financing burden borne by the lower income groups is less than their share of the community's income, whilst the share borne by the top income groups exceeds their share of the community's income. Comparing the share of income received by each income decile with its share of health care payments thus provides an alternative way of assessing progressivity. This is the approach adopted by Gottschalk *et al.* (1989) in their comparison of the health care financing systems of The Netherlands, the UK, and the US. Their results for the US, reproduced in Fig. 3.4, show that the American system is regressive. Thus, for example, the bottom income decile in 1981 received 1.4 per cent of (post-tax) income but made 3.9 per cent of health care payments.

Tabulations of the proportion of income spent on health care and of the shares of income and health care payments received and borne by different income groups do not enable one to answer the question of how much more (or less) progressive one system (or source of finance) is than another. At best they can indicate whether a system is progressive, regressive, or proportional. A more illuminating approach to assessing the progressivity of health care financing systems is to employ *progressivity indices* (Wagstaff *et al.* 1989). A variety of such indices have been proposed in the literature on tax progressivity (Lambert 1989). Two such indices—those of Kakwani (1977) and Suits (1977)—have been employed in the present study to enable comparisons to be performed both across countries and across financing sources. We outline each index in turn and then compare them.

Kakwani's index of progressivity

Kakwani's index is based on the extent to which a tax system departs from proportionality and can best be illustrated using Fig. 3.5(a). The curve labelled $g_{pre}(p)$ is the Lorenz curve for pre-tax income. The second curve, labelled $g_{tax}(p)$, gives the *tax concentration curve*, which plots the cumulative proportions of the population (ranked according to pre-tax income as with $g_{pre}(p)$) against the cumulative proportion of tax payments. If taxes are levied strictly in proportion to income, the tax concentration curve and the Lorenz curve for pre-tax income coincide. If the average tax rate rises with income (so that the tax system is progressive), the tax concentration curve lies outside the Lorenz curve for pre-tax income. The opposite is true if taxes are regressive. The degree of progressivity can therefore be assessed by looking at the size of the area between $g_{pre}(p)$ and $g_{tax}(p)$. If G_{pre} is the Gini coefficient for pre-tax income, and C_{tax} is the concentration index for tax payments, Kakwani's index of progressivity, π_K, is defined as

$$\pi_K = C_{tax} - G_{pre} \tag{3.1}$$

which is twice the area between $g_{tax}(p)$ and $g_{pre}(p)$. If the system is progressive, as in Fig. 3.5(a), π_K is positive. If, by contrast, the system is regressive, so that $g_{tax}(p)$ lies *above* $g_{pre}(p)$, π_K is negative. The value of π_K ranges from -2.0 (when all pre-tax income is concentrated in the hands of the richest person and the entire tax burden falls on someone else) to 1.0 (when pre-tax income is distributed equally and the entire tax burden falls on one person).

Suits' index of progressivity

The Kakwani index of tax progressivity is based on standard Lorenz and concentration curves. The Suits index, by contrast, is based on what Lambert and Pfähler (1988) call *relative* concentration curves. The index is illustrated in Fig. 3.5(b). The curve labelled $h_{pre}(y)$ is the relative concentration curve for pre-tax income. This plots the cumulative proportion of pre-tax income (starting at the bottom of the distribution) against the cumulative proportion of pre-tax income rather than against the cumulative proportion of the population (as is the case with

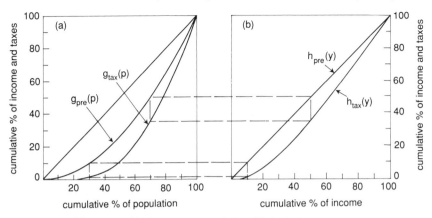

Fig. 3.5. (a) Kakwani index of progressivity; (b) Suits index of progressivity.

Kakwani's approach). Thus $h_{pre}(y)$ coincides with the 45° line and serves as the benchmark against which to assess progressivity. The curve labelled $h_{tax}(y)$ plots the cumulative proportion of pre-tax income (starting, as before, at the bottom of the distribution) against the cumulative proportion of tax payments borne by the households in the relevant part of the income distribution. If taxes are levied in proportion to income, $h_{pre}(y)$ and $h_{tax}(y)$ coincide, so that, for example, the bottom 10 per cent of pre-tax income goes to finance 10 per cent of tax payments. If the tax system is progressive, $h_{tax}(y)$ lies below the diagonal (the case illustrated). The opposite is true if taxes are regressive. The degree of progressivity can therefore be assessed by looking at the size of the area between $h_{pre}(y)$ and $h_{tax}(y)$. If H_{tax} is the relative concentration index for tax payments, the Suits index of progressivity, π_S, is defined as:

$$\pi_S = H_{tax} \tag{3.2}$$

which is twice the area between $h_{tax}(y)$ and $h_{pre}(y)$. If the tax system is progressive, as in Fig. 3.5(b), π_S is positive. If, by contrast, the system is regressive, so that $h_{tax}(y)$ lies *above* $h_{pre}(y)$, π_S is negative. The value of π_S ranges from −1.0 (when the entire tax burden falls on the poorest person) to 1.0 (when the entire tax burden falls on the richest person).

Properties of the Kakwani and Suits indices

Formby *et al.* (1981) have shown that the Suits index gives greater weight to departures from proportionality that occur amongst higher income groups than to departures from proportionality occurring amongst lower income groups. This is shown graphically by the lines joining Figs 3.5(a) and (b). Thus, for example, the departure from proportionality amongst the bottom 30 per cent of the population gets a smaller weight in the Suits index than in the Kakwani index: the area between the concentration curve and the benchmark curve is much smaller for the bottom 30 per cent in the case of the Suits index than in the case of the Kakwani index.[3]

A useful property of both the Kakwani and Suits indices is that the overall index for a system of two or more taxes is a weighted average of the indices for the individual components, where the weights are the proportions of the taxes in total revenue (Suits 1977). Thus, the progressivity characteristics of a health care financing system depend on the proportion of total revenues raised from each source and the degree of progressivity of each of these sources.

Another feature of these progressivity indices is worth mentioning. It is perfectly possible for a source of finance (or a tax) to be progressive (or regressive) at low income levels but regressive (or progressive) at high-income levels. Suppose, for example, that pensioners are exempt from social insurance contributions and tend to be located in the lower income groups. Suppose too that contributions are proportional (assume for simplicity to income) but only up to a ceiling. The exemption of pensioners makes the system progressive at low-income levels (the bottom income groups will tend to pay a relatively small fraction of their income towards health care) but regressive at high income levels (as a person's income rises above the ceiling, the proportion of their income they pay towards health will fall). The result is that the tax or payment concentration curve will cross from below the relevant benchmark curve (the Lorenz curve in the case of the standard concentration curve and the 45° line in the case of the relative concentration curve). This is shown in Fig. 3.6 in the case of the standard concentration curve. Calculating the Kakwani index as the difference between C_{tax} and G_{pre} in the case illustrated in Fig. 3.6 implies that the regressiveness at high incomes offsets—at least partially—the progressivity at low incomes. The result could, of course, be a zero value for the progressivity index. Similar remarks apply to the Suits index. In view of the relationship between the two indices shown in Fig. 3.5, it ought to be apparent that where the concentration curves cross their benchmark curves, it is possible for the Kakwani and Suits indices to have opposite signs. As will be seen, this does, in fact, happen in some cases in the country results reported below.

DATA, VARIABLE DEFINITIONS, AND INCIDENCE ASSUMPTIONS

Assigning the financing burden

As is evident from Table 3.1, very few taxes are earmarked for health care. Moreover, in many countries some *general* social insurance contri-

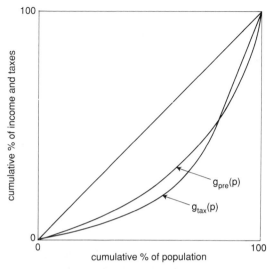

Fig. 3.6.   Intersecting Lorenz and tax concentration curves.

butions are used to finance health care. Some method is therefore required for deciding which non-earmarked payments actually go towards
the financing of health care. In the country reports in this volume, taxes
and social insurance contributions that are not earmarked have been
allocated *pro rata* according to the shares of the relevant revenues going
to finance health care. This procedure, which is—as Culyer (Chapter 17)
notes—somewhat arbitrary, is equivalent to weighting the progressivity
index of each tax or social insurance scheme by its share in total health
care expenditures.

Irrespective of whether or not a particular source of health care
financing is earmarked, the question arises as to who bears the burden of
the payment. Who, for example, bears the burden of—as distinct from
'who is liable to pay?'—contributions paid by employers towards social or
private health insurance schemes? In principle, one would like to bring
empirical evidence to bear on this issue, because it is well known that the
incidence of a tax depends on the relevant elasticities. For example, the
portion of the employer social insurance contribution that is borne by
the employee will depend on the elasticity of the labour supply curve
(Atkinson and Stiglitz 1987). As the relevant elasticities may be expected
to vary from one country to the next, it may well be sensible to adopt
different incidence assumptions for different countries. In practice, the
evidence on incidence is far from clear-cut and one is forced to opt for
the less ambitious option of making a set of necessarily arbitrary incidence assumptions. In principle, one could still adopt different sets of

incidence assumptions for different countries, but the reasons for varying the assumptions become less convincing. Because of this, all countries adopted—where possible—the same straightforward set of assumptions that has been adopted in previous studies such as that of Gottschalk *et al.* (1989): personal income tax and property taxes are assumed to be borne by the taxpayers concerned, corporate income taxes by shareholders, sales and excise taxes by consumers, and employee and employer social insurance contributions by employees.

Data and variable definitions

Typically—although not always—the rules governing health care payments (especially taxes and health insurance premia) apply to families or households rather than individuals. Thus, measuring the progressivity of health care financing systems requires household-level[4] data on pre-tax income and health care payments, with the latter broken down into: (1) taxation; (2) social insurance contributions; (3) private insurance premiums; and (4) out-of-pocket payments. The surveys used to analyse progressivity in the finance of health care in the 10 countries in the present study are listed in Table 3.2.

All authors employed gross (i.e., pre-tax) income as the benchmark against which to assess progressivity: gross income includes wage income as well as non-wage income (e.g., cash transfers, cash property income, etc.). Not all surveys contain information on pre-tax income, in which case countries have had to estimate it from data on post-tax income. In all but the American and UK country reports the gross income figure was converted to a per equivalent adult basis in order to take into account the variation in household structure that exists across families, with countries using whichever equivalence scale they felt to be appropriate.[5]

None of the surveys listed in Table 3.2 is sufficiently comprehensive to allow the entire financing burden to be allocated across income groups using only information recorded in the survey. Some surveys, for example, do not contain information on property taxes. Authors have had therefore to explore alternative data sources for at least some sources of finance, or else make guesses as to the distribution of the omitted categories.

Figure 3.7 shows the proportion of revenues allocated from each of five data sources. The first source is the *raw data* of the principal survey used in the country report—the survey listed in Table 3.2. This source is the most flexible, as authors were able to construct their income variable in line with the project's protocol. The second category is published *tabulated data* that have been derived from the principal survey by other researchers. The authors of the UK report, for example, have used tables published by the Central Statistical Office (CSO) based on data from the

Table 3.2. Surveys used in finance analysis

Country	Abbr.	Year	Survey(s)	Institution conducting survey	No. of households
Denmark	DK	1981	*Household Expenditure Survey*	Danmarks Statistik	2783
France	F	1984	*Family Expenditure Survey*	INSEE	11 977
Ireland	IRL	1987	*Household Budget Survey*	CSO	7705
Italy	I	1987	*Family Consumption Survey*	ISTAT	3164
Netherlands	NL	1987	*Household Expenditure Survey*	CBS	2750
Portugal	P	1981	*Family Income & Expenditure Survey*	INE	8054
Spain	E	1980	*Family Budget Survey*	INE	23 972
Switzerland	CH	1982	SOMIPOPS and SEVS surveys	National Science Foundation	3835
UK	UK	1985	*Family Expenditure Survey*	CSO	7000
US	US	1980	NMCUES	National Center for Health Statistics	6000

British *Family Expenditure Survey*. The disadvantage of pre-tabulated data is obvious: researchers have no option but to live with the definitions adopted by the persons who have done the tabulations. Households may, for example, have been ranked by income or equivalent expenditure, instead of equivalent income. The third category is *data from other surveys*. Sometimes the survey is in the same series but another year: the Irish and UK reports, for example, make use of data from previous years of their primary survey for some taxes. Alternatively, the survey can be another survey entirely: the authors of the Dutch report, for example, use tabulations of indirect taxes from a survey other than their principal survey. The fourth category comprises *estimated distributions*. This is where authors have not had access to data on the variable in question but have been able to estimate its distribution across income groups by using information from other studies. The authors of the Swiss report, for example, have estimated the distribution of semi-private insurance premia by drawing on econometric estimates of the income-elasticity of demand for this type of insurance. The fifth category comprises '*guesstimates*'. Some of these are more informed than others. Omitted indirect taxes, for example, have often been assumed to be distributed as the indirect taxes that have been allocated from survey data. Occassionally, no explicit assumption has been made. If only part of a category has been allocated on the basis of survey data, but the progressivity index has been weighted by the full share of the financing source, the implicit assumption is that the omitted part is distributed as the included part. If, by contrast, the source is omitted completely, the implicit assumption is that the source is distributed as the overall burden of included sources.

As is apparent from Fig. 3.7, most countries have managed to allocate over 90 per cent of revenues using raw survey data, tabulated data or data from other surveys. Exceptions to this are Ireland and Italy, where very nearly 90 per cent has been allocated from survey data, and Portugal and Switzerland, where the distribution of more than 20 per cent of revenues has had to be estimated or 'guesstimated'.

Table 3.3 indicates the proportions of each type of revenue that have been allocated on the basis of the survey data. For the most part the gaps are in the distributions of taxes, although in Switzerland and the UK the distributions of some non-tax revenues have had to be estimated or 'guesstimated'.

Computation of progressivity indices

The G_{pre}, C_{tax}, and H_{tax} indices are best calculated using microdata, in which case the simplest method of computation is the covariance method

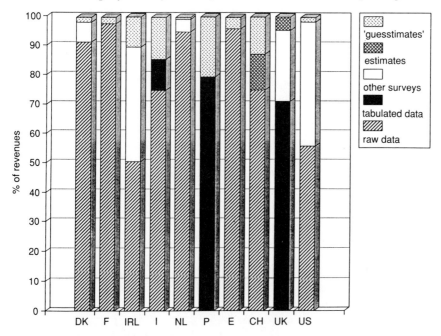

Fig. 3.7. Breakdown of data sources used in analysis of finance.

(Jenkins 1988). An alternative—but less accurate method—is to compute the indices from grouped data. If this is done, the simplest formula is derived on the assumption that the concentration curve is piecewise linear (Fuller and Lury 1977). This method assumes, however, that there is no variation in income (or health care payments) within each income class. A more accurate method which attempts to take this intra-class variation into account is that proposed by Kakwani and Podder (1976), which involves a non-linear approximation of the Lorenz or concentration curve.

EMPIRICAL FINDINGS ON PROGRESSIVITY IN HEALTH CARE FINANCING

Authors of the country reports in Part II have calculated both the Kakwani and Suits indices of progressivity. In most cases the two indices have the same sign, although in several cases the absolute magnitudes of the two indices differ. The differences, however, are not, on the whole, large enough to warrant the inclusion of both sets of results in this chapter. Only the Kakwani indices are reported.[6]

Table 3.3. Proportion of revenues allocated from surveys (per cent)

Country	Direct taxes (%)	Indirect taxes (%)	Social insurance (%)	Private insurance (%)	Direct payments (%)	Total (%)
Denmark	97	99	–	100	100	98
France	0	0	100	100	100	98
Ireland	64	100	100	100	100	90
Italy	86	49	100	–	100	86
Netherlands	61	100	100	100	100	99
Portugal	80	64	100	100	100	80
Spain	71	73	100	100	100	96
Switzerland	100	100	100	70	32	75
UK	100	100	100	0	100	95
US	100	75	100	100	100	98

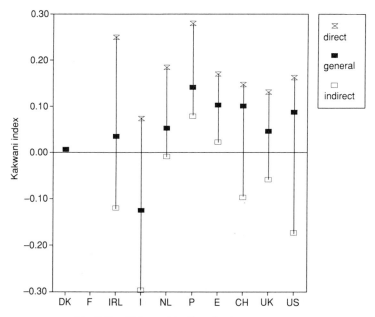

Fig. 3.8.   Kakwani indices for tax revenues.

Taxes

Figure 3.8 shows *inter alia* the progressivity characteristics of the direct tax revenues used to finance health care in each country. As noted above, most countries have not allocated direct taxes other than personal income tax, so most distributions reflect only this tax. Unsurprisingly, direct taxes are progressive in all countries, although the degree of progressively varies. According to Fig. 3.8, the countries with the most progressive direct tax systems are Portugal and Ireland, and the country with the least progressive system is Italy. The latter provides a nice example of the need to look beyond the rate structure when assessing progressivity: in 1987 the Italian personal income tax system contained no less than nine bands, but because so few people paid tax at the higher rates, the system was relatively unprogressive.

Figure 3.8 also shows the progressivity characteristics of the indirect tax revenues used to finance health care. Unsurprisingly, except in the cases of Portugal and Spain, indirect taxes are regressive, although as with direct taxes there is some variation in the degree of regressiveness across countries. The Italian indirect taxes appear as the most regressive, but it should be noted that the distribution reflects VAT (value-added tax) only and that households were ranked by equivalent expenditure rather than equivalent gross income. That indirect taxes were progressive in Spain and

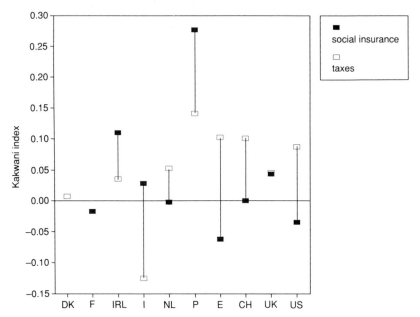

Fig. 3.9.   Kakwani indices for taxes and social insurance.

Portugal in the years in question is due to higher tax rates being levied on luxury goods.

In calculating the Kakwani indices for general tax revenues in Fig. 3.8 the indices for direct and indirect taxes have been weighted according to their importance in total tax revenues. Except in the case of Italy,[7] general taxes are at least proportional (Denmark) and are generally progressive, although—surprisingly—less so than direct taxes.

Social insurance

Figure 3.9 shows the variation across countries in the progressivity of social insurance and compares the latter with the progressivity of general taxation. In the three countries operating social insurance-based health care financing systems—France, the Netherlands, and Spain—social insurance is regressive.[8] This stems from the fact that contributions tend to be proportional to earnings only up to a ceiling. These systems would, however, be even more regressive if groups such as pensioners were not exempt from contributions (as in the Netherlands) or did not face reduced contribution rates (as they do in France). In Italy, where health-specific social insurance contributions still play a major role in the finance of public health care, social insurance is actually progressive. This is despite the fact that the marginal contribution rate actually *declines* with earnings. One reason may be that whilst contributions may be regressive on *earnings*, they may be proportional—or even progressive—on *income*. Alternatively, it may stem from the fact that different groups are treated differently within the social insurance system. Pensioners in Italy, for example, as in some other countries, are exempt from social insurance contributions. Or different professional groups may face different contribution schedules, with persons facing lower average contributions rates tending to have relatively small declared incomes.

The progressivity of the Portuguese social insurance scheme stems from the fact that although contributions to the scheme are earnings-related and compulsory, the scheme is not universal, covering and requiring contributions from only certain employees, the majority of these working in the public sector. Its progressivity is due to the fact that these workers tend to be in the higher income groups (the top decile alone contributed 42 per cent of the scheme's revenues). In both the UK and Ireland, where there are no earmarked social insurance contributions or where earmarking plays only a small role, social insurance is progressive, whereas in the US, where a percentage of social insurance is earmarked for public health care, social insurance is regressive.

Private insurance

In interpreting the results on private health insurance it is important to bear in mind the cover that private insurance buys in each country. Broadly speaking, three groupings emerge from Table 3.1: (1) countries where private insurance buys cover against public sector copayments (Denmark and France); (2) countries where private insurance is mostly taken out as supplementary cover (mainly 'double' cover) to that provided by the State (Italy, Portugal and the UK); and (3) countries where for the individuals concerned private insurance is (or is nearly) the sole source of cover (Ireland, the Netherlands, Spain, Switzerland and the US). In Ireland, the Netherlands, Spain, and the US, private insurance is generally taken out only by persons whose public cover is either restricted or non-existent, although in Ireland, Spain, and the US a small proportion of expenditures on private insurance is accounted for by persons with public cover purchasing supplementary insurance. In the US, persons purchasing private insurance as their sole source of cover make up the bulk of the population, whereas, in Ireland, the Netherlands, and Spain they comprised in 1987, 29 per cent, 39 per cent, and 15 per cent of the population, respectively. Switzerland is unusual (group 3) in that private insurance is bought by almost everyone.

Figure 3.10 shows the progressivity of private health insurance in each

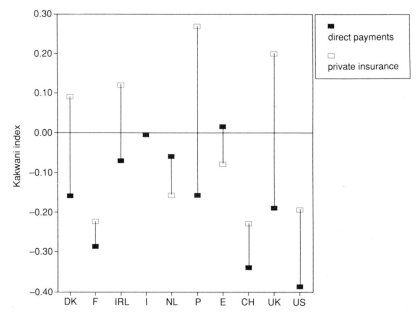

Fig. 3.10.   Kakwani indices for private health care expenditures.

country. The fact that private insurance against public sector copayments is progressive in Denmark but regressive in France reflects the fact that private insurance against public sector copayments is more widespread in France than in Denmark. This in turn reflects the higher copayments in France. Private insurance of a supplementary character is progressive: this suggests that such insurance is a 'luxury' good (a good for which the demand rises more than proportionately as income rises). By contrast, private insurance that is relied upon by the majority of the population for cover is highly regressive, as is apparent from the Swiss and American results. The highly negative Dutch index value stems from the fact that the figures include not only the genuinely private cover bought by the 39 per cent of the population, but also the non-catastrophic cover bought by the remaining 61 per cent from sick funds. Had only the former been included, private insurance would have emerged as being progressive as in Ireland, where private insurance is taken out mainly by the better-off.[9]

Out-of-pocket payments

As is evident from Fig. 3.10, out-of-pocket payments tend to be a highly regressive means of financing health care. In all countries in the study except Spain, such payments were regressive. There is, however, some

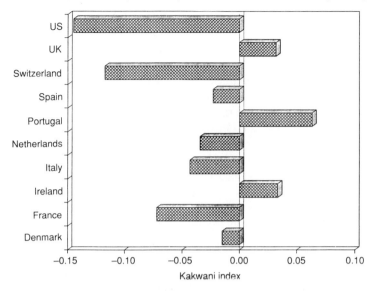

Fig. 3.11. Kakwani indices for overall financing burden.

variation across countries. That out-of-pocket payments were only mildly regressive in Ireland and the Netherlands in 1987 stems from the fact that the private cover taken out by persons in the higher income groups who did not have comprehensive public cover was either limited or required copayments. In Ireland, persons in the top 62 per cent of the income distribution were required to pay for general practitioner (GP) visits and prescription drugs in full, whilst in the Netherlands much of the expenditures associated with out-of-pocket payments were incurred by the privately insured in the upper half of the income distribution having insurance policies with substantial deductibles or excluding primary care. That out-of-pocket payments are so regressive in Switzerland and the US stems from the fact that—with the exception of Medicaid enrollees and some privately insured in the US—copayments are paid by all irrespective of their income.

Overall cross-country differences in progressivity of financing systems

By combining information on the revenue shares with the values of the progressivity index for each revenue source, it is possible to obtain a progressivity index value for each country's financing system overall (Fig. 3.11). It is striking that in only three countries—the UK, Ireland, and Portugal—is health care finance progressive. Also striking is that the progressivity indices in Fig. 3.11 fall into the same three clusters that emerged in the health care financing triangle in Fig. 3.3. The two countries with predominantly private financing systems—Switzerland and the US—have the most regressive structures overall. This is scarcely surprising in view of just how regressive private insurance and out-of-pocket payments are when used to finance such a large proportion of health care expenditures for such a large proportion of the population. The group of countries with the next most regressive financing systems are the countries operating the so-called social insurance model, notably France, Spain, and the Netherlands. That these countries' systems are less regressive than those of Switzerland and the US is partly because social insurance is less regressive than private insurance, partly because there is less reliance on out-of-pocket payments in the second group of countries, and partly because persons in the lower income groups in the latter countries tend to be less likely to be called on to make out-of-pocket payments. The final group of countries, which include Denmark, Ireland, Portugal, and the UK, rely mainly on tax-finance and have the least regressive financing systems. Indeed, in the UK, Ireland, and Portugal health care finance is, as has been noted, marginally progressive.

SUMMARY AND CONCLUSIONS

Health care is typically financed from a mixture of four sources: taxes, social insurance contributions, private insurance premia, and out-of-pocket payments. The precise mix varies from one country to the next. Amongst the countries that finance the bulk of their expenditures publicly, a distinction is made between tax-financed systems (Denmark, Ireland, Portugal, and the UK) and social insurance systems (France, the Netherlands, and Spain). Few countries finance the bulk of their expenditures privately: only in Switzerland and the US do private insurance premiums and out-of-pocket payments combined exceed 50 per cent.

On standard incidence assumptions, taxes are typically a progressive means of raising revenue. The overall degree of progressivity of taxation depends on the progressivity of each tax and the precise mix used. Typically direct taxes are progressive and indirect taxes regressive. Thus, in principle, if direct taxes are insufficiently progressive and/or there is a sufficiently strong emphasis on indirect taxes in the financing of health care, the tax burden overall can be regressive. Only in Italy, however, does this appear to be the case, although as the authors of the country report emphasise, this is a somewhat tentative conclusion. In all other countries the mix of taxes used to finance health care is progressive.

Social insurance, by contrast, tends to be a regressive method of raising revenue. This is typically because contributions are subject to a ceiling, although in some countries the marginal contribution rates themselves decline as earnings rise. There are, however, progressive elements to social insurance: for example, certain groups, such as pensioners, are typically exempt from contributions. Overall, however, social insurance tends to be regressive.

The same is true of private insurance in countries, such as Switzerland and the US, where the majority of the population has no public insurance cover. Indeed, private insurance is a more regressive method of raising revenue than social insurance, the reason being that whereas the latter is assessed on the basis of earnings, at least up to a point, the former is not. To the extent that private insurance premiums are adjusted for risk, premiums may actually be *negatively* related to income, as the worse-off tend to be especially sick. Only in countries like Britain and Spain where private insurance buys supplementary cover, and in countries like Ireland and the Netherlands where private insurance is taken out mainly by the better-off who have limited public cover, is private insurance progressive. This simply reflects the fact that private insurance in these countries is purchased only by the better-off. To the extent that further expansion of private insurance in these countries can only come about as a result of persons in the middle and lower income groups also taking out private insurance, such expansion would make private insurance less progressive. Indeed, at some point such expansion would render private insurance regressive, as it is already in Switzerland and the US.

Out-of-pocket payments are also generally a regressive form of health care finance. Such payments tend to be substantially more regressive than social insurance, and in countries where private insurance is widespread, they are even more regressive than private insurance premiums. In tax-financed systems, out-of-pocket payments are typically the only regressive element in the financing system, apart from indirect taxes. The regressiveness of out-of-pocket payments stems, of course, in part from the higher rates of sickness and medical consumption of the worse-off.

Given the above, it should come as no surprise that although tax-financed health care systems, such as those operating in Denmark, Ireland, Portugal, and the UK, tend to be mildly progressive, social insurance systems, such as those operating in France, the Netherlands, and Spain, and predominantly private systems, such as the American and Swiss systems, tend to be regressive, with the latter systems being particularly regressive.

NOTES

1. Switzerland is usually shown as being predominantly public (Maxwell 1981; OECD 1989). This is because the premiums paid to sickness funds for basic

health insurance cover are recorded under social insurance in the Swiss national accounts. This practice is misleading, as these premiums are neither compulsory nor earnings-related.

2. In the text, Hurst does remark that in the UK 'household income rises about $4\frac{1}{2}$ times between the second and ninth deciles whereas household tax contributions rose about seven-fold over this range' (Hurst 1985, p. 117).

3. We are indebted to the late Peter Ellemann-Jensen for this diagrammatic demonstration of the difference between the two indices.

4. Rules relating to the finance of health care, especially those concerning private health insurance, often apply to the family rather than the household. The latter, however, is typically the income-sharing unit and hence is arguably the more appropriate for assessing how health care payments relate to ability to pay.

5. The argument for employing different equivalence scales is that the circumstances of countries differ. The argument against this strategy is that use of different scales 'would be to invite the response that any inter-country differences emerging in the consequent results simply reflected these equivalence scale differences' (O'Higgins *et al.* 1990, p. 25). Health care payments were not equivalized in the calculation of the concentration indices.

6. The full set of results is reported in the Appendix to this chapter.

7. The extent to which the regressiveness of general tax revenues in Italy in Fig. 3.8 stems from the omission of indirect taxes other than VAT is unclear.

8. The progressivity index in the case of the Netherlands reflects only contributions to the AWBZ scheme for coverage against catastrophic expenses. Premiums paid by the bottom and middle income groups to sickness funds for non-catastrophic cover have been labelled as 'private', as these were included under the same heading in the Dutch *Household Expenditure Survey* as the private premiums paid by the top income group for the same cover. Because people pay either one premium or the other depending on their earnings, including the sickness fund premiums with the AWBZ premiums (which are paid by everyone), rather than private premiums would make social insurance more regressive and private insurance more progressive.

9. The top three deciles of equivalent gross income in Ireland accounted for 66 per cent of expenditures on private insurance premiums.

Appendix

Health care finance in 10 OECD countries

	Denmark 1981	France 1985	Ireland 1987	Italy 1987	Netherlands 1987	Portugal 1980	Spain 1980	Switzerland 1981	UK 1985	US 1981
Per cent from each source										
Direct taxes	49.4	0.0	28.5	19.6	2.1	20.4	7.6	31.6	38.3	23.1
Indirect taxes	35.8	2.3	39.3	22.7	4.5	45.6	6.4	7.4	31.2	6.6
Total taxes	85.2	2.3	67.8	42.3	6.6	66.0	14.0	39.0	69.5	29.7
Social insurance	0.0	75.5	7.3	37.7	65.7	5.2	61.7	1.5	17.0	14.4
Total public	85.2	77.8	75.1	80.0	72.3	71.2	75.7	40.5	86.5	44.1
Private insurance	0.9	7.5	10.0	0.0	20.2	0.6	3.0	40.9	4.8	26.3
Out-of-pocket	13.9	14.7	14.9	20.0	7.5	28.8	21.3	18.6	8.7	29.6
Total private	14.8	22.2	24.9	20.0	27.7	29.4	24.3	59.5	13.5	55.9
Total	100.0	100.0	100.0	100.0	100.0	100.6	100.0	100.0	100.0	100.0
Kakwani indices										
Direct taxes			0.250	0.074	−0.185	0.279	0.170	0.147	0.131	0.162
Indirect taxes		−0.017	−0.120	−0.297	−0.009	0.079	0.023	−0.097	−0.059	−0.174
Total taxes	0.007	−0.017	0.036	−0.125	0.053	0.141	0.102	0.101	0.046	0.087
Social insurance			0.110	0.028	−0.002	0.277	−0.063	0.000	0.043	−0.035
Total public	0.007		0.043	−0.053	0.003	0.151	−0.032	0.097	0.045	0.047
Private insurance	0.091	−0.224	0.120		−0.158	0.270	−0.079	−0.229	0.200	−0.195
Out-of-pocket	−0.159	−0.286	−0.070	−0.004	−0.059	−0.158	0.016	−0.339	−0.190	−0.387
Total private	−0.143	−0.265	0.006	−0.004	−0.131	−0.149	0.005	−0.263	−0.051	−0.296
Total	−0.015	−0.072	0.034	−0.043	−0.096	0.063	−0.023	−0.117	0.032	−0.145

	Denmark 1981	France 1985	Ireland 1987	Italy 1987	Netherlands 1987	Portugal 1980	Spain 1980	Switzerland 1981	UK 1985	US 1981
Suits indices										
Direct taxes			0.250	0.122	0.199	0.310	0.192	0.168	0.142	0.195
Indirect taxes			-0.140	-0.298	-0.016	0.085	0.019	-0.109	-0.069	-0.207
Total taxes	-0.002		0.024	-0.103	0.052	0.154	0.113	0.115	0.047	0.105
Social insurance		-0.030	0.080	0.007	-0.016	0.301	-0.084	0.000	0.028	-0.081
Total public	-0.002	-0.029	0.029	-0.051	-0.010	0.165	-0.048	0.111	0.043	0.045
Private insurance	0.097	-0.216	0.100		-0.169	0.292	-0.084	-0.233	0.250	-0.249
Out-of-pocket	-0.148	-0.293	-0.100	-0.036	-0.068	-0.157	0.013	-0.332	-0.210	-0.386
Total private	-0.133	-0.267	-0.020	-0.036	-0.142	-0.148	0.001	-0.264	-0.046	-0.322
Total	-0.021	-0.081	0.017	-0.048	-0.107	0.073	-0.036	-0.112	0.031	-0.160

Note: Indices for total taxes, total public, total private, and total calculated as weighted averages, with percentages in the top third of the table being used as weights. Dutch total indices taken from table 10.3, because social insurance in this table refers to AWBZ only.

4

Equity in the delivery of health care: methods and findings

Adam Wagstaff and Eddy Van Doorslaer

INTRODUCTION

In common with the majority of earlier literature on equity in the delivery of health care, the present study starts from the premise that health care ought to be distributed according to need rather than ability to pay. Attention is focused here on the horizontal version of this principle: that persons in equal need ought to treated the same irrespective of their ability to pay. Although this is the main focus of this chapter, evidence is presented first on inequalities in health.

INEQUALITIES IN HEALTH

As indicated in Chapter 2, equality of health is sometimes argued to be one of the yardsticks against which the equity of a health care delivery system might be judged. It is, after all, as Culyer and Williams note in their contributions to this volume, difficult to rationalize a concern about the distribution of medical care other than in terms of a concern about the distribution of health itself. Even if 'equality of health' is felt to be too stringent a definition of equity for the health care system (health is, of course, affected by many factors other than health care), inequalities in health are of interest in their own right and evidence on international differences in such inequalities is recognized as being potentially valuable (Fox 1990).

Measuring inequalities in health

Inequality in morbidity is measured in the present volume by means of an *illness concentration index* (Wagstaff et al. 1989). This index, as we have shown elsewhere (Wagstaff, et al. 1991 a), is closely related to the slope index of inequality (SII) of Preston et al. (1985), which involves computing a 'class gradient' by means of regression analysis. The SII has been used extensively in the literature on inequalities in health (Pamuk 1985,

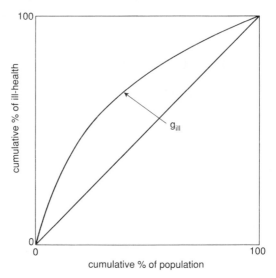

Fig. 4.1.   Illness concentration index.

1989; Wilkinson 1989) and, like our concentration index, has various advantages over the other measures of inequality encountered in this literature.[1]

In calculating the illness concentration index, individuals (or socio-economic groups) are ranked by their socio-economic status (as measured by their income or social class or socio-economic group, or whatever), beginning with the most disadvantaged. The illness concentration curve (labelled g_{ill} in Fig. 4.1) plots the cumulative proportions of the population (beginning with the most disadvantaged and ending with the least disadvantaged) against the cumulative proportions of illness. If illness is equally distributed across, say, income groups, g_{ill} will coincide with the diagonal. If poor health is concentrated in the lower income groups, g_{ill} lies above the diagonal. The illness concentration index—denoted by C_{ill} —is defined as minus twice the area between the concentration curve and the diagonal. Thus C_{ill} ranges from –1 (when only the most disadvantaged person is ill) to +1 (when only the least disadvantaged person is ill), and takes a value of zero when all individuals (or socio-economic groups) have the same morbidity irrespective of their income.[2]

Data and variable definitions

Measuring inequalities in morbidity calls for data at the individual level on whichever variable is used to rank individuals (equivalent income in the present study) and on morbidity. In most countries the obvious source of such data is a health interview survey (cf. Table 4.1). Only the UK and Ireland lack such surveys; in both cases a more general purpose household interview survey has been used.

One shortcoming of health interview surveys (and a potential advantage of the more general purpose surveys) is that their information on income and household structure can be somewhat limited. The Italian survey, for example, contained no information on the size and age structure of the respondent's family, which meant that, unlike the authors of the other reports, the authors of the Italian report were unable to express gross family income on a *per equivalent adult* basis.

Blaxter (1989) has proposed a useful schema for classifying morbidity measures according to the underlying conceptual model. She distinguishes between: (1) a *medical* model, in which ill health is defined in terms of a deviation from physiological norms; (2) a *social-interactional* or *functional* model, in which ill health is defined in terms of a lack of ability to perform 'normal' tasks or roles; and (3) a *subjective* model, in which ill health is defined in terms of the individual's perception. She then suggests how the various morbidity measures that crop up in health interview surveys fit into this schema: questions about chronic illness are argued to derive from the medical model; questions asking whether the individual's normal activities were affected by ill health in the recall period are argued to derive from the functional model; questions on self-assessed health (e.g., 'Do you consider your health to be good, quite good, or not good?') are argued to derive from the subjective model. Most country surveys contain questions deriving from each of Blaxter's models. There are, however, some exceptions, as is apparent from Table 4.2. In the French, Portuguese, and American surveys, for example, there is no question such as: 'Do you have any long-standing health problem or chronic illness?' The authors of the French country report have, however, been able to construct a proxy variable for chronic illness from a more general question concerning specific medical conditions with the assistance of physicians. All but the Irish survey contain information on functional health limitations, and all but the French, Irish, and Portuguese surveys contain a question on self-assessed health along the lines: 'Do you consider your health in general to be excellent, good, fair or poor?'

Empirical evidence on international differences in inequalities in health

We report below the values of the C_{ill} index of inequality for three different morbidity measures for adults only.[3] The first derives from Blaxter's 'medical' model and indicates whether or not the individual suffered from chronic health problems. The second derives from Blaxter's 'functional' model and indicates whether or not the individual suffered from a limiting

Table 4.1. Data sources for analysis of delivery systems

Country	Year	Survey	Institution conducting survey	Sample size (persons)	Income equivalized?
Denmark	1982/3	*Danish Health Study*	Odense University	3153	Yes
France	1980	*Health Interview Survey*	INSEE	21000	Yes
Ireland	1987	*SIDPUSS*	ESRI	8310	Yes
Italy	1985	*Health Care Consumption Survey*	Centro Europa Ricerche	2197	No
Netherlands	1981/2	*Health Interview Survey*	CBS	10319	Yes
Portugal	1987	*National Health Interview Survey*	Ministry of Health	35076	Yes
Spain	1987	*National Health Survey*	Social Investigations Center	16770	Yes
Switzerland	1981/2	*SOMIPOPS and SEVS surveys*	National Science Foundation	3835	Yes
UK	1985	*General Household Survey*	OPCS	25000	Yes
US	1980	*NMCUES*	National Center for Health Statistics	10396	Yes

Table 4.2. Morbidity indicators used in country reports

Country	Medical model	Functional model	Subjective model
Denmark	Chronic illness (yes/no). No. of chronic illnesses.	No. restricted-activity days. No. bed-days.	Health defined as 'not good' if respondent disagreed with statement: 'My health is excellent'.
France	Open list of 20 conditions later given ICD code by GPs and then classified into chronic and acute.	Restricted-activity days (yes/no).	
Ireland	Chronic illness (yes/no).	Limiting chronic illness (yes/no).	
Italy	Chronic illness (yes/no).	Restricted-actitivity days (yes/no).	Three categories in self-assessment: good, quite good, or not good. Latter used to defined health 'not good'.
Netherlands	Chronic illness (yes/no).	Restricted-actitivity days (yes/no).	Four categories in self-assessment: good, sometimes good/sometimes bad, fair, poor. Bottom 3 used to define health 'not good'.

Table 4.2. (*cont.*)

Country	Medical model	Functional model	Subjective model
Portugal		Chronic illness which limited activity in previous 2 weeks (yes/no). Bed-days (yes/no). No. bed-days. Days off work (yes/no). No. days off work.	Four categories in self-assessment: very good, good, fair, not good. Latter used to define health 'not good'.
Spain	List of 26 conditions later classified by principal components analysis into chronic and other.	Limiting chronic illness (yes/no). Restricted-activity days (yes/no).	
Switzerland	GP-diagnosed chronic condition (yes/no).	Limiting chronic illness (yes/no).	Four categories in self-assessment: excellent, good, fair, poor. Bottom two used to define health 'not good'.
UK	Chronic illness (yes/no).	Limiting chronic illness (yes/no).	Three categories in self-assessment: good, fairly good, or not good. Latter used to define health 'not good'.
US		Limiting chronic illness (yes/no).	Four categories in self-assessment: excellent, good, fair, poor. Latter used to define health 'not good'.

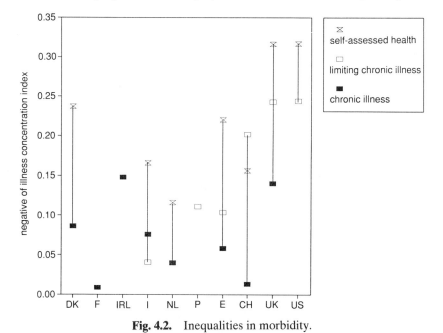

Fig. 4.2. Inequalities in morbidity.

chronic illness. The third derives from Blaxter's 'subjective' model and indicates whether or not the individual's own assessment of his or her health fell into what the authors have labelled the 'not good' category.

Cross-country differences in inequalities in morbidity

Inequalities in morbidity exist in all 10 countries and favour the rich. This is apparent from Fig. 4.2 (see also the Appendix to this chapter): no illness concentration index is positive. The degree of inequality depends, however, on morbidity measure chosen. In all countries, except Switzerland, inequalities in health are most pronounced when self-assessed health is used as the morbidity indicator. This is consistent with Blaxter's (1989) observation that self-assessed health has been found in several European health surveys to produce 'a remarkably steep and regular gradient by social class' (p. 217). Inequalities in limiting chronic illness tend to be more pronounced than inequalities in chronic sickness.

As is apparent too, there is considerable variation across countries in the inequality index. But interestingly the relative performance of countries is fairly insensitive to choice of morbidity indicator: the rank correlation between the self-assessed health inequality scores and the chronic illness inequality scores is particularly high ($r = 0.98$, $n = 6$, $P < 0.01$), although the rank correlation between the self-assessed health scores and the limiting chronic illness scores is lower ($r = 0.70$, $n = 5$, $P > 0.10$). It is striking that on both the self-assessed health indicator and the limiting chronic illness indicator, the UK emerges with a higher inequality score than any other European country, and that on the limiting chronic illness indicator only Ireland has a higher inequality index than the UK. What is also striking is the poor performance of the US: on both the self-assessed health indicator and the limiting chronic illness indicator its inequality score is much the same as the UK's. The only country which consistently has a low inequality score is the Netherlands. Switzerland and, to a lesser extent, Denmark also have low scores on the chronic illness indicator, as does Switzerland on the self-assessed indicator. Denmark, however, fares badly on the latter indicator, while Switzerland fares badly on the limiting chronic indicator.

Accounting for cross-country differences in inequalities in morbidity
Although the evidence on cross-country differences in inequalities in morbidity is clearly somewhat patchy, it is nonetheless interesting to try to discern whether there is any pattern in the results.

There is some evidence (although it is far from conclusive) to suggest that inequalities in morbidity are less pronounced in countries which spend a relatively large amount on health care. The US is, of course, an exception to this: it spends more *per capita* than any other country (Fig. 4.3) and yet appears to have the highest degree of inequality in morbidity. But if attention is restricted to the European countries, the picture changes: the correlations between health expenditures *per capita* and the inequality indices for chronic illness and self-assessed health are -0.74 ($P = 0.02$) and -0.60 ($P = 0.10$), respectively.[4] The sensitivity of this result to the inclusion of the US is apparent from Fig. 4.3. Thus higher health care spending in Europe seems to 'buy' some reduction in health inequality —a tentative finding that merits further investigation.

Although the above results are consistent with the view that the amount spent on health care and inequalities in morbidity are not unrelated, it is clear that variations in health care spending cannot explain all the differences in health inequality across countries. What explains, for example, the apparently high degree of inequality in morbidity in the US? One possibility is the high degree of income inequality in that country (Blaxter 1989; Wilkinson 1989). The results from the present study lend some support to the idea countries with a high degree of income inequality also tend to have a high degree of inequality in morbidity. The correlations between the Gini coefficient for equivalent pre-tax income (taken from the financing system analyses of the country reports) and the inequality scores for the three morbidity indicators are all positive. However, only in the case of self-assessed health (Fig. 4.4) is the coefficient significant at

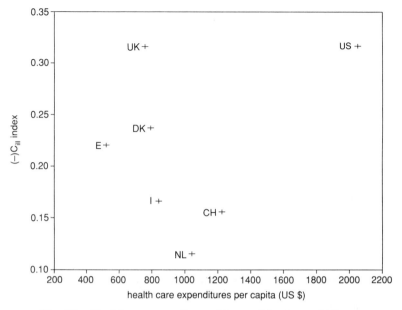

Fig. 4.3. Health care spending and inequalities in morbidity.

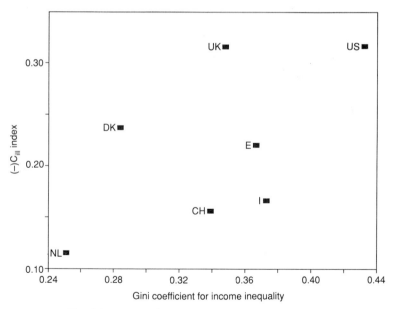

Fig. 4.4. Inequalities in income and in morbidity.

the 10 per cent level ($r = 0.58$, $P = 0.08$).[5] The evidence concerning the relationship between inequalities in health and inequalities in income is thus suggestive but far from conclusive.

EQUITY IN THE DELIVERY OF HEALTH CARE

We turn now to the issue of horizontal equity in the delivery of health care: the issue of how far people in equal need of health care receive the same treatment irrespective of their income. The organization of this section mirrors that of the previous section. Before discussing the issue of measuring equity in the delivery of health care, however, we summarize those differences in the health care delivery systems of the 10 countries which might be expected to have implications for the extent to which persons in equal need actually are treated the same.

Equity and the delivery of health care: cross-country differences

The degree of income-related inequity associated with any health care delivery system is likely to depend on the extent to which the incomes of consumers affect their health-related behaviour and that of health care providers.

The influence of income on the individual's own behaviour is likely to be greater the larger are the various financial and non-financial costs associated with making the initial contact with the health care sector and with receiving medical care once the initial contact has been made. Such costs are sometimes termed 'access costs' (Le Grand 1982; Mooney 1983), although the term is potentially confusing, because many of the costs associated with the receipt of health care are incurred *after* the individual has gained access to the health care system. The costs in question include out-of-pocket payments, transport costs, and the opportunity cost of time spent travelling and waiting. The magnitude of these access costs may well vary with income, as may the *effects* of such costs.

Variation in insurance cover is one reason why access costs may themselves vary across income groups. Some idea of within-country variation in insurance cover in each of the 10 countries can be gleaned from Table 4.3. In most countries insurance cover does not vary with income. In some countries, however, notably Ireland and the Netherlands, it is the better-off who have limited public cover. The US stands out as the only country where a substantial proportion of persons on low incomes have no insurance cover whatsoever. Davis (Chapter 18) reports that in 1986, 37 million Americans (15 per cent of the US population) had no insurance cover. Almost all of these had modest incomes. Indeed, one-third had incomes below the official poverty line. All, however, were either insufficiently poor to qualify for Medicaid or failed to meet other entry criteria (most working-age adults without children are ineligible). The high out-of-pocket payments required to receive medical care appears to have deterred persons in this group from seeking medical care. France is the only other country where some of the poorer members of the community lack comprehensive insurance cover. This stems from the fact that cover is related to occupation. As a result, a large number of single women (those who have never worked and who are not covered by a partner's policy) fall through the net.

Out-of-pocket payments may also vary across income groups (see Table 4.3). In some countries, the UK is an example, persons on lower incomes are exempted from public sector copayments. In other countries, however, the poor can end up facing larger out-of-pocket payments than the rich. This happens, for example, in France where the high *ticket modérateur* has resulted in *mutuelles* and private insurance companies offering insurance policies against public sector copayments. However, many French citizens—the so-called *nouveaux pauvres*—do not have or cannot afford insurance cover against copayments.

Other financial and non-financial barriers are also likely to be important and may also vary across income groups. The poor are likely to have to spend longer travelling to health care facilities than the rich, being more reliant on public transport and tending to live in areas where health care resources are relatively scarce (Le Grand 1982). They are also likely to spend longer waiting in the waiting room, being less likely to have a telephone at home with which to make an appointment. The poor are also likely to spend longer on any waiting list, being less likely than the rich to be able to 'go private', thereby bypassing any queue in the public sector. As is evident from Table 4.3, sizeable proportions of the populations of France, Ireland, Italy, Portugal, Spain, and the UK have private insurance which generally ensures easier access.

But even if utilization costs were invariant with respect to income, the *effects* of these costs would be likely to vary. Even if, for example, the nominal value of out-of-pocket payments were the same for everyone, the sacrifice in terms of forgone utility (and hence the deterrent effect) would probably be greater for the poor than for the rich. Evidence from the RAND health insurance experiment in the US suggests that this is indeed the case. Newhouse *et al.* (1981) remarked that: 'Our interim results indicate that the poor are not more responsive to cost sharing if the cost sharing is less for low income families, as in the experiment. However, our results do indicate that cost sharing *unrelated to income* would differentially affect lower income families' (p. 1505, italics added).

Provider incentives are also likely to be important in determining how

Table 4.3.   Access to health care in 10 OECD countries

Country	Year	Public cover	Cover of groups without public cover
Denmark	1981	95% of population choose comprehensive cover. Non-institutionalized among remaining 5% have limited public cover.	n.a.
France	1980	98% of population covered under the 3 main insurance funds, most of which provide comprehensive cover. Cover for remaining 2% available from special fund. Persons not opting for this scheme covered in principle by *Aide Médicale*, but in practice many discouraged by bureaucracy. Public hospital provides cover as last resort.	Negligible.
Ireland	1987	38% with lowest incomes all health care free. 47% with middle incomes not eligible for free GP services. 15% with highest incomes eligible only for hotel costs of public hospitals.	Almost all top 15% have private insurance, as do many of middle 47%.
Italy	1985	Universal and comprehensive.	n.a.
Netherlands	1987	Universal cover for catastrophic expenses. Persons with income less than Dfl49 150 (65% of population) have cover for non-catastrophic expenses.	Persons with income above Dfl49 150 typically have insurance cover for non-catastrophic expenses.

Cost sharing in public sector	Cover against public sector copayments	Use of private sector by groups with public cover	Direct payments to private sector
Copayments for dental care, prescription medicines, and physiotherapy. Limited public assistance for 5% with limited cover.	400 000 (10% of population) have private cover for public sector copayments.	None.	Negligible.
Ticket modérateur for ambulatory care and medicines. Small copayment for some inpatient care.	*Mutuelles* and private insurance companies provide cover for portion of public sector copayments.	No supplementary insurance cover. But use of private sector (including *secteur 2* GPs) on fee-paying basis.	Payments for GP, inpatient, and outpatient care.
47% with middle incomes liable for copayments for inpatient and outpatient care and full cost of GP care. 15% with highest incomes liable for inpatient hotel costs and full costs of inpatient, outpatient and GP treatment.	Included in private cover taken out by persons with limited public cover.	28% of population have supplementary private insurance cover, but public cover for some of these is not comprehensive.	Mostly by persons with restricted public cover.
Ticket modérateur for prescription drugs. Some groups (e.g., disabled) exempt.	None.	2.5% of population have supplementary private insurance cover. In addition, extensive use of private sector on fee-paying basis.	Extensive use of private sector on direct payment basis.
Copayments for medicines and for home nursing component of AWBZ-funded care.	None.	None.	Co-insurance and deductibles by groups without public sector cover for non-catastrophic expenses.

Table 4.3   *(cont)*

Country	Year	Public cover	Cover of groups without public cover
Portugal	1987	Universal and comprehensive. Double cover provided by compulsory occupational schemes for many public sector employees.	n.a.
Spain	1987	97% have comprehensive cover. Excludes dental care, opticians and mental care.	Of 3% without public cover persons without financial means covered by local government welfare programmes.
Switzerland	1981	Public cover limited to persons on low incomes.	Almost 99% of population have private cover with sickness funds. Three classes of cover, 1st (top) providing greater comfort in hospital.
UK	1985	Universal and comprehensive.	n.a.
US	1984	Medicare covers permanently and totally disabled, and 65+. Medicaid covers low-income pregnant women, single parents, children, elderly, and disabled persons, but not single persons or couples without children. 12 million Americans in 1986 below poverty line failed to qualify for Medicaid. Limited inpatient and outpatient care made available by public, private, and voluntary hospitals to persons on low incomes.	Private insurance provided mostly as tax-deductible fringe benefit to employees. Private plans typically unaffordable to those not covered by employer-provided cover. 31 million Americans in 1987 were without public or private cover.

Note: n.a. = not applicable.

Cost sharing in public sector	Cover against public sector copayments	Use of private sector by groups with public cover	Direct payments to private sector
Copayments for consultations, diagnostic tests, and medicines.	None.	2% of population have supplementary private insurance cover. In addition, extensive use of private sector on fee-paying basis.	Extensive use of private sector on direct payment basis.
Copayments for non-life-saving prescription medicines. Pensioners exempt.	None.	10–15% of population have supplementary private insurance cover. In addition, extensive use of private sector on fee-paying basis.	Extensive use of private sector on direct payment basis.
None.	None.	None.	Co-payments and deductibles for GP care and ambulatory care. Payments for items not covered, e.g., dental care.
Copayments for prescribed medicines, dental care, and opthalmic care.	None.	9% of population have supplementary private insurance cover.	Primarily by non-residents. No co-insurance and deductibles for privately insured.
Copayments for hospital and physician services for persons covered by Medicare. Minimal direct payments for persons covered by Medicaid.	Insurance against copayments possible.	Persons covered by Medicare also have private cover.	Some plans involve co-insurance and deductibles.

close a health care system comes to achieving 'equal treatment for equal need'. The most obvious way that the income of a patient might influence provider behaviour is if the provider is paid differently depending on whether the patient is being treated publicly or privately. As is clear from Table 4.4, in several countries some providers are paid in such a way that providing care to private patients is more profitable than providing care to public patients. Physicians, for example, may be paid on a fee-for-service basis for private patients, but by salary and/or capitation for public patients. Hospitals may receive a prospective budget for public patients but receive a fee for private patients. That these arrangements may well result in persons on different incomes but in equal need being treated differently is suggested by the work of Hooijmans and Rutten (1984). They examined regional differences in the Netherlands in the hospital utilization of (high income) privately insured and (low income) publicly insured, and found that—after controlling for other factors—specialist density had a positive influence on private hospital use but no effect on public hospital use. They interpreted this finding to be a consequence of the fact that the fees for treating private patients were twice those for treating public patients. The authors comment: 'In a region with a high number of specialists per bed, other things being equal, the specialists will have to treat more privately insured patients to reach the same level of income as in other regions' (p. 46).

Measuring inequity in the delivery of health care

Clearly, a simple comparison of the average amount of treatment received by different income groups or socio-economic groups (SEGs) reveals nothing about whether or not persons in equal need are or are not being treated the same, as 'need' (typically proxied in empirical work by self-reported health status) tends to be correlated with income and socio-economic status. Thus, for example, the fact that the rich privately insured in the Netherlands tend to have fewer GP contacts than the less well-off publicly insured[6] indicates nothing about any inequity in the Dutch health care delivery system, as the privately insured tend to be in better health than the publicly insured.

Le Grand's approach

One way of trying to overcome this problem is to compute the share of medical treatment (as measured, for example, by imputed expenditures) received by each income group or SEG and compare this with the group's share of 'need' (measured, for example, by ill health) (Le Grand 1978). If the expenditure shares of the top groups exceed their illness shares, whereas the opposite is true of the bottom groups, one concludes that there is inequity favouring the better-off. One interpretation of this approach is the following. Assume that all persons reporting themselves as ill are in equal need and that only persons who are ill receive health care. Then if horizontal equity is achieved, so that those in equal need receive the same amount of expenditure, the share of expenditure going to each group will be proportional to its share of persons reporting ill. If the share of expenditure received by the lower groups is less than their share of persons reporting ill, it must be concluded that the sick in the lower groups receive less expenditure than the sick in the higher groups. Equals are not being treated equally and this horizontal inequity apparently favours the better-off.

To *quantify* inequity using Le Grand's method one can employ illness and expenditure concentration curves (Wagstaff *et al.* 1989). In Fig. 4.5, individuals are ranked by their income, although the approach could be used where individuals are divided into SEGs. The curve labelled g_{ill} is the illness concentration curve defined earlier and provides the benchmark against which to assess the fairness of the expenditure distribution. The latter is represented by an expenditure concentration curve (labelled g_{exp} in Fig. 4.5), which plots the cumulative proportions of the population against the proportions of total expenditure received. In so far as the lower income groups are more intensive users of health care than the higher income groups, the expenditure concentration curve lies above the diagonal. If health care expenditures are allocated across income groups in proportion to their share of total ill health, the illness and expenditure concentration curves coincide. If those in lower income groups receive less medical care when ill than those in higher income groups, the expenditure concentration curve will lie below the illness concentration curve. The extent of inequity can be assessed by looking at the size of the area between the two concentration curves. Twice the area between the two concentration curves is equal to

$$HI_{LG} = C_{exp} - C_{ill},$$

where HI_{LG} is a Le Grand-type index of horizontal inequity, C_{ill} is the illness concentration index defined earlier and C_{exp} is an expenditure concentration index defined analogously to C_{ill}. The HI_{LG} index is positive if there is inequity favouring the rich, and negative if there is inequity favouring the poor (in which case g_{exp} lies *above* g_{ill}). It is worth noting that the two concentration curves may cross. Measuring inequity by the HI_{LG} index in this case implies that one is prepared to allow inequity favouring one group to offset inequity favouring another.[7]

Although Le Grand's approach *has* been employed in the country reports in this volume, it has been used to provide a point of departure rather than to generate reliable results. One reason is that it appears

Table 4.4. Anti-equity provider incentives in 10 OECD countries

Country	Year	Ambulatory care	Inpatient care
Denmark	1981	None.	None.
France	1980	Sector 2 GPs and specialists allowed to over-bill, subject to patient's agreement.	Some public hospitals house a private sector. Some private hospitals have limited public duty.
Ireland	1987	Higher fees for private patients than public patients.	Hospitals paid prospective budgets for publicly insured but FFS for privately insured and publically insured paying out-of-pocket.
Italy	1985	Specialists paid salaries for public outpatient visits and FFS for private visits. Full-time SSN specialists limited in amount they can earn from private patients, but part-time not limited. Recent change limits private consultation hours for full-time SSN specialists.	Ospedali convenzionati may receive higher fees for private patients than public patients.
Netherlands	1987	GPs and specialists paid capitation for sick fund patients but FFS for private patients.	Higher fees for private patients than public patients.

Portugal	1987	Salary in public care but FFS in private.
Spain	1987	Specialists paid salary for public patients and FFS for private patients.
Switzerland	1981	Physicians can charge higher fees for persons with 1st and 2nd class insurance cover.
UK	1985	None prior to 1991 reforms.
US	1984	Less generous reimbursment for Medicaid patients than others.

NHS doctors paid salary for NHS patients and FFS for private patients.	
Private hospitals paid per day by state and restrospectively by private insurance companies. Public sector GPs paid salary. Private sector GPs paid FFS.	
None.	
NHS doctors paid salary for NHS patients and FFS for private patients. Full-time NHS consultants limited in amount they can earn from private practice, but part-time not limited.	
Less generous reimbursment for Medicaid patients than others.	

Notes: FFS = Fee for service. NHS = National Health Service. SSN = Servizio Sanitario Nazionale.

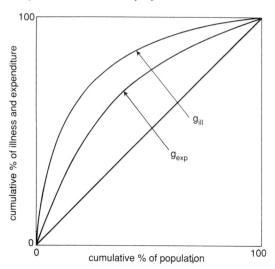

Fig. 4.5.   Le Grand-type index of inequity.

to contain an inbuilt bias towards the detection of inequity favouring the rich, the reason being that it implicitly assumes—unjustifiably, in our view—that the non-sick receive no health care (O'Donnell and Propper 1991 *a*; Wagstaff *et al.* 1991 *b*). The bias can be illustrated by means of the simple example in Table 4.5. Here, there are two equally sized income groups, rich and poor, and the sick are assumed—not unreasonably—to be concentrated amongst the poor. The rich non-sick and the poor non-sick are treated alike by the health care system, as are the rich sick and the poor sick, although the sick are assumed—again, not unreasonably—to receive more resources than the non-sick. It is apparent that, despite the equitable treatment of rich and poor, the poor's expenditure share is less than their illness share. Le Grand's method thus leads us to conclude wrongly that there is inequity favouring the rich.[8]

There is another problem with Le Grand's approach. The fact that the poor's expenditure share differs from their illness share (and likewise for the rich) may well stem not from inequity, or from the fact that the non-sick also receive medical care, but rather from the rich and poor having different demographic characteristics and the allocation of medical care reflecting these characteristics. Le Grand acknowledges this, but his standardized expenditure and illness shares, which indicate the shares each group would have received if it had had the same demographic characteristics as the population as a whole, appear to be unreliable, even if the sick *are* the only recipients of medical treatment (Wagstaff *et al.* 1991 *b*, *c*).

Table 4.5. Hypothetical distributions of illness and health care expenditures

Status	No. persons non-sick	No. persons sick	% of sick	US$ per person non-sick	US$ per person sick	Total expend. US$	% of expend.
Poor	30	20	66.7	50	100	3500	53.8
Rich	40	10	33.3	50	100	3000	46.2

Testing for inequity

Some authors have simply sought to *test* for inequity, rather than measure
its extent. The simplest approach is that adopted by Collins and Klein
(1980), who compare medical care utilization per person in the UK across
socio-economic groups within each morbidity category. An alternative is
to employ regression analysis. This has been particularly popular in the
American literature. L. Benham and A. Benham (1975), for example,
estimate regression equations of the form:

$$m_i = \pi_0 + \pi_1 y_i + \pi_2 h_i + \pi_4 x_i + u_i, \tag{4.1}$$

where m_i is imputed medical care expenditure of person i, y_i is income, x_i
captures demographic factors (it might, for example, be a dummy variable
to distinguish the elderly from the non-elderly), and the πs are coefficients. They find that the *t*-statistic on their estimate of π_1 is just below
the critical value in their 1963 equation but is well below the critical value
in their 1970 equation. This leads them to conclude that: 'the US
has moved in the direction of greater equity' (p. 101). Puffer's (1986)
approach, in his comparison of the UK and US, is similar, except that
interaction terms are introduced. His model is of the form:

$$m_i = \pi_0 + \pi_1 y_i + \pi_2 h_i + \pi_3 y_i \cdot h_i + \pi_4 x_i + \pi_5 y_i + u_i. \tag{4.2}$$

Equity is taken by Puffer to mean that π_1, π_3, and π_5 are all zero.

Potentially, these alternative approaches have important advantages
over that of Le Grand, although in practice the models have not always
been well specified. To illustrate the advantages and see the relationships
with Le Grand's approach it is convenient to ignore for the moment
demographic factors and write eqn (4.2) as:

$$m_i = \pi_0 + \pi_1 y_i + \pi_2 h_i + \pi_3 y_i \cdot h_i + u_i. \tag{4.3}$$

Suppose that y_i is a dummy variable taking a value of 1 if person i is rich
and 0 otherwise. Then eqn (4.3) is equivalent to the following regression
model

$$m_i = \begin{cases} \alpha_p + \beta_p h_i + u_{pi} & \text{if poor} \\ \alpha_r + \beta_r h_i + u_{ri} & \text{if rich,} \end{cases} \tag{4.4}$$

where $\alpha_p = \pi_0$, $\alpha_r = \pi_1 + \alpha_p$, $\beta_p = \pi_2$ and $\beta_r = \pi_3 + \beta_p$. The intercepts in
these equations, α_p and α_r, indicate the expected medical expenditures
received by a poor non-sick person and a rich non-sick person respectively, whereas the sums of the intercepts and the slope coefficients, $\alpha_p + \beta_p$
and $\alpha_r + \beta_r$, indicate the expected medical expenditures received by a poor
sick person and a rich sick person respectively. If, as is assumed by Le

Grand, the non-sick do not receive care (i.e., α_p and α_r are both zero), any discrepancy between the poor's expenditure share and its illness share must be attributed to differences across income groups in the amounts of expenditure received by the sick (i.e., differences in the β's). In this case, therefore, Le Grand's approach ought to give the same answer as the Collins–Klein approach, which in this case amounts to testing whether there is a significant difference between β_p and β_r, and the regression approach, which in this case involves testing the same hypothesis by testing the significance of the coefficient π_3 in eqn (4.3). But if the non-sick *do* receive medical care, the poor's expenditure share may, as was seen in the example above, differ from its illness share even if the rich and poor are treated alike in both morbidity categories, i.e., even if $\alpha_r = \alpha_p$ and $\beta_r = \beta_p$. By contrast, in the Collins–Klein approach, which in this case amounts to testing for significant differences both between α_p and α_r and between $\alpha_p + \beta_p$ and $\alpha_r + \beta_r$, and in the regression approach, which tests the same hypotheses by testing the joint significance of π_1 and π_3, one ought not to be able to conclude that the system is inequitable when it is in fact equitable.

The same logic applies when demographic factors are included as in eqn (4.2). The analogue of eqn (4.4) is:

$$m_i = \begin{cases} \alpha_p + \beta_p h_i + \delta_p x_i + u_{pi} & \text{if poor} \\ \alpha_r + \beta_r h_i + \delta_r x_i + u_{ri} & \text{if rich,} \end{cases} \tag{4.5}$$

so that if x_i is a dummy variable for the elderly, the expected expenditure received by, say, a poor non-sick person depends on whether he or she is elderly.[9] A poor person who is both healthy and young is expected to receive an amount of expenditure equal to α_p, for example, while his or her elderly counterpart is expected to receive an amount of expenditure equal to $\alpha_p + \delta_p$. Rich and poor will be treated alike within all age-morbidity categories if and only if $\alpha_r = \alpha_p$, $\beta_r = \beta_p$, and $\delta_r = \delta_p$, which can be tested using either the Collins–Klein approach or the regression approach.

Moreover, it is easy in these approaches to incorporate more detailed information on need. For example, suppose there are two morbidity indicators available: c_i (a dummy variable taking a value of 1 if individual i reports chronic health problems) and h_i (a dummy taking a value of 1 if individual i reports his health to be less than good). Then model (4.4) becomes

$$m_i = \begin{cases} \alpha_p + \beta_p c_i + \tau_p h_i + u_{pi} & \text{if poor} \\ \alpha_r + \beta_r c_i + \tau_r h_i + u_{ri} & \text{if rich,} \end{cases} \tag{4.6}$$

where one would expect the βs and the τs to be positive. Thus, a poor person who reports no chronic problems and reports his or her health as being good is expected to receive an amount of medical care equal to α_p, whereas a poor person who reports no chronic problems but nonetheless considers his health not to be good is expected to receive an amount of medical expenditure equal to $\alpha_p + \tau_p$. Rich and poor will be treated alike within all morbidity categories if, and only if, $\alpha_r = \alpha_p$, $\beta_r = \beta_p$, and $\tau_r = \tau_p$. This can be tested either using regression analysis via the single equation model analogue, namely:

$$m_i = \pi_0 + \pi_1 y_i + \pi_2 c_i + \pi_3 y_i \cdot c_i + \pi_6 h_i + \pi_7 y_i \cdot h_i + u_i, \qquad (4.7)$$

or alternatively by splitting the sample into different income-morbidity categories along the lines proposed by Collins and Klein. Including *both* demographic factors *and* several morbidity indicators is also straightforward.

Although, in principle, both the regression approach and the Collins–Klein approach do the same thing, the former has been used in the present study. An attraction of the regression approach is that it can easily accommodate the fact that in a typical distribution of medical expenditures, a large percentage of the population records zero utilization. The appropriate regression model in this case is a two-part model, the first part of which models the determinants of the individual's decision to seek care, whereas the second models the determinants of the amount of care received, given that a contact has been made (Manning *et al.* 1981; van Vliet and van de Ven 1985). The first part can be estimated by any of the estimation methods available for a regression model with a binary dependent variable: obvious candidates are the logit and the probit estimation methods. The second part of the model can then be estimated by ordinary least squares (OLS) using only those individuals recording positive utilization. The joint hypotheses $\alpha_r = \alpha_p$, $\beta_r = \beta_p$ and $\delta_r = \delta_p$ in eqn (4.5), for example, could then be tested using a likelihood ratio test,[10] bearing in mind that the log-likelihood for a two-part model is the sum of the log-likelihoods of the two parts of the model. Thus, one could estimate a two-part model (with interaction terms) for the entire sample, as in eqn (4.2), first with the relevant πs unrestricted and then again with the same coefficients restricted to be zero. Under the null hypothesis of no inequity twice the difference between the two models' likelihood values (denoted in the country reports in this volume by LR) is distributed with a chi-squared distribution with as many degrees of freedom as there are parameters that are restricted in the restricted model. An attraction of the two-part model is that it allows one to explore the possibility that income may not affect the likelihood of persons in a given degree of need seeking care but may affect the amount of care they receive once the contact has been made, or *vice versa*.

Although previous regression-based studies of inequity have been based on a single regression model, one could instead estimate separate equations for each income group, as in, for example, eqn (4.5), and then perform the relevant tests directly instead of indirectly via interaction terms. This would involve estimating separate two-part models for each income group, as in eqn (4.5), and then estimating the same model for the entire sample. The null hypothesis of no inequity can then be tested by a likelihood ratio test involving a comparison of the sum of the log-likelihood values for the models of the various income groups with the log-likelihood of the all-sample model.

Standardized expenditure curves and standardized concentration indices

A disadvantage of the testing approaches is that they do not lend themselves to the *quantification* of inequity. Yet quantification is clearly essential if cross-country comparisons are to be performed. The regression approach can, however, be extended to allow an index of inequity to be derived, providing one is prepared to accept a weaker definition of horizontal equity. So far, equity has been taken to mean that the intercepts and slope coefficients in the medical care equations should be the same for all income groups, i.e., in the case of eqn (4.4) $\alpha_r = \alpha_p$ and $\beta_r = \beta_p$. In other words, a health care delivery system cannot be said to be horizontally equitable if the rich and poor are treated differently in *any* morbidity category. But what if the rich are treated favourably in one morbidity category (e.g., the non-sick category) but the poor are treated favourably in the other (e.g., the sick category)? A less restrictive definition of equity would regard such a situation as horizontally equitable *on balance*, providing any favourable treatment afforded to the poor amongst the sick was sufficiently large to offset the favourable treatment afforded to the rich amongst the non-sick. But how large does 'sufficiently large' have to be before one can say that, on balance, no inequity exists?

To see the issues at stake, consider the model in eqn (4.4). (As should become apparent, the argument can be generalized to take into account *any* model of health care utilization.) The difference in the mean or expected medical care expenditures received by the rich and those received by the poor can be expressed as:

$$m_r - m_p = (\alpha_r - \alpha_p) + \beta_r(h_r - h_p) + h_p(\beta_r - \beta_p), \qquad (4.8)$$
$$\quad\;\; \text{(A)} \qquad\quad\; \text{(B)} \qquad\quad\; \text{(C)}$$

where h_r and h_p are the mean morbidity levels of the rich and poor respectively. In eqn (4.8), the term (B) represents the legitimate differences between the medical expenditures of the rich and poor that are attributable to the differences in mean health status. By contrast, terms (A) and (C) reflect inequity, (A) reflecting differential treatment amongst the non-sick and (C) reflecting differential treatment amongst the sick. Rather than requiring that there be no differential treatment in either morbidity category, one might say that inequity favours the rich in this case if the sum of the terms (A) and (C) in eqn (4.8) was positive. A problem with this, apart from the obvious problem of what one does when there are more than two income groups which we address below, is that weighting the differential treatment amongst the sick by the mean morbidity level of the poor is arbitrary and seems hard to justify.

An alternative approach to the weighting problem (Wagstaff *et al.* 1991 *b*) is to compute standardized expenditure figures along the lines proposed by van Vliet and van de Ven (1985). These standardized figures, which can be interpreted as the expenditures each income group would receive if it had the age distribution *and* the morbidity of the population as a whole, can be computed using the direct method employed by epidemiologists or by regression analysis. If OLS is used the two methods are equivalent and the standardized expenditures of the rich and poor respectively in the simple model in eqn (4.4) can be defined as:

$$
\begin{aligned}
m_r^+ &= a_r + b_r h \\
m_p^+ &= a_p + b_p h
\end{aligned}
\tag{4.9}
$$

where a_r is the OLS estimate of α_r, b_r is the OLS estimate of β_r, and so on, and h is the sample mean of h_i. The difference between these standardized means can be expressed as:

$$
m_r^+ - m_p^+ = \underset{(A)}{(a_r - a_p)} + \underset{(c')}{h(b_r - b_p)}.
\tag{4.10}
$$

In this decomposition, the degree of inequity affecting a given morbidity category is weighted by the fraction of the population in that category. Thus, the entire population is affected by any differences in the αs, whilst only the sick (a fraction h of the population) are affected by a discrepancy in the βs. Saying that inequity favours the rich if the sum of (A) and (c') is positive seems reasonable. It is evidently more general than the earlier definition of inequity (namely, $\alpha_r = \alpha_p$, and $\beta_r = \beta_p$), but subsumes it as a special case: if $\alpha_r = \alpha_p$, and $\beta_r = \beta_p$, it follows automatically that (A) + (c') = 0.

To obtain some idea of the *extent* of inequity one could, of course, simply compute standardized expenditure figures for all income groups, ideally using a two-part regression model, and then compare the values for the top and bottom groups. A more reliable approach is to use

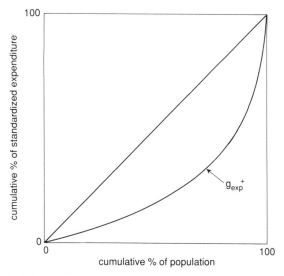

Fig. 4.6. Standardized expenditure concentration curve.

standardized expenditure shares and standardized expenditure concentration curves. Under an equitable delivery system, the standardized shares will be equal to each group's share of the population. Thus if, in the two-group case, the morbidity-standardized expenditure share of, say, the rich, is equal to its population share, it follows that:

$$(\alpha_r - \alpha_p) + h(\beta_r - \beta_p) = 0,$$

whereas if the rich's standardized expenditure share exceeds its population share, it follows that

$$(\alpha_r - \alpha_p) + h(\beta_r - \beta_p) > 0.$$

The opposite is true if the rich group's share is less than its population share. From the standardized expenditure shares for the various income groups one can plot a standardized expenditure concentration curve. This is the curve labelled g_{exp}^+ in Fig. 4.6 and plots the cumulative proportions of the population—again ranked according to income—against their standardized expenditure shares. If there is, on balance, inequity favouring the rich, g_{exp}^+ will lie below the diagonal (the case illustrated in Fig. 4.6), whereas the opposite will be true if there is inequity favouring the poor.

The *extent* of inequity can be measured by the concentration index for the standardized concentration curve. Thus an alternative index of inequity to HI_{LG} is:

$$HI_{WVP} = C_{exp}^+,$$

where C_{exp}^+ is the concentration index corresponding to g_{exp}^+. In the case illustrated, HI_{WVP} is defined as the ellipse-shaped area between g_{exp}^+ and the diagonal, expressed as a proportion of the area under the diagonal. In the case where g_{exp}^+ lies *above* the diagonal (i.e., where there is inequity favouring the poor), the concentration index is defined as the negative of the ellipse-shaped area as a proportion of the area under the diagonal. Thus HI_{WVP} is negative when there is inequity favouring the poor (the lower bound being –1), and is positive when there is inequity favouring the rich (the upper bound being +1). As is the case with the unstandardized illness concentration curve, g_{exp}^+ can cross its benchmark curve (the diagonal). In such cases, the HI_{WVP} index could register a value of zero even if the standardized expenditures vary across income groups. This would happen if the area between the concentration curve and the 45° line lying to the left of the cross-over point were equal to the corresponding area to the right of the cross-over. Such a situation might arise, for example, if the top and bottom income groups both have standardized expenditure figures that are above those of the middle groups. The implicit value judgement involved in using the HI_{WVP} index in this case is that inequity favouring one income group can offset inequity favouring another.

Data and variable definitions

The data sources for countries' analyses of equal treatment for equal need are the surveys listed in Table 4.1. 'Need' is proxied by the self-reported morbidity indicators listed in Table 4.2 'Treatment' has been proxied by imputed expenditures, as in Le Grand's (1978) study. Thus, in contrast to studies such as that of Collins and Klein (1980), studies in the present volume take into account not just whether an individual contacted the health care sector but also how much care was received. Moreover, in contrast to studies such as that of Puffer (1986), the studies in the present volume include not just primary care, but also specialist care and inpatient care. Dental care has been excluded on the grounds that the measures of need used do not, on the whole, reflect dental health. Medicines (prescribed and over-the-counter) were also excluded, because several surveys did not include sufficiently detailed information to allow expenditures to be imputed. In arriving at overall imputed expenditure, GP visits, specialist visits, and inpatient days (or, in some cases, hospital stays) have been weighted by their average cost. Except in situations where there was a clear difference between public and private sectors in the quality of

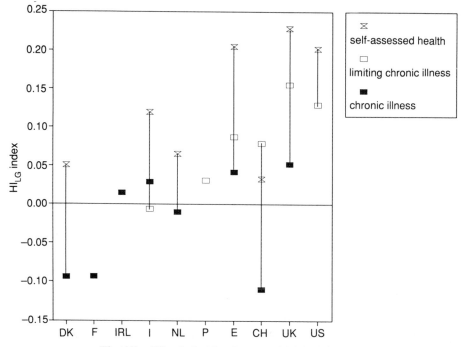

Fig. 4.7. HI_{LG} index for three morbidity indicators.

care delivered (i.e., in the likely improvements in health status), the same unit cost was used for both sectors.

Empirical evidence on international differences in equity in the delivery of health care

Replication of Le Grand's study

Although, as has been argued above, Le Grand's (1978) approach to analysing equity in the delivery of health care appears to be flawed, it does provide a useful reference point for the present study. Figure 4.7 and the Appendix to this chapter report the values for each country of the HI_{LG} index for the three morbidity indicators considered earlier for adults only.[11] Positive values of this index indicate that on balance any inequity favours the rich, whereas negative values indicate that on balance any inequity favours the poor.

Various points are worth noting about Fig. 4.7. First, the values of the HI_{LG} index are smaller in numerical value if chronic sickness is used as the morbidity indicator. This reflects the fact that inequalities in chronic sickness are less pronounced than inequalities in self-assessed health. Secondly, in only three of the six countries where information on the distributions of both self-assessed health and chronic sickness is available is the HI_{LG} index the same sign for both morbidity indicators. Thus, although the UK, Italy, and Spain the index indicates inequity favouring the rich irrespective of which indicator is chosen, in Denmark, the Netherlands, and Switzerland, the index indicates inequity favouring the rich if the self-assessed health indicator is used, but inequity favouring the poor if the chronic indicator is used. Choice of morbidity indicator thus appears to be of crucial importance in many countries in determining whether or not one detects inequity favouring the rich. Thirdly, although the sign of the HI_{LG} index is sensitive to the choice of morbidity indicator, the ranking of the various countries is relatively stable: indeed, the rankings in the case of the self-assessed health and chronic illness indicators are identical. The UK and Spain rank highest irrespective of the morbidity indicator used, and Denmark and Switzerland rank lowest.

Standardized concentration indices

In view of the apparent limitations of Le Grand's methodology, it would probably be unwise to attach much importance to the results of the previous subsection. Figure 4.8 shows the values of the alternative HI_{WVP} index when self-assessed health and chronic sickness are used as indicators of need. The most striking feature of the chart is that in all but four cases where need is proxied by self-assessed health or chronic sickness, the index values are *negative*. Only in the Spanish case is the HI_{WVP} index for the chronic indicator positive (and even then only marginally so), and only in the cases of the UK, Spain and the Netherlands is the index positive for the self-assessed health indicator. The fact that so many HI_{WVP} indices in Fig. 4.8 are negative whilst their HL_{LG} counterparts in Fig. 4.7 were positive provides some support for the earlier claim that Le Grand's method is likely to overstate the degree of inequity favouring the rich.[12] Taken at face value the results in Fig. 4.8 imply that if there is any inequity in the delivery of health care in these countries, it favours the poor rather than the rich. However, as we emphasize below, there is good reason to be wary about jumping to such a conclusion. Another noteworthy feature of Fig. 4.8 is that the ranking of the six countries for which there is information on both morbidity indicators is virtually the same irrespective of which of the two indicators is chosen: (in descending order) Spain, the Netherlands, the UK, Switzerland, Italy, and then Denmark. This ranking is somewhat different from the rankings of the same countries in Fig. 4.7, although Spain is near the top in both and Denmark is near the bottom in both.

One reason for not reading too much into the results in Fig. 4.8 is that

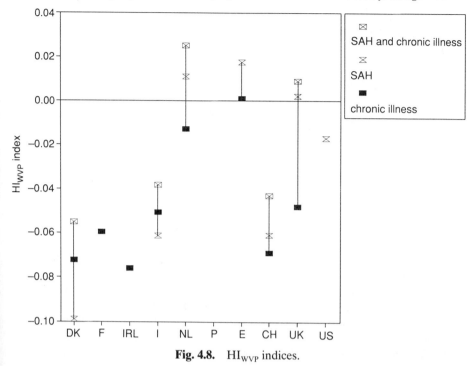

Fig. 4.8. HI_{WVP} indices.

it may well be the case that inequalities in health exist *amongst* the chronically sick and *amongst* those who perceive their health to be not good (O'Donnell and Propper 1991 *a*). Figure 4.8 also reveals that in all countries the HI_{WVP} index is larger in numerical size when the self-assessed health and chronic sickness indicators are used simultaneously than when each is used alone. The implication is that failure to take into account the extent of pro-rich inequalities in health *within* morbidity categories tends to result in an underestimate of the extent of inequity in the delivery of health care that favours the rich, or an overestimate of the extent to which if favours the poor.

Indeed, it seems highly unlikely that all such inequality is taken into account simply by including self-assessed health and chronic sickness simultaneously. Using data from the British *Health and Lifestyle Survey*, O'Donnell and Propper (1991 *a*) find that amongst persons reporting chronic illness, those in the lower income groups were more likely than their better-off counterparts to suffer from both more than one condition and relatively serious conditions, such as heart disease, angina and heart attack, and arthritis and rheumatism. By contrast, those in the lower income groups were least likely to suffer from less serious complaints such as skin disease, eczema and dermatitis, and migraine and chronic head-ache. Similar results are reported for the Netherlands in Chapter 10. This suggests that future work in this area ought to incorporate information not simply on whether chronic illness is reported but rather on the number and type of chronic conditions reported.

The results in Table 6.5 of the Danish country report indicate how sensitive the HI_{WVP} index is to the amount of information used in its calculation. When chronic sickness alone is used to calculate the index, its value is –0.072. When, in addition to chronic sickness, self-assessed health is included, the index rises to –0.055. Finally, when the number of chronic conditions is used (instead of simply whether or not the individual suffered from chronic sickness), and the number of activity-restricted days is included in addition to self-assessed health, the HI_{WVP} index rises to –0.031. It seems highly likely in the light of the UK and Dutch results noted above that if information on the *type* of chronic condition were to be included as well, the index would become larger and might even become positive.

The upshot of all this is that the HI_{WVP} indices in Fig. 4.8 appear to understate the degree of any inequity favouring the rich and overstate the degree of any inequity favouring the poor. Indeed, it is quite possible that the negative HI_{WVP} values are simply due to a failure to take into account the full extent of inequalities in health across income groups. What *is* implied by the discussion above is that incorporating more detailed in-formation on morbidity is most unlikely to cause any positive HI_{WVP} values to become negative. This suggests that any inequity in the delivery of health care in the UK, Spain, and the Netherlands does, indeed, favour the rich, but that this may be true of other countries as well.

Tests of inequity

Another reason for not reading too much into the results reported in Fig. 4.8 is that the index values are small in absolute value. This suggests that any inequity might not be too large to worry about. A sufficient—but not necessary—condition for the HI_{WVP} index to be zero is that the regression coefficients in models such as those in eqns (4.4), (4.5) and (4.6) are the same across all income groups.

Rather than report the LR statistics for all the various specifications estimated in all the country reports, Table 4.6 reports the LR test statistics and the associated HI_{WVP} values only for the most general specification for which the LR statistic was reported. These are, therefore, the specifications that capture as much income-related variation in morbidity as possible. Table 4.6 reports the LR test statistics for the first and second parts of the two-part model separately, as well as those for the combined model. It appears that in only one country (Denmark) does income

Table 4.6. Tests of inequity

Country	Variables in equation	HI$_{WVP}$	LR(1)	LR(2)	CV(1,2)	LR(Tot)	CV(Tot)	DF(Tot)
Denmark	CHRONIC, SAH (1)	−0.055	314	16	48	331	83	56
France								
Ireland	CHRONIC	−0.076	26	48	43	74	74	48
Italy	CHRONIC, ACUTE, SAH (2)	−0.036	54	74	57	129	103	72
Netherlands	CHRONIC, SAH (3)	0.025	38	60	57	98	103	72
Portugal								
Spain	CHRONIC, LIM CHRONIC, SAH, RADS	0.146	56	74	57	134	103	72
Switzerland	CHRONIC, SAH (1)	−0.043	20	32	48	53	83	56
UK	CHRONIC, LIM CHRONIC, SAH (1)	0.013	46	64	52	111	93	64
US	LIM CHRONIC, SAH (2)	0.028	36	874	52	908	93	64

Notes: SAH = self-assessed health. RADs = restricted activity days. Numbers in parentheses refer to number of dummy variables entered to capture self-assessed health. Figures for the US refer to results for the 18+ sample reported in the Appendix to Chapter 15. LR(1) and LR(2) are likelihood ratios for 1st and 2nd parts respectively. CV(1,2) is 1% critical value of chi-squared distribution for LR tests for 1st and 2nd parts. LR(Tot) and DF(Tot) are likelihood ratio and degrees of freedom for combined LR test statistics.

significantly affect the probability of an individual in a given degree of need seeking care, with the standardized probability rising with income. Surprisingly, perhaps, in all other countries the probability of seeking care —holding age, gender, and need constant—does not appear to depend on income. Income *does*, however, affect the amount of care received by those who use at least some health care: in all countries except Denmark and Switzerland the LR test statistic exceeds the 1 per cent critical value of the chi-squared distribution. Our evidence suggests, therefore, that amongst those who have entered the health care system, persons in equal need are not being treated equally. Indeed, the LR statistics for the two-part model *as a whole* (i.e., taking into account the effect of income on both the decision to seek care and the amount of resources received once contact has been made) suggest that inequity exists in the delivery of health care in all countries except the Netherlands and Switzerland. In these two countries the test statistic falls below the 1 per cent critical value. In the cases of Denmark, Italy, Spain, the UK and the US, the LR test statistic exceeds the critical value, suggesting that overall in these countries there *is* unequal treatment for equal need and that this inequity is income-related. In Spain, the UK, and the US, this inequity appears, on balance, to favour the better-off. The opposite appears to be true of Denmark and Italy. However, the earlier comments about the sensitivity of the HI_{WVP} values to the information included on need should be borne in mind. It is evident that the most decisive rejection of the null hypothesis of no income-related inequity is in the case of the US.

Accounting for cross-country differences

It would be unwise, in view of the sensitivity of the HI_{WVP} values to the amount of information used in its calculation, to attempt to draw firm conclusions about the extent to which any cross-country differences in inequity can be attributed to differences in health care delivery systems. Some tentative conclusions do, however, emerge. First, in the US there *does* appear to be inequity in the delivery of health care, which, on balance, favours the better-off. This is due to the fact that although the bottom income quintile fares relatively well given its high morbidity, the second income quintile fares particularly badly, which is presumably due to patchy insurance coverage amongst the relatively worse-off who are not covered by public programmes. Secondly, there appears to be inequity favouring the rich even in some countries where public cover is universal and comprehensive, notably Spain and the UK. At least in the UK it appears that this might to be due, at least in part, to the above-average private expenditures of the better-off. Thirdly, it appears that health care systems that do not have universal and comprehensive public cover are not necessarily those with the highest degree of inequity. Indeed, in both

Switzerland and the Netherlands, where public cover is either virtually non-existent (as in the case of Switzerland) or income-related (as in the case of the Netherlands), the null hypothesis of no income-related inequity could not be rejected at the 1 per cent level. Clearly, however, in view of the remarks above about the desirability of incorporating richer information on need into the analysis, further research into this and the other questions is necessary before firm conclusions can be drawn.

SUMMARY AND CONCLUSIONS

This chapter explored equity in the delivery of health care in 10 OECD countries using two alternative interpretations of equity—'equality of health' and 'equal treatment for equal need'.

Inequalities in health

In all countries morbidity was found to be unequally distributed, being concentrated amongst the worse-off. The extent of such income-related inequality was measured using an illness concentration index, a measure which is closely related to the relative index of inequality used extensively in the literature on inequalities in health. Inequalities in morbidity were found to be particularly pronounced in the case of self-assessed helth—a finding that is consistent with previous research in the field. Inequalities in limiting chronic illness were also found to be relatively pronounced in most countries. The relative performance of the various countries was found to depend only partly on the choice of morbidity indicator: countries in which there is a high degree of inequality in self-assessed health also tend to have a high degree of inequality in chronic illness, although countries with a high degree of inequality in limiting chronic illness are not always the countries with the highest degree of inequality in self-assessed health or chronic illness. Two countries stand out as having a particularly high degree of inequality in morbidity irrespective of the morbidity indicator used: Britain and the US. The Netherlands, by contrast, has a low inequality score on all morbidity measures.

The project's results suggest that—with the exception of the US— countries which spend a relatively large amount *per capita* on health care also tend to have a relatively low degree of inequality in morbidity. Our results also suggest that cross-country differences in inequalities in morbidity may be accounted for at least in part by differences in income inequality. These findings are, however, tentative.

Equity in the delivery of health care

Two main approaches were used to analyse 'equal treatment for equal need'. The first entailed an analysis of variations across income groups in standardized values of imputed medical expenditures. This approach asks, in effect: 'How much would each income group have received on average if its age structure and morbidity levels had been the same as those of the population at large?' The second approach involved a regression analysis of imputed expenditures to test the hypothesis that the relationship between the amount of medical care received and the determinants of utilization (morbidity, age, and gender) is the same for all income groups. This is equivalent to testing the hypothesis that imputed expenditures do not vary across income groups within each age–sex–morbidity category. A third approach used previously in studies of the UK National Health Service (NHS) was also used in the empirical analysis, but in view of its limitations, it is not, we believe, to be relied upon.

The results reported are somewhat sensitive to the choice of health indicators. When several health indicators are included simultaneously, the standardized medical expenditure distributions are less pro-poor or more pro-rich than when only one indicator is included at a time. This suggests that inequalities in morbidity exist even amongst, for example, the chronically sick. This is taken into account by the multiple-indicator standardization results. What is *not* taken into account in these results is the fact that the worse-off appear to be not only more likely to suffer from a chronic illness, but also more likely to suffer from several chronic illnesses at the same time, as well as from relatively serious illnesses. The inequity index values reported therefore almost certainly overstate any inequity favouring the poor and understate any inequity favouring the rich. This suggests that in countries where inequity favouring the rich was detected and the null hypothesis of no inequity was rejected (Spain, the UK, and the US), pro-rich inequity almost certainly exists. Further research is required before it can be established with any certainty whether inequity exists in the other countries and whether any cross-country differences can be related to differences in health care delivery systems.

NOTES

1. For an analysis of the properties of the various measures of inequality that have been employed in the literature on inequalities in health, see Wagstaff *et al.* (1991 *a*).
2. More generally, the index has a value of zero when there is no association

between morbidity and the individual's rank in the distribution of the variable used to rank persons or groups. A zero value of C_{ill} implies a zero value of the slope index of inequality and hence the relative index of inequality (Wagstaff *et al.* 1991 *a*, p. 550).

3. Index values for other morbidity indicators and for both adults and children are also reported in many of the country reports in Part II.

4. The correction between health expenditures and the inequality index for limiting illness is positive but not significant ($r = 0.10$, $P = 0.44$).

5. The correlations for the chronic illness and limiting chronic illness indicators are 0.33 ($P = 0.21$) and 0.24 ($P = 0.32$), respectively.

6. See, for example, van Vliet and van de Ven (1985).

7. Suppose, for example, that there are three income groups of equal size, all with the same mean illness. Suppose too that persons in the top and bottom groups receive on average US$100 of expenditure but persons in the middle group receive US$200. Then if follows that the illness concentration curve coincides with the diagonal while the expenditure concentration curve cuts the diagonal from below half way along each axis. If the HI_{LG} index is calculated as the difference between C_{exp} and C_{ill}, the index takes a value of zero in this case. This makes sense if one takes the view—as researchers in the field seem to—that what matters is not simply whether different income groups are treated differently, but rather whether there is any systematic pattern to this inequity: do the rich, for example, do better than the poor, in the sense that it is they who receive more than their fair share of medical care? In this particular case, the unfair treatment received by the poor is compensated by the fact that the rich also receive less than their fair share of medical care. Thus, there is, on balance, no income-related inequity.

8. Le Grand (1991) has challenged this conclusion, although his arguments have been questioned by O'Donnell and Propper (1991 *b*) and Wagstaff *et al.* (1991 *c*).

9. That factors other than ill-health may exert some influence over the receipt of medical care may in itself be considered to be inequitable. It certainly seems reasonable to argue that factors, such as educational attainment and insurance status, should not affect the receipt of medical care. Whether or not demographic factors ought to influence receipt of medical care is less clear. Where it is thought that 'need' may not have been captured fully by the health indicators used in a study, it might be argued that variables, such as age and gender, might be useful supplementary indicators of need. In which case there may be nothing inequitable about the fact that receipt of medical care depends on these variables. If, on the other hand, it is felt that need *has* been captured fully by whichever morbidity measures have been used, it might reasonably be argued that receipt of medical care should *not* depend on factors such as age and gender. But even if variables other than need indicators do affect the receipt of medical care, such inequity is of a different character from the income-related inequity being investigated here. Rather it concerns another aspect of horizontal equity in which equals are defined in terms of, say, age and gender, rather than need.

10. We are grateful to Carol Propper for her suggestions on the use of likelihood ratio tests.

11. Results for both adults and children are reported in many of the country reports in Part II.
12. It should be noted, perhaps, that the results in these two subsections are not strictly comparable, as the former are not age–sex standardized. However, note that, as indicated above, Le Grand's age–sex standardized approach still yields biased results.

Appendix

System characteristics and inequity in the delivery of health care

	Denmark 1982	France 1980	Ireland 1987	Italy 1985	Netherlands 1981	Portugal 1987	Spain 1987	Switzerland 1981	UK 1985	US 1980
Inequalities in health										
Chronic illness	0.086	0.009	0.148	0.075	0.040	–	0.058	0.013	0.140	–
Limiting chronic illness	–	–	–	0.041	–	0.111	0.104	0.202	0.243	0.244
Self-assessed health	0.237	–	–	0.166	0.115	–	0.220	0.156	0.316	0.317
Background characteristics										
Share of out-of-pocket payments (%)	13.9	14.7	14.9	20.0	7.5	28.8	21.3	18.6	8.7	29.6
Health care expenditure per capita, 1987 (US$)	792	1105	561	841	1041	386	521	1225	758	2051
Gini coefficient for pre-tax income	0.284	0.319	0.360	0.373	0.251	0.331	0.367	0.339	0.348	0.432
Le Grand inequity indices										
Chronic illness	–0.094	–0.093	0.015	0.029	–0.010	–	0.042	–0.110	0.052	–
Limiting chronic illness	–	–	–	–0.006	–	0.031	0.087	0.079	0.155	0.129
Self-assessed health	0.051	–	–	0.119	0.066	–	0.204	0.033	0.228	0.202
Standardized inequity indices										
Chronic illness	–0.072	–0.060	–0.076	–0.051	–0.013	–	0.001	–0.069	–0.048	–
Self-assessed health	–0.099	–	–	–0.061	0.011	–	0.017	–0.061	0.002	–0.017
Chronic illness and SAH	–0.055	–	–	–0.038	0.025	–	–	–0.043	0.009	–

Notes: Inequalities in health measured by negative of illness concentration index; SAH = self-assessed health. Health care expenditures from OECD (1989). Otherwise figures taken from country reports.

5

Policy implications of the COMAC-HSR project

Frans Rutten

INTRODUCTION

This chapter considers the results of the COMAC-HSR project reported in Chapters 3 and 4. In the next section current and possible future policies concerning equity in health care are identified and an attempt is made to assess the relevance of the project in this context. Following sections discuss the policy implications of the results reported in Chapters 3 and 4. Finally, we conclude and make recommendations for policy and research.

THE POLICY PERSPECTIVE

Equity in the finance of health care

One of the components of equity in health care considered earlier is (vertical) equity in the finance of health care. As explained in Chapter 2, focus here is not on the way in which the financing system may limit access to health care for particular groups (i.e., in case of large out-of-pocket payments for low income groups). Such effects show up when considering equity in the delivery of health care. The policy objective which underlies the concept of equity in the finance of health care, is the general concern for a fair distribution of incomes and, consequently, a fair distribution of the burden of paying for publicly financed goods and services (cf. Culyer, Chapter 17, who mentions four motives of interest concerning the distribution of payments for health care). As was stated in Chapter 2, and inferred from Table 2.1, policy statements on equity in the finance of health are somewhat vague. It can be observed, however, that equity considerations are prominent when national health reforms are being considered. Proposed health reforms in the US, Spain, and the Netherlands have been triggered, among others, by considerations of equity in the finance of health care and are aiming to change the distribution of health care payments over income groups. Furthermore, equity considerations played an important role in the British government rejecting proposals to reduce the role of tax financing of the National Health Service.

When considering health care financing a distinction between earmarked payments (health insurance premiums and out-of-pocket payments) and general taxation (direct and indirect) is useful. In the former, equity considerations may have a more direct bearing on health care financing policies than the latter, where the whole system of raising taxes is at stake. An exception to this is tax expenditure for private health insurance, where insurance purchase has a direct redistributive effect on the incidence of taxes. But even in the case of earmarked financing it may be necessary to widen one's equity perspective and to judge the equity characteristics of a particular health care financing system in the light of the whole system of raising revenue for the public sector. The social insurance systems, which have generally been found regressive, may in some countries coincide with highly progressive direct taxes (as in the Netherlands), which may lead to a positive judgement on equity in public finance in general.

Horizontal equity in the finance of health care has as yet received little attention in the project as well as in research in general. There is evidence of its presence in some systems, which are predominantly financed from social or private insurance. For instance, in Germany, people contribute between 8 and 16 per cent of income to their sickness fund, which has led to the mounting of a policy of achieving equalization between funds (Ham *et al.* 1990). The Dutch system has a high degree of horizontal inequity (Rutten and Janssen 1987), because the eligibility for sick fund insurance does not only depend on income, but also on employment status (employee or entrepreneur) and employer (government versus private enterprise). This adds to the horizontal inequity from social and private insurance operating in tandem, which was one of the reasons to propose fundamental health reform.

We observed a lack of explicit policy statements on the objectives on equity in finance in some countries, but at the international level the issue seems to be non-existent. There is, for instance, no mentioning of it in the European strategy for health for all in the year 2000 (WHO 1985).[1] An important international development in this context is, however, the establishment of an internal European market in the coming years. Until now social security in European Community member states is essentially a matter of the national authorities, although the European Commission is allowed to initiate research, promote co-operation between members and make recommendations on social policy (art. 118, Treaty of Rome). According to van Langendonck (1991) there is a political will to mark 'Europe 1992' with a strong social policy element. For instance, a Community directive might be issued to forbid certain sectors of the population to receive higher benefits at the same rate or at a lower rate of contributions, or allow them to pay lower contributions for the same or better benefits (horizontal inequity). Furthermore, the Community Social Charter, adopted by 11 of the 12 member states in December 1989, and the stronger competitive forces at the completion of the internal market in 1992 may lead to further harmonization of social security systems. Consequently, this may induce a European policy towards greater equity in the finance of health care. In this respect one may also point to the activities of the Association Internationale de la Mutualité, which also strives towards harmonization of health insurance systems in Europe.

In summary, we observe that there is a general concern that individual payments for health care are made according to ability to pay. Whether this means progressive, proportional, or regressive financing is not made explicit and may depend on the specific context in a country, for instance, on the progressivity of the tax system in general. We expect policies on the finance of health care to become more prominent as the issue gets high priority in European social policy in the coming decade.

EQUITY IN THE DELIVERY OF HEALTH CARE

The reduction of inequalities in health is a general policy objective, which can be promoted through various policies beyond those concerning health care. Reduction of inequalities in income, housing conditions, the working environment, etc., may contribute to reducing variation in health status among individuals, and policies aimed at eliminating these inequalities may help to achieve with general policy objective. In the COMAC-HSR project the focus is on equity in the delivery of health care as a means of contributing to the reduction of inequalities in health or, at least, helping to prevent an increase in inequalities in health as a consequence of external influences.

Policy statements on equity in the delivery of health care tend to be more explicit than those on equity in finance (cf. Table 2.1). Statements are typically terms of 'equal access' or 'the right to health care' and seem to refer predominantly to horizontal equity (equal treatment for equal need). Wagstaff and Van Doorslaer in Chapter 2 and Culyer in Chapter 17 provide arguments for considering 'equal treatment for equal need' rather than 'equality of access'. From a policy aspect one may argue that the latter is instrumental to the former and that it is the actual outcome of the process which needs to be assessed; others may see a greater role for people's own preferences and defend a focus on 'equal opportunity to receive treatment'. Both approaches provide information relevant for health care policy. A study of the European Science Foundation (Fox, 1989) concluded, on the basis of a survey, that class or income inequalities are less prominent in public debate than geographical inequalities. Indeed, at a more aggregate level regional differences have played a major role in policy discussions on equity. Some resource allocation mechanisms, like the implementation of the RAWP-formula for distributing resources to regions in the UK National Health Service, are targeted specifically at achieving equity. From a European perspective one may be interested in equity in the delivery of health care among EC member states. For an analysis at this level cross-country comparative data on average health status and actual benefits of the health care system should be made available. The project did not consider regional or national differences.

When assessing the degree of equity in the delivery of health care, one should select 'third' variables for which the relationship with expenditure, properly corrected for need, is assumed to inform us about discrimination. The obvious choice in the project was to take 'ability to pay', as measured by equivalent income, as a key 'third' variable. Discrimination on grounds other than income was not analysed in the present study, even though was recognize that other forms of discrimination/differential treatment may well be important (e.g., race in the UK and the US).

The policy perspective, from which horizontal equity in the delivery of health care is considered, may differ. In Europe, the interest of policy-makers is in the distribution of health care treatment over all levels of income groups regardless of the source of finance. This has been the starting point for the design of the study. It may be possible to take a more limited view and to consider only health care, which is publicly financed, or the distribution of the burden of payment for the least well-off in society.[2] The latter may apply to the US, where the market dominates resource allocation in health care, and public concern is concentrated on the poor (Medicaid) and the elderly (Medicare). In this case policy-makers may want to be informed on the performance of this safety net for the least well-off, which implies an analysis concentrating on public spending and on certain income and age groups. This could be carried out as an ancillary study to the project because a similar database can be used (using concepts from the poverty literature). In considering developing countries, equity in terms of social class or income seems closely related to geographical equity. In many developing countries, poverty has a significant regional dimension and, policies should be aimed at identifying deprived areas and take specific action there (World Bank 1990). In this case, studies on equity may select 'area', 'race', and 'sex' as third variables to test for discrimination.

At the international level there is the WHO policy of setting targets, which aim at 'the attainment by all citizens of the world by the year 2000 of a level of health that will permit them to lead a socially and economically productive life' (WHO 1985). This general policy has been translated to specific requirements to be met by Europe. The first of these specific targets concerns equity in health and reads:

... by the year 2000, the actual differences in health status between countries and between groups within countries should be reduced by at least 25%, by improving the level of health of disadvantaged nations and groups.

The implications for equity in health care are considered in targets 27 and 28. In target 27, resource allocation according to need and physical and economic accessibility are discussed. Target 28 concerns primary care and states that the primary care system should give special attention to high-risk, vulnerable, and deprived individuals and groups. The results of the project, as reported in this volume, seem particularly relevant for monitoring whether resources are allocated according to need regardless of ability to pay. Given the uniqueness of the work performed, future replications of this research effort would be necessary to measure progress as demanded in target 1 of the European strategy. Although the current project also provides data on the financial accessibility of health care (see Chapter 3), the next phase of the COMAC-HSR project could include a more comprehensive analysis of equality of access and a detailed study on horizontal equity on the finance side, and this too would be extremely relevant for monitoring developments in relation to target 27.

IMPLICATIONS OF THE RESULTS OF THE PROJECT

The most important achievement of the COMAC-HSR project is that for the first time comparable quantitative data on equity in health care for 10 countries are available and that clear methodological guidelines are in place for further studies. As we expect that a growing concern for equity aspects in national and international health care policies will develop, the need for the type of information provided by the project will increase and new studies could be initiated making use of the experience gained.

Below, the policy implications of the results a reported in Chapters 3 and 4 will be discussed.

Equity in the finance of health care

The results of Chapter 3 suggest that there are three groups of countries with quite different characteristics of health care financing. First, countries with health care systems, which are predominantly financed from taxes, have either progressive (the UK, Ireland, and Portugal) or mildly regress-ive (Denmark) systems. Policies to change these equity characteristics would need either to effect the whole tax system or to influence the share of out-of-pocket payments or private insurance.

The second more heterogeneous group of countries, which is character-ized by the social insurance model, have moderately regressive financing systems, with France being more regressive, and the Netherlands being less regressive than the average. Here, the opportunities for modifying the equity characteristics of the financing system are greater because revenues raised are earmarked for health care. As each country relies on various sources and has various revenue-raising schemes, calibration to attain a desired degree of vertical equity would be relatively easy. The problem of horizontal inequity, however, is expected to appear more frequently than in the tax-based financing group,[3] as is also suggested by the reported evidence on the Dutch and German systems. In conclusion, the project's results suggest that proposed changes in financing in these countries should be better judged a priori on their implications for both vertical and horizontal equity, given the relative regressiveness of the systems and their vulnerability for horizontal inequity.

The US and Switzerland, which are largely financed from private sources and have particularly regressive systems, constitute the third group. To the remarks made above on the social insurance-based systems, could be added that the comparatively large regressivity of finance in these countries may be a cause for concern in itself, as it is in the US (see Chapters 15 and 18) and in Switzerland, where a referendum on increas-ing the share of taxes in health care financing is to be held.

The methodology for characterizing equity in finance can be usefully employed to analyse the equity implications of health care reforms that have already been implemented as well as those that have as yet only been proposed. Van Doorslaer *et al.* (1991 *a*) analysed the equity im-plications of the proposed health care reform in the Netherlands (van de Ven 1991). This plan seeks to establish universal health insurance coverage while at the same time diminishing government regulation and stimulating competition among health care insurers and providers. They found that the progressive effect of extending public health insurance coverage (from 65 per cent to 100 per cent) was more than offset by the introduction of a flat premium next to an income-related premium to pay for public insurance and by the reduction of the public insurance package.[4] Similar studies are being initiated for other countries having experienced or expecting reform (e.g., Spain, the UK, and France). Also, minor changes in health care financing, such as the 'Plan Seguin' to increase co-payments for non-essential drugs in France, or the possible introduction of tax relief on private health care insurance in the UK need careful moni-toring of their implications for equity. The relative regressivity of each financing system may help to establish the urgency of estimating the a priori equity implications of proposed changes in health care finance.[5]

Finally, the present study very clearly shows the relative progressivity of each revenue-raising mechanism: direct taxes are progressive, indirect taxes and social insurance are mildly regressive, and private insurance and out-of-pocket payments are highly regressive. The actual degree depends on the characteristics of the revenue system and on the actual income groups, from which revenues are raised. Although the global progressivity characteristics of each financing method are rather obvious, detailed analysis, as in the present project is necessary to predict the actual performance of a complex mixture of different financing mechanisms, which is at the basis of most of our health care systems.

Equity in the delivery of health care

The results of Chapter 4 suggest that in none of the 10 countries is there clear evidence that the amount of medical care received by persons in equal need depends on their income. The authors mention some caveats relating to the measurement of utilization of care and of need, and this may indeed confuse the issue. But even when the results are to be accepted, it is important to think about the mechanisms behind inequity in the delivery of health care as these may work in different directions and provide clues for policies reducing inequity. Table 5.1 suggests possible mechanisms and their effect on the degree of horizontal equity.

The first five demand-side mechanisms have rather unambiguous effects on the distribution of health services (except for the second, which may work either way but is likely to be pro-rich) and are well documented (e.g., Acton 1985; Van Doorslaer 1987; Janssen 1989). Time prices are expected to be more important when there is shortage of supply or when health care organization is relatively poor, both of which may be correlated with the level of funding of a health system. As regards financial prices the evidence from the US (Chapter 15) clearly suggests these to be important as lack of insurance (in the lower part of the income distribution) is reported to be an important determinant of lower medical care consumption. Furthermore, the pro-rich distribution of health services in Portugal may be partly explained by the relative large share of out-of-pocket payments in that country.

The last three mechanisms in Table 5.1 are a combination of supply and demand forces. There is little evidence in the literature about the way in which consumer and provider incentives may lead to a pro-rich distribution of health services and the directions indicated in the table are therefore tentative. As suggested in Chapter 4, provider incentives may play a role as remuneration schemes often differ for public and private

Table 5.1. Possible mechanisms underlying inequity in the delivery of care

Mechanisms the rich may:	Effect on inequity		
	Pro-poor	Pro-rich	Unclear
1. be more aware of health disturbance		x	
2. be better informed about care-seeking options			x
3. spend less time for travelling and waiting		x	
4. face higher time prices	x		
5. face lower financial prices relative to their income		x	
6. be more rapidly referred to specialist care and may jump queues (own preferences and provider incentives)		x	
7. acquire treatment demanding a shorter stay in hospital and requiring less absence from work (own preferences and provider incentives)			x
8. consume more diagnostic services (own preferences and provider incentives)		x	

patients. The latter will be even more obvious when providers work simultaneously in both public and private sectors, as is the case in several countries (e.g., UK, Portugal, the Netherlands). If, in addition, capacity is scarce, the incentives generated by such circumstances hold the danger of discrimination against the lower income groups. Patients' preferences may lead to the higher income groups being able to satisfy their demand for quick referral and high quality care demanding less absence from work. In the Netherlands, Hooijmans and Rutten (1984) found that the bed supply elasticity of hospital use for the higher income groups was much lower than for the lower income groups in a situation where there was large regional variation in bed supply. They concluded that higher income groups were better able than lower income groups *to resist* the strong incentives to fully exploit hospital capacity.[6] We conclude by observing that the mechanisms as set out in Table 5.1 may work in both directions and that the project may not be able to identify inequalities because they may offset each other at the group level (but not necessarily for an individual).

In contrast to the former case of equity in the finance of health care where we considered only national policies, inequity in the delivery of health care may be redressed by a variety of policies at various levels of decision-making within the health care sector. These may range from financial policies limiting out-of-pocket payments or changing provider fee schedules to health education programmes for the less educated or changes in the organization of health care provision. More specifically, it would be advisable to make systems more responsive to consumers, and there are several policy initiatives that may help to achieve this. There is a general trend towards strengthening of management in health care and allowing a greater role for insurance organizations or health authorities through 'managed care' arrangements. Closer examination of treatment decisions, development of standards, and guidelines and health services accreditation, are other instruments that may help to diminish inequality in treatment. More detailed and refined research is necessary to not only confirm the finding of the project but also to identify the effects of the mechanisms underlying the distribution of health care services across income groups.

RECOMMENDATIONS FOR POLICY AND RESEARCH

Summarizing our observations above we arrive at the following recommendations:

- The observed variation in progressivity in the finance of health care should be considered now that further harmonization of social security systems is part of European policy after 1992. As changes in financing health care are occurring rapidly in various countries the monitoring of current developments using the COMAC-HSR project's methodology is recommended.

- Measures curtailing demand, such as cost-sharing and introducing limits on the choice of providers, and also measures on the supply side, such as restraining finance, making reimbursement conditional on performance, and the introduction of 'managed care' structures, have a potential impact on the access to health care for different income groups and may change the equity characteristics of the system. As these actions are often triggered by a concern for efficiency, a priori estimation of their effects on equity should precede their implementation.

- The WHO policy towards health for all in the year 2000 and the related targets concerning equity in health and in health care for Europe clearly call for careful monitoring of developments in the member states; this can only be successful if there is information on developments, which is accessible, reliable, and comparable across countries.

- It is recommended to establish a closer link between researchers and policy-makers, both at the national and international level. Given the WHO policies and the EC plans toward greater harmonization in social security as mentioned above, co-operation between the international research groups conducting the project and these international agencies is called for.

- Finally, in spite of all efforts to use similar definitions and protocols in the national studies, data limitations may prevent researchers from reaching a sufficient level of comparability of results over countries. There is still considerable variation in design and operationalization of variables among national surveys relating health care expenditure, health status, and income. It may be worthwhile to investigate the possibility of conducting a European survey on the distribution of payments and expenditure in health care over income deciles.

NOTES

1. Except for a short statement on 'economic accessibility' in target 27.
2. See the Rawlsian stance mentioned by Williams in Chapter 16.
3. Note that horizontal inequity may also be present in a tax-based system (e.g., self-employed versus salaried).
4. A reduction in the public insurance package implies that private insurance payments or out-of-pocket payments have to be made to acquire the services which are no longer in this package. The effect of this is regressive.
5. For examples, France, Switzerland, and the US which show largely regressive financing.
6. The figures in the study relate to 1973, when hospital managers faced marginal revenues per patient day well in excess of marginal costs and physician's fees for private patients were about three times as high as for publicly insured patients. Since then the incentive schemes have changed drastically.

Part II

Equity in the finance and delivery of
health care in 10 countries

6

Denmark

Terkel Christiansen

INTRODUCTION

The pursuit of equity in the area of health care has a long tradition in Denmark as well as in the other Scandinavian countries. A main characteristic of Danish health policy over many years has been 'equal and free (or almost free) access to various health-related services for all irrespective of economic means and social status' (Indenrigsministeriet og Sundhedsstyrelsen 1985).

THE DANISH HEALTH CARE SYSTEM

Financing and delivery of health care in Denmark

The organization and financing of the Danish health care system today is the same as during the 1980s. Only minor changes in the organizational structure took place during this decade. The public health care system is organized at three administrative levels: national; regional (counties); and local (municipalities). Alongside this public system there is a private sector with general practitioners, specialists, dentists, physiotherapists, chiropractors, and pharmacists. In general, those practising in the private sector negotiate an agreement with the public financing authorities concerning the conditions of delivering their services to the population. The regional level is responsible for providing all hospital services and much primary health care. In principle, each county has a unified hospital service with a certain division of tasks between the existing hospitals. At the local level, the municipalities are responsible for a number of primary health care tasks, such as district nursing, health visiting, school medical examinations, nursing homes, and home help. Each of the three administrative levels finance their budgets through various taxes and duties. It is

The author's colleague, Peter Ellemann-Jensen, participated in the planning phase of the present paper before his death in 1990. I am, however, responsible for the content of the paper. The study has been supported by a grant from the Danish Social Science Research Council (14-5301).

Table 6.1.   Distribution of health care financing (percentage, 1981)

Direct taxes (%)			55.2
Personal		52.4	
State	19.7		
Regional	6.5		
Local	19.8		
Other	6.4		
Corporate		2.7	
Indirect taxes (%)			42.4
Compulsory fees and fines			0.3
Social security contributions			2.1
Total (%)			100.0
Total (Dkr millions)			185 379

Source: Danmarks Statistik (1987).

of note that no earmarking is used, and thus health care, like almost all other expenditure and transfer programmes is financed through general taxation. Some consumer contribution to health care is also involved, especially for dentistry, prescription drugs and physiotherapy.

In this chapter, health care expenditure figures refer to 1981. At the local level, municipal budgets were financed by a proportional income tax on individuals and corporations, and taxes on real estate. The counties' budgets were financed through a proportional income tax, whereas various types of taxes and duties were levied at the national level. Among the most important of these were a progressive personal income tax and taxes on goods and services, including a value-added tax (VAT). Other sources of national financing included wealth tax, corporation tax, and social security contributions. In 1981, the relative shares of the various types of taxes and duties for the combined three public sector levels are shown in Table 6.1. In 1981, the total tax incurred was 45.3 per cent of GNP in market prices.

To achieve a greater degree of equity among geographical areas, a scheme for the transfer of funds both between municipalities and between counties has been instituted. In 1981, this fiscal equalization across counties was based on the deviation of each particular county's tax base from the average tax base for all counties in the preceding year. The tax base was defined as taxable income plus 10 per cent of the land value. Another type of transfer was a government transfer involving both counties and municipalities. These transfers were based on indicators of standard expenses, such as the number of inhabitants in specific age groups and the standard number of hospitals days, and they amounted to more than Dkr20 billion in 1981, or about 15 per cent of the combined municipality and county budgets. During the last decade, however, government transfers have been reduced. Because of this method of financing public expenditures and transfers, it is somewhat arbitrary to calculate, for example, a specific household's contribution to health care.

Any person having permanent residence in Denmark has a right to receive health care through tax-financed public health insurance. Each year a resident can choose between two forms of insurance: either group 1 or group 2. Those who choose group 1 are allocated to a general practitioner (GP) of their choice, in their local area. Children under 16 are covered by their parents' insurance. Almost 95 per cent of the adult population were group 1 members in 1981, and were entitled to free medical services from GPs and, when referred by a GP, free care from private specialists, physiotherapists, etc. In this way, group 1 membership supports the family doctor principle, which also implies that the doctor acts as a gatekeeper to the secondary health care sector. Some of the remaining 5 per cent are not covered by public health insurance, but are either in military service, or living in an institution with a doctor on call. The remainder are members of group 2, and may visit a specialist without prior referral from a GP. However, they do not receive free medical care, although public health insurance covers an amount equal to the relevant service fee for group 1 members. Public health insurance covers or subsidizes the cost of health care delivered outside hospitals and of prescription drugs, whereas hospital care is financed through allocation of annual funds.

Private health insurance can be taken out through Denmark, a non-profit health insurance company that almost exclusively covers the health insurance market. Usually, people take out this insurance to help cover their copayments for prescription drugs, dentistry or physiotherapy. In 1981, Danmark had more than 400 000 members (a figure that has risen rapidly since then), and has paid Dkr202 million in claims (Pedersen 1989).

Equity in Danish health care policy

In 1973 the sickness funds were abandoned, and a general tax-financed public health insurance was established. The public documents relating to the preparation of this reform (Socialreformkommissionen 1969) and the passing of the law in parliament (Folketingets Forhandlinger 1970/71)[1] show the legal acceptance of the principle of equity in health care. In these documents, eligibility regarding access to health care services and progressivity in financing were discussed.

The law of Public Health Insurance was submitted to parliament in

1971 by the liberal party Minister of Social Affairs. In the 'Comments to the law proposal' (Folketingestidende 1970/71),[2] the Minister stated that: 'The proposal presented here is based on attitudes that are similar to those of the majority of the members of the Social Reform Commission. Briefly, these attitudes are the following: Access to health care in case of illness ought to be available to the whole population . . .'

Later, in the comments to the proposed law it was stated: 'The more it is recognized that society has a responsibility for the total social and health-related services, the more it seems obvious that the administration of the services should be unified, that the services are to be offered to the whole population, and that the expenses are to be financed in the same way that expenses for other public services are financed, that is, by means of taxes and duties that are adjusted to each individual's ability to pay. The majority of the Social Reform Commission based their proposal in their [. . .] report on such attitudes, and the government concurs with these attitudes.'[3]

At the first reading of the bill, the Minister of Social Affairs declared: 'The intention of this proposal is, as you may know, that the Public Health Insurance is to be financed in proportion to income, and that means that people with lower incomes are going to pay less than today, while people with higher incomes are going to pay more, an attitude which I am glad to find supported here in Parliament.'[4]

PROGRESSIVITY OF HEALTH CARE FINANCE IN DENMARK

Data, variable definitions, and incidence assumptions

The analysis presented here is based on a combination of data from two surveys carried out in the 1980s. These surveys are briefly described below.

The 1981 *Household Expenditure Survey* conducted by the central statistical bureau (Danmarks Statistik 1985, 1986), was based on 2783 households, and data were collected through a combination of an initial interview and household accounts for a single month, supplemented with other statistical information at Denmarks Statistik. The survey is representative of Danish households and contains detailed data on income, direct and indirect taxation, insurance premiums, and use of health services. However, the aggregate use of health services was not distributed evenly over income groups, but was influenced by a few individuals who had had long periods of hospitalization.

The 1982–3 *Danish Health Study* conducted by a team at Odense

University (Bentzen *et al.* 1988) was based on a sample of 1200 households. Like the expenditure survey, it is representative of Danish households. The survey contains detailed information on health and use of services. However, information on income included only earned income generated through work as an employee or via self-employment. Transfer incomes for pensioners and students were imputed.[5]

The analysis of the distribution of payments was based on data from the *Household Expenditure Survey*, whereas data on the use of health services came from the *Danish Health Study*. The incidence assumptions adopted were the same as those adopted in the COMAC-HSR study. Computation of equivalent household income was based on the following OECD-recommended equivalence scale: 1st adult = 1; 2nd adult = 0.7; each child = 0.5. A comparison of equivalent household income by decile from the two surveys shows that the two distributions follow each other rather closely. When using the linear approximation method, the Gini coefficient is 0.2841 for the *Household Expenditure Survey* and 0.3066 for the *Danish Health Study*. When using the non-linear approximation method, the Gini coefficients are 0.2887 and 0.3111, respectively.

Empirical results

The costs of health care in Denmark amounted to approximately 7.3 per cent of its GNP in 1982, a figure that declined to 6 per cent at the end of the decade (MEFA 1984, 1990). Table 6.2 shows the distribution of expenditures by source of finance and by decile of equivalent household income. It appears from the bottom rows of the table that insurance and direct payments play a somewhat subordinate role in the financing of health care. The table also shows Gini and concentration indices, and Kakwani and Suits indices of progressivity. Columns [1]–[3] are based on data from the *Household Expenditure Survey*. Contributions to health care through taxation are based on an assumption of pro rata financing. The distribution of general taxation by decile follows the income distribution rather closely and, consequently, the concentration coefficient for health care expenditures through taxes is almost equal to the Gini coefficient for the pre-tax income distribution. The positive value of the Kakwani progressivity index indicates that payment through taxation is slightly progressive, whereas the opposite is indicated by the Suits index. The difference between the two indices may be ascribed to the different nature of the two indices. The payment of insurance premiums for voluntary insurance is also progressive. It should be noted that this source of finance accounts for a negligible percentage of the total. Direct payments were pieced together from the data of the *Danish Health Study* on payments for pharmaceuticals and dentistry, and data from the *Household*

Table 6.2. Distribution of equivalent household income and health care payments (percentage, 1981).

Income decile	Pre-tax income	Taxes[1]	Insurance premiums	Total direct payments	Total payment
	[1]	[2]	[3]	[4]	[5]
Bottom	3.11	2.26	1.74	8.32	3.10
2nd	4.45	3.13	2.81	6.84	3.64
3rd	5.86	5.73	4.78	9.02	6.18
4th	7.40	8.02	8.80	6.98	7.88
5th	8.76	9.68	6.05	8.60	9.50
6th	10.08	11.17	8.16	9.75	10.95
7th	11.38	12.29	12.03	11.39	12.16
8th	12.90	13.05	13.04	11.89	12.89
9th	14.86	14.65	15.08	10.69	14.10
Top	21.20	20.02	27.51	16.53	19.60
Index					
Gini/Conc.	0.2887	0.2961	0.3793	0.1311	0.2717
Kakwani		0.0074	0.0906	−0.1586	−0.0170
Suits		−0.0018	0.0969	−0.1484	−0.0237
Average					
Dkr		8040	99	597	8736
%		92.0	1.1	6.9	100.0
Macroweights[2]		85.2	0.9	13.9	100.0

Note: The Gini index value of 0.2887 was used to calculate the Kakwani indices. The table includes all types of health care including prescription drugs. Nursing homes are excluded.
[1] Around 3 per cent of the total revenue, originating from corporate taxes etc., are ignored.
[2] From MEFA (1983).

Expenditure Survey on other direct payments. For each decile, the average amount of payment for pharmaceuticals and dentistry and for other purposes were simply added together to attain a total amount of direct payment. Total direct payments appear to be regressive. Overall, the distribution of total payments follows the distribution of pre-tax income rather closely, and the Kakwani index is close to zero, indicating proportionality.

The relative concentration curves corresponding to Table 6.2 are shown in Fig. 6.1. The relative concentration curve for the imputed tax payment cuts the 45° line from below, indicating that taxation is progressive at lower income levels and regressive at higher income levels. As it can be seen, the differences between the curves are small (cf. the values of the Kakwani and the Suits indices in Table 6.2). The relative concentration

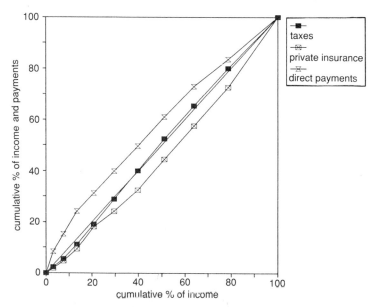

Fig. 6.1. Progressivity of health care finance, Denmark.

curve for insurance premiums, which lies below the 45° line clearly indicates progressivity, whereas the relative concentration curve for direct payment indicates regressivity.

EQUITY IN THE DELIVERY OF HEALTH CARE IN DENMARK

Data and variable definitions

The analysis of the delivery of health care is based on the *Danish Health Study*. Various measures of morbidity are used to indicate the need for health care. The correlation between these measures is shown in Table 6.3. Measures 1 and 2 pertain to functional limitations; measures 3 to 4 to self-reported illness; and measure 5 to subjective health perception.

Table 6.3 also includes a measure, 'current health', that is a Likert-scaled self-assessment of present health status. The items included are coded so that a high score on the 'current health' scale is favourable to good health. Notice that item 5 is one of the items included in the 'current health' scale. The 'current health' scale has high reliability and validity properties (Christiansen 1990) and can be regarded as the most general measure of health status. Although measures (4) and (5) are related to

Table 6.3. Product-moment correlation between various measures of morbidity

Measure	All age groups				18+ years
	1	2	3	4	5
1. No. of activity-restricted days					
2. No. of days confined to bed	0.52 (3076)				
3. No. of chronic illnesses per person*	0.31 (3044)	0.19 (3032)			
4. No. of chronically sick persons	0.14 (3044)	0.11 (3032)	0.64 (3133)		
5. No. of persons with 'health not good'	0.30 (2245)	0.23 (2244)	0.43 (2260)	0.19 (1545)	
6. Current health	−0.37 (2036)	−0.26 (2035)	−0.48 (2050)	−0.21 (1353)	0.86 (2050)

Note: The number of morbidity cases are given in parentheses.
* Number of chronic illnesses checked off from a list of chronic illnesses.

the number of unhealthy persons, the other measures are related to the 'amount' of unhealthiness per person. All measures, except 'current health', are ratio-scaled and thus eligible for inclusion in analyses of inequity, using the method of concentration curves.

Unstandardized distribution of morbidity and health care

The distribution of expenditure on health care for adults is shown in column [3], Table 6.4. Expenditures include costs of visits to GPs, specialists, and outpatient departments, and hospitalization. A uniform pattern does not emerge: the second quintiles especially, have high values due to the above average use of hospitalization. The concentration indices show a certain amount of inequity favouring the lower income groups. When children are included, C_{exp} increases to −0.1127. The distribution of various measures of morbidity by income group can be seen from columns 4 to 8 in Table 6.4: the distributions by quintiles are shown for adults only. Values of the concentration index and the inequity index are shown in the lower part of the table. The bottom line of the table shows the inequity index when children are included.

In general, the C_{ill} measure indicates health inequalities to the disadvantage of the lower income groups, as can be seen from the negative

Table 6.4. Distribution of health care expenditures and various measures of health (18+ years)

Income quintile	No. in sample	Sample (%)	Expendit. (%)	Activity-restricted days per person	Days confined to bed per person	No. of chronic illnesses per person	'Chronically sick' per 100	'Health not good' per 100
	[1]	[2]	[3]	[4]	[5]	[6]	[7]	[8]
Bottom	474	19.5	28.18	6.76	2.32	1.88	66	20
2nd	497	20.5	29.94	8.01	2.28	1.98	71	23
3rd	483	19.9	15.74	4.92	1.63	1.36	52	14
4th	488	20.1	15.19	4.76	1.59	1.18	48	9
Top	484	20.0	10.92	3.44	1.38	0.98	47	6
Average Dkr								
n	2426		3590					
Conc. index								
C_{exp}			−0.1891					
C_{ill}				−0.1434	−0.1105	−0.1612	−0.0859	−0.2370
HI_{LG} (adults)				−0.0457	−0.0786	−0.0279	−0.0941	0.0500
HI_{LG} (adults and children)				−0.0530	−0.0709	−0.0259	−0.0668	

Note: The concentration indices were found by the covariance method. 'Activity-restricted days' and 'days confined to bed' refer to a 6 month time period.

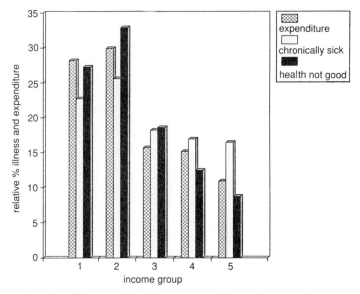

Fig. 6.2.   Illness and health care expenditure shares, Denmark.

values of the index. The picture varies, however, depending on which measure is used, and the indicators do not decrease uniformly with rising income. The greatest concentration coefficient is found for the subjective measure 'health not good' followed by 'number of chronic illnesses per person'. The HI_{LG} index is negative for all need indicators, except for 'health not good', but the positive value deviates only slightly from zero. The range for adults is from –0.09 to 0.05. The indices change slightly when children are included, and the range is now from –0.07 to –0.03. In Fig. 6.2 the shares of health care expenditure are compared to the shares of morbidity as measured by 'health not good' and 'chronically sick'. Expenditures in the second income group are relatively high and higher than the corresponding share of 'chronically sick', but slightly below the share of persons reporting 'health not good'.

Standardized expenditure distribution

In a two-stage standardization procedure, the estimated expenditure in each income group is found as the product of the estimated probability of a positive usage of health care, and the estimated amount of health care, given that usage is greater than zero. Results of standardization for age, sex, and various health measures are shown in Table 6.5 for adults. When standardized for age, four age groups are used (18–34, 35–44, 45–64, and 65+ years). Column [3] shows results from standardization with both the

Table 6.5. Distribution of health care expenditures standardized for age, sex, and health (18+ years, percentage)

Income quintile	Health measures used for standardization					
	Chronically sick	Health not good	Chronically sick + Health not good	Chronically sick + Health not good + Activity-restricted days	Health not good + Activity-restricted days + No. of chronic illnesses	Activity restricted days + Chronically sick + Current health
	[1]	[2]	[3]	[4]	[5]	[6]
Bottom	17.68	23.12	23.87	25.02	24.86	20.85
2nd	29.38	25.67	23.21	21.20	21.49	20.03
3rd	22.93	20.82	13.11	17.14	18.40	16.75
4th	12.80	15.72	22.38	21.22	18.49	20.23
Top	17.21	14.66	17.43	15.41	16.76	18.14
HI_{WVP}	−0.0724	−0.0989	−0.0550	−0.1121	−0.0311	−0.1446

Note: Columns [1]–[2], direct standardization; columns [3]–[6], two-stage standardization.

'chronically sick' and the 'health not good measure'; the resultant HI_{WVP} index is negative. Results from standardization with three morbidity indicators are shown in columns 4 to 6. In column [4], the measure 'activity-restricted days' is added to the two measures used in the previous analysis, and the resultant HI_{WVP} index decreases. In column [5], the 'health not good' measure is used along with 'activity-restricted days' and 'number of chronic illnesses'. In this case, the index increases compared to the findings in the previous analysis. In the column [6], results from standardization with the three measures 'current health', 'chronically sick', and 'activity-restricted days' are shown. 'Current health' is used instead of 'health not good' to standardize for health (cf. column [4]). In general, the results from the analyses using the HI_{WVP} index show inequity favouring the lower income groups. This finding is in contrast to one of the findings based on the HI_{LG} index. However, the magnitude of the implied inequity varies by the measures of morbidity included in the analyses from –0.03 to –0.14.

Test of inequity

In the tests reported below, interaction terms between income and other variables used for standardization are tested separately from the income group 'dummies'. The tests are devised for adults only.

In the first test, a probit model is estimated for all individuals and includes four income group dummies (and one omitted group), four age groups dummies, a gender dummy, and two morbidity dummies plus interaction terms between income and age, gender, and morbidity dummies. The morbidity dummies are 'chronically sick' and 'health not good'

The likelihood function for this model, when estimated for all individuals, is denoted lnProbit(1), whereas the likelihood function for an estimation of an ordinary least squares (OLS) model, for individuals with positive expenditure only, is denoted in OLS(1). The likelihood function for the whole model is denoted $lnL(1) = lnProbit(1) + lnOLS(1)$. In the second model, the four income dummies are excluded, but the interaction terms were kept. The log-likelihood functions are denoted lnProbit(2), lnOLS(2), and lnL(2) respectively. Finally, in the third model, all income terms in the first model are omitted. The likelihood functions are denoted lnProbit(3), lnOLS(3), and lnL(3) respectively. The tests are based on the following test statistics: (a) the test statistic for income group dummies (autonomous terms):

$$LR(2,1) = 2(lnL(2) - lnL(1)), \tag{6.1}$$

which is approximately χ^2_r distributed, with r being the difference between number of parameters in models 2 and 1; and (b) the test statistic for all income terms (autonomous and interaction):

Table 6.6. Tests of inequity: results

Model	lnProbit	lnOLS	lnL	Parameters
1	−1250.7	−12 451.8	−13 702.5	34
2	−1252.6	−12 451.8	−13 704.4	31
3	−1407.6	−12 460.1	−13 867.7	6

$$LR(2,1) = 2(13\,704.4 - 13\,702.5) = 3.8; r = 6, P < 0.50$$
$$LR(3,1) = 2(13\,867.7 - 13\,702.5) = 331.4; r = 56, P < 0.0005$$

$$LR(3,1) = 2(\ln L(3) - \ln L(1)), \tag{6.2}$$

which is approximately χ^2_r, distributed, with r being the difference between number of parameters in models 3 and 1. (See Table 6.6.)

The test statistic for the pure autonomous income terms, denoted $LR(2,1)$, is not statistically significant when a chi-squared test is used. However, the test statistic $LR(3,1)$ for all income terms (autonomous and interaction) is highly significant. Thus, differences in expenditure exist between income groups that are not accounted for by the standardization.

SUMMARY AND DISCUSSION

From official documents, it appears that equity considerations concerning both finance and delivery were primary motivations in the public policy decisions leading to the formation of the present Danish health care system. With respect to delivery, equity is expressed in terms of access.

This study has been based on two surveys, both of which are relatively small. The survey analysing health care delivery used information for earned income only and imputed transfer income for pensioners, the unemployed, and students. It was demonstrated here, however, that the Gini coefficients were almost equal for the income distribution in the two samples. The small size of the samples was a particular problem in standardization on the delivery side, due to a substantial variation among individuals in the use of health care during the observation period. As a consequence, the results must be interpreted with caution. Data were collected by survey method and based on interviews with private households. Individuals living in institutions were therefore not included, although they are known to be relatively heavy users of health care. It can be expected that the reported retrospective use of health care was incomplete, especially for individuals in older age groups who were too sick to be interviewed, or who had died. The older age group was under-represented in the sample, and although a weighting scheme was applied, one would anticipate that those who were included were the most healthy.

Of the total cost of health care, 85 per cent was financed through general taxation (Table 6.2). A pro rata payment for health care purposes through taxation was assumed. The overall distribution of payment appears to follow the distribution of income rather closely, and the Kakwani as well as the Suits indices are close to zero, indicating almost proportionality in the finance of health care.

On the delivery side, various measures of morbidity were used as indicators of the need for health care. In general, inequity favouring the lower income groups was found (Table 6.4). The measures 'health not good' and 'chronically sick' are key measures for the present study. As is apparent from Table 6.3, the correlation between the two measures was relatively low. A joint distribution of the two measures showed that, although 40 per cent reported chronic illness, only 14 per cent reported 'health not good'. Consequently, the two measures included a different number of people with ill health. Moreover, neither of the two indicators of need for health care coincided with the number of people receiving health care. An average of 56 per cent reported use of health care during the previous 6 months; the correlation between use of health care and 'chronically sick' is 0.30, whereas the correlation between use of health care and 'health not good' is 0.23. Based on this evidence, it is tempting to prefer the 'chronically sick' measure as an indicator of the need for health care.

One might suspect that self-assessment depends on what the individual expects regarding health status, for example, given age. As a consequence, perceived health would not decline in proportion to, for example, a biological assessment of health status. This problem, which is associated with the 'current health' measure, also relates to the measure of perceived health based on one item only (that is, the 'health not good' measure). Moreover, several of the measures cannot be expected to be highly valid indicators of the individual's need for health care, because with health care, persons with ill health may be restored to good health. As the various measures are measures of different aspects of ill health, it is of no surprise that most correlation coefficients are not impressively high.

In the unstandardized analyses, the index of inequity, HI_{LG}, shows a negative value when the 'chronically sick' measure is used, but use of the 'health not good' measure results in a positive index value. Although the Le Grand approach showed inequity favouring the upper income groups in one case, the standardization approach, suggested in Chapter 4, showed results that imply inequity favouring the lower income groups no matter how expenditure was standardized for morbidity.

In the analysis of standardized expenditures, based on a two-stage regression approach, various measures of morbidity were used. The measure 'number of chronic illnesses per person' is a more refined measure than 'chronically sick', and consequently is assumed to be a more adequate measure of need for service. The results in Table 6.5 show that inequity is less when 'number of chronic illnesses per person' is used compared to the 'chronically sick' indicator. The 'current health' measure is a more refined measure than the dichotomized measure 'health not good'; and because it is a scale based on a number of items, it can be expected to be a more reliable measure than one based on a single item. It appears that the implied inequity favouring the lower income groups increases compared with the results in Table 6.5, column 4. This result was unexpected, and no explanation seems to be readily available.

It should be considered whether the applied measures of need are measures of the same amount of need across income and age groups. A priori, it might be expected that a chronic condition implies a greater need among the older age groups than among the younger. As the older age groups are concentrated in the lower income groups, the apparent inequity favouring the lower income groups, when the 'chronically sick' measure of need is used, might simply be a reflection of the lower income groups having a greater need for service than expressed by the need indicator. With a more complete coverage of the older age groups in the survey, it would be expected that a group with more sickness and a high use of health care would be included. This broader inclusion would influence the measure of inequity, but it is not possible, a priori, to determine exactly how. Compared with other age groups, pensioners have a relatively high share of capital income. If more comprehensive data on income were available, some pensioners would probably have moved to higher income groups. It can be assumed that this would have decreased, in absolute value, the concentration indices for both morbidity and expenditure. Here, again, the possible influence on the index of inequity cannot be settled a priori.

NOTES

1. Folketingets Forhandlinger 1970/71, column 2785, 3412, 7066, and 7196. Folketingstidende, Tillæg A, column 2433, Tillæg B, column 2217; Tillæg C, column 1007.
2. Folketingstidende 1970/71, Tillæg A, column 2451.
3. Folketingstidende 1970/71, Tillæg A, column 2451.
4. Folketingets Forhandlinger 1970/71, column 3441.
5. Detailed information is available from the author.

Appendix

Translated questionnaire items

1. Activity restricted days

About how many days during the last 6 months have you been so ill that you could not carry out your usual activities (job, work around the house and garden, school, kindergarden, etc.)? Days

2. Days confined to bed

About how many days during the last 6 months have you been so ill that you were confined to bed? Days

3. Chronic illnesses

In the following I mention a number of health problems which for some people are lasting problems. Please indicate whether or not members of the household have any of these. (A list with 36 conditions were read, see Bentzen *et al.* 1988.)

4. Current health

The scale is composed of 9 items with the following response categories: Agree entirely; Agree; Don't know; Disagree; Disagree entirely.

1. According to the doctors I have seen, my health is
2. I feel better now than I ever have before.
3. I am somewhat ill.
4. I am not as healthy now as I used to be.
5. I'm as healthy as anybody I know.
6. My health is excellent.
7. I have been feeling bad lately.
8. Doctors say that I am now in poor health.
9. I feel about as good now as I ever did.

6. Health not good

This measure was based on item (6) above (My health is excellent'). 'Health not good' included individuals who responded 'Disagree' or 'Disagree entirely'.

7

France

Claire Lachaud and Lise Rochaix

INTRODUCTION

The French health care system was established in 1945 with the clear objective of guaranteeing health for all. Equality of access was therefore a founding principle, but so was the rather more individualistic principle of autonomy of the consumer—freedom of choice. The result is a rather hybrid system which attempts to reconcile solidarity and liberalism through collective financing, coupled with the coexistence of a public and a private sector for the delivery of health care.

The administrative complexity of the French health care system generates potential inequity and an analysis of this, however difficult, can therefore be useful. It is also timely for at least two reasons: first, the general economic situation with its growing unemployment deprives a small but increasing fringe of the French population from social insurance; secondly, recent pressure from cost containment policies is increasingly seen as a threat to the solidarity principle.

In this chapter, the methodology of the COMAC-HSR project[1] is adopted in order to shed light on the equity characteristics of the French health care system.

THE FRENCH HEALTH CARE SYSTEM

The French system of social insurance (*Sécurité Sociale*) is based on the principles of insurance and solidarity. Risk-sharing applies, as in insurance, but contributions are compulsory, related to income rather than risk, and give entitlement to open-ended benefits for the insured and his or her family. The system is three-tier, between: the sick and the healthy; the young and the elderly; and the poor and the wealthy. It is then divided into three main branches, *Assurance Maladie* (health

The authors are grateful to the URA 934 for the support given to this project over the period 1989–91. We would like to thank INSEE, and, in particular, Mr. Mormiche and Mme de la Godelinais for providing us with the raw data.

insurance); *Assurance Vieillesse* (pension funds); and *branche famille* (family benefits).

Another salient feature of the French social security system is the emphasis on occupational rather than national solidarity. The system is mainly financed collectively through contributions from employers and employees levied by the various occupational regimes. The resulting fragmentation of solidarity (within an occupational group rather than nation-wide) makes an assessment of the distributive effects of the health care insurance system only tentative.

Cover for health insurance is virtually comprehensive: 98 per cent of the total population is covered under three main national health insurance funds: salaried workers (75 per cent)—the *Régime Général*; agricultural workers (8 per cent); and self-employed (7 per cent). The remaining 10 per cent of the population is covered by no less than 15 different special funds. For salaried workers, contributions are compulsory and paid by the employee (30 per cent) and his or her employer (70 per cent), although respective shares can vary from one occupational fund to another.

In 1989, 74.4 per cent of health care expenditures[2] was financed by *Sécurité Sociale*: state and local authorities contributed 1.3 per cent through earmarked taxes; households and their private insurances contributed 18 per cent; and the remaining 6.3 per cent was financed by *mutuelles* (non-profit-making 'friendly' insurance companies, where subscription is voluntary).

For ambulatory care and drugs, the insured generally pays the service charge in full and is refunded on the basis of a fixed rate, depending on the occupational regime. It is usually 75 per cent for medical services and 70 per cent, on average, for pharmaceutical goods. The remaining copayment, the so-called *ticket modérateur* can be partly or totally refunded by private complementary insurance schemes (including the *mutuelles*). At least 10 per cent of the insured who suffer from long-term severe illnesses, such as cancer, are totally or partially exempted from the copayment. On the other hand, the copayment can reach as high as 40 per cent for some pharmaceuticals which are considered non-essential (*médicaments de confort*). A small proportion of pharmaceuticals is actually non-refundable.

For hospital expenditures, however, *Sécurité Sociale* acts as a third-party payer and patients only pay the copayment, which cannot exceed 20 per cent of the total bill, exclusive of expensive specialized services. The same applies to diagnostic hospital services provided on an outpatient basis and for expensive drugs and laboratory tests. In fact, only 4 per cent of hospital resources are actually directly financed by households, and about 15 per cent of hospital days bear a copayment.

Health care delivery for its part is characterized by the coexistence of a public and a private sector. However, for hospitals, the relationship is rather complex: on the one hand, public hospitals carry out a public obligation (mainly in terms of opening times), but they contain a private sector. On the other hand, private hospitals (*cliniques privées*) are a highly heterogenous group, and some have a public obligation, whereas others are run on a profit basis only. The second important characteristic of the delivery side is that patients have free access to both primary care (general practitioners) and secondary care services (specialists, outpatient consultations in hospitals, and inpatient care).

Inequity may stem from the very structure of the finance system where benefit entitlement is related to occupation rather than medical need. The system caters for the family through the extension of the insured's benefits, and for the unemployed and the retired workers through special funds, but it is biased against those who have never had a regular occupation.[3]

Inequity can also stem from the different types of financial incentives facing patients: for example, the partial refund for ambulatory care on the one hand, compared to a third-party payer coverage for hospital expenditures on the other, may generate different health care consumption patterns between income groups.

PROGRESSIVITY OF HEALTH CARE FINANCE IN FRANCE

Data and variable definitions

The 1984 *Family Expenditure Survey* carried out by INSEE (Institut National des Statistiques et Etudes Economiques) was used for the finance side.[4] From the 11 977 households surveyed, 11 136 remained after excluding those with poor or incomplete responses (841, i.e., 7 per cent). The notion of income used is that of pre-tax income per equivalent adult, after exclusion of social security payments. The equivalence scale chosen is that generally used by INSEE (1 for the head of the household; 0.7 for another adult; 0.5 for a child). The estimation methods used for each of the items considered on the finance side are as follows.

Social contributions

For salaried workers in the *Régime Général* and for other special régimes,[5] health insurance contributions have been obtained in the following way: the health insurance contribution base has been estimated by adding all employees' and employers' social contributions to the income declared in the survey. These social contributions include health insurance, pension fund contributions, family benefits, and widows' contributions. With the knowledge that health care contributions represent 5.5 per cent of this base for employees and 12.6 per cent for employers, the health insurance social contributions are then obtained. The estimation method of the health insurance contribution base is shown in Appendix 7.1. For independent workers, the calculation of the contribution rates takes into account the financial ceiling.[6]

Income tax

The share of income tax in the total financing of health insurance is minimal (2.3 per cent in 1985) and will not be considered.

Direct payments

Information was recorded on hospital stays during the six months prior to the survey period and for the duration of the survey. For the other health care episodes, the data were collected for the duration of the survey only. Ambulatory care consumption is measured by general practitioners' (GPs) and dentists' consultations and home visits, as well as services provided by ancillary staff.

Due to the possibility of some services being paid directly by the *Sécurité Sociale* acting as third-party payer, it is sometimes difficult to establish out-of-pocket expenses. The amount reported in this survey may sometimes correspond to the total cost of the service (in which case the insured will be refunded a certain amount), or only to the copayment. An estimation of out-of-pocket expenses has been attempted which also includes a correction for the potential later refund of the copayment by a complementary health insurance (cf. Appendix 7.2 for more details). However, in view of the imprecise nature of these estimates, our results must be interpreted with care.

Complementary insurance premiums

The premiums correspond to the contributions paid to the complementary health insurance companies, either of the *mutuelle* type or purely private.

Empirical results

Table 7.1 shows results for each decile, and the relative proportions for income distribution and payments for each type of contribution can be compared. The non-linear estimations of the concentration indices are available for each type of payment. In general, the progressivity indices emphasize the regressive structure of payments. Figure 7.1 shows the relative concentration curves corresponding to the various types of payments, and illustrates their progressivity or regressivity.

Table 7.1. Distribution of health care financing (percentage, 1984)

Income decile	Pre-tax income	Insurance premiums	Employee contrib.	Payroll tax	Tot Publ [3]+[4]	Direct payments	Total payments
	[1]	[2]	[3]	[4]	[5]	[6]	[7]
Bottom	2.25	10.76	1.56	1.05	1.22	9.23	1.33
2nd	4.66	6.92	4.72	4.38	4.50	8.22	4.53
3rd	5.81	7.38	5.84	5.85	5.85	10.34	5.88
4th	6.91	9.18	7.31	7.24	7.26	9.54	7.29
5th	8.09	9.58	9.05	9.28	9.20	11.06	9.21
6th	9.41	8.81	9.95	10.36	10.22	11.31	10.22
7th	10.82	9.51	11.70	12.31	12.10	8.25	12.06
8th	12.58	10.43	13.21	13.93	13.68	9.80	13.64
9th	15.14	11.12	15.28	15.88	15.68	10.29	15.62
Top	24.32	16.31	21.38	19.72	20.28	11.96	20.21
Macroweights		7.68			77.28	15.05	100
Non-linear approximations							
Index							
Gini	0.3262	0.0949*	0.3086	0.3095	0.3091	0.0327*	0.3063
Kakwani		−0.2240*	−0.0176	−0.0167	−0.0171	−0.2862*	−0.0720
Suits		−0.2161	−0.0262*	−0.0311*	−0.0295*	−0.2926	−0.0810*

Note: * This is the linear approximation, when the concentration curve crosses the diagonal or when the concentration curves cross each other.

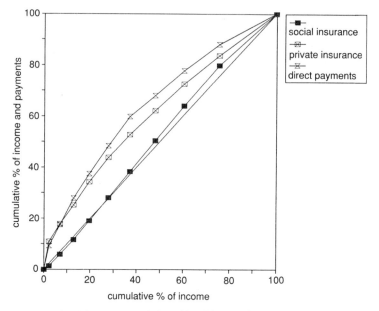

Fig. 7.1. Progressivity of health care finance, France.

The pre-tax income distribution is unequal, with a Gini coefficient of 0.3262. The first decile receives 2.25 per cent of total income, whereas the last receives 24.32 per cent.

The structure of the insurance premiums distribution is clearly regressive. The first five deciles contribute 43.82 per cent of total payments, whereas only receive 27.72 per cent of total income. As a result, the absolute and relative concentration curves are respectively below and above the relevant benchmark curve. The non-linear estimation of the Kakwani index is not given here because the corresponding concentration curve crosses the diagonal for the lowest income decile.

For the bottom decile, the subscription rate to complementary health insurance is rather high (10.76 per cent of the total), which can be partly explained by the high student cover (see Volatier 1990). However, more research is needed to explain this rather unexpected result.

Employees' contributions are very slightly regressive. The first five deciles receive 27.72 per cent of total income, and pay 28.48 per cent of employees' contributions. Likewise, employers' contributions are slightly regressive. The first five deciles pay 27.8 per cent of employers' contributions. Taken together (column [5] in Table 7.1), employers' and employees' contributions have consequently a slightly regressive structure. This can be explained by the ceiling still imposed on independent workers' health insurance contributions.[7] But in view of the limited size of this group, its influence on the whole regressive nature of the system should remain marginal.

Direct payments have a regressive structure. The top decile only contributes 11.96 per cent, although receives 24.32 per cent of total income. The first five deciles bear 48.39 per cent of all direct payments, whereas they receive 27.72 per cent of total income. It must be noted, however, that total direct payments represent 2.62 per cent of all contributions to the health care system, which is much less than expected. This is clearly related to the short time period covered by the survey, leading to an under-reporting of individual consumption. These estimates are therefore rather inprecise, and the results for out-of-pocket payments are to be interpreted with caution.

The total payments column is derived as the weighted average of the three components defined, using adjusted macroweights.[8] Overall, total contributions (health insurance contributions, column [5], complementary insurance premiums, column [2], and direct payments, column [6], display a regressive distribution.

Sensitivity analyses have been carried out in order to test the impact on the progressivity/regressivity structure of some of our assumptions. The first is concerned with the inclusion of payroll tax in the definition of gross income in order to link more closely ability to pay and payments, which include this tax. The second tests the sensitivity of the results to the choice of quintiles rather than deciles. The results do not alter the main findings. In the first case, the concentration indices vary marginally, whereas in the second, the absolute value of these indices is lowered, with no change of sign.

EQUITY IN THE DELIVERY OF HEALTH CARE IN FRANCE

Data and variable definitions

The 1980 *Health Interview Survey* (HIS) used for the study of equity on the delivery side is still the most recent and exhaustive survey, carried out by INSEE on a nationally representative sample of 7323 households (21 000 individuals).[9] Information is available on the number of general practitioners' and specialists' services, and the expenditure incurred by the household, as well as the number and duration of hospital stays. General health status at the beginning of the survey is recorded by an open list[10] of 20 conditions (e.g., whether chronic or acute, light or severe). Morbidity during the survey is recorded for each medical event by including a motive for consultation, in the interviewee's own formulation, later translated back in the WHO ICD classification by a group of experts working for the survey team.

Choice of different need indicators

Unfortunately, the HIS does not provide a scale of self-reported morbidity which could be used as a proxy for Blaxter's (1989) *subjective* model. Neither does the survey contain questions, such as: 'Do you suffer from a chronic or an acute illness?', or 'Do you suffer from a long-standing illness?', as is the case in other countries.

As a result, a morbidity indicator had to be constructed as a proxy for a need indicator, using indications on self-reported morbidity. A classification method defined by Béland (1990) on the basis of ICD codes has been applied to the opening list of conditions in order to distinguish between chronic and acute conditions. In addition, this method allowed conditions to be further classified into severity levels: life-threatening versus light morbidity conditions. The classification's general principles are outlined in Appendix 7.3. The following set of indicators were then derived.

- Indicator A: chronic conditions.
- Indicator B: acute conditions.
- Indicator C: light morbidity conditions (not life-threatening).
- Indicator D: severe morbidity conditions (life-threatening).

The individual is said to suffer from a chronic (acute) condition if he has declared at least one chronic (acute) condition. The same reasoning applies for the two levels of severity defined. In addition, information on interruptions of activity (yes/no) has been used as a proxy for Blaxter's *functional* model (indicator E).

A preliminary analysis using the chronic indicator, displayed a sickness ratio of 688 per 1000, which is much higher than in other countries. Clearly, the fact that the list is longer in France, containing both benign and severe conditions leads to a bias. Indeed, when patients see a condition written explicitly in the questionnaire, they are more likely to report it. The analysis has been redone, after excluding a number of conditions[11] which do not seem to appear explicitly in other countries' opening lists. After correction, the sickness ratio for chronic conditions is 530/1000, and is comparable to the European average.

The results presented here were derived from the whole sample: 21 000 individuals, 13 753 of whom remained after excluding the under 18-year-olds, as well as individuals for whom no income variable was available.

Table 7.2. Unstandardized distribution of morbidity and expenditure (percentage)

Income decile	Expendit.	Chronic conditions (A)	Acute conditions (B)	Light conditions (C)	Severe conditions (D)	Interrupted activity (E)
Bottom	15.91	10.08	9.92	9.68	13.14	8.46
2nd	11.90	11.02	10.54	10.92	10.98	9.06
3rd	8.44	9.97	10.01	9.95	11.23	8.79
4th	11.24	9.91	9.74	9.80	11.23	9.82
5th	10.24	9.82	9.95	9.77	10.73	11.06
6th	9.01	9.42	9.77	9.50	7.65	9.65
7th	7.96	10.23	9.84	10.22	10.12	11.33
8th	8.22	9.73	9.81	10.00	9.13	11.33
9th	8.59	9.42	9.77	9.64	6.72	11.28
Top	8.49	10.41	10.65	10.51	9.07	9.22
C_{exp}	−0.102					
C_{ill}		−0.0088	0.000376	−0.000217	−0.0833	0.0383
HI_{LG}		−0.0931	−0.102	−0.102	−0.0187	−0.140

Income variable and equivalence scale

The individual's equivalent income was constructed (after social security contributions), using income declared in the survey. In most cases, this will represent pre-tax income, which is the standard type of income reported in France, but the survey is not very explicit in this respect. The equivalence scale used is the same as for the finance side.

Estimation of total cost

The average costs of medical services have been estimated using published data. The items of medical consumption considered are physicians' and specialists' visits, and hospital stays.[12] The cost of public and private hospitals have been imputed slightly differently because they reflect a structural difference which has an impact on quality—public hospitals usually deal with more severe cases.[13]

Unstandardized distribution of morbidity and health care

Table 7.2 shows the Le Grand unstandardized analysis, using the five morbidity indicators. The HI_{LG} coefficient of horizontal inequity is negative for all indicators which shows inequity favouring the poor. Indeed, the top three quintiles consume less compared to their morbidity shares, irrespective of the morbidity indicator chosen. More importantly, expenditures are concentrated in the bottom income decile (15.91 per cent), as expected, and the share of expenditure is greater than the relevant share of morbidity, for all morbidity indicators.

A comparison of results across the five morbidity indicators is useful so that the nature of this inequity can be explained. The life-threatening morbidity indicator (D) is very sensitive to the singularity of the French health care system where the poor tend to consume more hospital services at a later stage, a finding confirmed in the literature (cf. Charraud 1988) and explained partly by cultural factors and partly by the different financial incentives facing patients, (hospital services being virtually free compared to ambulatory care services). The higher share of expenditure of the first income decile is clearly related to the treatment of severe conditions (shown by indicator D), which is usually carried out in hospital and is more expensive.

Standardized expenditure distribution

The purpose of this analysis is to standardize medical care consumption per quintile by age (four groups), sex, and morbidity indicator(s), by means of a two-part regression model.

The results on French data showed a poor fit of the probit model per quintiles, as evidenced by a log likelihood ratio chi-squared test. Indeed, the expected probabilities of having a positive expenditure for each quintile were found to be substantially different from those which could have been expected by looking at the ratio of individuals with positive consumption over the whole sample.[14]

Consequently, the direct standardization method is used (cf. Van Doorslaer and Wagstaff 1989), rather than the two-part regression model, but it is carried out in two parts, in order to take into account the high frequency of zero medical care expenditure among individuals. Indeed, if it is the case that a standardization carried out by regression without the probit specification is biased, so too should be a direct standardization which would not reflect this particular feature of medical expenditure. For this reason, the standardization is in two parts:

1. In the first part, the standardized probability that an individual i in quintile k has a positive expenditure is derived:

$$P_k^+ = \sum_{h=1}^{2} \sum_{l=1}^{2} \sum_{j=1}^{4} f_{hlj} \cdot P_{khlj},$$

where P_{khlj} is the proportion of individuals with positive medical expenditure in quintile k, with health status h, gender l, and age j; f_{hlj} is the

Table 7.3.   Standardized distribution of expenditure (percentage). (Two-part direct standardization)

Income quintile	Indicator					
	A	B	C	D	E	A,D,E
Bottom	25.93	25.72	25.96	25.73	26.95	27.44
2nd	18.77	18.78	18.85	18.54	18.81	18.74
3rd	18.99	18.95	18.97	19.00	18.30	18.03
4th	16.86	17.15	16.78	16.89	16.24	15.49
Top	19.45	19.40	19.45	19.84	19.70	20.29
HI_{WVP}	−0.0595	−0.0571	−0.0603	−0.0537	−0.0683	−0.0702

proportion of individuals in the whole sample with health status h, gender l, and age j.

2. In the second part, the standardized conditional level of expenditure is derived for each quintile, conditional on expenditure being positive:

$$m_k^+ = \sum_{h=1}^{2}\sum_{l=1}^{2}\sum_{j=1}^{4} f_{hlj}^c \cdot m_{khlj}^c,$$

where c indicates that the proportions are calculated using the censored sample; m_{khlj}^c is the mean of medical expenditure for people in the censored sample in quintile k, with health status h, gender l, and age j; f_{hlj}^c is the proportion of individuals in the censored sample with health status h, gender l, and age j.

The product of these results yields the standardized health care expenditure per quintile.

Table 7.3 shows the results from this two-part direct standardization, using the five morbidity indicators separately and a combination of three of them.

When standardizing with one morbidity indicator, the results display a strong inequity favouring the poor. The higher percentage of standardized expenditure is to be found in the bottom income group (more than 25 per cent of expenditure for all morbidity indicators). The other quintiles have an even distribution of expenditure, with the exception of the top quintile whose share of expenditure is slightly higher. Consequently, the HI_{WVP} index of horizontal inequity is negative, showing inequity favouring the poor.

A standardization using more than one indicator of morbidity does not

Table 7.4.   Testing the hypothesis of absence of income-related inequity

Indicator	A	B	C	D	E
Degrees of Freedom	24/13 752	24/13 752	24/13 752	24/13 752	24/13 752
F value	1.348	1.410	1.344	2.260	3.813
$P > F$	0.1185	0.0878	0.1211	0.0004	0.0001

Table 7.5.   Testing Le Grand's hypothesis

Indicator	A	B	C	D	E
Degrees of Freedom	5/13 752	5/13 752	5/13 752	5/13 752	5/13 752
F value	20.153	21.974	21.849	19.353	29.471
$P > F$	0.0001	0.0001	0.0001	0.0001	0.0001

alter these results. As an example, the analysis has been carried out with the chronic (A), the life-threatening morbidity (D), and the interruption of activity indicator (E).[15] Again, the distribution of the share of expenditure has the same pattern.

In conclusion, all the analyses carried out with the various morbidity indicators show inequity favouring the poor.

Test of inequity

Because the probit model did not seem to fit the data, the regression based F-test has not been performed. Instead, the F-test has been carried out using a general ordinary least squares (OLS) model, at the risk of deriving biased estimates. This bias is not worrying, provided that it does not affect income groups differently. Considering the standardized results shows that irrespective of the morbidity indicator chosen, the non-negative medical care expenditure probabilities show little variation across income groups. The hypothesis made hereafter is that the estimation bias (which should induce a bias in the F-test), if it does exist, equally affects the income groups.

The regression model adopted follows closely that outlined in Chapter 4. The same quintiles were used as in the two-part direct standardization, with identical age and sex categories, as well as the two health categories of each of the morbidity indicators.

A first set of results is shown in Table 7.4 and tests the absence of income-related inequity (all income coefficients equal to zero). This hypothesis is rejected for morbidity indicators D and E, whereas it is accepted at 10 per cent for A, B, and C. There is, therefore, evidence of income-related inequity.

A second set of results (Table 7.5) tests Le Grand's (1978) assumption that the non-sick receive no care. The results are unambiguous, and irrespective of the morbidity indicator chosen, the hypothesis is rejected: the non-sick also consume medical care. These results show the potential biases of Le Grand's method and the value of the Wagstaff *et al.* (1991 *b*) approach used here.

The analyses carried out using different approaches and different morbidity indicators corroborate the main finding of an inequity favouring the poor on the delivery side of the French health care system. The sensitivity analysis also clearly shows that lower income groups suffer from more severe conditions requiring more expensive treatments.

CONCLUSION

This chapter has analysed the equity consequences of the way in which health care is financed and delivered to the French population. The possible existence of vertical inequity on the finance side has been documented by an analysis of the 1984 *Household Expenditure Survey*. The results indicated that overall, the French system is slightly regressive, mainly due to health insurance contributions.

Horizontal inequity in favour of the lower income groups was found, using the 1980 *Health Interview Survey*. This result is robust to any of the specifications of the need indicator, although its magnitude is lower for the high severity indicator, which seems to capture the different consumption patterns among income groups in France.

NOTES

1. See Chapters 2 and 3, Part I, for a presentation of the methodology.
2. The distribution for the study period (1984) were as follows: 75.5 per cent for *Sécurité Sociale*; 2.3 per cent for the state and local authorities; 17.1 per cent for households and their private insurance 14.7 per cent and 2.4 per cent respectively; and 5.1 per cent for the *mutuelles*.
3. However, a 1953 extension of the former *Aide Médicale Gratuite* (free medical assistance) serves as a financial net for those excluded from the system and in need of medical care.
4. This survey is undertaken every five years and was carried out from June 1984 to July 1985. It provides information on budget shares in order to analyse households' living standards and consumer behaviour, using daily records, one of which concerns health directly.
5. Ideally, average payments should be computed for each of the various occupational regimes, but the limited information available in the survey regarding the nature of the health insurance cover prevents an exact evaluation of these

contributions. The same rates were therefore used across the board, this methodological choice being justified by the fact that the *Régime Général* covers 75 per cent of all insured and that the contribution rates of the various regimes do not differ markedly.

6. The contribution rate is 3.1 per cent below the financial ceiling of the *Régime Général* (Ffr8490, 1 July 1984) and 8.75 per cent and up to five times this amount.

7. Employees' and employers' health insurance contributions paid to the *Régime Général* were originally subject to a financial ceiling which limited the progressivity of contributions for the very high levels of income. This ceiling was removed for employers from January 1984 and for employees from January 1980. This measure has favoured an income redistribution from the rich to the poor. Independent workers for their part are still subject to this ceiling.

8. Note that the State's 2.3 per cent share has been omitted.

9. The data were collected over one year in four successive periods of 12 weeks, from March 1980 until April 1981.

   Although representative, this survey suffers a number of limitations. First, part of the population is under-represented. This is the case for the institutionalized population in hospices, convents, and old people's homes, which is excluded because of the sampling method adopted here (place of residence). Secondly, the total number of hospital stays recorded in the 1980 survey is rather limited: 675 hospital stays during the survey period, and 2384 for the previous year.

10. The interviewee is given the opportunity to declare a condition not mentioned on the list.

11. Some of the illnesses that seemed benign, compared to those reported in other countries, have been excluded, using information published on the 1980 health survey giving the number of cases identified for each condition (sleep problems, dental problems, constipation, and sight problems).

12. The choice of the time reference period is three months. Because the 1980 survey covers hospital stays for the duration of the survey and the previous year, and medical events are only recorded for the duration of the survey, the amounts for hospitalizations were divided by 5 in order to harmonize time periods.

13. The average fees used are: Ffr49,70 for GP treatment, Ffr63,39 for specialist, Ffr277 per day for private hospitals, and Ffr510 per day for public hospitals (1980 prices).

14. Furthermore, these probabilities vary substantially, depending on the number of morbidity indicators used in the standardization. They are too low if only one indicator is used, and too high if more than one indicator is used.

15. The low severity indicator is not included in view of its high correlation with the chronic indicator.

Appendix 7.1

Estimation of the health insurance contribution base

The method consists in estimating the health insurance contribution base using the income notion declared during the interview: income before tax but after social contributions and cash transfers. This requires a knowledge of the different contribution rates of the *Sécurité Sociale*. The following table summarizes the rates for the different types of payments:

	Age	
	under 65	over 65
Contribution without ceiling (%)	18.2	18.1
Contribution with ceiling (%)	23	17.3

The intervals between a pre-tax income equal to the ceiling (of Ffr8490 in 1984) and post-tax income can be calculated as follows: for a person over 65 years old, we obtain a post-tax income of Ffr: 5484.54 (8490 · (1 − 35.4%), and for a person under 65 years old, post-tax income is Ffr4992.12.

Thereafter, let y' be any given post-tax income, and y any given pre-tax income then:

> If age > 65, and $y' < 5484.54$, then $y = y' / (1 - 35.4\%)$;
> otherwise, $y = (y' + 17.3\% \cdot 8490) / (1 - 18.1\%)$.
> If age < 65, and $y' < 4992.12$, then $y = y' / (1 - 41.2\%)$;
> otherwise, $y = y' + 23\% \cdot 8490) / (1 - 18.2\%)$.

Appendix 7.2

Estimation of out-of-pocket expenses

The estimation of out-of-pocket expenses varies according to the item of medical care consumption considered, and is carried out in the following way.

For hospital expenses, the amount declared in the survey is assumed to correspond to the copayment before potential refunding by a complementary health insurance. Hospital payments include both those made during the 6 months prior to the survey and the 14 days covered during the survey period and they are converted in monthly amounts.

For the remaining items of medical care consumption (dentists, GP visits, laboratory tests, and ancillary staff) an arbitrary criterion is used and payments (E) are compared with the average fee (P) for the corresponding item. If $E < P$, the E is considered a copayment, whereas when $E \geq P$, an average reimbursement rate is used to derive the copayment.[16]

To account for the subsequent reimbursement of the copayment by complementary medical insurances, final direct payments made by each decile are revised downwards, using the percentage of complementary health insurance contributions purchased by that particular decile.

NOTES

16. The fees chosen correspond to Ffr65 for GPs' and dentists' consultations (with a corresponding rate of reimbursement of 75 per cent), Ffr50 for ancillary staff services (65 per cent), Ffr20 for pharmaceuticals (70 per cent), and Ffr50 for laboratory tests and X-rays (70 per cent).

Appendix 7.3
The Béland classification methodology

Diagnostic classification is a recurrent problem in health services and health care systems research. Existing classifications are either too elaborate or designed for particular purposes which do not necessarily suit those of the undertaken research.

The classification method proposed by Béland (1990) and used here groups the most frequent diagnostics encountered in medical care practice into eight categories.

The objective was to obtain a concise classification of medical diagnostics which would also be relevant for hospital care. The starting point was the Schneeweiss and Coll classification (1983) which has been developed for ambulatory care. Their list of 92 diagnostic categories has been given independently to two medical experts, asking them to identify preventive diagnoses, traumas, acute illnesses, chronic illnesses, and psychiatric conditions. Within each of these five categories, the two physicians had to decide whether the diagnoses referred to life-threatening conditions or not: 71 out of 92 diagnoses were classified without difficulty. For the remaining 21, each expert was asked to reconsider his choice in the light of his collegue's diverging opinion. Finally, the few diagnoses on which opinions still diverged were discussed between the two experts to arrive at a unique classification.

For psychiatric diagnoses and traumas, additional information was used from ICD codes. The complete classification now comprises the following eight categories: severe preventive, light preventive, severe acute condition, light acute condition, severe chronic condition, light acute condition, traumas, and psychiatric illnesses, for which no severity index exists. This index should be available shortly, as well as diagnostics excluded from the original Schneeweiss and Coll (1983) classification. Note that apart from the severity index, the diagnoses are not ordered on a continuum, but grouped in discrete classes.

8

Ireland

Brian Nolan

INTRODUCTION

This chapter presents the results of an analysis of equity in the financing and delivery of health care in Ireland, applying the methodology developed in the course of the COMAC-HSR project. The data on which the paper is based come from two large-scale surveys: the *Household Budget Survey*, carried out by the Irish Central Statistics Office in 1987 (for the financing side), and the *Survey of Income Distribution, Poverty and Usage of State Services* carried out by The Economic and Social Research Institute in the same year (for the delivery side). The results from an equity perspective presented here can be placed in the context of the Irish health services utilization and financing patterns analysed in detail in Nolan (1991).

THE IRISH HEALTH CARE SYSTEM

The way in which health care financing and delivery are organized in Ireland is described in the *Report of the Commission on Health Funding* (1989) and in Nolan (1991). The system is a complex one, with different groups in the population having different entitlements to free or subsidized care, and with care being delivered by public and private sectors which are interwoven rather than distinct. It is necessary to first outline the structure of entitlement to free or subsidized medical care set up by the state. This structure has been altered as detailed below, but we first describe the system which operated up to mid-1991. The population was divided into three entitlement categories as follows:

1. *Category I* had full entitlement to free medical care financed by the state, covering general practitioner (GP) care, prescribed medicines, and hospital outpatient services, and inpatient maintenance and treatment.

2. *Category II* were entitled to maintenance and treatment in public hospitals (subject to a IR£10 per night charge) and to hospital out-

patient services (subject to a IR£10 charge for the first visit for a particular condition) but not to GP care or (most) prescription medicines.[1]

3. *Category III* were entitled only to maintenance in public hospitals (subject to the IR£10 per night charge), they were liable for consultant services as well as for outpatient and primary care.[2]

The entitlement category into which a person and his/her dependants fall is determined on the basis of income limits/means tests.[3] In 1987, the year to which the data used in this paper apply, about 38 per cent of the population were in Category I, 47 per cent were in Category II, and 15 per cent were in Category III.[4] Category III was abolished in June 1991, Category II entitlements being extended to that group. The analysis in this Chapter relates to the situation before that change.

Primarily because those in Category III had only limited entitlement to hospital care, the state also set up a monopoly health insurer, the Voluntary Health Insurance Board (VHI). This operates at arms-length from the state and currently provides health insurance, for the most part covering hospital care, to about 29 per cent of the population. Given that only 15 per cent of the population were in Category III, clearly many people in the other categories, with full, or close to full, entitlement to public hospital care, nonetheless choose to pay 'extra' to obtain VHI cover. The dominant factor in producing this demand appears to be the ease of access to 'private' hospital care—in either private or public hospitals—enjoyed by those with insurance. (The fact that premiums are fully tax-deductible may be an important contributory factor in such demand.)

With a substantial proportion of health care either provided free (or at a low charge) by the state or covered by health insurance, there still remains a significant element paid for out-of-pocket by households. This includes, most importantly, GP care and (most) prescription medicines for those not in Category I. Expenditure on non-prescription medicines is also significant, as is spending on dental care.

State expenditure on health care is itself financed largely through general taxation, with a small proportion provided by social security contributions. Social security contributions are at a relatively low level in Ireland. A special Health Contribution of 1.25 per cent, levied on earnings, goes to fund general health services, and the dental treatment of insured workers is covered by the Social Insurance Fund. These account for only about 10 per cent of public expenditure on health service provision, the remainder being financed out of general taxation.

How then is health care—financed by the state, health insurance, or out-of-pocket—delivered? General practitioner care is provided by independent professionals, most of whom treat both patients in Category I, who are entitled to free GP care, and the remainder of the population.

For Category I patients these GPs are remunerated by the state, now through a capitation system introduced in 1989. In 1987, however, they were paid by the state on a fee service basis, which is also the way in which patients outside Category I are themselves charged.

Hospital services are provided predominantly through publicly financed rather than private hospitals, although there is a small private hospital sector. Some of these publicly financed hospitals are fully owned and managed by the state (through local area health boards), whereas others are owned and run by religious orders or voluntary trusts. In these public hospitals, though, there is an important distinction between treatment in public wards and in private or semi-private accommodation. People in Categories I and II are entitled to treatment in public wards (free for Category I and subject to a per-night maintenance charge for Category II). Those either willing to pay out-of-pocket or with health insurance cover usually obtain care in private accommodation from a consultant of their own choice. The hospital consultant most often treats both 'public' and 'private' patients. Thus, both 'public' and 'private' hospital care is often provided by the same hospital and consultant—there is no clear divide between public and private delivery in the hospital sector. Hospital outpatient services are similarly provided for the most part by publicly financed hospitals.

The final aspect of the Irish health services which merits discussion is the role given to equity in the stated goals of the system. Health policy and, the organization and objectives of the health services were recently reviewed in an official consultative document produced by the Department of Health (1986), *Health: the wider dimensions*. In considering equity as an objective, this review stated that, in the context of health policy, equity 'is taken to relate to the distribution of available health services over the population on the basis of need and an equitable sharing of the cost of providing such services . . . Access to needed health services is guaranteed to the whole community, with individuals being asked to pay on the basis of their financial means' (p. 18). The existing eligibility system is seen as clearly discriminatory in favour of those in the lower socio-economic groups, although some anomalies in the application of the income tests to determine eligibility are noted. The review goes beyond the notion of equity in terms of access and the distribution of health resources, though, to discuss 'equality in health', which it states would imply that 'each individual is offered the same opportunity to enjoy good health' (p. 18). Clear inequalities in health, between age/sex groups and socio-economic groups, are noted, and a basic objective 'should be to frame policy responses on a broad front, based on a full analysis of these differences, which promote equality in health' (p. 18). The health sector is seen as only one element of the national policy response required, with a particularly important role in stimulating debate about health inequalities.

PROGRESSIVITY OF HEALTH CARE FINANCE IN IRELAND

Data, variable definitions, and incidence assumptions

In examining distributional aspects of the financing of health care, detailed information is required on direct household expenditures on health care and health insurance and, crucially, the household's contribution to public expenditure on health care, through the taxes and social security contributions it pays, must also be estimated. The *Household Budget Survey* (HBS) carried out by the Central Statistical Office (CSO) in 1987 provides this level of detail on Irish households. It covered a random national sample of 7705 households, and published results show, *inter alia*, average direct household expenditure on different types of health care and on health insurance and average income tax and social insurance contributions paid, by households classified by gross income decile (CSO 1989). Results are not published on an equivalent income basis, but for this Chapter, special tabulations were obtained from the microdata tapes.

The budget survey itself presents no data on indirect taxes, but the CSO also produces an analysis of the redistributive effects of taxes and benefits based on the HBS, corresponding closely to the similar exercise published by the UK CSO on the basis of the *Family Expenditure Survey*. This allocates indirect taxes to households on the basis of their expenditure patterns using the conventional incidence assumptions that such taxes are borne fully by the consumer. The results for 1987 are not yet available, so for indirect taxes we have had to rely on the distributional pattern shown by the previous exercise which used 1980 data (CSO 1983).

Empirical results

This section considers the importance of the various sources of health service financing and their distributional pattern. As described above, these sources are:

(1) general taxation;
(2) social security contributions;
(3) health insurance; and
(4) out-of-pocket household expenditure.

In arriving at total current state expenditure on health service provision, the starting point is non-capital expenditure by the Department of Health, which in 1987 was IR£1221.5 million.[5] From this we must subtract expenditure on income maintenance for certain groups (which is administered by the Department but constitutes social welfare rather than health care), and conversely some health services funded by other departments ('treatment benefits' administered by the Department of Social Welfare) must be included.[6] This produces a total for public expenditure of IR£1133 million, of which about 10 per cent is financed by social security contributions and the remainder out of general taxation.[7]

Health insurance expenditure, almost all by the VHI, amounted to IR£150 million in 1987.[8] Based primarily on the Household Budget Survey the CSO have estimated that household expenditure on health care (net of insurance premiums and refunds) amounted to about IR£225 millions.[9] Thus, aggregate expenditure on health care was about IR£1508 million (8.4 per cent of GNP), and was financed as follows:

- General taxation   67.8%
- Social insurance   7.3%
- Health insurance   10.0%
- Household expenditure   14.9%

Compared with other countries, this financing structure has a relatively high share coming from general taxation. Social insurance is much less important than in France, Germany, Italy, and the Netherlands; private insurance is quite important and out-of-pocket expenditure is about the middle of the range.

We now turn to the distributional pattern associated with each financing source, based on the 1987 HBS. Households are ranked by equivalent gross income, the equivalence scales used being based on the relativities implicit in Irish social welfare payment rates, where if a single adult is 1, each extra adult in the household is 0.66 and each child is 0.33. (These scales have been employed in recent research on poverty and income distribution in Ireland, see, for example, Callan *et al.* 1989.)

For each decile, the average amount paid in income tax, social insurance, health insurance, and out-of-pocket expenditure on health services can be derived directly from the survey. As already noted, the distributional pattern of indirect taxes has not yet been estimated by the CSO for 1987, and the present exercise therefore uses earlier CSO results—based on the 1980 HBS—to estimate indirect taxes by decile. [10] Given the importance of indirect taxes—accounting for over half of Irish tax revenue—and the dominance of general taxation in health service financing, the pattern shown here must therefore be treated with some caution. Income and indirect taxes taken together account for about

85 per cent of all tax revenues.[11] (Property and corporation taxes are much less important in Ireland compared to other countries; they are not included in the CSO's redistributive exercises and no attempt is made here to allocate them among households.)

Table 8.1 shows the distribution of health care payments from each source among households classified by gross equivalent income decile, together with the share of gross equivalent income going to each decile. For general taxation, income tax and indirect taxes are shown separately. The distribution of total taxation is a weighted average of the two in accordance with their relative importance as revenue sources, which means that indirect taxes are weighted 0.58 and income tax 0.42. The table shows that, as is generally the case, income tax falls relatively heavily on high-income groups, who pay a share greater than the percentage of income they receive, whereas lower income groups pay a proportion of indirect tax greater than their share in income. Table 8.1 also shows the Gini coefficient for the various revenue sources, and the Kakwani and Suits progressivity indices. These also indicate that income tax is progressive and indirect tax regressive, so that total tax is slightly progressive, the shares paid in tax by the various deciles being close to their shares in income.

The table shows that (employees') social insurance contributions are progressive, although less so than income tax. The same is true of health insurance premiums, which is not surprising given the role of health insurance in the Irish system. Household direct expenditure on health care is regressive, although less so than indirect taxes. Total health care payments, then, have a distribution similar to that of total taxes and gross equivalent income itself. On the basis of the Kakwani and Suits indices, total payments are slightly progressive. The concentration curve for payments does not lie outside the Lorenz curve for income throughout, however, they (barely) intersect towards the top, with the bottom 80 per cent of the distribution having a slightly larger share in total payments than in income. Clearly, the two distributions are very similar and health care payments are close to proportional.

EQUITY IN THE DELIVERY OF HEALTH CARE IN IRELAND

Data and variable definitions

The *Household Budget Survey* cannot be used as a data source for this analysis as no information on health status is obtained, but an alternative is available in the *Survey of Income Distribution, Poverty and Usage of*

Table 8.1. Distribution of health care financing (percentage, 1987)

Income decile	Pre-tax income	General taxation			Social insurance	Insurance premiums	Household expendit.	Total payments
		Income tax	Indirect tax	Total tax				
Bottom	2.9	0.1	5.1	3.0	0.3	2.4	4.1	2.9
2nd	4.2	0.2	4.9	3.0	0.9	1.1	3.5	2.7
3rd	4.9	0.5	5.1	3.2	1.4	1.2	3.1	2.9
4th	5.7	1.5	6.7	4.5	3.4	2.5	6.2	4.5
5th	6.8	3.6	9.1	6.8	7.0	4.5	8.5	6.8
6th	8.4	7.1	11.1	9.4	11.0	8.8	12.1	9.9
7th	10.3	10.8	12.4	11.7	13.8	13.7	14.3	12.4
8th	12.9	14.8	13.1	13.8	16.6	16.7	14.0	14.3
9th	16.6	21.8	15.4	18.1	20.2	22.5	17.4	18.6
Top	27.3	39.5	17.1	26.5	25.4	26.5	16.8	25.0
Total health care payments (%)	–	28.5	39.3	67.8	7.3	10.0	14.9	100.0
Index								
Gini/Conc.	0.36	0.61	0.24	0.39	0.47	0.48	0.29	0.39
Kakwani	–	0.25	-0.12	0.03	0.11	0.12	-0.07	0.03
Suits	–	0.25	-0.14	0.03	0.08	0.10	-0.10	0.02

State Services, carried out by the Economic and Social Research Institute in 1987. This covered 3300 households and gathered in-depth information on household income and, *inter alia*, on utilization of health services of various kinds during the previous year (see Callan *et al.* 1989, for a full description of the sample). The utilization data covered the number of GP visits, prescriptions filled, visits to outpatient clinics or day surgery, nights spent in hospital, and visits for dental treatment, sight or hearing tests in the previous 12 months, for each household member. Comparison of sample data with the limited national aggregates available indicate that the sample represents the population's characteristics and health service utilization levels well, although there may be some under-representation of GP visits, possibly due to recall problems (see Nolan 1991).

The survey also sought limited information on health status. Each adult (where possible) was asked 'Do you have any major illness, physical disability or infirmity that has troubled you for at least the past year or that is likely to go on troubling you in the future?' To provide information about psychological health, adults were also asked a shortened version of the widely used General Health Questionnaire (GHQ), comprising 12 items (see Whelan *et al.* 1990). Because these questions were asked only of adults, the results here refer only to those aged 18 or over.

Health care expenditure/ benefit is now attributed to each person on the basis of their reported utilization of care of different types, multiplied by the estimated unit cost of each type of care. These unit costs are estimated using aggregate data on overall expenditure and utilization levels for different services, as described in detail in Nolan (1991). The types of care covered and their estimated unit costs are:

- GP visits—IR£5 per visit;
- outpatient consultations—IR£25 per visit;
- day surgery visits—IR£80 per visit;
- hospital inpatient stays—IR£140 per night;

The categories of expenditure just described account for about 55 per cent of total health care spending. Expenditure on long-term institutional care, psychiatric care, dental care, and prescription medicines are not included in the exercise for the reasons discussed in Chapter 4.

Unstandardized distribution of morbidity and health care

Allocating expenditure among individuals in the sample on the basis of their reported utilization over the previous 12 months and the estimated unit costs, a total expenditure figure for each person is derived. In order to assess the resulting distribution of health care expenditure, individuals are firstly categorized by the equivalent gross income quintile of their household. Table 8.2 shows the percentage of health care expenditure going to the individuals in each quintile. The bottom two quintiles receive higher shares of expenditure, and the top three quintiles lower shares, than their population share of 20 per cent. The bottom two quintiles each have 26–27 per cent of total expenditure, whereas the top three each have only 15–16 per cent.

In order to relate the distribution of health expenditure to that of 'need', we employ the measure of chronic illness. Table 8.2 also shows where the ill are located in the equivalent income distribution. They are found to be relatively heavily concentrated towards the bottom, in the second quintile containing 30 per cent of all persons reporting chronic illness, and the bottom quintile containing 24 per cent. This pattern is closely related to the age composition of the quintiles, as will be shown.

Comparing the distribution of health care expenditure with that of persons reporting chronic illness, then, the bottom quintile receives a higher proportion of spending than its proportion of the ill—27 per cent compared with 24 per cent. The opposite is the case for the second quintile, which receives 26 per cent of expenditure but has 30 per cent of the ill. The third quintile also has a higher proportion of the ill than of expenditure, but the top two quintiles receive a higher proportion of expenditure than their proportion of persons reporting chronic illness. The concentration indices C_{exp} and C_{ill} are both negative, indicating that lower quintiles have higher proportions of both expenditure and illness than their share in the population. The two indices are close in value—C_{exp} is −0.1333 where C_{ill} is −0.1482. Thus, the HI_{LG} index is 0.0149, indicating slight inequity favouring higher income groups. If, however, expenditure is averaged over those reporting chronic illness only, the bottom and the top two quintiles have above-average expenditure, whereas the second and thrid quintiles from the bottom have below-average expenditure per person ill.

Standardized expenditure distribution

The importance of standardizing for the differences in age and sex composition between the quintiles, as well as the proportion ill, has been emphasized in the EC comparative project. The approach described in Chapter 4 to deriving standardized expenditure by quintile, which entails calculating weighted mean expenditure distinguishing four age categories, male/female, and chronically ill/not ill, is now implemented with the Irish data.

Table 8.3 shows standardized expenditure figures derived in this way. The picture revealed is rather different to that produced by simply examining expenditure per person ill. Standardized expenditure per person is

Table 8.2. Unstandardized distribution of morbidity and expenditure (1987)

Income quintile	Sickness rate (per 1000)	Chronically ill (%)	Expendit. per person (IR£)	Expendit. per person ill (IR£)	Total expendit. (IR£'000)	Expendit. (%)
Bottom	168	24.3	321.2	1912	533.8	27.1
2nd	209	30.3	311.5	1489	517.7	26.3
3rd	125	18.2	187.8	1492	312.1	15.8
4th	93	13.5	188.5	2019	313.3	15.9
Top	94	13.7	176.4	1871	293.3	14.9
Conc. index		−0.1482				−0.1333
HI_{LG}						0.0149

Note: $n = 8310$.

Table 8.3.   Standardized distribution of expenditure (1987)

Income quintile	Expendit. per person (IR£)	Share of expendit. (%)
Bottom	300.8	26.1
2nd	229.6	19.9
3rd	190.0	16.5
4th	215.9	18.7
Top	215.7	18.7
Conc. index		−0.076

now clearly higher for the bottom quintile than the other quintiles. Whereas the second and third quintiles both had relatively low mean expenditure per person ill, when standardized the third quintile is now seen to do significantly worse than the second.

Only the bottom quintile receives a higher share of standardized expenditure than its share in the population. This is reflected in the concentration index, which has a value of −0.076, indicating some inequity favouring the poor.

Test of inequity

This section considers the results of some regression-based tests for inequity across income groups using the same sample data. This involves regressing health care expenditure on a set of variables comprising age group, sex, whether reporting chronic illness, and income quintile. The full model includes both the income quintiles themselves and interaction terms between these quintiles and the other explanatory variables. Equations are also estimated excluding the interaction terms, the main effects, and both the main and interaction income terms. Thus, the main and interaction income effects can be tested both separately and in combination. As a considerable number of individuals in the sample have zero health care expenditures, estimating the model relating expenditure to the independent variables for the whole sample by ordinary least squares (OLS) may lead to biased results. The two-stage procedure is therefore adopted where the probability than an individual has positive expenditure is modelled by estimating a probit equation, and the level of expenditure for those with positive expenditure is then fitted by OLS.

Table 8.4 shows the log likelihood values for the estimated equations when these models are applied to the Irish data. Calculating the test values for the restrictions that the income effects do not add significantly to the explanatory power of the model, this is below the critical value for

Table 8.4. Regression-based tests for income-related inequity (1987)

	(1) No income variables	(2) Main income variables	(3) Interaction income variables	(4) Full model
Log likelihood				
Probit	−5366	−5363	−5358	−5353
OLS	−44 126	−44 119	−44 103	−44 102
Total	−49 492	−49 482	−49 461	−49 455
No. of independent variables	5	9	25	29
Likelihood ratio compared with (4)	74	54	12	
Degrees of freedom	48	40	8	
Critical value				
at 5% level	65.5	55.8	15.5	
at 1% level	74.5	63.7	20.1	

the chi-square test at both 5 per cent and 1 per cent significance levels for the main income variables alone (model 2) and for the interaction terms alone (model 3). Comparing the model with *no* income terms (Table 8.4, column 1) with the full model, the test statistic is very close to the critical value at the 1 per cent level, but above that at the 5 per cent level. Thus, at the 1 per cent level the hypothesis of no income-related income inequality cannot be rejected on the basis of the test. At the 5 per cent, level this is not the case, and the estimated coefficients in the full model would suggest that any such income-related inequity is 'pro-poor' in favour of the bottom quintile.

Discussion

In summary, then, standardized mean health care expenditures suggest that in the Irish case the bottom quintile receives a relatively high share of expenditure, having controlled for differences in composition including the numbers reporting chronic illness. Regression-based tests also suggest that if there is any income-related inequity, it is in favour of the bottom quintile. Such a finding requires a good deal of further analysis before it can be interpreted as having strong implications as regards equity. Crucially, the extent to which differences in health needs have been adequately taken into account requires in-depth investigation. The self-reported measure of chronic illness used here represents an advance on what has been available in previous Irish studies of health care financing and utilization, but is clearly crude and limited. More sophisticated measures of health status—available for some of the other countries in the EC project—hold out some prospect of more satisfactory assessment of differences in health care needs.

Even with such measures, however, strong conclusions as regards equity may remain elusive. Using unit costs for different types of health care which are uniform across the population, the distribution of health care expenditures will be dominated by the utilization pattern for hospital inpatient stays. If differences across income groups in the incidence or length of hospital stays which do *not* arise from genuine differences in health care needs are to the identified, we require rather sensitive indicators of needs in which a great deal of confidence can be placed—otherwise, the fact/length of a stay may itself be a superior measure of need. Nonetheless, such comparisons across income groups can be suggestive, if perhaps not conclusive, as regards the distribution of expenditure relative to need, and can highlight the importance of exploring, in depth, the ways in which any such apparent inequities are produced.

SUMMARY AND CONCLUSIONS

This chapter has examined the distribution of health care financing and expenditure in Ireland in 1987. Health care financing in Ireland is dominated by state expenditure financed from general taxation, which accounts for over two-thirds of all health care expenditure. Social insurance contributions finance only about 7 per cent, health insurance accounts for 10 per cent, and household direct expenditure for 15 per cent. Overall, the distributional pattern of financing among households classified by equivalent gross income appears to be mildly progressive. This reflects the balance between indirect tax and household expenditure, which are regressive, and income tax, social security contributions, and health insurance premiums which are progressive. The figures used for indirect tax had to be estimated on the basis of 1980 data.

The analysis of health care delivery, based on the 1987 ESRI *Survey of Income Distribution, Poverty and Usage of State Services*, showed a relatively high share of expenditure going to the lower income quintiles. Those reporting chronic illness were also relatively heavily concentrated in the bottom quintiles, however. Averaging expenditure over the chronically ill, the bottom and top two quintiles were above average, whereas the second and third quintiles were below average. This can be a misleading basis on which to compare income groups, however. Further standardization for age, sex, and illness produced standardized expenditure per person which was substantially above average for the bottom quintile. On balance, mild inequity in favour of those on lower incomes was indicated by the concentration index for standardized expenditure. Regression-based tests also suggested that any income-related inequity was not substantial and, to the extent that it was indicated, favoured the poor.

The crucial element in the analysis of equity in the distribution of health care expenditure is the measurement of health care needs, as only differences in expenditure across income groups which do *not* arise from variation in needs are to be seen as inequitable. Further progress in the analysis of equity will depend crucially on improving the measure of needs. The observed differences between income groups in mean health care spending on both the chronically ill and the 'non-ill' need to be separated out, by type of utilization and by the individual's characteristics, so that the source of the differences can be identified. Much more information about variation in health status and 'needs', both among the healthly and among the ill, will be required before any firm conclusions about the distribution of expenditure relative to needs can be reached, but the analysis can nonetheless be suggestive.

The use of uniform unit costs for a particular utilization type in allocating expenditure also raises some interesting issues. Averaging all spending on GP care over the total number of consultations implicitly assumes, in the Irish context, that a 'free' visit, financed by the state, is 'worth' the same as a visit paid for out-of-pocket at a higher rate by the individual. In the case of GP consultations this may be reasonable, but what about hospital impatient treatment: is a night spent in a public ward of a public hospital 'worth' the same as one spent in a private bed or a private hospital? Clearly the answer depends on what one is attempting to measure, and in focusing on equity in health care delivery it would not appear appropriate to value the private bed more highly simply because of the 'hotel' aspects of the facilities available. However, there may also be differences in the health care *per se*, although identification and valuation of these clearly poses major difficulties.

NOTES

1. Expenditure on prescribed medicines above a certain ceiling is reimbursed by the state.
2. The IR£10 charges for Categories II and III were introduced during 1987 and their full effect is not reflected in the data analysed here.

3. Membership of Category I is determined on the basis of a family means test. For Category II versus III, however, an individual earnings' ceiling is applied.
4. Department of Health (1988), p. 90.
5. Department of Health (1989), Table J1, p. 101
6. For 'treatment benefits' see *Report of the Commission on Health Funding* (1989), Table 4.1, p. 43.
7. Health Statistics (1988), Table J2, gives the sources of funding for the IR£1,221.5 million spent by the Department of Health. Adding in treatment benefits and ignoring EC receipts, we arrive at a total of £127 million from social security contributions, the remainder being Exchequer-financed.
8. *Report of the Commission on Health Funding*, Table 4.1, p. 43.
9. *Report of the Commission on Health Funding*, Table 4.1, p. 43.
10. The distribution of indirect taxes, by *original* (i.e., pre-transfer) household income decile in 1980, from the CSO's redistributive exercise, is given in Murphy (1984). UK data suggest the distribution by gross or disposable income is slightly more even over the deciles.
11. It is worth noting that they account for a significantly smaller share of total government expenditure because of the size of the Irish Exchequer current budget deficit in that year, as through much of the 1980s.

9

Italy

Pierella Paci and Adam Wagstaff

INTRODUCTION

Prior to the reforms in the late 1970s public health care in Italy was financed largely through employment-based sickness funds and provided mainly by non-profit organizations.[1] In 1975 coverage against inpatient care costs was increased from 95 per cent to 100 per cent when responsibility for public hospital services was transferred to the state. In 1978 the government created a national health service—the Servizio Sanitario Nazionale (SSN)—and cover for ambulatory care and medical goods was increased to 100 per cent. The SSN was to be financed eventually out of general taxation, although it was accepted that in the short term there would be some reliance on earnings-related health-specific social insurance contributions as under the old sickness fund system. In contrast to the British National Health Service (NHS), it was accepted that the private sector would play a part in the provision of SSN-financed health care.

One of the factors motivating these reforms was a desire to promote equity or fairness. The Act of Parliament setting up the SSN talks of 'ensuring the equality of citizens with their dealings with the health service' (Ministero di Grazia e Giustizia 1978). The question arises as to whether the reforms have been successful in promoting equity in the finance and delivery of health care—a question that has received very little attention to date. The question also arises as to how successful Italy has been in achieving equity in health care compared to other countries. In this chapter we employ the methodology of the COMAC-HSR project in an attempt to shed light on these issues.[2]

THE ITALIAN HEALTH CARE SYSTEM

In 1987 Italy spent Itl70 293 billion on health care, equivalent to 7.2 per cent of its GDP.[3] Of this, Itl56 222 billion (79.3 per cent) was publicly

The authors are grateful to the Centro Europa Ricerche (CER) in Rome, and in particular to Stefania Gabriele, for providing data from the CER *Health Care Consumption Survey*, to Ugo Ercolani and George France for help in obtaining data on Italian health care expenditures, to Guido Citoni for help on the Italian health care system and for making his version of the Istat *Family Consumption Survey* available to us, to Orazio Paci for help with the Italian tax system, and to Eddy van Doorslaer for comments on an earlier version.

Table 9.1.   Distribution of health care financing (1987)

	Overall health care financing				SSN financing	
	Itlbn	%	Itlbn	%	Itlbn	%
Social insurance	26 484	37.7			26 484	46.4
Health-specific			22 298	31.7		
General			4186	6.0		
General taxation	29 738	42.3			29 738	52.1
Direct: personal			13 776	19.6		
Direct: corporate			2229	3.2		
Indirect: VAT			6697	9.5		
Indirect: duty, etc.			7037	10.0		
Private expenditures	14 071	20.0			813	1.4
Ticket modérateur			813	1.2		
Private sector			13 258	18.9		
Total	70 293	100.0	70 293	100.0	57 035	100.0

Notes: Social insurance is net of fiscalization. The figure of Itl26 484 billion taken from lower part of table S3, Relazione Generale 1988. Split between health-specific and general calculated from upper part of same table, with *altre entrate* ignored in total. Only items 3 and 4 included under 'general'. General taxation total calculated as residual obtained after deducting social insurance from total public expenditures. Split amongst general revenues taken pro rata from table II-2 of Ministero del Tesoro (1988). All direct taxes except ILOR, IRPEG, and *minori* have been classified as personal income tax. IRPEG is corporate income tax.

financed.[4] The majority of the Itl14 071 billion of privately financed expenditure[5] bought private health care; only Itl813 billion went on SSN copayments (the *ticket modérateur*).[6]

The public sector: the Servizio Sanitario Nazionale

Although the 1978 reform envisaged the SSN being financed out of general taxation, the SSN is still heavily dependent on direct health contributions. This dependence has been somewhat reduced by *fiscalizzazione* (fiscalization): a policy designed to reduce the cost of labour—and increase employment—in targeted industrial sectors and regions, involving the central government shifting the onus of the financing of part of the relevant social contributions from employers in those sectors and regions on to general taxation.

The various sources of finance for the SSN in 1987 are presented in Table 9.1. When fiscalization is allowed for the share of social insurance contributions in SSN expenditure is 46 per cent. Most of these contributions are health-specific, although some general social insurance contributions are also used to finance the SSN. The proportion of SSN expenditure financed by out-of-pocket payments is minimal: the 1.4 per cent in Table 9.1 derives from the *ticket modérateur* on prescription drugs from which groups, such as the disabled, the blind, and the chronically ill, are exempt.[7] The remaining 52 per cent of SSN expenditure is financed out of general taxation. Of this, 13 per cent (Itl7420 billion) is attributable to *fiscalizzazione*. The remainder includes central government contributions to the health service fund—the Fondo Sanitario Nazionale (FSN)—as well as payments by central government to cover the persistent gap between SSN expenditure and the resources of the FSN. The Itl29 738 billion financed by general taxation has been allocated pro rata to direct and indirect taxes.

Funds collected by the central government are allocated via regional governments to local health authorities—Unità Sanitarie Locali (USL)—which have responsibility for the provision of health care. Inpatient care is provided either by hospitals run by the USL or by hospitals operating under contract to the state—*ospedali convenzionati*. In 1985, the latter supplied 18 per cent of SSN-financed bed-days 11 per cent of inpatient cases.[8] Specialist care, diagnostic tests, and other non-general practitioner ambulatory care is provided on a referral basis (except in the cases of gynaecology and paediatrics) either by USL employees or by the private sector operating under contract to the state. The latter is, in fact, the dominant source of supply: of the Itl2746 billion spent by the SSN in 1987 on non-GP ambulatory care, as much as Itl2120 billion (77 per cent) was supplied by the private sector on a contractual basis (Ministero del Tesoro 1988, pp. 166–70). Primary care is provided by independent GPs. Despite the importance of the private sector in the provision of SSN-ambulatory care, the bulk (86 per cent in 1985) of expenditures by the USL is spent in SSN institutions (Ministero del Tesoro 1988).

The private sector

Although private health insurance is growing rapidly in Italy (during the period from 1977 to 1987 the number of private health insurance policies in existence grew at an average annual rate of 40 per cent (Buratti 1990)), it is still relatively uncommon. In 1987 there were 461 693 private insurance policies in existence (Buratti 1990). Assuming that each policy covered a household of average size[9] gives a coverage rate of 2.5 per cent —a much smaller figure than, for example, the UK figure of 9 per cent quoted by O'Donnell *et al.* (Chapter 14).[10] Private health insurance in Italy is tax deductible for the employer only (Dirindin 1991).

As is to be expected, given the lack of private insurance cover in Italy, the private sector is small and caters mostly for the affluent. In 1985, roughly 17 per cent of specialist consultations, 13 per cent of diagnostic tests, and 8 per cent of hospital stays took place in the private sector, but use was much more common amongst the well-off (Bariletti *et al.* 1986). Out-of-pocket payments to specialists are tax deductible in full.

Equity in Italian health care policy

Equity has long been an explicit objective of health care policy in Italy. Indeed, as has been noted, a desire to promote equity was one of the factors motivating the 1978 reform. The SSN Act of 1978 begins with the words 'The Republic protects health as a basic right of the individual . . .', and in the same article talks of 'maintaining and restoring the mental and physical health of all persons regardless of their individual circumstances' (Ministero di Grazia e Giustizia 1978). It also talks of 'ensuring the equality of citizens with their dealings with the health service'. Documents discussing the 1978 reform talk a great deal about the principles of *general solidarity* and *universality* (Carloni 1988).

To our knowledge, the only previous analyses of equity in health care in Italy, apart from our own preliminary results reported elsewhere (Wagstaff *et al.* 1989), have been the studies of Bariletti *et al.* (1990), Citoni (1990), and Dirindin (1991).[11] Bariletti *et al.* focus on the delivery of health care and use the same survey as us; however, they simply report the distributions of morbidity and health care utilization across income groups. Citoni, by contrast, who also focuses on the delivery of health care, employs similar methods to those of the COMAC-HSR project, but employs a different data set and stratifies by social class rather than income. The study by Dirindin is an income redistribution study similar in spirit to the Swiss study of Leu and Frey (1985), although not as comprehensive.

PROGRESSIVITY OF HEALTH CARE FINANCE IN ITALY

Data, variable definitions, and incidence assumptions

Our analysis is based on a 10 per cent random sample of the 1987 *Family Consumption Survey* (FCS) conducted by the Italian government's Institute of Statistics (Istat 1989). Our sample size, after excluding cases with missing information, is 3164.

We measure a household's 'ability to pay' by its pre-tax (i.e., gross) income per equivalent adult. The latter has been estimated using the net income of each household member and the relevant tax and social insurance contribution schedules. In the absence of information on the source of income, we have assumed that all income derives from earnings (in the case of those in the labour force) and pensions (in the case of pensioners). We have made no attempt to go beyond what Istat has already done to correct any under-reporting of income. Finally, to convert a household's gross income to equivalent gross income we have used the formula:

$$E = G/S^e,$$

where E is equivalent income, G is gross income, S is the size of the household, and e is an equivalence elasticity, which we have set at 0.40 (Buhmann *et al.* 1988).

The health care payments whose progressivity we wish to examine are: (1) health-specific social insurance contributions; (2) general social insurance contributions; (3) personal income tax; (4) other taxes, including corporate income tax, VAT, and duty; (5) direct payments to the SSN (the *ticket modérateur*); and (6) payments for private medical care.

Items (1) and (2) are not recorded in the FCS and therefore had to be estimated. In the case of dependent workers both types of social insurance contribution are paid by both the employee and employer, with the employer being liable for most of the contribution. We have assumed that both the employee's *and* employer's social insurance contributions are borne by the employee and have taken into account that different professional groups face different contribution schedules. We have not been able to take into account that some workers have had their employer contributions fiscalized and have assumed instead that the employer contributions are reduced for *all* workers pro rata and that to finance *fiscalizzazione* taxes are increased for everyone pro rata. Item (3) is also excluded from the FCS and has had to be estimated. In calculating income tax payments we have taken into account the family circumstances of each household.

The items listed under (4) were also omitted from the FCS. In the case of VAT we have built on results obtained by Di Nicola (1990). Although his figures were also obtained from the 1987 FCS, the shares of VAT paid by each decile relate to deciles of equivalent *expenditure* rather than equivalent *income*. Moreover, the equivalence scale is different. In the case of duty and other indirect taxes we have assumed that the distribution is identical to that of VAT. In the case of corporate income tax we have made two alternative assumptions: (1) that the distribution mirrors that of VAT (an assumption that might be a reasonable first approximation if corporate income tax is borne by consumers), and (2) that the distribution mirrors that of personal income tax (an assumption that might be a reasonable first approximation if corporate income tax is borne by shareholders).

Item (5) was also estimated. The FCS records expenditure on prescription drugs and over-the-counter (OTC) drugs under one heading. We have assumed estimated expenditure on prescription drugs to be a constant fraction of this combined expenditure, where the fraction is national expenditure on prescription drugs as a proportion of national expenditure on prescription on OTC drugs combined.

Finally, item (6) was calculated from the FCS as the sum of expenditure on medical fees, hospital fees, diagnostic fees, and nursing home fees, OTC medicines, ophthalmics, and other items of health care.[12] It should be noted that the FCS substantially underestimates aggregate expenditure on these items of expenditure.[13] Although we have weighted the distribution of private expenditures according to the aggregate figure rather than the figure implied by the FCS, it is possible that the FCS distribution is quite different from the true distribution.

Empirical results

It may be verified that the concentration curve for health-specific social insurance contributions (cf. Table 9.2) cuts the relevant benchmark curve (the Lorenz curve in the case of the Kakwani 1977 index and the 45° line in the case of the Suits 1977 index) from below. This implies that health-specific contributions are progressive at low-income levels but regressive at high-income levels. Both the Kakwani and Suits indices suggest that on balance health-specific contributions are mildly progressive, although the Suits index gives a much smaller progressivity value. The difference stems from the fact that the Suits index places a greater weight on the regressiveness of the system at higher income levels than does the Kakwani index. By contrast, the concentration curve for general social insurance contributions lies everywhere below the relevant benchmark curve: this is reflected in the positive Kakwani and Suits indices.

The apparent progressivity of health-specific and general social insurance contributions is somewhat surprising, as both are known to be regressive for a given individual (indeed, the *marginal* rate actually declines with income). A similar result has, however, been reported by Bernardi *et al.* (1990). We suspect that the apparent progressivity of the social insurance system stems from an interaction between the differential treatment across professional groups in the social insurance system and the position of these groups in the income distribution. If pensioners (who are exempt from social insurance) and the self-employed (who, on the assumption of full backward shifting, have the lowest average contribution rates) are those reporting relatively low incomes (due almost certainly to under-reporting in the case of the self-employed), the system as a whole might

Table 9.2. Distribution of health care financing (percentage, 1987)

Income decile	Pre-tax income	Health social insurance	General social insurance	Personal income tax	Indirect taxes	Ticket mod.	Private sector	Total (I)	Total (II)
		[1]	[2]	[3]	[5]	[6]	[7]	[8]	[9]
Bottom	1.9	0.7	1.1	7.7	8.2	6.6	6.7	5.0	5.0
2nd	4.0	2.2	2.2	1.0	8.7	5.8	2.7	3.6	3.4
3rd	5.1	4.3	4.2	2.6	9.1	8.1	6.7	5.6	5.3
4th	6.2	5.8	5.6	3.6	9.3	11.3	4.9	6.0	5.9
5th	7.4	8.1	7.6	5.0	9.5	8.5	5.5	7.3	7.2
6th	8.6	10.0	9.2	6.2	9.8	9.3	5.3	8.3	8.1
7th	10.1	11.9	10.9	8.0	10.1	9.8	6.9	9.7	9.6
8th	12.0	14.5	13.7	10.1	10.5	11.5	11.9	12.1	12.1
9th	15.3	17.0	15.7	14.3	11.1	13.1	13.2	14.3	14.4
Top	29.3	25.5	29.8	41.3	13.7	15.9	36.2	28.1	29.0
Rev. weight (I)		31.7	6.0	19.6	22.7	1.2	18.9	100.0	
Rev. weight (II)		31.7	6.0	22.8	19.5	1.2	18.9		100.0
Index									
Gini/Conc.	0.3730	0.3980	0.4186	0.4473	0.0760	0.1490	0.3702	0.3276	0.3395
Kakwani		0.0251	0.0456	0.0743	−0.2970	−0.2500	−0.0027	−0.0453	−0.0335
Suits		0.0016	0.0363	0.1217	−0.2981	−0.2320	0.0369	−0.0369	−0.0235

Note: Indices calculated by means of linear approximation.

appear to be progressive even if the schedules facing all individuals are regressive.[14]

Turning now to personal income tax, it is evident from Table 9.2 that this component of the health care financing system is progressive, indeed more so than either type of social insurance contribution. That personal income tax is progressive in Italy comes as no surprise: in 1987 the income tax schedule contained no less than nine tax brackets. What *is* surprising is that the low degree of progressivity. Our result, is, however, in line with the results reported by Bernardi *et al.* (1990) and Lugaresi (1990), and seems to be due to the fact that comparatively few people find themselves in the higher tax brackets.

The concentration curves for 'indirect taxes' (based on Di Nicola's distribution of VAT payments across deciles of equivalent expenditure) lie everywhere above the relevant benchmark curve. The index values suggest that VAT in Italy is highly regressive, irrespective of which index of progressivity one uses.

As is evident from Table 9.2, the *ticket modérateur* in Italy is also highly regressive. This, of course, comes as no surprise. The concentration curve in this case lies everywhere above the relevant benchmark curve and the Kakwani and Suits indices are fairly similar.

This is not true of the final component of the health care financing system: out-of-pocket payments to the private sector. Here, the concentration curve crosses the relevant benchmark curve from above, suggesting that such payments are regressive at low income levels but progressive at high income levels. The reflects the fact that payments made by persons in the higher income groups are primarily for private medical care, the consumption of which rises steeply with income. Whether, on balance, private payments are regressive or progressive depends on whether one opts for the Kakwani index or the Suits index. The difference stems from the fact that the Suits index attaches less importance than the Kakwani index to any departure from proportionality (in this case regressiveness) at low income levels.

In Table 9.2, columns [8] and [9] present the distribution of total payments for health care on two alternative assumptions about the distribution of corporate income tax. In column [8] it has been assumed that the distribution mirrors that of VAT, column [5], whereas in column [9], it has been assumed that the distribution mirrors that of personal income tax. Predictably, the second of these assumptions makes the health care financing system as a whole appear less regressive than the former. However, even under the more progressive assumption concerning the incidence of corporate income tax, the Italian health care financing system is regressive. In view of the near-proportionality of payments to the private sector, it should come as no surprise that the SSN financing system is even more regressive than the system as a whole.

EQUITY IN THE DELIVERY OF HEALTH CARE IN ITALY

Data and variable definitions

Our analysis is based on the 1985 *Health Care Consumption Survey* (HCCS) conducted by the Centro Europa Ricerche (CER) (Bariletti *et al.* 1986). We have re-weighted the sample ($n = 2197$ after deletion of cases with missing information) to make it more representative of the Italian population.

Our measure of income is family disposable income. Because families were allocated to income ranges and because the survey does not contain information on the structure of the respondent's family, we were unable to convert family income to a per equivalent adult basis.

The HCCS contains morbidity measures from each of Blaxter's (1989) models. From the *medical* model it contains information on whether the respondent suffered from a chronic illness and, if so, which. From the *functional* model the survey contains information on: (a) whether chronic sickness was limiting (did it cause normal activities to be interrupted?); and (b) the number of days in which the respondent had to interrupt his or her normal activities due to chronic and/or acute sickness (we have used only information on whether or not the respondent reported some days of restricted activity). From the *subjective* model, the HCCS contains a question on self-perceived health: 'Do you consider your health to be good, quite good, or not good?' In the analysis below we have distinguished simply between those who considered their health to be 'not good' and the remainder of the sample. In addition to these measures of morbidity, we also use information on whether or not the respondent had suffered from acute sickness in the previous three months.

We estimated health care expenditure using information on the respondent's utilization of: (1) GP services; (2) specialist services; and (3) hospital care. We were able to identify the type of doctor consulted in roughly 90 per cent of physician visits. Visits known to have been to a GP were then weighted by the cost per GP consultation. This was calculated at Itl24 851 and was arrived at by multiplying the number of GP consultations per 100 population by the population of Italy in 1985, and dividing the resulting figure into public expenditure on general medical services for 1985.[15] Visits known to have been to a specialist were all weighted by the public sector's cost per specialist consultation, irrespective of whether the consultation was in the public or private sector. The cost was calculated at Itl50690 and was calculated by multiplying the number of specialist consultations per 100 population by the product of the proportion of physician consultations that took place in the public sector and the population of Italy in 1985, and then dividing the resultant figure into public expenditure on specialist services for 1985.[16] For the remaining 10 per cent of visits, where the type of doctor consulted was unknown, we weighted visits by the average cost per physician visit, calculated as a weighted average of the cost per GP visit and the cost per specialist visit, where the weights are the share of each type visit in the total number of physician visits in Italy in 1985. In the absence of data on the costs in public hospitals, we have weighted hospital stays by the average unit cost in 1985 of *ospedali convenzionati*.[17] Average cost per case was calculated at Itl4001375 and was obtained by dividing total public expenditure on services provided by *ospedali convenzionati* by the total number of SSN-financed cases treated, the latter being calculated from information on the mean length of stay, the stock of beds, and the bed-occupancy rate.[18]

Unstandardized distribution of morbidity and health care

Irrespective of one's choice of morbidity measure, inequalities in health in Italy exist and favour the rich (cf. Table 9.3). A couple of points are, however, worth noting. First, for none of the health indicators does the percentage reporting illness decline monotonically with income. The income gradients are, in other words, not unambiguous. Secondly, there are differences in the values of the illness concentration indices. The index corresponding to the 'health not good' measure is larger in absolute value, indicating that inequalities in health are more pronounced if self-perceived health is used as the measure of morbidity. This is consistent with the findings of Blaxter (1989). Also consistent with Blaxter's findings is the small value of the concentration index for the restricted activity days measure. One result that is *not* consistent with Blaxter's findings is that in our sample there is more inequality in chronic illness than there is in limiting chronic illness. This difference may be attributable to differences in the wording of the question. The UK *General Household Survey*, for example, asks whether chronic illness *limits* the respondent's activities in any way. The HCCS, by contrast, asks whether chronic illness has led to the *interruption of normal* activities.

It can be verified that the concentration curves for the 'health not good' and chronic sickness indicators lie everywhere above the expenditure concentration curve, so that according to Le Grand's approach, inequity

Table 9.3. Unstandardized distribution of morbidity and (percentage, 1985)

Inc. range (Itlm)	Pop. (%)	Total reporting (%)					Total expendit. (%)
		Chronic illness	Limiting chronic illness	Restricted-activity days	Acute illness	Health not good	
<12	22.4	29.2	26.9	24.3	28.2	36.8	27.0
12–18	14.4	14.4	11.9	12.5	14.0	13.6	13.9
18–25	20.3	17.7	18.3	19.7	18.5	16.2	19.2
25–50	22.4	20.4	26.4	22.8	18.3	18.6	20.0
>50	20.4	18.3	16.5	20.6	20.9	14.7	19.9
Conc. index		−0.0753	−0.0406	−0.0046	−0.0540	−0.1661	−0.0467
HI_{LG}		0.0286				0.1194	

exists irrespective of the measure of need chosen and this inequity favours the rich. The extent of inequity is inevitably greater if the 'health not good' indicator is chosen, as inequalities in self-assessed health (SAH) have been seen to be more pronounced than inequalities in chronic sickness. These findings are confirmed by the values of HI_{LG} in Table 9.3.

Standardized expenditure distribution

To calculate standardized expenditure figures a two-part regression model was estimated for each income group as described in Chapter 4. We standardized for age, sex, and health. Our age categories were: (a) 18–29; (b) 30–44; (c) 45–59; and (d) 60+. Health was measured in four different ways: (1) by the chronic sickness indicator; (2) by the SAH indicator; (3) by both; and (4) by SAH (broken down into three categories: good, quite good, and not good), chronic sickness, and acute sickness.

Table 9.4 shows the logit and ordinary least squares (OLS) coefficients for the first of these specifications for the sample as a whole and for each income group separately. By substituting the sample means of the dummy variables into the logit equation and the censored sample means (i.e., the means of those reporting positive expenditures) into the OLS equations, one obtains the standardized probability of a contact being made with the health care sector and the standardized expenditure conditional on a contact having been made. Multiplying one by the other gives the standardized expenditure figures for each income class. The same procedure was used with the other morbidity indicators.

The resulting values of the HI_{WVP} index for the chronic and SAH indicators (Table 9.5) are smaller than the corresponding values of the HI_{LG} index; indeed, both are negative. This result is consistent with the claim that Le Grand's approach is biased towards the detection of inequity favouring the rich. Surprisingly, however, the HI_{WVP} index is more negative in the case of the SAH indicator. When both indicators are used simultaneously, the HI_{WVP} index increases substantially (although it remains negative) and becomes even less negative when all health indicators are entered simultaneously. This implies that even amongst the chronically sick there are inequalities in self-assessed health in favour of the rich; because of this, the use of one indicator alone results in the failure to capture the full extent of inequalities in need across income groups. The result is still, however, a pro-poor distribution.

Test of inequity

Under an equitable health care delivery system the coefficients of the logit and OLS equations would be the same for all income groups. This

Table 9.4. Regression results

	Sample means		Sample / Entire sample		Income group 1		Income group 2		Income group 3		Income group 4		Income group 5	
	All	Pos. expendit.	Logit	OLS	Logit	OLS	Logit	OLS	Logit	OLS	Logit	OLS	Logit	OLS
Constant	1	1	0.158	578 561	−0.193	407 968	1.182	624 098	−0.508	436 247	0.624	662 294	−0.162	575 748
Age 30–44	0.26	0.24	−0.087	−51 907	0.106	−69 110	−0.386	5762	0.021	−61 991	0.038	−22 003	−0.147	−169 589
Age 45–59	0.25	0.25	−0.206	−65 149	−0.285	197 252	−0.497	−125 006	−0.122	−109 615	−0.24	−107 237	−0.147	−119 373
Age 60+	0.24	0.31	0.003	−108 467	−0.15	−121 114	0.994	51 192	0.099	−252 131	−0.642	−9890	0.117	−109 422
Female	0.52	0.6	0.43	−80 244	0.64	−165 170	0.711	−48 125	0.359	31 953	0.592	−46 445	0.087	−71 945
Chronic	0.24	0.35	0.635	−29 052	1.18	184 995	0.129	−200 620	0.795	93 233	0.565	−54 635	0.508	−183 596
Good health	0.52	0.37	−1.207	−268 882	−0.85	−110 830	−2.164	−385 775	0.674	−192 570	−1.834	−369 160	−0.701	−127 760
Quite good health	0.37	0.44	−0.557	−218 810	−0.45	−139 928	−1.732	−316 201	0.041	−57 055	−0.94	−388 591	−0.024	−55 045
Acute	0.16	0.29	1.776	63 254	1.756	163 840	0.781	109 991	3.057	9777	1.915	59 717	1.739	−63 862
Expected conditional expenditure				280 458		313 734		261 039		274 088		289 898		273 846
Pred. prob. pos. expendit.			0.478		0.504		0.489		0.673		0.467		0.466	
Expected expendit.				133 969		158 104		127 614		184 533		135 408		127 566
Log likelihood			−1303	−14 442	−226	−3018	−198	−2077	−272	−3129	−295	−3260	−285	−2921

Table 9.5. Standardized distribution of expenditure

Inc. range (Itlm)	Pop. (%)	Unstand. expendit. (%)	Standardized expendit. with health indicator (%)			
			Chronic	SAH	Chronic & SAH	All
<12	22.4	27.0	27.2	26.4	23.9	24.0
12–18	14.4	13.9	13.5	15.2	16.5	12.4
18–25	20.3	19.2	19.0	17.7	17.0	25.4
25–50	22.4	20.0	21.6	25.2	26.3	20.6
> 50	20.4	19.9	18.7	15.6	16.2	17.6
HI_{WVP}			−0.0506	−0.0612	−0.0383	−0.0364
No. of restrictions			48	48	56	72
LR test statistic			89	61	113	129
Chi-squared crit. value			74	74	83	103

restriction can be tested using a likelihood ratio test, as described on Chapter 4. The values of the test statistic (LR) and critical values of the chi-squared distribution are shown in Table 9.5. The hypothesis of no inequity is rejected at the 99 per cent level in all specifications except where the 'health not good' indicator is used alone.

SUMMARY AND DISCUSSION

In 1987, 38 per cent of total health care expenditures in Italy (46 per cent of SSN expenditures) were financed out of social insurance contributions (85 per cent of which were health-specific), 42 per cent (53 per cent of SSN expenditures) out of general taxation, and 20 per cent via out-of-pocket payments. The vast majority of the latter (94 per cent) were payments to the private sector, the rest being payments to the SSN via the *ticket modérateur*. Our results show social insurance to be mildly progressive, even though contribution schedules are regressive for a given individual. We argued that our result may be spurious and due to the fact that the self-employed face lower average rates than employees (assuming backward shifting of the employer's contribution) and are especially likely to under-report their income (for which we have made no allowance). Our results also show personal income tax to be mildly progressive, apparently due the fact that although there were as many as nine levels in the income tax schedule in 1987, very few people paid tax at the higher rates. Both of the remaining sources of finance of the SSN—taxes other than personal income tax and the *ticket modérateur*—were found to be regressive. Payments to the private sector were found to be regressive at low-income levels but progressive at high-income levels. Whether on balance such payments are deemed to be progressive or regressive was found to depend on which index of progressivity was chosen. Overall, the Italian health care financing system is regressive, as is the financing of the SSN. From the point of view of promoting equity on the financing of health care, the 1970s reforms appear, therefore, to have been only marginally successful.

Turning to the delivery of health care, we found that irrespective of which measure of morbidity is chosen inequalities in health exist in Italy and favour the rich. These inequalities are most pronounced when self-assessed health is used as the measure of morbidity and least pronounced when the activity-restricted days measure is used. In our replication of Le Grand's analysis we found inequity in the delivery of health care that favoured the rich irrespective of whether we measured need by self-assessed health or by chronic illness. By contrast, the method proposed by Wagstaff *et al.* (1991 *b*) gave rise to a pro-poor picture irrespective of which morbidity indicator was used. The absolute value of the HI_{WVP}

index was, however, small when all three morbidity indicators were used simultaneously. Nonetheless, the income effects in the two-part regression model were statistically significant at the 99 per cent level in all specifications except where the 'health not good' indicator was used alone. Our results need, however, to be interpreted with some caution, because it is possible that the use of three health indicators simultaneously is still insufficient to capture the full extent of inequalities in health. It may be the case, for example, that the poor in Italy, as in the UK (O'Donnell and Propper 1991 *a*), are more likely than their better-off counterparts to suffer from more than one health problem, and from relatively serious problems. If this is the case, there may well be pro-rich inequity that we have failed to capture.

NOTES

1. See Buglione and France (1984) and Ferrera (1986) for useful summaries of the reforms.
2. The data, variable definitions, and results are described in more detail in Paci and Wagstaff (1991).
3. For sources see 4–6.
4. From: Servizio Centrale della Programmazione Sanitaria, quoted on p. 5 of *Il Sole 24 Ore*, 10 January 1990. This figure, which includes Itl54 542 billion of current expenditure (Ministero del Tesoro 1988) and Itl1680 billion of capital expenditure, is marginally higher than the Itl56 110 billion quoted in OECD (1989).
5. From: National Accounts. This figure, which is slightly lower than the Itl14 780 billion quoted in OECD (1989), includes the following categories of expenditure: medicines (Itl4558 billion); spectacles, contact lenses, syringes, orthopaedic and other equipment, and other medical materials (Itl768 billion); payments to private hospitals, clinics, and nursing homes (Itl3618 billion); fees paid to physicians and nurses, payments for diagnostic tests, and physiotherapy costs (Itl5109 billion).
6. From: Ministero del Tesoro (1988), p. 171.
7. In 1987, two out of five of prescriptions in Italy were exempt (Centro Europa Ricerche 1988).
8. From: tables SA-11-HS-005 and SA-11-HS-006, Ministero della Sanità (1986 *a*).
9. This is likely to result in an overestimation of the coverage, as health insurance is likely to be more popular amongst northern Italians, who have smaller families.
10. There is, however, a quasi-private health insurance scheme operated for managers, known as Fondo Assistenza Sanitario Integrativa (FASI). This scheme is compulsory and entitles the insuree to care in an *ospedale convenzionato*.
11. There is, in addition, the regional analysis of Quirino (1991).
12. We have not been able to allow for the fact that some of these expenditures are tax-deductible.

13. When grossed up, the FCS figure gives an aggregate figure of Itl8668 billion. The National Accounts figure, by contrast, is Itl13 258 billion. Both exclude the Itl813 billion spent on the *ticket modérateur*. When this is included the National Accounts figure is very close to the figure in OECD (1989).

14. For a more detailed discussion of this issue see Paci and Wagstaff (1991).

15. The information for these calculations were taken from Bariletti *et al.* (1986) and table SA-11-SR-CS4, Ministero della Sanità (1986 *b*).

16. See Note 15 for sources.

17. In Paci and Wagstaff (1991), we also report results obtained using information on the number of inpatient days rather than the number of spells. The results show a less pro-rich distribution of health expenditures, due to the fact that the inpatient treatment received by the top income group is frequently provided by the private sector where spells are shorter (15.6 days in 1985 compared to 18.4 days in public hospitals and 20.2 days in *ospedali convenzionati* (Istat 1986, p. 156)).

18. The information for these calculations were table SA-11-SR-CS4, Ministero della Sanità (1986 *b*), and table SA-11-HS-006, Ministero della Sanità (1986 *a*).

10

The Netherlands

Eddy Van Doorslaer, Adam Wagstaff, and Richard Janssen

INTRODUCTION

In the Netherlands—as in many other European countries—equity concerns have always been an important motivation for government intervention in the way health care services are financed and delivered.[1] Despite a long tradition of government intervention in health care, the uneasy coexistence of a public and private insurance sector has continued to foster political debate concerning radical reforms. In particular, the persistent and pronounced medical consumption differentials (see van Vliet and van de Ven 1985) and the alleged lack of financial solidarity between the publicly and the privately insured have often been cited as sufficient reasons for concern about the equity characteristics of the system.

This chapter builds on two earlier reports (Van Doorslaer and Wagstaff 1989; Wagstaff and Van Doorslaer 1989) on equity in the delivery and the finance of health care in the Netherlands. The results differ from previous work because a more recent year (1987) and a more refined algorithm for the calculation of health care payments is used in the analysis of the distribution of the financing burden. It also applies a more sophisticated standardization method (i.e., a two-part regression model and more health indicators) in the analysis of the health care expenditures distribution.

THE DUTCH HEALTH CARE SYSTEM

Equity considerations in health policy documents

Explicit policy statements on equity in health care can be found in the report, *Limits to Care* (Ministerie van Welzijn, Volksgezondheid en Cultuur, 1988), which describes the official government viewpoint based on three requested reports of the main health advisory bodies (the Health

The authors are grateful to the Dutch Ministry of Health for financial support to the project *Burden and benefit distribution of health care*, to the Dutch Central Bureau of Statistics for providing the datasets used, and to Jan van Emmerik and Edwin Thieman for help with the computations.

Insurance Council, the National Council on Public Health, and the Health Council). *Limits to Care* discusses the principles on which priority-setting in health care is to be based. It mentions two principles for an equitable distribution of health services: solidarity and equality. Solidarity is interpreted to mean that 'society forces the individual to contribute money to support the worse-off in society' (p. 20). Equity (*billijkheid*) is interpreted as 'everyone has equal access to health services' (p. 21). If, due to scarcity, equal access is untenable and priorities are to be set then medical need could serve as a selection criterion for who is to be treated first.

The Dutch health care financing rules (described in more detail in the next section) illustrate that it is apparently felt that contributions to health care should be proportional to ability to pay, but this requirement is subject to some restrictions, as is indicated by the existence of exemption categories and maximum premium levels. Moreover, the fact that some households with wage levels above the sickness fund threshold result in paying substantially smaller proportions of their income than households with wages below that level is widely regarded as an undesirable and an inequitable consequence of the dual insurance system. It has also been one of the factors underlying the proposed reforms to the system (van de Ven 1990). Clearly, the key term in common use in the Netherlands— and indeed in many other Western European health care systems (Hurst 1991 *a*)—to indicate concerns about equity in the financing of health care payments is *solidarity*.

The interpretation of the equality principle is more problematic. Access to health care should be equal but need can be a criterion when choices have to be made. The Dutch Constitution gives every citizen the right to health care. This egalitarian principle has been interpreted as follows: 'This principle demands compensation, whereby inequality in the distribution of health services is used to reduce inequality in health. This is in line with Aristotle's rule that equity not only requires that equals are treated equally, but also unequals unequally' (Leenen 1984). This interpretation provides some support for adopting the horizontal equity principle adopted in this chapter to analyse the delivery of health care.

Financing of health care services

Health care in the Netherlands is financed from five sources. Table 10.1 shows the relative shares of these sources in total health care costs in 1987. There are two categories of social insurance contributions. The first, AWBZ (Exceptional Medical Expenses Act), is a genuine public insurance scheme in the sense that it covers the entire population for expenses incurred for three types of care: 'catastrophic illness' (i.e., illness requiring long-term institutional care), outpatient mental care, and home

Table 10.1. Dutch health care financing (1987)

Source	Dfl million	%
Social insurance		
AWBZ	9028	26.2
Sickness fund	12 556	36.4
Civil servants	1100	3.2
Total	22 684	65.7
General taxation	2288	6.6
*Private insurance**	6966	20.2
Direct payments	2579	7.5
Total	34 517	100.0

Source: Commissie Structuur en Financiering van de Gezondheidszorg, 1987, table 3, p. 225.
* We have assumed that 10 per cent of the private insurance payments (i.e., 777 of the 7740Dfl million reported in the source) were direct payments.

Table 10.2. Social insurance contributions (percentage, 1987)

Contributions	Pensioners	Employees	Self-employed	Social security recipients
A. AWBZ[1]	0	4.55	4.55	0
B. Sickness fund[2]				
Worker	3.05	5.05	0	5.05
Employer	3[3]	5.05		

[1] The AWBZ premium is subject to a maximum of Dfl0.0455 · Dfl62 500 = Dfl2844 per wage-earner
[2] The sickness fund premium is subject to a maximum of (Dfl0.0505+Dfl0.0505) · Dfl41 860 = Dfl4605 per wage-earner. The threshold wage level is Dfl49 150.
[3] Plus 10.1 per cent over any occupational pension on top of statutory pension.

nursing. AWBZ contributions are a fixed percentage of income (4.55 per cent) up to a ceiling of Dfl2843 per wage-earner. These contributions are paid by the employer for employees. Self-employed pay the premium themselves and pensioners are exempt.

The second type of social insurance, sickness fund cover, is compulsory only for employees with a wage below a threshold wage level (Dfl49 150 in 1987) and for social security recipients and the elderly with an income below the same threshold level. These contributions cover most other types of health care and are a fixed proportion (5.05 per cent) of wages (for employed) or income up to another (lower) ceiling (Dfl41 860) (see Table 10.2). The employer's contribution for wage-earners is also 5.05 per cent of the gross wage. In 1987, these funds covered 61 per cent of the population (Central Bureau of Statistics 1989). There is another compulsory health insurance scheme specific to employees of non-central government (provinces and municipalities) covering 6 per cent of the population. Because its premiums are mainly income-related and subscription to the scheme is compulsory for these civil servants, it is best regarded as social insurance.

The self-employed and wage-earners with a wage above the cut-off wage level (33 per cent of the population) have to obtain private insurance cover from one of the private insurance companies. Premiums are not income-related but are becoming increasingly risk-related (e.g., according to age). The privately insured often elect not to be covered for certain types of care and/or to bear some fixed amount of treatment costs via deductibles in return for a premium reduction.

Direct health care payments by households can be supplementary to any of the above categories of insurance but are primarily paid by the privately insured with less than full coverage. The remaining 13.7 per cent of total health care expenditures is financed out of general taxation.

Delivery of health care

In principle, both publicly and privately insured patients have direct access to all health care providers. However, the sickness fund-insured can be on the patient list of one general practitioner (GP) only who is paid a capitation fee. The privately insured have free choice of GP and pay fee-for-service. In order to see a specialist, the sickness fund-insured first have to obtain a referral card from their GP. Specialist fees and hospital bills are higher in the private than in the public sector despite the fact that the services delivered are virtually identical. As explained above, most care is provided free to sickness fund-insured whereas the privately insured may have to pay all or part of the fees directly out-of-pocket.

PROGRESSIVITY OF HEALTH CARE FINANCE IN THE NETHERLANDS

Data, variable definitions, and incidence assumptions

The empirical analysis is based on data taken from the 1987 *Household Expenditure Survey* of the Netherlands Central Bureau of Statistics (CBS). We measure a household's 'ability to pay' by its pre-tax income per equivalent adult using the following formula:

$$E = G/S,$$

where E is equivalent income, G is gross income, and S is the CBS equivalence factor which depends on the number of adults and children in the household, and the age of the eldest child (Schiepers 1988). The sample size used contains 2750 households.

Of the five sources of health care finance listed in Table 10.1 we have been able to include about 95 per cent directly from the survey data. The remaining 4.5 per cent represent taxes other than personal income tax, i.e., indirect taxes (48 per cent of all tax revenues) and corporate income tax (20.5 per cent of all tax revenues) (see Centraal Plan Bureau 1988, p. 127). In order to allocate these, we had to make rather stringent assumptions. We assumed that all were distributed according to the calculations of the Social and Cultural Planning Bureau for 1977 for the indirect (mainly sales and excise) tax distribution with respect to equivalent net income on the basis of another dataset (Sociaal en Cultureel Planbureau 1981). This implies that we assumed that corporate income taxes were completely shifted on to prices. Direct personal income tax payments were reported per household in the survey.

Direct payments and insurance premiums were recorded in the survey but sickness fund premiums had to be adjusted (i.e., doubled) to take into account the employer contribution. Finally, AWBZ premiums, which are wholly paid by the employers had to be estimated (according to the rules described above) for all household members who were employees.

Empirical results

Table 10.3 indicates the proportion of total payments from each source of finance borne by each decile of equivalent income together with the relevant indices.[1] The column for total payments has been derived as the weighted sum of the other five columns with the weights being the proportions of total revenue indicated at the bottom of the table. These shares are derived from Table 10.1 and may deviate from the shares actually observed in this particular survey. Because, in 1987 in the Netherlands, 31.5 per cent of all tax revenues were accounted for by personal income tax, we calculated the weight to be given to this type of tax payment as 0.315×6.6 per cent = 2.1 per cent, and the remainder (4.5 per cent) as other taxes.

It can be proved that the concentration curve for the total health care payments lies between the diagonal and Lorenz curve for income, reflecting the overall regressiveness of the system. As is apparent from Fig. 10.1, the relative concentration curves for insurance premiums and direct payments lie everywhere above the 45° line. Both of these payments are therefore unambiguously regressive. Insurance premiums are regressive because in the lower deciles these are mainly sickness fund premiums, which are proportional with wages up to the threshold level, whereas in the higher deciles they consist largely of private premiums which are

Table 10.3. Distribution of health care financing (percentage, 1987)

Income decile	Pre-tax income	Insurance premiums	AWBZ premiums	Personal income tax	Indirect taxes	Direct payments	Total payments
Bottom	3.8	5.3	1.8	1.0	1.9	4.7	4.1
2nd	5.5	8.0	4.7	2.4	6.2	5.2	6.7
3rd	6.7	10.0	7.5	4.2	7.4	7.4	8.9
4th	7.7	9.8	8.4	5.7	8.4	7.9	9.1
5th	8.6	11.1	9.7	7.0	9.3	11.5	10.6
6th	9.6	10.1	10.6	8.5	10.2	11.3	10.3
7th	10.9	10.6	12.1	10.5	11.2	11.1	11.1
8th	12.3	11.0	12.9	12.2	12.4	11.2	11.6
9th	14.3	12.5	15.2	15.4	14.2	13.2	13.4
Top	20.6	11.4	17.0	33.1	18.8	16.5	14.1
Total revenue (%)		59.8	26.2	2.1	4.5	7.5	100.0

Linear approximations

Index

Gini/Conc.	0.2509	0.0932	0.2488	0.4355	0.2424	0.1915	0.1553
Kakwani		−0.1578	−0.0022	0.1846	−0.0085	−0.0594	−0.0956
Suits		−0.1687	−0.0161	0.1987	−0.0163	−0.0679	−0.1067

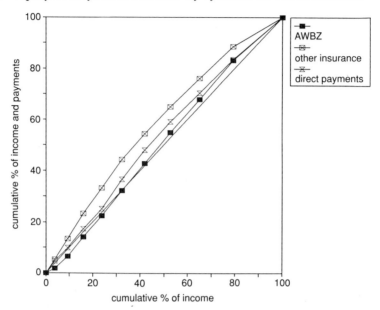

Fig. 10.1.   Progressivity of health care finance, the Netherlands.

unrelated to income. With the (important) exception of the lowest decile, this seems to result in a fairly even distribution of the insurance premium contributions across the deciles.

Because of the lower degree of full insurance coverage, the (mainly privately insured) top income deciles do pay a larger share of out-of-pocket payments but the distribution is still regressive. From a comparison of the relative concentration curves it can also be verified that insurance premiums are unambiguously more regressive than out-of-pocket payments: the latter curve 'Lorenz dominates' the former in the sense that the latter's relative concentration curve lies everywhere below that of the former (Hemming and Keen 1983). The values of the Kakwani and Suits indices mirror these conclusions.

The relative concentration curve for AWBZ contributions crosses the 45° line from below. This implies that AWBZ contributions are progressive at low income levels but regressive at high income levels. It is striking that the three deciles whose share of AWBZ contributions is less than their share of pre-tax income are the two bottom deciles and the *top* decile. This is explained by two characteristics of the AWBZ contribution schedule: (1) pensioners and certain types of social security recipients are exempt from AWBZ contributions and these groups tend to be concentrated in the bottom deciles; and (2) there is a maximum AWBZ premium per wage-earner. Overall, the AWBZ system is close to proportional according to both indices, although the Suits index is lower than the Kakwani. This reflects the higher weight the Suits index attaches to the departure from proportionality occurring amongst the higher income groups (the relative concentration curve crosses the diagonal before the concentration curve crosses the Lorenz curve).

Personal income tax is, unsurprisingly, progressive, but this source accounts for less than 5 per cent of allocated health care payments. The distribution of the indirect tax payments is very similar to that of the AWBZ payments—roughly proportional—but the deviations from proportionality in the top deciles are reflected more markedly by the Suits index.

The last column of Table 10.3 indicates the progressivity characteristics of the system as a whole: because of the dominating influence of insurance premiums, the system overall is regressive. Interestingly, the Suits and Kakwani indices are of similar order of magnitude, −0.1067 and −0.0956, respectively. Both are higher than the values we obtained for 1981, but the two sets of results cannot be compared because of the differences in the methods used to arrive at these results.[2]

INEQUITY IN THE DELIVERY OF HEALTH CARE

Data and variable definitions

The data used here were taken from the combined 1981–2 *Health Interview Survey*.[3] This is conducted each year by the Central Bureau of Statistics (CBS) on about 10 000 individuals. It asks all members of a family or household about their health, use of medical care services, and income. We restricted our analysis to adults (people aged 18 or over) but used the information on all household members in order to convert gross household income to a per equivalent adult basis. The equivalence scale used was the CBS scale (Schiepers 1988). After deletion of children (for children under 16 information was provided through proxy interviews with the parents) and cases with missing values, the remaining sample size was 10 319.

Three different morbidity measures were used as indicators of need: (1) the presence of (at least one) chronic condition or handicap mentioned in a checklist; (2) self-perceived health status in general; and (3) the number of restricted-activity days over the last two weeks.

Annual health care expenditure per person was not recorded in the survey but had to be estimated using information on: (1) the number of GP visits over the past three months; (2) the number of specialist visits in the past three months; and (3) the number of days in hospital in the last year. The latter was (arbitrarily) divided by four to convert it to a quarterly

Table 10.4. Unstandardized distribution of morbidity and expenditure (percentage)

Income decile	Expendit.	Chronic illness	Health not good	Restricted-activity days
Bottom	6.8	9.5	10.5	8.3
2nd	14.6	12.4	15.0	11.2
3rd	12.1	11.6	13.4	8.8
4th	11.4	10.2	11.2	8.8
5th	10.7	10.1	9.7	10.5
6th	9.5	9.5	8.9	9.8
7th	8.9	9.0	8.2	10.3
8th	8.5	9.6	8.5	11.2
9th	8.8	8.7	7.6	10.2
Top	8.7	9.5	7.2	11.0
Conc. index	−0.0499	−0.0399	−0.1154	0.0331
HI_{LG}		−0.0100	0.0654	−0.0830

basis. Each category of consumption was then weighted by its estimated unit cost in 1981–2 (Dfl27, Dfl75, and Dfl458, respectively)[4] and the three items were then summed to arrive at an estimate of quarterly expenditure per person.

Unstandardized distribution of morbidity and health care

Table 10.4 shows the percentages in each (equivalent) income decile reporting morbidity according to the three measures, and the corresponding concentration indices.[5] The gradients in ill-health observed in this table are less clear than the ones obtained by Wagstaff *et al.* (1991 *a*) with the same data for eight (non-equivalent) income groups but the concentration indices are very similar. With the (important) exception of the (younger) bottom decile, the lower half of the income distribution seems to account for a larger share in both health care expenditure and the first two morbidity indicators (percentage with chronic illness and less than good health). This is not true for the third indicator (restricted activity days) which is reported more often by the higher income deciles and therefore shows a positive concentration index. The finding that health inequalities are most pronounced in self-perceived health is consistent with the findings of Blaxter (1989) and Wagstaff *et al.* (1991 *a*).

O'Donnell and Propper (1991 *a*) reported evidence for the UK that 'for a given level of self-reported morbidity, individuals in the lower income groups are more likely to suffer multiple and more serious conditions'

(p. 17). Mackenbach (1991) recently reviewed the Dutch empirical evidence on socio-economic inequalities in health and noted that the negative association between income and health is more marked for the more severe chronic conditions and physical handicaps. Ooijendijk *et al.* (1991) analysed the CBS health interview survey data for 1983–8 and found a significantly negative association between socio-economic status (as measured by education, occupation, and income) and the following reported conditions: chronic bronchitis and other lung diseases; heart disorders; a group of abdominal disorders; rheumatic complaints; and accidents. Positive associations were found for sinusitis and chronic skin disorders. These findings are confirmed by our dataset which is a subset of the CBS data. The appendix shows the prevalence of each type of chronic condition by income quintile.

In addition, a comparison of the imputed expenditure and morbidity distributions using Wagstaff *et al.*'s (1989) HI_{LG} index suggests different results depending on the morbidity indicator used. Negative values are obtained for chronic illness and restricted activity days, which suggests some inequity favouring the poorer groups. However, according to the 'health not good' indicator the higher income groups obtain a larger share of the expenditure than their illness share, as shown by the positive index value. In the next section, we will explore whether these findings on inequities are affected when standardization is applied along the lines suggested in Wagstaff *et al.* (1991 *b*).

Standardized expenditure distribution

In order to limit the number of regression equations to be estimated, we restricted the calculation of standardized health care expenditure to quintiles. For each quintile, standardized expenditures were calculated as the product of the expected probability of having positive expenditure and the expected expenditure, conditional on expenditure being positive using the two-part regression results reported in Table 10.5. By applying the quintile-specific logistic regression coefficients to the total sample means of the regressors, we obtain the standardized (or expected) probabilities per decile of having positive health care expenditure. Similarly, by applying the ordinary least squares (OLS) regression coefficients to the (censored) sample means, the standardized conditional expenditure per quintile is obtained. The product of these two gives the standardized expenditure for each quintile in the bottom row of Table 10.5.

The quintile distribution of both standardized and unstandardized expenditure is shown Table 10.6. Column [3] shows the results using the two-part regression model standardization. It can be seen that the main effect of the standardization is to raise the share of expenditure going

Table 10.5. Calculation of mean standardized expenditure per quintile using two-part regression model

Regression coefficient	Sample means		Quintile									
	Total	Positive expendit.	1		2		3		4		5	
			Logit	OLS	Logit	OLS	Logit	OLS	Logit	OLS	Logit	OLS
Constant	1	1	-0.6842	314.85	-0.523	209.16	-0.6393	286.93	-0.6337	166.94	-0.7448	248.01
Chronic condition	0.2945	0.4188	0.6354	59.47	0.9188	156.46	0.8928	-81.552	0.9408	38.66	0.6798	197
Age 18–34	0.3985	0.3677	-0.2154	-205.88	-0.1597	-44.98	-0.0573	-104.4	-0.045	-36.27	0.0323	36.53
Age 35–44	0.1778	0.1578	-0.1552	-85.33	-0.4434	-112.46	-0.3341	-149.03	-0.2137	-26.33	-0.2065	64.13
Age 45–64	0.2767	0.293	-0.4387	-141.94	-0.2713	-52.88	-0.1656	-120.47	-0.1744	53.36	-0.1928	-56.02
Female	0.5043	0.5813	0.7033	40.58	0.6294	16.92	0.6757	23.66	0.6004	14.62	0.7902	-167.15
Health fair	0.1487	0.222	1.0135	20.94	1.0033	126.21	1.1287	337.5	1.2827	148.22	1.2631	129.66
Health varies	0.0732	0.1102	1.0255	239	0.7685	401.37	1.1302	287.5	0.9319	398.03	1.2343	51.27
Health poor	0.0232	0.038	1.5185	542.56	1.3083	-299.4	1.0956	1190	1.129	639.52	1.8534	666.07
Expected conditional expenditure				284.19		295.61		321.15		290.84		300.232
Pred. prob. pos. expendit.			0.4710		0.5208		0.5280		0.5317		0.5245	
Expected expendit.				133.85		153.96		169.59		154.65		157.46

Table 10.6.   Distribution of unstandardized and standardized expenditure

Income quintile	No. in quintile	Unstandardized expendit. (%)	Standardized expenditure (%)		
			Full model	Chronic condit.	Health not good
	[1]	[2]	[3]	[4]	[5]
Bottom	2064	21.3	17.4	18.9	18.8
2nd	2064	23.6	20.0	22.1	21.5
3rd	2063	20.1	22.0	21.2	22.3
4th	2064	17.4	20.1	18.8	20.0
Top	2064	17.5	20.5	18.9	21.0
	10 319				
Conc. index		−0.0553	0.0249	−0.0128	0.0110

to the three top quintiles, and to lower those of the first two quintiles. As a consequence, the negative concentration index now turns positive indicating any inequity would not favour the lower but rather the higher income classes! However, a closer look at the percentage distributions reveals that, after standardizing for the presence of a chronic condition, the subjective health rating, and age and sex composition, the bottom quintile is now getting less than its fair (population) share of the expenditure, whereas the third quintile is getting more. This points to some inequity favouring the better-off but the question remains whether its magnitude is important enough to cause concern. This will be tested formally in the next section by means of a likelihood ratio test.

We also performed the same standardization procedure using only the dummy for the presence of a chronic condition (column 4) and the 'health not good' dummy (column 5) in turn as the sole health indicator in the regressions. It can be seen that with the 'chronic condition only' standardization, the concentration index remains negative, indicating inequity favouring the poor. This seems to confirm that the dichotomous chronic illness variable insufficiently captures the need differences as they are reflected, not only in the presence, but also in the type and number of chronic conditions. In so far as the lower income groups tend to suffer from increasingly severe conditions, the (inadequate) need standardization based on the chronic illness dummy will tend to be biased towards inequity favouring the poor. Standardizing for the 'health not good' dummy makes the HI_{WVP} index positive, although it is lower than in the full model standardization.

Table 10.7.   Likelihood ratio tests of model restrictions

Model	LL Logit	LLOLS	LLSum	LR	r	χ^2 $(P = 0.01)$
1	−6367.3	−42 889.1	−49 256.4			
2	−6386.4	−42 919.2	−49 305.6	98.5	72	103.8

Notes: 1 = full model: four health dummies, all interactions; 2 = restricted model: no quintile dummies or interactions.

Test of inequity

Table 10.7 shows the summary results of two two-part regression models for health care expenditure which were estimated for the entire sample. Model 1 is the complete model including all variables used in the two-part models of Table 10.6 plus their interactions with four income quintile dummy variables. To test for the statistical significance of income-related inequity, this model was compared to the restricted model 2 in which 2 × 36 = 72 parameters (the coefficients of all income dummies and their interactions with other variables) were restricted to be zero. The resulting log likelihood ratio test statistic value is 98.5, which does not exceed the 1 per cent critical value of the chi-square distribution with 72 degrees of freedom, which is 103. We therefore cannot reject the null hypothesis of no income-related inequity at the 99 per cent confidence level. However, it does exceed the 5 per cent critical value which equals 93—in fact, it approximately equals the 2.5 per cent critical value. This result suggests that the inequity in the Dutch health care delivery system favouring the higher income groups—as implied by Table 10.6—has limited statistical significance.

CONCLUSION AND DISCUSSION

In this chapter we have analysed the equity consequences of the way(s) in which health care in the Netherlands is financed by and provided to Dutch citizens. Progressivity analysis of CBS *Household Expenditure Survey* data for 1987 revealed that overall the Dutch health care financing system is regressive. Whether the extent of regressivity is of concern can only be answered by policy-makers. It would certainly be helpful if comparable figures for other countries become available. Given the finding that the AWBZ payment schedule is roughly proportional to income, the government proposals for a substantial extension of the share financed from this source give rise to the expectation that the proposed so-called Dekker reforms (Commissie SFG, 1987) may reduce the regressivity of the system. In addition, the abolition of the distinction between publicly and privately insured may remove some of the currently existing horizontal inequities.

The possible existence of horizontal inequity in the provision of health care services was examined using 1981–2 data from the CBS *Health Interview Survey*. No clear gradient was found in the distribution of health care across income groups. It appears that the middle classes receive a slightly larger share of Dutch health care expenditure on GPs, specialists, and hospitals, and this pattern remained even after standardizing for age, sex, and a number of health indicators. A formal likelihood ratio test showed this inequity favouring the middle and higher income classes to be close to statistical significance. This result, however, proved to be sensitive to the choice of health indicator in the standardization for need: when only the presence of at least one chronic condition was used as morbidity indicator the concentration index changed sign, indicating inequity favouring the lower income classes. A closer examination of the number and type of reported chronic conditions suggested that this finding may be due to inadequate need adjustment when only those with and without a chronic condition are distinguished, thereby biasing the results towards inequity favouring the poor.

Clearly there seems to be room for improvement of the methodology on the delivery side, particularly in the measurement of need. In this regard the possibilities offered by the CBS *Health Interview Survey* have not yet fully been exploited. When combining the samples for several years of the survey, it should be possible to consider more homogenous need categories (e.g., individuals with the same chronic condition) to explore the extent of unequal treatment for equal need.

NOTES

1. The indices in Table 10.3 were calculated from the grouped data in the table using the linear approximation method (see e.g., Fuller and Lury 1977).
2. The main differences are: (1) the use of another equivalence scale; (2) the separate estimation of payments for all household members with more refined rules; and (3) the inclusion of personal income tax payments.
3. A publication, in English, describing the survey methods and the first five year results is: Netherlands Central Bureau of Statistics (1988).
4. The unit costs were calculated by dividing national expenditure on the service in question by the estimated total number of consumption units (e.g., GP visits, hospital days, etc.). No distinction was made in placing a monetary value on public or private patient consumption units, assuming that the real resource costs are the same.
5. All indices in Table 10.4 have been calculated using the linear approximation method (cf. Fuller and Lury 1977).

Appendix

Prevalence of reported chronic conditions by income quintile.
(CBS *Health Interview Survey* 1981–2, n = 10 319)

Condition	Income quintile					Total
	1	2	3	4	5	
Asthma/chronic bronchitis	34.4	28.1	27.7	19.9	24.2	26.8
Sinusitis	3.9	1.9	2.4	4.8	5.3	3.7
Heart disorder	29.1	38.2	18	16.5	16	23.5
Stroke (and consequences)	2.4	2.9	3.4	1	0.5	2
Varices	11.6	14	11.2	12.1	8.2	11.4
Haemorrhoids	11.1	11.1	10.7	9.2	9.7	10.4
Stomach or duodenal ulcer	6.8	6.8	4.9	2.9	2.4	4.7
Other stomach complaints	12.6	7.3	6.8	5.8	11.1	8.7
Large intestine	12.1	15.5	12.6	13.1	8.7	12.4
Gallstones, gall bladder, liver	5.8	5.3	4.4	5.8	4.8	5.2
Hernia	1.5	1	1	1.5	1.9	1.4
Kidney stones	3.4	3.4	8.7	4.4	3.4	4.7
Chronic cystitis	1.9	3.9	3.9	1.9	3.9	3.1
Prostate complaints	1.5	3.4	1.5	1.5	0.5	1.6
Prolapse	1.5	2.4	2.4	3.4	2.9	2.5
Diabetes mellitus	22.8	27.1	9.7	7.8	7.8	15
Thyroid disorder	7.3	2.9	3.9	3.4	8.2	5.1
Back complaints	47	41.6	43.7	36.3	41.2	42
Arthritis, rheumatism	41.2	40.2	35.4	32.5	26.6	35.2
Epilepsy	2.9	2.9	2.9	4.8	5.3	3.8
Migraine, serious headache	14.5	14	16.5	32.5	26.6	20.8
Chronic skin disorder	4.4	8.7	10.2	14.5	13.6	10.3
Cancer	5.3	3.4	2.4	1.9	7.3	4.1
Accident consequences	13.6	9.2	12.6	7.8	7.8	10.2
Other	110	100.2	84.4	86.7	73.6	91

11

Portugal

João Pereira and Carlos Gouveia Pinto

INTRODUCTION

In the late 1970s, together with other southern European countries such as Greece and Italy, Portugal took a decided step to change the financing of its health care from a predominantly social insurance base to a tax-financed National Health Service. An argument put forward at the time was that such a change would lead to both greater equity in the burden of payments borne by different income groups and in the provision of treatment to persons with differential economic resources but similar levels of need. In the 1990s, it is clear that political options with regard to health care financing and delivery have changed. As elsewhere in Europe, greater emphasis is now placed on increasing the relative share of direct payments and insurance contributions *vis-à-vis* tax financing, and on increasing the scope of competition in the provision of services. These developments have been defended strictly on the grounds of *efficiency*, namely the bureaucratized nature of an NHS-type system, and its lack of cost-saving and quality-promoting incentives to providers and users. Curiously, the questions of how the burden of payments and incidence of benefits are distributed across income groups have virtually been ignored in the recent public debate. In part, this may reflect the paucity of empirical knowledge on the subject. Apart from preliminary work leading up to this chapter, there are no earlier studies in Portugal which measure the attributes examined here, namely vertical equity in financing and horizontal equity in the delivery of health care. Our results, and their eventual comparison with those from other countries, can, therefore, go some way to redressing the imbalance in the debate.

The chapter is organized as follows. In the following section we describe basic aspects of the provision and finance of health care and discuss the legal and political specification of health equity objectives in Portugal. The third and fourth sections present the empirical analyses of equity in the financing of health care and in its delivery. In both cases, the datasets

We would like to thank António Correia de Campos, Alan Maynard, and the editors and other contributors to this volume for comments on earlier drafts. Financial support from the National Council for Scientific and Technological Research (JNICT) and the Portuguese Health Economics Association (APES) is gratefully acknowledged.

used and the specification of empirical variables are described, in order to permit informed reasoning in international comparisons. The final section summarizes and concludes the empirical analyses.

THE PORTUGUESE HEALTH CARE SYSTEM

Finance and delivery of health care in Portugal

If one were asked to describe the Portuguese health care system of recent years it would be tempting to categorize it as conforming to a national health service model (i.e., universal coverage of the population, national tax financing and national ownership or control of factors of production). In 1979, the National Health Service was indeed instituted with a political commitment that it become the preponderant mode of health care financing and provision. Yet one would be hard pressed to describe the system which existed throughout the 1980s (the period to which the empirical analysis in this paper refers) as being of the NHS-type. This is best exemplified by confronting the NHS's main objectives—universality, generality, and gratuity at the point of use—with actual evidence.

Although the NHS claims to be *universal*, there coexist a number of occupational insurance schemes—overwhelmingly non-voluntary and in the public sector of the economy—which tend to cover the better-off socio-economic groups. In terms of family income, more than half of the top 5 per cent of earners and a mere 3 per cent of the bottom decile enjoy such coverage (Pereira 1988). Evidence from various sources shows that around a quarter of the population are effectively outside the NHS (Freixinho 1990; Pereira and Pinto 1990). The delivery and payment of care in the insurance funds is similar to that in other countries: users are free to purchase care wherever they wish; most use the private sector or contracted services for ambulatory care and the NHS for non-elective surgical interventions; and the funds pay contracted services on a fee-per-item basis and reimburse patients or cofinance the use of privately provided care. The insurance part of financing is also similar to that in other countries in that employees contribute a small proportion of their income, but with an important qualification. This is that, effectively, an important proportion of expenditures throughout the 1980s were part financed by state taxation, due to the insurance funds operating over-whelmingly in the public sector of the economy. Private insurance, as such, is a negligible part of total health care financing.

With regard to the NHS providing a *general* service of health care to patients the evidence is inconclusive. There exists a perennial under-utilization of equipment, either because of shortages in the supply of

Table 11.1. Health care utilization by sector (percentage, 1987)

	NHS	Private	Other
	[1]	[2]	[3]
Consultations	67.0	26.7	6.3
GP consultations	76.5	17.8	5.7
Dental consultations	15.5	77.1	7.4
Specialist consultations	47.8	44.1	8.1
Family planning consultations	61.7	33.9	4.4
Antenatal consultations	61.9	35.0	3.2
Child deliveries	87.6	7.4	5.0
X-rays	47.5	44.2	8.2
Laboratory tests	29.5	66.4	4.1
Hospital stays	72.8	22.2	5.0

Notes: Column [3] includes services contracted to occupational health schemes within companies, armed forces health care, associations, etc.

All consultations refer to the last visit within a three month reference period, except for family planning consultations which are the last consultation with no reference period and antenatal visits which refer to the last child born and currently under 5 years of age.

Diagnostic use refers to last use in a three month reference period.

Hospital stays are taken from the 1985 NHIS, which refers to the population in the Lisbon region. Private sector use is generally higher for diagnostic tests and child deliveries in this region but roughly the same for sonsultations.

Source: Calculated from *National Health Interview Survey*, Ministério da Saúde (1987).

human resources or laxity in administrative controls on providers who work simultaneously for the NHS and the private sector. Physicians are plentiful by international standards but there are extreme shortages in some specialties (e.g., dentistry and ophthalmology). Nurses are few, with scarcely one for each doctor, compared to a ratio of 6:1 in the UK (OECD 1985). There is also a wealth of evidence showing an unequal spread of human and material resources throughout the territory (Campos 1987).

An indication that the NHS may not provide the sufficiently wide range of services it promises is indicated in Table 11.1. It shows that the NHS is predominant in the provision of hospital stays and general practitioner (GP) and mother and child care but takes a minor role in specialist and dental consultations as well as diagnostic services, where it commonly reimburses private providers. Although such information raises more questions than it answers, it is fair to assert that private provision plays an important role in the delivery of health care in Portugal and that it does so where the NHS has willingly or unwillingly failed to carry out its intended general role.

The idea that the Portuguese health care system is *free at the point of use* and overwhelmingly financed by taxation is not totally borne out by the evidence. OECD figures show that, among the 12 EC countries, Portugal has the lowest share of public health care expenditure in GDP (OECD 1990). In 1980, almost 30 per cent of all expenditures were out-of-pocket (rising to 40 per cent in 1987), a figure significantly higher than those of other countries acknowledged to have a national health service, such as the UK or Italy. One would expect with this evidence, and other things being equal, that money prices of care have a stronger rationing role in Portugal than in other countries where health care is designated to be free at the point of consumption. It is true that a high share of out-of-pocket expenditures may simply reflect the strength of the insurance funds but there is evidence that NHS users also face significant money prices. In particular, most individuals using the NHS face flat-rate copayments for consultations and diagnostic tests and pay a large and rising proportion of the cost of drugs. The latter payment varies with the therapeutic value of the drug in question with exemptions operating only in relation to the product (i.e., if it is perceived to be life-saving) rather than patient characteristics (e.g., age or income).

The final piece of the puzzle in explaining patterns of finance and delivery of care is provided by information on the ownership and control of the factors of production. With regard to labour, for example, doctors and nurses have not been required to exercise their duties on a full-time basis and tend overwhelmingly to work for the NHS in the morning, as salaried civil servants, and in private practice in the afternoon, on a fee-per-item of service or contractual basis. Autonomous market or NHS provision was, until 1989, virtually non-existent. Individuals who consult doctors in a private setting, either because they have insurance coverage or are willing to pay the rates set by the market, will be seen by the same practitioners who in the morning provided the same types of care in a public institution. The incentives generated by these circumstances go some way to explaining the utilization and expenditure patterns previously described. Due to laxity in regulation, doctors are motivated to supply minimum standards of care in NHS work-settings in order to augment the potential market share of private practice.

In summary, although Portugal is commonly believed to have had throughout the 1980s a system of the NHS type, the incentives built in to this structure were such that it tended to operate in a fashion not dissimilar to countries where there is collective provision of a basic level of care complemented by private individual purchase.

Health–equity objectives

The political and legal specification of health–equity objectives in Portugal is described in detail by Pereira (1990). There, it is argued that three seemingly distinct objectives have emerged. In the Constitution there seems to be implicit an objective in terms of the *access of all citizens to health promoting commodities*, of which health care is but one. This ambitious aim has not been clarified in subsequent documents, where the emphasis has been on health care, rather than health *per se*. The National Health Service Law, for example, states that 'access to the NHS is guaranteed to all citizens, independently of their economic or social status' (Assembleia da República 1979). Given that in the justification for the Law it is also suggested that the NHS should have 'universal characteristics, in which all citizens have access, in equality of circum-stances' (ibid.), the equity objective seems best interpreted in terms of *equality of access to NHS care for equal need*. More recently, the issue was complicated by a pronouncement of the present government which seems to imply that it aims to assure *equal opportunity of access to health care, both public and private.*

Despite the differences between these objectives it is possible to identify some common strands among them. First, they suggest that there exists a *specific concern* for questions of distribution in the health domain. Secondly, the attainment of equity in health care appears to require *equal* access between socio-economic groups to a general range of services. It does not imply merely that the poor should have available a basic level of care nor that all should have access to a limited range of services. Finally, there is a concern that equity should obtain in the *processes* of health production and health delivery, and not simply in their outcomes (absence of morbidity and service utilization).[1]

It is worth noting that there are no explicit pronouncements on equity in the *finance* of health care. This does not mean that it is unimportant or that equitable financing objectives are not implicit in Portuguese health care. For instance, equal access appears to imply that lower income groups should not face economic barriers when and if they require health care. Furthermore, in aiming to be financed by a taxation system that is necessarily progressive, the NHS, as the principal form of providing health care, has an implicit goal of payments being related to ability to pay.

PROGRESSIVITY OF HEALTH CARE FINANCE IN PORTUGAL

Data, variable definitions, and incidence assumptions

The empirical analysis of the income distribution of health care financing is based on data from the *Family Income and Expenditure Survey* (FIES) for 1980–1, the last year for which data are available. The sampling and data collecting techniques are similar to those employed in other countries that carry out this type of survey. Between March 1980 and February 1981, 8054 households were studied, corresponding to 26 792 individuals. This sample is representative of the non-institutionalized civilian population of Continental Portugal as a whole (i.e., excluding the Azores and Madeira Islands). The data arrived in the form of cross-tabulations of average income, taxation, transfers, and expenditures per decile groups of households ranked by gross household income. From this information it was possible to construct the various distributions and progressivity indices presented in the following section.

We measure a household's 'ability to pay' by its gross income (i.e., factor income plus transfers) per equivalent adult. This was obtained by the following formula:

$$E = G/S^e,$$

where E is equivalent income, G is average reported gross income, S is average household size, and e is an equivalence elasticity. The rationale for this approach, is provided by Buhmann *et al.* (1988), who show that various equivalence scales drawn from different countries can be represented quite well by a single parameter (e), the family size elasticity of need. This elasticity varies between zero (no adjustment for family size) and 1 (corresponding to per capita income). It is, therefore, higher when economies of scale within the family are lower. In the light of Portuguese research on equivalence scales, we have set e = 0.60 (Santos 1984; Teekens 1990; Pereira 1992).

With regard to health care payments, from the discussion in the previous section one can identify four main sources of finance, which are disaggregated in the analysis which follows; (1) general taxation which finances, wholly, the NHS and, partly, the social insurance schemes which operate in the public sector of the economy; (2) social insurance contributions to occupational schemes in the public sector; (3) private insurance premiums; and (4) direct payments by users (i.e., copayments in the NHS and out-of-pocket payments by insured and non-insured persons for private medical care).

Tax payments have been imputed to the income deciles on the basis of 14 per cent of state expenditures going to finance health care. Direct taxes reported in the survey include all income and property taxes, with the exclusion of corporate tax. In 1980, revenues from this tax accounted for around 20 per cent of direct tax revenues. Social security contributions have not been included as they constitute an autonomous state revenue which is not used to finance health care. We have assumed that all income and property taxes are borne fully by owners of the factors of production.

The allocation of indirect tax financing is complicated by the fact that in the early 1980s, there were various such taxes in operation; some of them lump-sum, others proportional; a variety of exempted goods; and so on. Yet one cannot simply ignore them because, in 1980, they accounted for 61 per cent of all fiscal revenues. Only one comprehensive study of tax incidence by income groups is available for Portugal (Tanzi and de Wulf 1976), but it draws on data from 1967–8 which is clearly outdated. We have instead allocated indirect taxes to the income deciles on the basis of effective tax rates for seven classes of goods and services calculated by Domingues *et al.* (1984) for 1979. Their study includes taxes which comprise 64 per cent of all indirect tax revenues. The effective tax rates have been applied directly to the relevant expenditures (by income decile) reported by the surveyed households in the 1980–1 FIES. We have, therefore, assumed that the full burden of indirect taxation is borne by consumers. On the whole, roughly 70 per cent of all tax revenues have been allocated.

Household contributions to social and health insurance schemes could not be readily extracted from the data available and we suspect that, as in most income and expenditure surveys, they may be slightly under-valued. Private insurance premiums were straightforward enough to extract from the expenditure data, but by far the greater proportion of total contributions are effectively payroll taxes in the public sector of the economy. Consulting the questionnaire, which is not geared to eliciting health-related information, we have opted to attribute 20 per cent of contributions to social insurance schemes, as health-related financing. The remainder is considered to cover other risks, such as unemployment, handicaps, and retirement allowances. Of the estimated contributions, 75 per cent were allocated to social insurance financing, and the remaining 25 per cent was added to insurance premiums.

Direct payments are computed net of reimbursements and health insurance premiums, and once again are derived directly from the grouped data available to us.

Empirical results

Table 11.2 indicates the proportion of health care payments from each source of finance borne by each decile of equivalent income. It is instructive to consider, first of all, the progressivity of the taxation system. Direct taxes (column 2) are clearly progressive, a conclusion which is confirmed by analysis of the Kakwani and Suits indices. Indirect taxation (column 3) also emerges as progressive, although far less so than its direct counterpart. This result is probably surprising in an international context but is consistent with previous findings by Tanzi and de Wulf (1976) and Domingues *et al.* (1984). It can be put down essentially to high marginal tax rates applied to so-called luxury goods, a feature of the Portuguese tax

Table 11.2. Distribution of health care financing (percentage, 1980–1)

Income decile	Pre-tax income	Health care payments						
		Direct taxes	Indirect taxes	Total taxes	Social insurance	Insurance premiums	Direct payments	Total payments
	[1]	[2]	[3]	[4]	[5]	[6]	[7]	[8]
Bottom	3.10	0.23	1.97	1.43	0.18	0.38	5.81	2.63
2nd	4.59	0.54	3.41	2.52	0.55	0.50	8.84	4.25
3rd	5.86	1.46	4.32	3.44	1.26	1.22	8.00	4.67
4th	6.82	2.94	6.11	5.13	3.18	2.95	8.07	5.91
5th	8.00	5.25	7.36	6.71	4.29	4.17	8.61	7.19
6th	9.25	7.08	8.44	8.02	6.44	7.22	10.27	8.62
7th	10.66	8.49	10.77	10.07	10.57	11.73	9.34	9.88
8th	12.32	11.75	12.64	12.37	12.45	11.44	10.19	11.75
9th	15.10	18.05	15.67	16.41	19.31	19.23	14.32	15.89
Top	24.29	44.22	29.29	33.91	41.77	41.18	16.53	29.20
Total revenue (%)		20.4	45.6	66.0	5.2	0.6	28.2	100.0
Index								
Gini/Conc.	0.3091	0.5883	0.3883	0.4501	0.5858	0.5786	0.1512	0.3737
Kakwani		0.2791	0.0792	0.1409	0.2766	0.2695	-0.1579	0.0646
Suits		0.3100	0.0845	0.1542	0.3012	0.2922	-0.1574	0.0749

Notes: Decile groups of households are ranked by gross household income.
Indices calculated using linear approximation method.

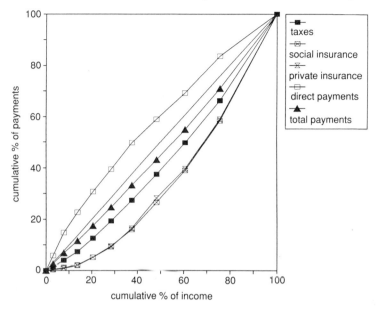

Fig. 11.1. Progressivity of health care finance, Portugal.

system for many years. The taxation system as a whole (column 4) reveals Kakwani and Suits indices in the order of 0.14 and 0.15, respectively, meaning that it favours the less well-off. In effect, this implies that the rich support a higher than proportional burden of tax-financed health care.

The proportions of both social and health insurance contributions (columns 5 and 6) rise steeply with income and have a distribution similar to that found for direct taxes. This is attributable to the fact, noted earlier, that supplementary health insurance, whether on an occupational or private basis, is essentially a middle class phenomenon.

The proportion of direct health care payments (column 7) reveals a relatively flat section between the second and eighth deciles; otherwise it rises with income. Overall, however, out-of-pocket payments are clearly regressive in relation to income. The lowest decile receives 3.1 per cent of equivalent income but expends 5.8 per cent of net direct payments on health care; the highest decile, which receives 24 per cent of equivalent income, accounts for only 16.5 per cent of direct payments.

Column [9] presents the proportion of total health care payments.[2] It appears that they are slightly progressive in relation to income, a result which is supported by the Kakwani and Suits indices which show positive values relatively close to zero.

Figure 11.1 which shows the relative concentration curves corresponding to the data in Table 11.2, indicates that taxation and insurance contributions are unambiguously progressive, that direct payments are unambiguously regressive, and that total health care payments are progressive. It is significant, however, that the latter appear to be almost proportional to the ability to pay of very low-income households but progressive as higher income levels are attained. Thus, a policy objective which regards health care as a merit good and aims that the very poorest groups should pay a less than proportionate share of payments relative to income would not find a great deal of comfort in these results.

EQUITY IN THE DELIVERY OF HEALTH CARE

Data and variable definitions

The data used here are drawn from the *National Health Interview Survey* (NHIS) for 1987. This is a population-based survey representative of the non-institutionalized population of Continental Portugal. Its sampling and data gathering techniques are similar to those used in the American NHIS, upon which it is based. The survey has been conducted at regular intervals by the Portuguese Ministry of Health since 1983, although 1987 is the only year for which data are available for the country as a whole. In that year, 41 585 individuals were surveyed. The present study makes use of a subsample of those individuals ($n = 35\,076$), after exclusion of persons living in multi-family households, and those with missing information on the income variable. In conformity with other country reports, the main part of the analysis is restricted to adults ($n = 29\,540$), although later we also present results for the sample as a whole.

The income measure used in the analysis is gross family income per equivalent adult. Like many health surveys, the NHIS obtains rather crude income data. Families are asked to indicate on a card showing 10 monthly and yearly gross income groupings that which best represents their own. Each individual is then attributed his or her family income category. Although the family is widely accepted as the most plausible unit of analysis in terms of income pooling for health care consumption, the lack of a continuous income variable precludes the construction of exact population/income percentiles, which are often the basis for analyses of income distribution. This problem is nevertheless minimized once the income variable is equivalized with recourse to a common scale. Following the methodology described in the first part of the chapter income per equivalent adult was obtained from:

$$E_{ik} = G_{ik} / S_k^e,$$

where E_{ik} is equivalent income, G_{ik} is the mid-point of the monthly income grouping to which individual i in the kth family is allocated, S_k is family size, and e is an equivalence elasticity of value 0.60.

The method we have used to identify aggregate utilization by each individual is slightly different to that followed by most other country reports in this volume. The same three categories of service are considered: (1) GP consultations; (2) specialist consultations; and (3) hospital stays. They are, however, valued differently, according to whether care was consumed in the public or private sectors.[3] A practical reason for following this approach is that, in Portugal, private consumption is proportionately the highest of all EC countries, even though there exists a comprehensive NHS. Individuals make a rational choice to consume care outside the NHS because they perceive benefits to be higher. In this context it does not seem reasonable to assume that the value of a unit of health care is identical regardless of the setting in which it is provided.[4]

In the empirical analysis, publicly provided health care has been valued at the prices which the NHS charges to insurance schemes when their beneficiaries use state services. These are, by statute, a close approximation to NHS unit costs. Consumers of NHS care have been identified, in the survey, by their last contact with the health service. If it was under the NHS, then it is assumed, for a given individual, that all consultations and numbers of days in hospital in the reference period were also experienced in similar circumstances. Number of GP and specialist visits are reported in the survey for the past three months, and have been converted to a two weekly basis; the number of days in hospital are reported directly for the two week reference period.[5] Multiplying the number of utilization units, on an individual basis, by their respective prices yields the imputed expenditure by each person consuming NHS care.

Privately supplied health care, on the other hand, has been valued directly by consumer expenditures. In Portugal, the consumer generally pays the provider directly and may then be reimbursed depending on whether he or she is covered by an insurance scheme. The NHIS asks respondents extensively about the exact amounts spent on health care in a two week reference period. Expenditures on GP and specialist visits and on hospital stays are, therefore, taken from these replies as measures of utilization. The value of total health care utilization is then computed by summation of two relevant categories of expenditure. Thus, for any individual, utilization is measured by the sum of his expenditures in the private and public sector.

A person's need for health care is measured here by six different indicators of self-reported morbidity. The first of these—designated CHRONIC—measures the proportion of respondents who suffered incapacity or restricted activity in a two week reference period due to an illness which had been present for over three months. It is not strictly comparable to the 'chronic illness' variables used in other reports in this volume, as it misses individuals who suffered no restricted activity but who nevertheless suffer from a chronic condition which requires regular surveillance by a GP or specialist. On the positive side, the indicator chosen has the advantage of identifying those who are more likely to be in need of health care in the same period to which health care utilization is referred; the two weeks preceding enquiry.

The second variable—ALLSICK—measures the proportion of persons who described themselves as either incapable of carrying out certain activities or more simply as ill or off-colour in a two week reference period. It thus comprises a greater number of persons than the first variable: besides the chronically sick, the acutely ill, and those who simply did not feel well, are also included.

The remaining four indicators are based on questions which measure the number of disability days experienced by respondents. These are arguably less open to subjective variation between individuals than conventional self-assessment techniques. Kravits and Schneider (1975), for example, found that self-assessment questions of the type: 'Do you consider your health to be good, fair or not good?' tended to under-state the health status of Blacks in the US whereas Newman (1975) found that disability days were the most important predictor of medical care use. Equally important, these indicators generally provide an opportunity to measure the intensity of illness and not merely its prevalence, a point which is highlighted later. BEDRIDDEN and OFFWORK, respectively measure the proportion of persons who were confined to bed or did not attend work or school for health reasons. Like the indicators described earlier they are measures of prevalence. BEDDAYS and OFFWORKDAYS, on the other hand, are intensity-of-illness indicators, based on the same survey questions. They measure the number of days, in a two week reference period, that an individual experienced a particular dysfunction.

Empirical results

Unstandardized distribution of morbidity and health care

Table 11.3 shows the unstandardized distribution of morbidity and health care expenditure for the adult population (aged 18 or over) surveyed by the NHIS. Consider first the distribution of morbidity. All six indicators display inequality in the burden of illness: the poor always report a higher than proportionate share; whereas the reverse is true of the rich. There is, nevertheless, some variation in the degree of inequality brought out sharply by the concentration indices at the bottom of the Table 11.3.[6] There is least inequality in the indicator ALLSICK, which includes all those who did not feel well; whereas the indicators that measure dysfunctions (i.e., if a person missed work due to illness or was confined to bed) reveal the highest levels of disparity between income groups. The pattern is even more pronounced when one considers the intensity of illness. The two poorest groups, for example, account for 65 per cent of days confined to bed, whereas the two richest groups account for a mere 19 per cent. These results support the argument put forward in O'Donnell and Propper (1991 *a*), that for a given level of self-reported morbidity, individuals in poorer income groups are more likely to suffer multiple and more serious conditions.[7]

The figures in Table 11.3 also show that the distribution of expenditure is skewed towards lower income groups. This suggests that although the poor experience a greater burden of illness they are nevertheless compensated by a large share of health care benefits. A question arises as to whether this compensation is sufficient to assure equal treatment for equal need. Wagstaff *et al.* (1989) have suggested that the extent of inequity defined as such might be measured by the HI_{LG} index, which compares the concentration curves for expenditure and morbidity. The indices reported in Table 11.3, show that—whichever indicator of morbidity is chosen—there is always inequity favouring the rich. The degree of inequity, however, varies considerably, depending on the particular measure of need being employed. If, for example, one considers all persons who felt unwell the index is 0.0100, whereas if number of days confined to bed is chosen, it rises to 0.1809. Most European work on horizontal inequity has thus far used prevalence measures of need, such as the first four indicators in Table 11.3. If it is accepted that intensity-of-illness measures, such as BEDDAYS and OFFWORKDAYS, provide a more objective and accurate indication of need, then the results show that, at least for Portugal, inequity is likely to be greater than is often suggested.

A further salient feature of Table 11.3 is the large share of illness and expenditure which the second income group accounts for. This result is largely explained by the different age structures of the income classes. Equivalization of income has projected a large proportion of the aged into the second quintile. Whereas all other income groups have age distributions which are roughly similar, the second quintile has an average age 10 years older than the population mean. In Pereira (1992) the results presented above were standardized for age and sex. Two unambiguous effects were revealed: the morbidity distributions became less unequal although still favouring the better-off in every case; the distribution of expenditure, on the other hand, became more homogenous with the rich now deriving a larger share of the benefits of health care consumption. The effects of these opposing tendencies on measured horizontal inequity was consequently of little impact, with the HI_{LG} indices having broadly similar values to the unstandardized results.

Standardized expenditure distribution

The results presented up to now essentially follow Le Grand's (1978) analysis of horizontal inequity. Wagstaff *et al.* (1991 *b*) have suggested an

Table 11.3. Unstandardized distribution of morbidity and expenditure (percentage, adults only)

Income quintile	Population	Expendit.	ALLSICK	CHRONIC	OFFWORK	BED/RIDDEN	OFFWORK DAYS	BED DAYS
Low	16.8	19.3	18.6	21.4	21.0	23.3	22.0	22.0
2nd	23.5	29.3	29.6	27.2	22.8	38.7	23.2	42.8
3rd	19.4	17.1	19.1	19.3	20.4	16.7	22.6	16.7
4th	19.6	16.6	17.3	17.0	20.1	12.1	18.8	10.5
High	20.8	17.6	15.4	15.0	15.7	10.1	13.3	8.0
Conc. index		−0.0803	−0.0930	−0.1108	−0.1594	−0.2260	−0.1946	−0.2639
HI_{LG}			0.0100	0.0278	0.0807	0.1430	0.1159	0.1809

alternative method (see also Chapter 4 of this volume) which essentially consists of standardizing the expenditure distribution by age, sex and morbidity. The results of this procedure, namely the calculation of standardized expenditure for the four prevalence of sickness indicators, are presented in Table 11.4.[8] The values of expenditure per person ill are very much as one would expect: lowest for the ALLSICK indicator and highest for persons who were confined to bed in all or part of the two weeks preceding enquiry. Noticeably, the chronic sick also reveal high level of expenditure.

With regard to the actual distribution of health care consumption benefits (proxied as before by expenditure) there are two distinct patterns. When the ALLSICK and CHRONIC indicators are employed the incidence of benefits is roughly U-shaped, with the two bottom quintiles as well as the top revealing the highest expenditure per person ill. A different pattern emerges, however, for the other two indicators, with benefits being highest for the rich, particularly when standardization is carried out with the 'days off work' indicator. These results are also supported by the concentration indices which reveal both negative and positive values. Therefore, one is led tentatively to conclude that there is horizontal inequity favouring the poor for the first two illness indicators but that it favours the rich when the OFFWORK and BEDRIDDEN measures are used.

The results presented above clearly demand closer scrutiny. From what has been said beforehand it would seem that, indicators based on illness days are the more objective. Evidence drawn from studies that compare survey-based indicators strongly favours such measures for validity and reliability. This is not surprising given that individuals are asked to report experiences that incapacitate them from performing normal tasks rather than simply being asked to indicate whether they feel sick or not sick. Therefore, from this standpoint the alternative standardized expenditure approach still suggests that the delivery of health care in Portugal is inequitable. This conclusion has, nevertheless, to be qualified, as the 'bedridden' expenditure curve actually crosses the 45° line, making it difficult to establish the existence of inequity. The 'offwork' curve, on the other hand, indicates a distribution of health care benefits favouring the rich. A possible interpretation is that active lower to middle income persons are more likely to forego health care consumption in the face of similar levels of illness. This would again point to inequity.

Results for adults and children

The analyses carried out in the previous sections were also replicated for the entire sample. In principle, this procedure should permit the establishment of whether inequity is greater for adults or for children, particulary as information on all family members was used to convert

Table 11.4. Distribution of expenditure, standardized by age, sex, and 4 morbidity indicators (adults only)

Equivalent income class	Population (%)	ALLSICK		CHRONIC		OFFWORK		BEDRIDDEN	
		Expendit./ pers. ill	Expendit. (%)	Expendit./ pers. ill	Expendit. (%)	Expendit./ pers. ill	Expendit. (%)	Expendit./ pers. ill	Expendit. (%)
Low	16.8	1697	18.2	4584	18.7	3731	15.1	6540	17.1
2nd	23.5	1697	25.6	4488	25.6	3420	15.0	6377	23.4
3rd	19.4	1455	18.1	3878	18.3	3279	16.8	6162	18.7
4th	19.6	1412	17.8	3742	17.9	3938	23.2	6297	19.3
High	20.8	1526	20.4	3862	19.5	4461	29.9	6601	21.5
Conc. index			-0.0320		-0.0421		0.0504		0.0013

gross family income to a per equivalent adult basis. The results are presented in Tables 11.5 and 11.6.

The distribution of illness is consistently less unfavourable to the poor when both adults and children are considered. But at the same time the poor also seem to obtain a relatively smaller proportion of health care benefits as proixed by expenditure. Consequently, measured horizontal inequity, using the Le Grand approach, turns out to be roughly similar to that found for the subsample of adults. A different picture is painted by the standardized expenditure approach. In this case, the degree of inequity is increased if children are included. Given that this approach standardizes by illness category it is likely that the results are indicative of the greater propensity of richer parents to take their children to a doctor under conditions of equal need for care. From the researchers point of view it also shows that—if possible—it would be prudent to include childrens' use of health care in evaluating equity.

CONCLUSIONS

This chapter has examined the achievement of equity in the financing and delivery of health care in Portugal, using data drawn from the 1980–81 *Family Income and Expenditure Survey* and the 1987 *National Health Interview Survey*. It was shown that the financing of Portuguese health care is apparently slightly progressive: that is, low income households pay a smaller proportion of their income towards health care than the rich, although the departure from proportionality is not very great. The results also reveal how policy choices in the future may affect the distribution. For instance, a switch from general taxation finance to any framework that implies more direct payments will, *ceteris paribus*, lead to a more unequal distribution of payments, with the poor bearing a greater share of the health care financing burden.

With regard to the delivery of care our results show that, in Portugal the distribution of adult illness is generally unfavourable to poorer income groups, with the difference being accentuated if one considers the extent of morbidity rather than simply its existence. Poor adults are nevertheless compensated by a larger share of health care expenditures when compared to richer groups. Such asymmetries become less pronounced once the results are standardized for the age and gender structures of the population.

Horizontal equity was measured through two alternative methods. In the first, sometimes referred to as the Le Grand approach, the delivery of health care in Portugal is unambiguously favourable to the better-off. This method has, however, been increasingly criticized for ignoring health care

Table 11.5. Unstandardized distribution of morbidity and expenditure (percentage, adults and children)

Equivalent income class	Population	Expenditure	ALLSICK	CHRONIC	OFFWORK	BEDRIDDEN	OFFWORK DAYS	BED DAYS
Low	18.3	19.8	18.9	21.6	21.3	22.6	22.5	22.4
2nd	21.7	26.8	27.9	26.5	21.7	35.4	22.6	40.3
3rd	20.0	17.8	19.8	19.7	21.5	18.5	22.8	17.7
4th	20.1	17.3	17.7	17.2	19.9	12.9	18.5	11.1
5th	19.8	18.3	15.7	15.1	15.7	10.6	13.5	8.6
Conc. index		−0.0574	−0.0744	−0.0965	−0.1248	−0.1950	−0.1622	−0.2374
HI_{LG}			0.0171	0.0392	−0.0720	0.1377	0.1094	0.1801

Table 11.6. Distribution of expenditure, standardized by age, sex, and 4 morbidity indicators (adults and children)

Income quintile	Population (%)	ALLSICK		CHRONIC		OFFWORK		BEDRIDDEN	
		Expendit./ pers. ill	Expendit. (%)	Expendit./ pers. ill	Expendit. (%)	Expendit./ pers. ill	Expendit. (%)	Expendit./ pers. ill	Expendit. (%)
Low	18.3	1732	19.9	4947	20.1	3702	16.6	6260	18.0
2nd	21.7	1642	24.4	4658	22.5	3270	14.0	6117	20.9
3rd	20.0	1487	18.7	4256	19.0	3391	17.7	6114	19.3
4th	20.1	1465	18.5	4164	18.6	3974	23.0	6361	20.2
High	19.8	1635	20.4	4487	19.8	4743	28.6	6932	21.6
Conc. index			−0.0183		−0.0246		0.0639		0.0201

consumption by those who do not describe themselves as in need of health care. Although followers of the Le Grand methodology could reasonably argue that one is objectively interested in whether those in need obtain equal treatment, the critiques have aroused sufficient interest to warrant attention. Consequently, horizontal equity was also measured using the approach adopted in Chapter 4 of this volume. Although the results produced by this method are less conclusive, they still point to inequity favouring the rich, however, to a reduced degree *vis-à-vis* the Le Grand approach. Replicating both analyses for the entire sample (i.e., without excluding children), revealed the necessity of using information on persons of all ages if one is to arrive at a rigorous evaluation of the horizontal equity within a particular country's health system.

NOTES

1. The empirical analysis presented here on equity in the delivery of health care does not address the access objective explicitly, concentrating rather on equal *utilization* for equal need. Nevertheless, it does provide information on *realized* access, a concept with established traditions in health services research (cf. Aday and Anderson 1980).
2. The sum of health care payments for the ith decile group is calculated by:

$$TP_i \, a(DT_i + IT_i) + SI_i + PI_i + DP_i,$$

   where TP, total health care payments; a, per cent of general taxation allocated to health care (14.00 per cent); DT, direct taxes; IT, indirect taxes; SI, social insurance contributions; PI, private insurance premiums; and, DP, direct health care payments. Each funding source is also weighted by National Accounts Figures, i.e., the 71.2:28.8 ratio of public-to-private financing suggested by OECD figures for the year 1980 (OECD 1990). This procedure largely explains the difference between the results in Table 11.2 and those presented in Pereira and Pinto (1990), where actual survey proportions were used to calculate total health care payments.
3. Other country reports apply a system-wide unit cost of production to value each type of care consumed.
4. There is an alternative justification for our approach discussed in Pereira (1992).
5. The NHIS regularly inquires the number of days individuals spent in hospital over the past 12 months. Unfortunately, in 1987, this question was omitted, so that it is only possible to identify persons who were hospitalized in the two weeks preceding enquiry. Therefore, the results for hospital care are based on a relatively small sample (203 individuals who reported hospital stays).
6. All indices in Table 11.3 and in the tables following have been calculated using the linear approximation method (cf. Fuller and Lury 1977).
7. See also Pereira (1988) for further evidence for Portugal in terms of health inequalities related to income, occupational class, and education.
8. Four age groups were used for age standardization: (1) 18–34 years; (2) 35–44; (3) 45–64; and (4) 65 and over.

12

Spain

Marisol Rodríguez, Samuel Calonge, and Joana Reñé

INTRODUCTION

Other than the manifest interest of the COMAC-HSR project in itself, and its use as a comparative instrument, we must stress that, in Spain, this type of study is unusual. Equity aspects of the Spanish health care system have received little research and, only from the point of view of *geographical* inequity in the distribution of resources (expenditures, doctors, hospitals, etc.), and not from the aspect of equity associated with income.

THE SPANISH HEALTH CARE SYSTEM

Like many others, the Spanish health care system is a rather complex structure due to the superposition of a fairly large number of agencies and institutions which participate in the financing, production, and management of health care services. This superposition is the result of historical evolution in which the different 'layers' of public intervention in health eventually crystallized not always replacing the previous ones.

Apart from the Ministry of Health and Consumption, which is in charge of defining the national health policy and executing certain public health programmes, the Social Security is at the centre of the system, now covering practically all the population.[1] This includes civil servants and the military who benefit from special social security schemes. Compared to the general scheme, their financial arrangements are quite similar, but there are substantial differences in the delivery of care: mainly a much wider choice between providers, either public or private. This privilege is one of the sources of inequity in the delivery of health care in Spain. In addition, because or the process of decentralization, started in 1979, four Spanish regions (Andalucia, Catalonia, the Basque country, and Valencia) now have jurisdiction over health services which were previously in the hands of the central government and the Social Security. This decentralization

The authors gratefully acknowledge the financial help received from a FISSS grant and the support and facilities provided at the Department of Health and Social Security of the Generalitat de Catalunya.

entails certain variations in the delivery of health care between regions, but not in its financing. Provincial governments do not play an important role in the field of health care, although municipal governments do have jurisdiction over local public health and preventive activities. There exist, too, a good number of private non-profit-making entities who maintain control over the production and delivery of an important part of services that are contracted out by the Social Security. The private profit-making sector is also quite sizeable.

Finance and delivery of health care in Spain

The Social Security is financed by workers' and employers' contributions (6.16 per cent and 33.10 per cent of gross salary earnings, respectively, in 1980), and state allocation from general taxes (9.5 per cent of the total Social Security budget that year). Health care expenditures from central and local governments are all financed from general taxation (local government specific taxes are negligible in Spain). In addition, private expenditures for health care are quite important.

Considering all the participating institutions and their sources of income, the final financing mix of the system in 1980 was: (1) 61.7 per cent social insurance contributions; (2) 14 per cent general taxes; and (3) 24.3 per cent private insurance and out-of-pocket payments (Coll 1985). The volume of (3) has diminished slightly during the decade. One of the reasons is the increase in the Social Security coverage. On the other hand, transfers from general taxation to the Social Security have increased steadily.

Although the General Health Act of 1986 maintains all three sources of finance (art. 79), several additional proposals advocate a gradual fall in social insurance contributions and an increase in the share of general taxes (Ministerio de Trabajo y Seguridad Social 1985). The General Budget Act of 1989 adopted these proposals, rearranging the financing mechanisms of the Social Security system, so that 79 per cent of public health expenditures were financed through general taxation. The idea behind the reform was to clarify and separate the aims of the different areas of the Social Security and, thus, to adapt the financing flows (Elola 1991). It was argued that, because under the General Health Act health care was considered a right of the citizen, its financing should be mainly through taxes, breaking the earlier link with the employment situation and salaries.

Access to public health care is organized and channelled through INSALUD, the Social Security's managing agency for health concerns. The benefits provided are very extensive, and the main exclusions are mental health, dental services other than extractions, and protheses such as spectacles. The only cost-sharing is for pharmaceuticals, for which the patient has to pay 40 per cent of the cost; pensioners are excluded from such payments, as are also some life-saving products.

Each patient is registered for a specific general practitioner (GP), and can only change him or her in certain circumstances. Except for emergencies, the GP must always be the first point of contact with the health care system; it is the GP who can refer the patient to the appropriate specialist, or directly to hospital admission.

This rigidity, above all in the choice of specialist, constitutes a powerful incentive for patients to leave the public sector and seek a private consultation with the specialist of their preference; and, of course, for specialists to establish their private practice out of public-duty hours, where most of them are paid on a salary basis. Obviously, the possibility of rejecting the system and going to a private specialist is associated with ability to pay. This introduces, therefore, an important factor of inequity in the *access* to care—which does not necessarily mean inequity in the actual quality of care received. This, together with the fact that satisfaction with primary care is generally low, is one of the main reasons for having a private insurance policy. Indeed, between 10 to 15 per cent of households have double coverage, frequently using the public one for hospitalization (satisfaction with regard to public hospital services is much higher) and private insurance for consultations.

Concerning private expenditures, and in order to be able to extract equity considerations, a distinction must be made between those that are substitutes for the public sector and those that are complementary. The first are expenditures that the families could avoid by using the alternative services offered by the public sector. However, they imply a waiving of a right, because of dissatisfaction regarding public medicine, difficult access —due to distance, waiting lists, etc.—or other reasons.[2] Complementary expenditures apply to services not covered (dentists, outpatient mental care, and protheses) or covered only in part (*ticket modérateur* for medicines); therefore, these are expenditures which families cannot avoid should they need or want to use the service. In 1980, it was estimated that, on average, 42 per cent of private expenditures were complementary to the public sector, whereas 58 per cent belonged to the substitute type (Rodríguez 1990). Indeed, what is more interesting, the proportion of income spent on both types of expenditures remains quite stable across income deciles—only the bottom and top deciles depart significantly from this pattern, in the sense that both have a higher proportion of substitute expenditures. These figures suggest an equity corollary: the existence of a number of risks not covered or covered only in part imply a threshold for private expenditures under which it is difficult not to spend. Obviously, the relative burden of this threshold is higher the lower the family income.

Equity in Spanish health care policy

The landmark in the organization of health care was the 1986 General Health Act (GHA). Equity goals are given in art. 3.2, 'Public health care will be extended to cover all the Spanish population. Access and services will be carried out in conditions of effective equality', art. 3.3, 'Health policy will be oriented towards the overcoming of geographical and social imbalances'; and art. 12. 'Public powers will address their policy of expenditures in health towards the correction of health care inequalities and towards the guaranteeing of equal access to the public health services in the whole of the Spanish territorry . . .' The guarantee of equal access has been interpreted as the extension of coverage to all the population, irrespective of the labour requirements contemplated by the Social Security rules. However, the priority given during that time to the process of decentralization of power and services in favour of the regional governments, and the criteria established for their financing, has resulted in functions mainly directed towards the guaranteeing of *equal expenditures per person* in all regions (GHA, art. 82). However, even this goal, which does not warrant equal access for equal need, as no adjustment for population structure or other variables are taken into account, is still far from being accomplished (Elola *et al.* 1990).

PROGRESSIVITY OF HEALTH CARE FINANCE IN SPAIN

Data, variable definitions, and incidence assumptions

Our analysis is based on the *Family Budget Survey* of 1980–1 (1980 prices) covering 23 972 Spanish households[3] (i.e., 0.24 per cent). The survey, conducted by the National Institute of Statistics (INE), contains information on net income, savings, expenditures on goods and services, and socio-economic characteristics of the household and its members.

Calculation of gross equivalent income

As we only had net income, this had to be converted into gross income. However, given the evidence of extensive under-reporting of income, we decided not to use reported income but *estimated income* as the basis for conversion. (The method used for the estimation of income is described in the Appendix.) Then, income gross of taxes was calculated as estimated income/(1 − t), where t is the effective tax rate (after discounting for deductions) paid by the different income brackets as reported by the Ministerio de Economía y Hacienda (1983). Similarly, we have added social insurance contributions, assigned after differentiating between salary earnings and self-employment income, as the latter attract lower rates. Finally, the per adult equivalent income was calculated by using the formula:

$$EI = GI / FS^e,$$

where EI is equivalent income, GI is the estimated gross income, FS is the size of the household, and e is the elasticity factor measuring the economies of scale within the household. Following the findings of Buhmann *et al.* (1988), we have chosen the value e = 0.4. The resulting distribution of equivalent income does not differ significantly from the distribution obtained using the scale defined by the British Royal Commission on the distribution of income and wealth, which we also used.

Calculation of health care payments

In 1980, total health care expenditures were estimated at pta850 800 million (Coll 1985). This includes hospital care (but not nursing homes), all types of ambulatory care, public health activities, administration costs, and some research and teaching costs. As we saw in the previous section, these expenditures were financed by a mix of social insurance contributions, general taxes, and private payments, which we have allocated as follows.

1. To impute social insurance contributions, we differentiated self-employed and salaried income in each household. To the former we applied the corresponding rate and for the latter we assumed that employers' contribution as well as employee's are borne by the employee. In this case, the rates applied were taken from Argimón and González (1987) who have estimated this incidence assumption for different years.

2. For direct taxation, personal income taxes was assigned only; this accounts for 71 per cent of total direct taxation. The tax base is income gross of taxes (but not of social insurance contributions), to which we applied the effective tax rate of the corresponding income bracket (Ministerio de Economia Hacienda 1983). With regard to indirect taxation, in 1980 VAT had not yet been implemented, instead there were more than 10 different sales and excise taxes. We have been able to impute approximately 73 per cent of their total revenue that year. The allocation was carried out according to the consumption structure of the household, using the incidence rates for the different subgroups of consumption calculated by Alvarez *et al.* (1989) with the same household survey. In total, we have been able to allocate a little more than 60 per cent of the total tax revenue, which we deemed would give us sufficient

accuracy taking into account that, in 1980, the proportion of general taxation directed to the financing of health care was only 6.6 per cent.

3. Private payments made by households have been taken from the *Family Budget Survey*, which contains quite detailed and accurate information on 17 different items of health care expenditures. This has enabled us to differentiate between direct payments for visits, drugs, etc., and indirect payments for insurance premiums.

Empirical results

In Table 12.1 we compare the income share of each decile with its share of each source of health care finance. We see, first of all, that the distribution of equivalent income is unequal, for example, the top decile receives 12 times more income than the bottom one. The Gini coefficient equals 0.367. By contrast, income taxes are clearly progressive, with the ninth and, above all, the tenth deciles being the only ones that contribute more than their income share: the top decile paid 50 times more income taxes than the bottom one. The structure of indirect taxation was also slightly progressive. Consequently, the Kakwani index for total taxes is positive (0.102). Social insurance payments actually borne by employees were clearly regressive as we can see in column [5], with the tenth decile deviating most from its proportional share: although it had 12 times more income it paid only 7 times more social insurance contributions. Thus, the Kakwani index is negative: −0.063. Taking into account the great importance of social contributions in the public financing of health, total public payments in Spain are, as expected, also regressive. When we get to the ninth decile, only 72.1 per cent of the income but 76.6 per cent of the public payments are accounted for. The degree of regressiveness of public financing of health is shown by a Kakwani index of −0.032. Private health expenditures appear to be proportional, a result that is a combination of regressive private premiums and progressive direct payments.

In sum, adding the public and private sources of finance, the system is slightly regressive with a Kakwani index for total payments of −0.023. We also investigated the effect on the indices upon using the microweights of the different financial sources as they were derived from the survey instead of the macroweights. As the main difference was a slightly higher proportion of social insurance contributions, the consequence was a slightly more negative Kakwani index of −0.0616. The respective concentration curves for income and payments appear in Figure 12.1, as expected, the cumulative payments curve lies inside the Lorenz curve. Finally, the Suits index for total payments is notably more negative than the Kakwani index, conveying a higher degree of regressiviness. This is

Table 12.1. Distribution of health care financing (percentage, 1980)

Income decile	Pre-tax income	Health care payments									
		Income tax	Indirect tax	Total tax [2] + [3]	Social insurance	Public payments [4] + [5]	Private dir. payments	Private insurance	Private payments [7] + [8]	Total payments [6] + [9]
	[1]	[2]	[3]	[4]	[5]	[6]	[7]	[8]	[9]	[10]
Bottom	2.2	0.3	1.7	0.7	2.2	1.9	1.6	3.9	1.9	2.0
2nd	3.8	1.4	3.2	2.0	4.1	3.7	3.5	5.2	3.7	3.7
3rd	5.0	2.8	4.6	3.4	5.7	5.3	4.3	6.0	4.5	5.1
4th	6.3	4.2	6.0	4.8	7.2	6.7	6.2	6.7	6.2	6.7
5th	7.3	5.5	7.2	6.0	8.4	8.0	7.8	8.2	7.8	8.0
6th	8.8	7.1	8.9	7.7	10.1	9.7	9.4	8.4	9.3	9.6
7th	10.2	9.0	10.7	9.5	11.8	11.4	10.2	10.3	10.2	11.1
8th	12.5	12.0	13.2	12.4	13.9	13.6	13.2	13.1	13.2	13.5
9th	15.9	16.9	16.8	16.9	16.2	16.3	15.4	16.2	15.5	16.1
Top	27.9	40.9	27.9	36.6	20.4	23.4	28.5	22.2	27.7	24.2
	100.0	100.0	100.0	100.0	100.0	100.0	100.0	100.0	100.0	100.0
Total revenue (%)		7.6	6.4	14.0	61.7	75.7	21.3	3.0	24.3	100.0
Index										
Gini/Conc.	0.3671	0.5368	0.3901	0.4881	0.3045	0.3336	0.3832	0.2882	0.3714	0.3439
Kakwani		0.1697	0.0230	0.102	−0.0626	−0.032	0.0161	−0.0789	0.005	−0.0232
Suits		0.1922	0.0188	0.113	−0.0839	−0.048	0.0130	−0.0837	0.001	−0.0357

Note: Indices calculated using linear approximation method.

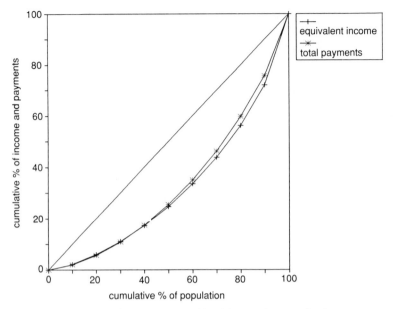

Fig. 12.1.   Progressivity of health care finance, Spain.

not surprising given that the Suits index gives greater weight to departures from proportionality occurring in the higher income groups, and that is clearly the case in Spain, as shown in Table 12.1.

Discussion

The main conclusion of our analysis is that, in 1980, the financing of health care was regressive in Spain. This stems mainly from the fact that almost 62 per cent of total funding derived from social insurance contributions, which are quite regressive. There are various reasons for this:

1. Social insurance contributions can, in fact, be considered as a tax on wage earnings, and wage earnings constitute a much higher proportion of income in the lower and middle income groups (except in the very low ones who live on pensions or other transfers) than in the higher income groups.

2. The premium rate is constant, *but* there is an upper ceiling in the wage base that varies according to the professional category. Therefore, the more the wage surpasses that ceiling, the lower is the average rate.

3. The previous two factors are reinforced by the incidence assumption regarding employers' contributions.

By the same token, our conclusion concerning the progressivity of the system would probably be reversed if the analysis was carried out in 1992, following the reform in the financial structure of health care; a reform which has greatly decreased the role of social insurance contributions in favour of general taxation.

The progressivity of indirect taxes that we have found lies, most probably, in the difference in the structure of consumption across the income groups. For example, the proportion of expenditures on food, with a tax rate near 3 per cent, goes from 44 per cent in the bottom decile to 20 per cent in the top decile, whereas the proportion of expenditures on transport and communication, which attract an average tax rate a little over 23 per cent, represent only 5 per cent in the bottom income group but 16 per cent in the top group. The introduction of VAT in 1986 may have changed this, although there are still important differences in the rates imposed on some goods, for example, motor cars.

By contrast, there are reasons to doubt the relatively high degree of progressiveness of income tax in Table 12.1. Tax evasion is—and it was even more so in 1980—a widespread practice in Spain, affecting capital, professional, and entrepreneurial earnings much more than wages, where taxes are already deducted at source and cannot be easily hidden. It has been estimated that, in 1980, 62 per cent of what would have been the actual wage earnings according to the national accounts were reported in income tax declarations, but only 24 per cent was declared of all the other types of earnings (Lagares 1989). Therefore, given that capital, professional, and entrepreneurial earnings represent a higher proportion of income in the higher income groups than in lower income groups, it is in those higher income sectors where tax evasion is more prevalent.

Finally, regarding private health expenditures and their slightly positive progressivity index, one should remember the comments made in the first section about the 'unavoidability' and relative higher burden the lower the family income of some of these payments.[4]

EQUITY IN THE DELIVERY OF HEALTH CARE IN SPAIN

Data and variable definitions

Here we used data from the 1987 *National Health Survey*. This was a comprehensive survey, conducted by the Social Investigations Centre, which includes information on health status, utilization, and socio-demographic characteristics for the population aged over 16. The survey contained information on the income category of the household rather than exact income. We had therefore, to break down the 12 existing categories into quintiles. The problem arose because, upon summing the categories it was impossible to decide on the approximate quintile cut-off point without having an additional breakdown criterion. We chose, therefore, the educational level of the head of household as an additional criterion because we believe it is a fairly good indicator to household income. This two-dimensional breakdown procedure enabled us to construct a rough income distribution by quintiles. Finally, in order to obtain equivalent income, and given that the survey did not provide information about the household structure but only its size, we adjusted gross household income to natural logarithm of family size as an equivalence factor. The use of this weighting factor is reasonable because it is highly correlated with several scales used in the literature (Buhmann *et al.* 1988).

As our proxy for utilization of medical care, we used health care expenditures associated with hospital episodes[5] and physician visits, differentiating between GPs and specialists. Average costs were imputed dividing national expenditure in each service category by the estimated number of consumption units according to the *National Health Survey*. The visit to a specialist was assumed to cost 5.1 times more than a visit to the GP (INSALUD 1990). To measure 'need', we selected four indicators which try to capture different aspects of health. First, the *chronic conditions*, which are associated with long-term health problems, rather than to an individual's health at a given moment in time. We built a chronic illness dummy variable which takes a value of 1 if the respondent declares any one of nine conditions: cholesterol, rheumatism and arthritis, dental problems, varicous veins, persistent foot trouble, nervous diseases and mental sickness, migraines, stomach complaints, and hypertension.[6] The survey also provides information on functional impairments; whether or not chronic conditions had limited the normal activities of the individual in the past year. *Limiting chronic* (= 1, limited normal activies) is, then, our second indicator, and, like the previous one, it conveys a permanent health dimension. Other indicators are related to subjective aspects of health. Therefore, as a third indicator, we diferentiated *not good* and the remaining categories in a self-evaluation of health (very good, good, fair).[7] Finally, out of the remaining proxies for health, we selected restricted-activity days (RADs) in the last two weeks prior to the survey as one directly measurable concept of *acute illness*.

Unstandardized distribution of morbidity and health care

We present unstandardized results for each of the variables mentioned above, in Table 12.2. The associated expenditure and illness concentration curves are shown in Fig. 12.2. All concentration curves lie above the diag-

Table 12.2. Unstandardized distribution of morbidity and expenditure (percentage)

Income quintile	Population	Expendit.	Chronic illness	Limiting chronic	Health not good	Reporting RADs
Bottom	19.8	21.8	22.7	25.9	30.7	28.7
2nd	20.9	20.4	23.1	23.5	29.4	22.6
3rd	19.1	17.9	17.8	16.4	14.1	16.7
4th	20.0	20.1	19.0	19.3	16.1	19.6
Top	20.1	19.8	17.4	14.9	9.7	14.4
C_{ill}		−0.0164	−0.058	−0.1036	−0.2204	−0.1333
HI_{LG}			0.041	0.087	0.204	0.117

Note: RADs = restricted-activity days.

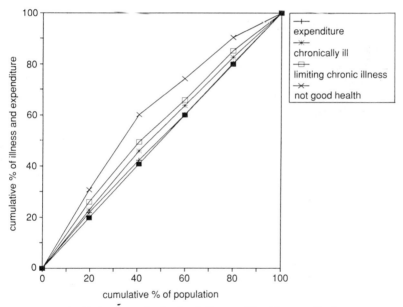

Fig. 12.2. Inequity in the delivery of health care, Spain.

onal, indicating that the illness and expenditure distributions tend to be concentrated in the lower income groups. Moreover, the expenditure curve lies below the illness curve for each morbidity group, implying that the share of resources received by the worse-off is less than their sickness share. This suggests that the system fails to achieve equity amongst income groups. The HI_{LG} index values also support this finding, inequity

Table 12.3.   Standardized distribution of expenditure (percentage)

Income quintile	Population	Chronic	Limiting chronic	Health not good	RADs
Bottom	19.8	20.8	19.7	19.9	20.2
2nd	20.9	20.0	19.7	19.3	19.9
3rd	19.1	18.2	18.4	18.6	18.2
4th	20.0	20.4	20.4	21.0	20.5
Top	20.1	20.6	21.8	21.2	21.2
HI_{WVP}		0.001	0.020	0.017	0.011

Note: RADs = restricted activity days.

being particularly pronounced when self-assessed health is used to measure need.[8]

Standardized expenditure distribution

We next compared the above unstandardized results to the results obtained using the standardization proposed by Wagstaff *et al.* (1991 *b*), both through the direct method and the two-part regression model (see Tables 12.3 and 12.5 respectively). Looking at the inequity indices calculated via the direct procedure, the standardization for age,[9] sex, and ill health status results in a tendency towards equity. In the case of the chronic illness indicator, the two bottom income groups have a slightly higher cumulative proportion of health expenditure than the corresponding figures for population, but so do the two top quintiles. The small value of the standardized expenditure concentration index indicates an equitable distribution for this health measure. The same is true of the limiting chronic illness indicator. For example, the degree of inequity falls from 0.08 to 0.02 when we move from the HI_{LG} index to the HI_{WVP} index. Also, the standardization tends to smooth the outcomes for the remaining indicators. There, the standardization effect becomes even more patent.

Based on the estimations of the two-part model, and in order to assess the degree of inequity considering simultaneously all four health indicators, we again calculated the standardized HI_{WVP} index (see Table 12.5). The result ($HI_{WVP} = 0.14$) shows clear inequity in the distribution of resources.

Test of Inequity

We have also tested inequity across income groups using a two-part regression model considering all four health indicators. In this model, the decision to demand medical care and the amount of expenditure are modelled separately. For each quintile, we applied a probit model to estimate the conditional probability of any individual having positive expenditure. The level of expenditure is then modelled by linear regression taking into account individuals with positive expenditure. This set of equations (see Table 12.4) constitutes the alternative hypothesis. The same process is replicated for the whole sample, the null hypothesis. To assess differences due to income, a structural stability test across income groups is implemented via the likelihood ratio principle comparing the two hypotheses mentioned. The result of the test (Table 12.5) leads us to reject the null hypothesis, that is to say, there are important differences in the pattern of health consumption across income groups, or put in another way, inequity related to income.

Discussion

In order to conclude this state of our study, the following considerations are to be taken into account. First, the results relative to equity as regards the delivery side of health care do not depend on the choice of ill health indicators used in the analysis. Indeed, whatever be the variable employed to characterize 'need' and the procedure used in order to investigate the existence or non-existence of equity in the system (shares approach, concentration curves and indices, expenditure per person ill across income groups), it is feasible to arrive at the conclusion that there exists a certain degree of inequity in the system in favour of the better-off. However, the extent of this inequity becomes less important when we consider those same results once they have been standardized (see the HI_{WVP} index). In a systematic manner for all indicators, the inequity lies in the second and third quintiles, that is, the standardized expenditure share for those income groups is below the corresponding population proportions. Secondly, the smoothing effect of the standardization is to be expected given the age and sex distribution across income quintiles. Older people are more concentrated in the two poorest income groups, the average ages of which are 48 and 51 compared to the sample average age of 44. Moreover, it is likely that the standardization effect on expenditure is influenced by the sex standardization, bearing in mind that women are greater consumers of health care. In our sample, the proportion of females in the bottom and the top quintiles is 56.6 per cent and 47.6 per cent respectively. Finally, the expenditure distribution is U-shaped across income groups in the standardized results for all four health indicators. The reason why the expenditure share regarding income does not decrease monotonically, but presents a turning-point in the third quintile is due to a change in the type of consumption. Although quantity

Table 12.4. Two-part regression model estimation

Regression coefficient	Quintile 1		Quintile 2		Quintile 3		Quintile 4		Quintile 5		Whole sample	
	Probit	OLS	Probit	OLS	Probit	OLS	Probit	OLS	Probit	OLS	Probit	OLS
Constant	-1.10	7019.7	-1.12	6790.3	-1.19	7127.0	-1.12	6118.0	-1.16	6287.7	-1.14	6678.3
	(-18.3)	(13.2)	(-16.6)	(12.0)	(-21.7)	(13.9)	(-22.3)	(14.0)	(-24.1)	(13.9)	(-46.8)	(30.7)
Chronic	0.25	-1031.9	0.27	-997.7	0.27	-1896.7	0.22	-1917.9	0.15	-1581.8	0.23	-1449.8
	(4.5)	(-2.2)	(4.6)	(-2.1)	(4.8)	(-3.8)	(4.2)	(-4.5)	(2.8)	(-3.3)	(9.4)	(-7.0)
Light-chronic	0.37	1013.0	0.28	1510.7	0.22	1922.1	0.41	1889.9	0.47	2261.9	0.35	1698.6
	(6.3)	(2.3)	(4.4)	(3.4)	(3.1)	(3.7)	(6.4)	(4.2)	(6.7)	(5.0)	(12.2)	(8.1)
RADs	0.05	80.3	0.05	-8.3	0.08	-140.3	0.06	-64.6	0.08	66.8	0.06	-5.3
	(7.3)	(2.0)	(6.2)	(-0.2)	(9.0)	(-2.9)	(7.5)	(-1.4)	(8.0)	(1.2)	(16.7)	(-0.2)
Health not good	0.51	1406.9	0.49	1389.0	0.65	1980.7	0.49	2236.5	0.51	-29.1	0.51	1424.0
	(7.3)	(3.1)	(6.5)	(2.9)	(6.5)	(3.2)	(5.3)	(4.1)	(4.4)	(-0.1)	(13.4)	(5.9)
Age 2	-0.11	-237.0	-0.10	-1514.7	-0.17	-1155.9	-0.06	36.1	-0.04	-1154.1	-0.09	-736.1
	(-1.2)	(-0.3)	(-1.5)	(-1.8)	(-2.3)	(-1.7)	(-0.7)	(0.1)	(-0.6)	(-1.8)	(-2.7)	(-2.4)
Age 3	-0.06	-2299.0	0.007	-2388.8	-0.11	-1304.2	0.03	-1179.2	-0.03	-1332.0	-0.02	-1738.5
	(-0.8)	(-4.3)	(0.09)	(-4.0)	(-1.6)	(-2.3)	(0.5)	(-2.4)	(-0.4)	(-2.4)	(-0.9)	(-7.3)
Age 4	0.05	-2928.2	0.10	-3395.9	0.23	-2087.1	0.18	-2018.2	0.12	-540.3	0.12	-2568.8
	(0.6)	(-5.3)	(1.4)	(-5.9)	(2.6)	(-3.1)	(2.4)	(-3.6)	(1.3)	(-0.7)	(3.6)	(-10.1)
Sex	0.12	-866.8	0.10	-257.7	0.21	-71.5	0.16	159.7	0.18	540.9	0.15	-178.6
	(2.4)	(-2.2)	(1.9)	(-0.6)	(3.9)	(-0.1)	(3.3)	(0.4)	(3.5)	(1.2)	(6.6)	(-0.9)
L-liked	-1795	-9189	-1620	-8077	-1522	-7054	-1732	-8397	-1601	-7078	-8298	-39832
R²		0.08		0.08		0.08		0.08		0.06		0.07
N:	3445	915	3098	809	3304	702	3466	839	3447	704	16770	3969

Note: The *t*-ratio is in brackets. RADs = restricted activity days.

Table 12.5. Distribution of expenditures for all four indicators. (Standardized results using two-part regression model)

Income quintile	P (Exp. > 0) [1]	E (Exp. > 0) [2]	Total exp. [1] × [2]	Expendit. (%)
	[1]	[2]	[3]	
Bottom	0.22	5114.6	1128.5	19.3
2nd	0.21	4948.7	1054.7	18.0
3rd	0.21	5475.2	1157.9	19.8
4th	0.23	5000.2	1190.9	20.4
Top	0.22	5932.3	1314.6	22.5
HI_{WVP}				0.14
Likelihood ratio test		$\chi^2_{72} = 134$		

consumed remains quite stable across the income groups (with the exception of the bottom quintile which has a slightly higher number of visits and hospitalizations), the fourth, but above all the fifth quintile, consume many more specialist visits in comparison with GP visits than the other quintiles. For instance, visits to the specialist account for 40 per cent of total visits in the top quintile, whereas the proportion is only half in the bottom group. As specialist visits are five times more expensive than GP visits, total expenditures are higher.

CONCLUSION

We observed that the distribution of health resources is not equitable, albeit to a small degree. Nevertheless, if we take into account other factors that are generally believed to bear a great influence on the well-being and health of individuals, such as preventive medicine, we suspect that our final balance would be more negative. For example, the top quintile made 50 per cent more visits to the dentist in the last three months than the bottom group. However, this issue has not been explored in detail, or have we investigated the possible impact of the use of public medicine versus private on equity. Our data show that visits to a private doctor were more frequent for the better-off, but we do not have enough elements to assess this fact.

NOTES

1. In 1987, the year for our delivery side analysis, the percentage of the population with social security coverage was 97 per cent. Of the remaining 3 per cent, the less well-off were covered by the local governments' welfare programmes. In 1989, this group was also included in Social Security coverage.
2. Obviously, they are not perfect substitutes, and the difference is precisely what people buy.
3. Although in the title the word used is 'family', the actual unit of analysis in the survey is the household, defined as all the persons living under the same roof and sharing a common budget.
4. Another point worth mentioning is the fact that these expenditures are deductible from income tax. Although we have not been able to take this into account on an individual basis, it has been indirectly considered by using the effective tax rates (after accounting for deductions) instead of the theoretical rates of the tax schedule in our calculations. Moreover, as private expenditures are almost proportionally distributed across income groups, these deductions would not change the relative shares in the income tax distribution very much.
5. We chose the hospital episode as a consumption unit rather than the length of stay. Criticism can be made regarding both concepts. Whereas the former implies losing information about the number of stays, the latter implies applying the same average cost throughout the period, despite the fact that the marginal cost of the last days in hospital is usually lower. Nevertheless, we chose the hospital episode because our interest lay in whether or not the patient received treatment, and this is not necessarily better the longer the stay.
6. These chronic conditions are those which bore statistical significance in a factorial analysis of multiple correspondence out of a list of 26 conditions (Murillo and González-Valcárcel 1990).
7. The question put forward is the following: 'During the past 12 months, would you say your health has been very good, good, fair, not-good?'
8. This fact is consistent with other findings and with the supposition that strong differences in self-perceived health across income groups can partly be explained to differences in attitudes towards health.
9. We used four age categories: 16–35; 35–44; 44–64; >64.

Appendix

Estimation of income from reported income

A common problem in most expenditure surveys is that of mis-reporting —generally under-reporting—of income, due to psychological or sociological reasons. This was also the case in our *Family Budget Survey* 1980–1, where, on average, Spanish households stated they spent 14.4 per cent over their declared income which, in turn, was 30 per cent below the figures given by the national accounts. Moreover, savings, which were independently estimated through a series of separate questions in the survey, were positive.

In order to overcome this contradiction and try to come closer to what must be the true situation we corrected reported income using the method developed by the Instituto Nacional de Estadística (1977). The procedure is as follows:

1. We accepted the expenditures declared by the households as being true (although they also may have mis-reporting problems, they are usually less serious) and we adjusted a lognormal function by the maximum likelihood method. The estimated mean comes very close to the average expenditures reported by the households, indicating a good adjustment.

2. We selected a set of 'honest households' defined as those for which the relative difference between the sum of expenditure plus savings and reported income was not higher than 5 per cent in absolute value.

$$\left| \frac{(\text{Exp} + \text{S}) - \text{RI}}{\text{Exp} + \text{S}} \right| \leq 0.05$$

3. For this set we assumed the following relationship between expenditure and reported income:

$$\text{Ln Exp} = \alpha + \beta \ln \text{RI}, \tag{12.1}$$

with the results: $\alpha = 0.94346$; $\beta = 0.92744$; $R^2 = 0.91$.

4. The α and β parameters thus estimated were considered valid for all households and were applied in order to obtain the logarithm of estimated income:

$$\text{Ln EI} = \alpha' + \beta' \ln \text{Exp}, \tag{12.2}$$

where $\alpha' = -\alpha/\beta'$ and $\beta' = 1/\beta$.

5. Finally, household estimated income derives from:

$$EI = Exp \left(\ln EI + \tfrac{1}{2}\sigma^2\right), \tag{12.3}$$

where $\tfrac{1}{2}\sigma^2$ is a correction applied to go from a lognormal to a normal distribution.

13

Switzerland

Robert E. Leu and Michael Gerfin

INTRODUCTION

Equity and solidarity are key issues in the current political debate concerning the Swiss health care system and possible reforms to it. Equal access to medical care has always been a basic principle which has been strongly supported by all political parties and is reflected in the legal framework. Because the health care system is highly decentralized, assigning most of the responsibilities to the 26 cantons, these legal statements exist predominantly on the cantonal level. For example, the communities are compelled by cantonal law to guarantee access to those who need it but cannot afford it (Undritz 1987, p. 21). However, no such consensus exists with respect to health care financing. The conservative parties favour financing schemes which promote efficiency but are regressive (such as a high share of private financing, high co-insurance rates, and deductibles). By contrast, the parties with a strong social committment support financing schemes which are progressive (high share of tax-financing, low co-insurance rates, and deductibles, free care). In the 1980s, the actual development was characterized by a decreasing share of tax-financing and increased co-insurance rates, thus increasing the regressiveness of the financing system. However, this development is likely to be reversed in the near future. A referendum is pending, proposing a massive increase in the share of tax-financed health care, and seems to have a good chance of winning the vote. These developments should be kept in mind when interpreting our empirical findings which related to the situation in 1982.

We used data from the first nation-wide representative health survey (SOMIPOPS), which was carried out in 1981–2 (see Gutzwiller *et al.* 1985) and from the corresponding *Income and Wealth Survey* (SEVS 1982)[1] covering the same households (see Leu *et al.* 1988). The SOMIPOPS data, for a sample of 3835 adults, contain detailed information on health status, factors affecting health (health behaviour environmental variables), health care utilization, health insurance premiums, as

The authors would like to thank Rainer Kensy for skilful research assistance at a preliminary stage of this study, and Eddy Van Doorslaer and Adam Wagstaff for many helpful comments.

well as a host of socio-economic and demographic characteristics. The *Income and Wealth Survey* provides detailed information on income, wealth, and taxes paid for the same individuals.

THE SWISS HEALTH CARE SYSTEM

The Swiss health care system is characterized by a complicated mix of private and public elements on both the delivery and the financing sides. Hospital care is to a large extent provided by public hospitals, producing 83 per cent of all hospital services. Private hospitals account for only 15 per cent of all hospital beds. By contrast, ambulatory care is mainly provided by physicians privately, except for emergency treatment which is offered by both hospitals and private doctors.

The organization of the health care system mirrors the country's extremely decentralized political structure: the responsibility for health lies primarily with the cantons (of which there are 26) and, to a lesser extent, the local communities. The federal government has only a few responsibilities in the health field, such as supervision of food quality, legislation and control of narcotic substances, control of infectious diseases, radiation protection, licensing of physicians, and legislation concerning the sickness funds and the social security system. Even in these areas, however, the federal government restricts itself in many instances to the process of establishing legislation, which is then carried out on a cantonal or communal level or by private organizations (Swiss Medical Association, Health Leagues, etc.).

Within the limits set by federal legislation the cantons are free in how they organize their health systems. Not surprisingly, therefore, one encounters a wide variety of different approaches. Some cantons, for example, provided hospital care entirely through public hospitals, whereas others do not have any public hospitals. Instead they subsidize private hospitals. Some have introduced prospective financing schemes for hospitals, others automatically cover any hospital deficit. The communities are mainly engaged in home care (SPITEX) as well as in providing welfare programmes for the elderly and the poor. They are obliged to guarantee care to all those who need it but cannot afford it.

A similar mix of private and public elements prevails on the financing side. Health care is financed through three channels: (1) taxes (direct and indirect, federal, cantonal, and communal); (2) health insurance premiums; and (3) direct payments. The bulk of health insurance is provided by the sickness funds. These are basically private health insurance companies which are subject to public regulation and, in return, receive considerable subsidies. At the moment, there are about 450 such funds. This number is shrinking rapidly due to an accelerating concentration process which is mainly caused by differing risk and, hence, premium structures. Public regulation of these funds includes standards of minimal coverage, conditions for membership (entry into and change of sickness fund), criteria according to which premiums may be differentiated, and the maximum level of copayments to be paid by the insured. In 1982, there was a maximum co-insurance rate of 10 per cent for ambulatory care and a deductible (franchise) of Swfr30–50 for the first physician visit of a treatment episode. No copayment is necessary for hospital care provided that the patient is treated according to his or her insurance category.

The sickness funds offer three insurance categories: minimum coverage (third class); semi-private (second class); and private (first class). The main difference for the patient is a different comfort level during hospital stays. The difference with respect to the health care system is that first and second class patients fully cover their hospitals costs, whereas third class patients do not. General insurance basically covers treatment costs, sometimes for specified hospitals only (for example, cantonal hospitals, unless a required treatment is not available). Dental care is generally excluded from all types of health insurance: 95 per cent of all dental care costs are paid directly out-of-pocket. Although membership is not compulsory, over 99 per cent of the population have health insurance. Low income groups are eligible for premium subsidies.

Complementary to these sickness funds, there are three compulsory public insurance systems: (1) on-the-job accident insurance (SUVA); (2) insurance against the risks of accidents and disease during periods of military service (MV); and (3) disability insurance (IV). Finally, health insurance coverage can be bought from private insurance companies which are not part of the sickness funds because they do not fulfil the regulatory requirements and, therefore, are not eligible for the subsidies. Accordingly, either their premiums or their co-insurance rates or deductibles tend to be higher.

The structure of health care expenditure and the sources used to finance it are shown in Fig. 13.1 for 1982, the year to which our analysis applies. Total health care expenditure amounted to Swfr14.6 billion in that year (see Gygi and Frei 1985), accounting for 7.1 per cent of GNP (up from 2.8 per cent in 1950 to 7.5 per cent in 1987). Of this expenditure, 52 per cent was spent on hospital care including investments, teaching, and research, 32 per cent on ambulatory care including drugs, physio- and psychotherapy, chiropractors and laboratories, and 16 per cent on dental care, public health programmes, and home care. Dental care alone accounted for roughly 10 per cent of total health expenditure. Of total medical care expenditure, 39 per cent was financed through taxes, 31 per cent of these

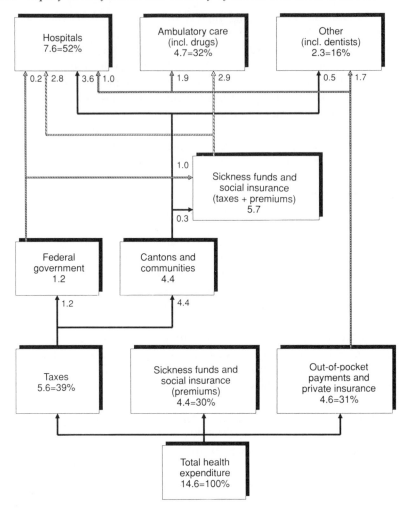

Fig. 13.1. Total health expenditure and sources, 1982 (Swfr billions).

were contributed by cantons and local communities, and 8 per cent by the federal government. Of the total expenditure, 30 per cent was covered by the publicly regulated sickness fund premiums and the compulsory social insurance contributions,[2] and the remaining 31 per cent were financed through direct payments, premiums for first and second class insurance and premiums for insurance with private, non-subsidized companies.

PROGRESSIVITY OF HEALTH CARE FINANCE IN SWITZERLAND

Data, variable definitions and incidence assumptions

As explained above, health care in Switzerland is financed through three channels: taxes, health insurance premiums, and direct payments. Information on most direct taxes is available per household from the *Income and Wealth Survey*. Direct taxes which are not contained in the household tax files (corporation income and capital taxes), as well as indirect taxes and other government revenues, are imputed according to a study of fiscal incidence by Frey and Leu (1983, p. 11). Sickness fund premiums are recorded in the SOMIPOPS health survey. The survey data also contain information on co-insurance rates and deductibles. However, no information is available for the remaining items of the category: 'Direct payments and private insurance', including expenses for dental care and premiums for private and semi-private insurance (additional cover). This implies that about 25 per cent of the total financing cannot be allocated to income groups. Because the analysis employed in this volume is based on the distribution of the various financing sources across income groups, distributional assumptions are necessary for the missing sources to ensure comparability with the other studies. These assumptions are chosen as follows: (1) missing direct payments are distributed as those elements of direct payments that are included in the data; (2) premiums for additional cover are distributed half way between an equal distribution across income deciles and a distribution that is proportional to income.[3] Using these assumptions we calculate the progressivity indices which are described in Chapter 3 for each financing source.

The overall progressivity of the financing system is determined as the weighted sum of the individual progressivity indices. The weight attached to each financing source is its respective share of financing the health care system according to the official statistics. The shares of direct taxes, indirect taxes, social security contributions, and basic cover premiums can be easily computed using Gygi and Frei (1985). To determine the distributions of direct payments and premiums for additional cover further assumptions have to be made.[4] The resulting distribution is shown in Table 13.1.

In assigning the burden of the tax-financed part of medical care to the households in the sample, we have taken into account the detailed structure of the revenue systems on all three levels of government. As is well established in the public finance literature, formal and effective tax incidence need not coincide. In order to impute the burden of the tax-financed part of health expenditure on households we use a set of incidence

Table 13.1. Distribution of health care financing (percentage)

Income decile	Pre-tax income	Direct taxes	Indirect taxes	Total taxes	Social insurance	Basic cover premiums	Additional Cover premiums[1]	Total premiums[2]	Direct payments	Total payments
	[1]	[2]	[3]	[4]+[2] +[3]	[5]	[6]	[7]	[5]+[6]+ [7]+[8]	[9]	[10]
Bottom	2.0	0.8	2.8	1.2	2.0	7.5	6.0	7.1	11.1	5.5
2nd	4.5	2.4	5.8	3.0	4.5	8.3	7.2	8.0	10.3	6.5
3rd	5.8	3.7	7.2	4.4	5.8	8.7	7.9	8.5	8.8	6.9
4th	6.9	4.9	8.4	5.6	6.9	9.2	8.4	9.0	9.6	7.7
5th	7.8	5.9	9.3	6.6	7.8	9.4	8.9	9.3	10.1	8.4
6th	9.0	7.5	10.0	7.9	9.0	10.4	9.5	10.1	10.5	9.3
7th	10.4	9.0	11.0	9.4	10.4	11.2	10.2	10.9	9.2	10.0
8th	12.0	11.7	12.0	11.7	12.0	10.9	11.0	10.9	10.0	11.1
9th	14.6	15.2	13.6	14.9	14.6	11.4	12.3	11.7	9.2	12.5
Top	27.1	39.0	20.0	35.5	27.1	12.6	18.6	14.4	11.4	22.1
Total revenue (%)		31.6	7.4	39.0	1.5	28.5	12.4	40.9	18.6	100.0
Index										
Gini/Conc.	0.339	0.487	0.242	0.394	0.339	0.088	0.161	0.110	−0.088	0.222
Kakwani		0.147	−0.097	0.103	0.000	−0.251	−0.178	−0.229	−0.339	−0.117
Suits		0.168	−0.109	0.117	0.000	−0.258	−0.177	−0.233	−0.332	−0.112

Notes: Linear approximation used.
[1] In the additional cover column each decile's proportion has been derived as the average of its proportion of income and its proportion in an equal distribution (10%).
[2] Total premiums column derived as weighted average of basic cover and additional cover premiums.

assumptions for the various types of public revenues which has been proposed in past studies of fiscal incidence (see Frey and Leu 1983, Leu *et al.* 1985). These assumptions are summarized in Chapter 3 of this volume.

Empirical results

Table 13.1 shows the distribution of pre-payment income and of the various sources of finance across income deciles as well as the corresponding progressivity indices. Both the Kakwani and the Suits index (−0.12 and −0.11, respectively) indicate that the overall payment system is regressive. This overall result arises from opposing effects. Direct taxes are progressive, whereas indirect taxes are regressive. Total tax incidence is still progressive. Social insurance contributions are proportional to income. Direct payments and premium payments for basic cover are rather strongly regressive. According to our assumption, the premiums for additional cover are also regressive. Consequently, the incidence of all insurance premiums taken together is regressive. The overall Kakwani and Suits indices are relatively small in numerical value compared to the other countries covered in this volume. Only the US seem to have a more regressive financing system for medical care than Switzerland. This is not surprising given the high share of private financing of both health care systems.

The above results depend crucially on: (1) distributional assumptions for 25 per cent of the financing sources, and (2) rough estimates of some of the shares of the financing sources in the official statistics. For example, if we use the alternative assumption that the premiums for additional cover have an income elasticity of 1, we obtain a Kakwani index of −0.09, instead of −0.12 for total payments. If we assume that dental care is distributed proportional to income we obtain a Kakwani index of −0.08 for total payments. The combination of these alternative assumptions leads to a Kakwani index of −0.06. Thus, the results in Table 13.1 are rather sensitive to distributional assumptions. However, the general result that the financing of health care in Switzerland is regressive remains unchanged.

Discussion

The overall incidence on the financing side depends on the shares of the various sources employed to finance medical care. Since the beginning of the 1980s the share of tax-financed medical care has decreased, whereas the share financed by insurance premiums has increased. This implies that the system of financing health care has become more regressive in recent years. The lesson for public policy emerging from our results is the following: if equity in the financing of health care is a goal of health policy, the share of medical care financed via taxes should be increased. A recent referendum brought forward by the sickness funds proposes exactly this. Equivalently, the financing system could be changed in such a way that health insurance premiums are tied to income, thereby introducing a progressive element into the premium structures.

EQUITY IN THE DELIVERY OF HEALTH CARE IN SWITZERLAND

Data and variable definitions

Empirical indicators for medical treatment and need are required to investigate equity on the delivery side of the health care system. We use health care expenditure as indicator of the amount of treatment a person received during the study period. As the data do not contain direct information on this variable, it had to be constructed by multiplying utilization in physical units (general practitioner visits, visits to specialists, hospital spells, and consumption of prescribed medicines) with its averaged unit costs. The latter was calculated using the information provided by Gygi and Frei (1985). Summing up the health care expenditure over all utilization categories for every individual in the sample provides total health care expenditure per person which is used subsequently in our analysis.

We employ five morbidity indicators as empirical proxies for need. These include:

(1) self-rated illness;
(2) chronic impairment;
(3) physician-diagnosed chronic illness;
(4) symptoms of 4 major chronic diseases;
(5) major illness (combines 2–4).

All these indicators are dummy variables, taking the value 1 if a person has bad health, is impaired or is suffering from one of the diseases, and zero otherwise. A more detailed description of these indicators is contained in the Appendix.

As our income variable we used adult equivalent gross income which is calculated using the SKÖF (Swiss Conference for Public Assistance) equivalence scale. This scale is officially used in Switzerland and takes the following values: one adult = 1; two adults = 1.5; two adults and one child

= 1.89; two adults and two children = 2.11. Each additional child increases the scale by 0.25. Individuals are ranked according to their adult equivalent gross income which is also used to define the income quintiles used in the analysis.

Unstandardized distribution of morbidity and health care

In a first step we investigated the unstandardized distribution of the five morbidity indicators and health care expenditure across income quintiles. Table 13.2 shows the number of individuals in each quintile (as the percentage of all individuals) reporting the respective morbidity. It consistently indicates for all five morbidity indicators that morbidity is highest in the lowest quintile. This is especially pronounced for the indicators 'self-rated illness' and 'chronic impairment'. This impression is confirmed by the corresponding values of C_{ill} (see Chapter 4, for a definition). With respect to the chronic conditions, it is interesting to note that 'physician-diagnosed chronic illness' is considerably less prevalent in the bottom quintile than the other two indicators for chronic conditions, 'chronic impairment' and 'symptoms of 4 major chronic diseases', which are self-reported. Note also that 'major illness', which is a combination of the three indicators of chronic conditions, is mainly determined by 'Physician-diagnosed chronic illness'.

Table 13.2 also shows the values for the unstandardized HI_{LG} (= C_{exp} − C_{ill}) which is based on Le Grand (1978) and serves as a reference point for the following results. HI_{LG} varies both in absolute size and in sign for the different morbidity indicators: we obtain positive values for HI_{LG} for 'self-related illness' and for 'chronic impairment', implying inequity favouring the better-off, whereas the indices for the other morbidity indicators imply inequity favouring the poor. However, as is shown in Chapter 4, HI_{LG} would appear to be a flawed measure for assessing equity in the delivery of health care.

Standardized expenditure distribution

In this section we analyse expenditure shares that are standardized for age, gender, and morbidity (need). Chapter 4 of this volume contains a detailed discussion on standardization. With the standardized expenditure shares we constructed the standardized concentration curve for expenditure. The measure of equity, HI_{WVP} is twice the area between the concentration curve and the diagonal (Wagstaff *et al.* 1991 *b*). We compute the standardized expenditure shares with respect to two morbidity indicators: 'self-rated illness' and 'major illness'. We use these indicators for two reasons: (1) their distribution across the sample is quite different (see

Table 13.2. Number of individuals in each income group reporting morbidity as a percentage of the total number reporting this morbidity

Income quintile	Population	All adults reporting 'health not good'	All adults reporting 'major illness'	All adults reporting 'physician-diagnosed chronic illness'	All adults reporting 'chronic impairment' (OECD scale)	All adults reporting 'symptoms of 4 major chronic diseases'
Bottom	20.00	31.00	22.16	21.32	34.11	27.13
2nd	20.00	20.29	18.72	18.25	22.05	19.74
3rd	20.00	18.83	19.32	19.52	16.76	19.89
4th	20.00	16.55	20.11	20.23	14.43	17.01
Top	20.00	13.33	19.69	20.68	12.65	16.23
C_{ill}		−0.156	−0.014	0.003	−0.202	−0.098
C_{exp}		−0.123	−0.123	−0.123	−0.123	−0.123
HI_{LG}		0.033	−0.019	−0.120	0.079	−0.025

Table 13.2), and (2) 'self-rated illness' is a *subjectively* perceived indicator, whereas 'major illness' is mainly determined by *physician-diagnosed* chronic disease. The standardized expenditure shares are computed using: (a) each indicator separately, and (b) both indicators simultaneously. In the former case we employ the direct standardization method (cf. Chapter 4, p. 000). In the latter case the regression approach to standardization is used.

Standardization was carried out using four age groups: 20–34 years, 35–49 years, 50–64 years, and 65 + years. HI_{WVP} is calculated using the non-linear approximation proposed by Kakwani and Podder (1976). We obtain HI_{WVP} = −0.061 for 'self-rated illness' and HI_{WVP} = −0.069 for 'major illness' (see Table 13.3). In contrast to the HI_{LG} indices, the values for HI_{WVP} consistently indicate inequity favouring the lower income groups. Although their distribution is quite different, the HI_{WVP} values are almost identical for the two morbidity indicators.

Measuring need can be improved by incorporating both morbidity indicators simultaneously in the computation of the inequity index. As it is not possible to apply the direct standardization in this case we used the regression approach to standardization instead, employing the two-part regression model (cf. Chapter 4, p. 74). In the first part, the decision to seek care is modelled. The second part models the determinants of the amount of health care, including only the observations with positive health care expenditure. This model assumes that the two equations are independent (i.e., that there is no selectivity bias). This assumption is tested and cannot be rejected against a selectivity corrected specification. The model is also tested against a Tobit specification in which it is assumed that the effect of the right-hand-side variables is the same in the selection process and in the determination of expenditure. The Tobit specification is rejected in all cases. Detailed test results are presented in Leu and Gerfin (1991).

The model is estimated separately for each income quintile, using Probit for the first part and Ordinary Least Squares (OLS) for the second. The estimation results are shown in Table 13.4. The variables are defined as follows: SELFILL and MAJORILL are the two morbidity indicators, AGE_j (j = 1, 2, 3) is the jth age group (the fourth age group is omitted), and GENDER equals 1 for males. As expected, the morbidity indicators are the most important variables in describing health care expenditure. The age and gender coefficients are mostly insignificant. When significant, the coefficients for GENDER have the expected negative sign.

The estimated coefficients allow the calculation of a standardized expenditure share for each quintile (cf. Chapter 4). Using these standardized expenditure shares we calculate HI_{WVP} = −0.041. Thus, the value of

Table 13.3. Unstandardized and standardized distribution of health care expenditure

Income quintile	Unstandardized	Standardized for age, gender, and 'Major illness'	Standardized for age, gender, and 'Self-rated illness'	Standardized for age, gender, and both morbidity indicators
Bottom	0.293	0.231	0.217	0.206
2nd	0.202	0.235	0.246	0.230
3rd	0.189	0.189	0.203	0.208
4th	0.166	0.179	0.164	0.174
Top	0.150	0.167	0.170	0.183
Conc. index	−0.123	−0.069	−0.061	−0.041

Table 13.4. Two-part estimation results

Variable	Quintile 1		Quintile 2		Quintile 3		Quintile 4		Quintile 5	
	Probit	OLS*	Probit	OLS*	Probit	OLS*	Probit	OLS*	Probit	OLS*
Intercept	0.67 (4.43)	358.05 (1.56)	0.88 (4.57)	73.94 (0.13)	0.81 (4.06)	80.91 (0.15)	1.05 (4.97)	575.23 (3.39)	1.11 (5.16)	951.55 (4.08)
Self-rated illness	0.58 (2.21)	1171.60 (5.50)	0.43 (1.81)	1764.40 (3.30)	0.99 2.59	644.39 (1.38)	0.53 (1.60)	1067.67 (7.08)	0.42 (1.29)	548.35 (2.41)
Major illness	0.91 (5.51)	294.39 (1.47)	0.83 (5.31)	611.96 (1.48)	0.80 (5.22)	1015.50 (2.83)	0.67 (4.24)	306.45 (2.88)	0.93 (6.33)	387.35 (2.61)
Age 1	0.35 (2.04)	590.10 (2.54)	0.23 (1.21)	638.09 (1.19)	0.32 (1.46)	438.22 (0.80)	0.36 (1.56)	267.30 (1.55)	0.03 (0.12)	-69.61 (0.29)
Age 2	0.26 (1.32)	403.85 (1.54)	0.17 (0.88)	-11.66 (0.02)	0.15 (0.71)	462.79 (0.91)	0.15 (0.71)	28.08 (0.17)	-0.21 (0.98)	-394.66 (1.85)
Age 3	0.08 (0.35)	-0.01 (0.00)	-0.06 (2.27)	1419.92 (1.99)	0.02 (0.08)	111.71 (0.18)	0.32 (1.26)	-61.50 (0.34)	-0.23 (1.00)	-257.95 (1.13)
Gender	-0.05 (0.34)	43.41 (0.24)	-0.38 (3.07)	145.21 (0.37)	-0.18 (1.37)	36.99 (0.11)	-0.37 (2.44)	-264.10 (2.54)	-0.29 (2.15)	-248.12 (1.72)

Notes: Absolute *t*-values are in parentheses.
* Only observations with positive expenditure.

Table 13.5.   Test for the impact of income

Model	LLProbit	LLOLS	SumLL	Likelihood ratio statistic	df	$\chi^2_{0.01,df}$
1	1629.5	32 389.7	34 019.2			
2	1632.9	32 391.4	34 024.3	10.2	8	20.1
3	1635.8	32 405.0	34 040.8	43.2	48	73.7
4	1639.4	32 406.4	34 045.8	53.2	56	83.5

Notes: 1, full model; 2, autonomous terms dropped; 3, interaction terms dropped; 4, all income-related variables dropped.

HI_{WVP} is lower in absolute terms than when each indicator is taken into account separately.

Test of inequity

The regression approach allows one to test the hypothesis that there is no income-related inequity. This can be achieved by estimating the two-part model for the whole sample, including income group dummies and inter-action terms of these dummies with the standardizing variables. In this specification, income influences health expenditure through the quintile dummies (i.e., the autonomous terms) and the interaction terms. To test for these effects separately, the model is estimated dropping: (1) the autonomous terms, and (2) the interaction terms. In a final test, all income-related coefficients are dropped. These restrictions can be tested using a likelihood ratio test. The log likelihoods are determined as the sum of the log likelihood of the probit estimation and the log likelihood of the OLS estimation. Table 13.5 contains the relevant log likelihood values, the resulting test statistics, the degrees of freedom, and the critical Chi-square values. The results indicate that the restrictions cannot be rejected in all three cases at the 1 per cent significance level. This suggests that there is no income-related inequity in the distribution of health expenditure in Switzerland and that the egalitarian goals of the Swiss health policy on the delivery side are being achieved.

Discussion

Some caveats apply to these results. One major problem of this type of study is measurement of need. The five morbidity indicators used in our paper constitute an arbitrary selection. Therefore, the results cannot be generalized. This is even more the case in those sections of this chapter where only one or two of these indicators are taken into account. Moreover, these indicators are all dummy variables and do not express severity of illness. With the exception of 'self-rated illness', they all indicate the presence of at least one out of several diseases which may differ largely in type, intensity, and costs of treatment required. Judging equity on the delivery side by relating total health expenditure to a few arbitrarily selected health indicators requires restrictive assumptions about variations in treatment costs by diagnosis. One possibility of improving the analysis would be to carry it out for specific diagnostic categories, taking into account only the disease-specific treatment cost. However, the data needed for this type of approach are not presently available in Switzerland. Similar measurement problems occur with respect to treatment. In this chapter, treatment is measured by health expenditure. However, as this variable was not directly available in the data it had to be constructed using average prices per treatment category, thereby ignoring quality aspects that might be important. Equivalent gross income is used to indicate the financial status of the persons in the sample. As has been increasingly recognized in the recent literature on poverty this may be misleading as the distribution of wealth is not taken into account. In addition, the usual caveats with respect to the validity of income data based on tax files apply. For these and other reasons discussed in Chapter 4, our results are preliminary.

SUMMARY AND CONCLUSIONS

The results of our study on equity in the delivery and finance of health care in Switzerland can be summarized as follows:

1. Both the Kakwani and the Suits indices imply that the system of financing health care, taking all financial sources into account, was regressive in 1982.

2. The overall incidence on the financing side depends on the shares of the various sources employed to finance medical care. Since the beginning of the 1980s, the share of tax-financed medical care has decreased, whereas the share financed by insurance premiums has increased. This implies that the system of financing health care has become more regressive in recent years.

3. The lesson for public policy from the above is the following: if equity in the financing of health care is a goal of health policy, the share of medical care financed via taxes should be increased. Equivalently, the financing system could be changed in such a way that health insurance premiums are tied to income, thereby introducing a progressive element into the premium structures.

4. We find higher morbidity rates for the lower income groups with respect to the selected morbidity indicators used in this study.

5. The age, gender, and morbidity standardized concentration indices imply that health care is distributed slightly unequally in favour of the lower income groups. However, statistical tests indicate that the degree of inequity is not significantly different from zero. Thus, the delivery of health care in Switzerland seems to be equitable according to our results. Further research is required, however, to determine whether these results are robust to the inclusion of more detailed information on need.

NOTES

1. SOMIPOPS, Socio-Medical Indicators for the Population of Switzerland. Project No. 4.350.0.79.08 of the National Research Programme No. 8, Swiss National Science Foundation. SEVS, Schweizerische Einkommens- und Vermögens-stichprobe. Swiss National Science Foundation, Project No. 1.455.0.81.
2. It should be emphasized that the basic cover premiums are private. It is rather confusing to combine them with the compulsory social insurance contributions in the official statistics, thus making international comparisons difficult.
3. Assumption (1) corresponds to an income elasticity of zero; assumption (2) corresponds to an income elasticity of 1. For a different data set, Zweifel (1983) estimated the elasticity of the demand for additional insurance with respect to labour income. He obtained values ranging from 0.2 to 0.8, depending on the kind of additional insurance. This suggests that asumption (2) might indeed be an upper limit for the distribution of the omitted items.
4. The assumptions are that all dental care (approximately 9.5 per cent of total expenditure), all medicines not covered by the basic cover (approximately 5 per cent of total expenditure), and all unallocated 'other expenditure' (approximately 2.3 per cent of total expenditure) are direct payments. The copayments are approximately 1.5 per cent of total expenditure. We then get a very rough estimate of 18.6 per cent of total expenditure for direct payments and 12.4 per cent of total expenditure for additional insurance (cf. Gygi and Frei 1985, pp. 90–92).

Appendix

The construction of the morbidity indicators

1. 'Self-rated illness'. The question 'How are you right now?' could be answered: excellent, good, fair, or poor. Those answering fair or poor are classified as 'self-rated illness'.

2. 'Chronic impairment'. This indicator was constructed using 10 questions, such as: 'Do you have difficulties with climbing stairs?' 'Difficulties with walking 400 metres?' 'Difficulties with carrying 5 kilos?' etc. Four answers were possible. Those answering 'I cannot do it' or 'I have great difficulties' to one of the 10 questions are classified as 'chronic impaired'.

3. 'Physician-diagnosed chronic illness'. 22 diagnosed disease were combined to construct this indicator, e.g., tuberculosis, arthritis, heart attack, high blood pressure, or cancer. If at least one of these diseases was diagnosed, the indicator takes the value 1.'

4. 'Symptoms of 4 major chronic diseases'. These are angina pectoris, rheumatism, chronic bronchitis, and intermittent claudication. The indicator takes the value of 1 if a person reports sysmptoms for at least one of the above diseases.

5. 'Major chronic illness'. This indicator combines 2 to 4. It equals 1 if at least one of the indicators 2–4 equals 1.

In constructing the morbidity indicators we were assisted by Dr E. Zemp of Basel University Hospital, Switzerland.

14

United Kingdom

Owen O'Donnell, Carol Propper, and Richard Upward

INTRODUCTION

This chapter presents evidence on departures from equity in the finance and delivery of health care in the UK. Following the methodology proposed in this volume, we examine equity in the finance and the delivery of health care separately and thus do not examine the net redistributive impact of the UK health care system. On the finance side, we review the progressivity of the finance of health care in the UK. Since health care in the UK is primarily financed from taxation, the analysis is predominantly an assessment of the progressivity of general taxation. On the delivery side, we examine the extent to which the allocation of health care in Britain is consistent with the National Health Service (NHS) policy objective of 'equal treatment for equal need'. Previous studies of this issue in the UK have yielded contradictory results. Le Grand (1978), using data from the 1972 *General Household Survey*, found evidence of substantial inequity in favour of the middle classes. Collins and Klein (1980), using data from the same survey but for a later year (1974), could find no evidence of inequity. We have argued elsewhere that, in part, these conclusions may reflect methodological differences between the studies (O'Donnell and Propper 1991 *a*).

Our chapter has the same format as other country reports in this volume. We therefore begin with a description of the UK health care system before examining equity in the finance and delivery of health care.

THE UK HEALTH CARE SYSTEM

In 1985, the UK spent approximately 6.7 per cent of its GNP on health care (Office of Health Economics 1987). Health care is predominantly

We are grateful to the ESRC for financial support in part provided under project number R000231635. We are grateful to the Office of Population Censuses and Surveys for the GHS data and to the ESRC Data Archive for granting us access to this and the HLS data. We would like to thank Maria Evandrou for data support. We alone are responsible for remaining errors.

financed and provided through the public sector. The majority of health care is supplied by the public NHS. Publicly financed NHS expenditure accounted for 86.5 per cent of total expenditure on health care in 1985[1] (OHE 1987). All of this expenditure is raised through general taxation. (User charges for NHS services are treated as private payments and accounted for only 3 per cent of total NHS financing.)

The NHS comprises hospital and community health services and family practitioner services (general practitioners (GPs), dentists, pharmaceuticals, and opticians). Doctors in the hospital sector are salaried employees. In the primary care sector GPs contract with the health service to provide care for a defined population and derive their income from a mixture of salary, capitation payments, and some fee-for-service payments. The recent reforms of the NHS, initiated in the White Paper 'Working for Patients' (Cmd 555), seek to divorce the purchasers of health care (District Health Authorities and GP budget holders) from the providers (public and private hospitals and community services) (Culyer *et al.* 1990). The aim is to introduce greater competition in the delivery of health care while maintaining a tax financed service. It is too early to assess the impact of these reforms, but, in principle, they offer greater opportunities for the private sector in the delivery of health care in the UK (Propper and Maynard 1990).

At present, a limited private sector exists. In terms of total size this sector is dwarfed by the NHS, total expenditure on the former being approximately £1 billion and on the latter £17 billion in 1985 (OHE 1987). However, the specialization of the private sector in the provision of acute surgical treatment means that its contribution to this type of care is quite large, especially in more affluent regions (Nicholl *et al.* 1989). Approximately 9 per cent of the population are covered by private health insurance (Laing 1987). The White Paper reforms introduce tax relief on private health insurance premiums for people over the age of 60, which is expected to increase, although not dramatically, the number covered by private insurance (Propper and Maynard 1990).

Despite any incentives provided in the 1989 White Paper to increase private finance and/or delivery of care, the principles on which the NHS was established reflect an egalitarian concept of equity. The White Paper introducing the NHS stated: 'The Government ... want to ensure that in future every man, woman and child can rely on getting ... the best medical and other facilities available; that their getting them shall not depend on whether they can pay for them or any other factor irrelevant to real need' (Cmd 6502).

This commitment to the allocation of health care on the basis of need, rather than ability to pay, was reiterated in the 1989 White Paper.

PROGRESSIVITY OF HEALTH CARE FINANCE IN THE UK

The progressivity of the financing of health care in the UK is largely determined by the progressivity of the tax system.[2] In this section, the distributional impact of the UK tax system in 1985 is examined before assessing the progressivity of other sources of health care finance in the UK.

The Central Statistical Office (CSO) publishes tables annually showing the distribution of the tax burden across the population ranked by income (CSO 1986). These tables are generated from data collected in the annual *Family Expenditure Survey* (FES). The figures reported in this chapter are derived from the published CSO tables.

Households are ranked according to their unadjusted gross household income and decile groups formed. On the basis of certain incidence assumptions,[3] tax payments are allocated to each group. The results are presented in Table 14.1. Both the Kakwani and Suits indices for income tax are positive, indicating that this is a progressive source of finance.[4] The indices are again positive for National Insurance (NI) contributions but the lower absolute values indicate that this is closer to a proportional tax. National Insurance contributions are paid by both employees and employers. The CSO estimates are based upon the assumption that the incidence of the employers' contributions are borne by consumers. An alternative incidence assumption (used in most of the other studies reported in this volume) is that employers shift the incidence of NI contributions on to employees, in the form of lower gross wages. O'Higgins and Ruggles (1981), using 1971 FES data, compared the progressivity of employers' NI contributions under both incidence assumptions. They found that the assumption used by CSO (forward shifting on to consumers) results in employers' NI contributions being regressive, whereas the alternative assumption results in proportionality. Hence, if the alternative assumption had been employed, the distribution of NI contributions would have been more progressive than is indicated in Table 14.1.

The distribution of indirect tax revenues in relation to incomes results in a negative value for both the Kakwani and Suits indices, indicating that these taxes are regressive. Overall, the Kakwani and Suits indices, reflecting the relationship between the distribution of total tax payments and incomes, are positive, indicating a progressive tax system. However, both indices are close to zero (0.068) and so the overall departure from proportionality is slight.

The published CSO tables, used to generate the data presented in Table

Table 14.1. Distribution of tax payments (percentage, 1985)

Income decile[1]	Gross income	Income Tax[2]	National insurance[3]	Indirect tax[4]	Total tax	Post-tax income
	[1]	[2]	[3]	[4]	[5]	[6]
Bottom	2.23	0.03	0.83	2.60	1.19	2.72
2nd	3.20	0.35	1.13	3.74	1.83	3.85
3rd	4.29	0.84	2.02	5.45	2.88	4.94
4th	5.85	3.00	4.58	7.25	4.97	6.23
5th	7.58	5.60	7.76	8.69	7.22	7.72
6th	9.32	7.72	10.42	10.28	9.23	9.32
7th	11.19	10.72	12.91	11.29	11.35	11.10
8th	13.46	14.01	15.97	13.87	14.32	13.03
9th	16.67	19.76	19.12	15.51	17.96	16.08
Top	26.21	37.98	25.25	21.32	29.03	25.01
Total tax revenue (%)[5]		41.88	18.61	39.51		

Non-linear approximations

Index

Gini	0.380	0.575	0.449	0.311	0.448	0.349
Kakwani		0.195	0.069	−0.069	0.068	
Suits[6]		0.213	0.051	−0.079	0.068	

Notes: [1] Decile groups of households ranked by gross household income.
[2] Net of tax relief at source.
[3] Approximately one-third of employers' NI contributions are fully forward shifted on to consumers. The rest are unallocated. All employees' NI contributions allocated.
[4] Excluding rates.
[5] These figures are the percentages of total allocated tax revenues and were calculated from CSO (1986), table 2.
[6] Based on relative concentration curves, which were estimated using linear interpolation.
Sources: Columns [1]–[4] and [6]: CSO (1986), table 6. Column [5]: average of columns [2]–[4] weighted by percentage of revenue.

14.1, do not provide a complete description of the progressivity of health care finance in the UK. The CSO allocated only 74 per cent of all taxes paid by UK residents to income groups. Whether the whole tax system is progressive or regressive is dependent upon the distribution of the burden of the remaining unallocated taxes. Also omitted from the data presented in Table 14.1 are the distributions of non-tax sources of health care finance; that is, direct user charges and private health insurance premiums. Unfortunately, data on the distributions of CSO unallocated taxes, direct user charges, and private insurance premiums are not readily available in a form consistent with that presented in Table 14.1. It is difficult, therefore, to give a complete description of the progressivity of health care finance in the UK. However, some data are available which allow examination of the sensitivity of the progressivity indices presented in Table 14.1 to the exclusion of the three remaining sources of health care finance.

The taxes unallocated by CSO are: commercial and industrial rates, part of VAT, corporation tax, capital tax, petroleum revenue tax, and two-thirds of employers' NI contributions. O'Higins and Ruggles (1981), using 1971 FES data and various incidence assumptions, succeeded in allocating these taxes.[5] They found, on the basis of the allocation of 100 per cent of tax revenues, the tax system was broadly proportional, whereas the CSO estimates showed a progressive system.

In order to provide a 'guesstimate' of the likely impact on the tax progressivity indices presented in Table 14.1 of the inclusion of CSO unallocated taxes, we use the O'Higgins-Ruggles results to calculate Kakwani and Suits indices for unallocated taxes in 1971. These indices are then weighted according to the proportion of tax revenues accounted for by CSO unallocated taxes in 1985 and a weighted average of the progressivity indices for (CSO) allocated and unallocated taxes is used to give an estimated index of progressivity for the whole tax system.

This exercise is obviously deficient in a number of respects. The UK tax system in 1985 differs markedly from that in 1971. One might expect that the progressivity of CSO unallocated taxes will have changed over the period. Additionally, in the O'Higgins-Ruggles study households are ranked by their original income (i.e., pre-income transfers and tax) rather than gross incomes, as in the case in Table 14.1. In order for Kakwani and Suits indices based on such rankings to be valid, one must assume that income transfers do not produce re-rankings in the income distribution. This is obviously unrealistic. However, O'Higgins and Ruggles provide the only indication of the distribution of CSO unallocated taxes. We use their results in order to give a very rough estimate of how the results presented in Table 14.1 might differ if 100 per cent of taxes had been allocated. This sensitivity analysis is intended to improve the comparability between the UK results and the others presented in this volume.

Using the O'Higgins-Ruggles results, the Kakwani and Suits indices for CSO unallocated taxes are estimated to be −0.0185 and −0.0245, respectively. The negative values indicate CSO unallocated taxes were regressive in 1971. We assume this was also the case in 1985. A weighted average of the progressivity indices for allocated and unallocated taxes produces estimates of the Kakwani and Suits indices for the whole UK tax system in 1985 of 0.046 and 0.044, respectively. Comparison with the value of the indices for CSO allocated taxes of 0.068 indicates a slight reduction in the progressivity of the system. Once again, it must be emphasized that these are no more than best guesses of the impact of including taxes not allocated by CSO.

Over-the-counter (OTC) payments for medical and surgical goods

Table 14.2. Distribution of payments for prescriptions and OTC medicines (percentage)

Income group[1]	Population	Gross income	Prescriptions and OTC payments
Poorest	10.4	1.89	4.27
2	12.1	3.65	5.90
3	12.2	5.73	9.99
4	13.2	9.10	13.62
5	12.0	11.08	13.87
6	15.6	18.82	17.64
7	13.0	20.5	17.97
Richest	11.5	29.24	16.73
Index			
Kakwani			−0.19
Suits			−0.21

Notes: [1] Bands of gross household income.
Source: *Family Expenditure Survey Report* (1985), tables 1, 5, and 22.

provides another source of health care finance. These payments fall into two categories: (1) charges for medicines and medical appliances issued through NHS prescriptions; (2) and pharmaceuticals and medical goods purchased without a prescription. The latter group accounts for two-thirds of all over-the-counter (OTC) medical purchases in the UK. Data on the distribution of these payments by income group are available from the FES, the same data source used to generate the CSO tax distribution tables and, consequently, Table 14.1. The proportion of total prescriptions and OTC payments for medicines accounted for by eight income groups are presented in Table 14.2. The income groups comprise different ranges of gross household income. Both the Kakwani and Suits indices for these health care payments are negative, indicating a regressive means of finance.

Payments for private health care are the final source of health care finance in the UK. The vast majority of private health care is financed through medical insurance. Unfortunately, no data are available which allow examination of the distribution of medical insurance premiums across income groups.[6] The 1987 *General Household Survey* (GHS) provides information on individuals covered by medical insurance. Table 14.3 shows the proportion of all individuals (and households) covered by private health insurance accounted for by each gross income decile. These figures illustrate that the distribution of health insurance coverage in the UK is highly pro-rich.

Table 14.3. Distribution of private health insurance (PHI) cover (percentage)

Income decile[1]	Gross income	All persons covered by PHI	All households covered by PHI
Bottom	1.72	0.45	0.74
2nd	2.46	0.51	0.74
3rd	3.54	0.58	1.18
4th	5.03	1.16	1.15
5th	7.00	2.83	4.13
6th	9.08	5.60	7.39
7th	11.16	7.46	8.42
8th	13.67	13.45	14.49
9th	17.26	19.74	19.49
Top	29.09	48.22	42.28
Index			
Conc.	0.43	0.66	0.60
Kakwani		0.23	0.17
Suits		0.29	0.21

Notes: [1] Ranked by gross household income.
Source: *General Household Survey* (1987).

In calculating progressivity indices for private health insurance payments from these data, we have assumed premiums paid do not vary with income. This is obviously unrealistic as premiums are generally related to characteristics such as age, which indicate health risks. On the basis of this simplifying assumption, we have calculated progressivity indices for the distribution of both individuals and households covered by medical insurance. Using the former implies the assumption that premiums are constant across individuals but vary across households in direct proportion to the number of individuals covered by a policy. Using the latter distribution implies the assumption that the premium paid by a household is invariant to the number of persons covered by the policy. The true distribution will lie somewhere between these two extremes. Using insurance coverage as an indication of payments also implies the assumption that the incidence of employer-provided insurance is shifted on to the salaries of employees.

Whatever distribution is examined, the Kakwani and Suits indices are positive and quite large, indicating that the finance of health insurance in Britain is highly progressive. This is unsurprising given that private insurance is mainly purchased by the rich as a supplement to NHS coverage.

The overall progressivity of the system can be assessed by taking a weighted average of the progressivity indices for each of the sources of finance. The relevant weights are the proportions of total health care finance raised through each source.

The estimated overall Kakwani and Suits indices, shown in Table 14.4, for total health care finance are 0.032 and 0.031, respectively, which suggests that health care finance in Britain is only very slightly progressive. The impact of including sources of finance other than CSO allocated taxes is to reduce the value of the progressivity indices by more than half. However, these indices have been calculated using data from two different surveys and three different years and must be treated as best estimates likely to be subject to some error. The index which is likely to contain most error is that for CSO unallocated taxes, because this was calculated from 1971 data. The true value of the progressivity indices will be greater or less than those presented in Table 14.4 depending on whether the taxes which CSO do not allocate were less or more regressive in 1985 than in 1971. The index for private health insurance may also be subject to some error as no data on premiums paid were available. However, given the low weight attached to this source, any error is unlikely to have a dramatic effect on the overall index of progressivity.

It is interesting to compare the progressivity of different sources of health care finance. The near proportionality of the complete system is maintained by a progressive income tax which accounts for 27 per cent of total finance. Any reduction in the proportion of revenues accruing from this source would involve a move towards regressivity. Similarly, increases in finance through OTC payments would induce greater regressivity. It should be pointed out that the fact that private health insurance is a progressive means of finance in Britain does *not* imply that greater reliance on this source of revenue would induce greater progressivity. An expansion of private insurance is likely to involve increasing coverage among the middle and lower income groups which would make this source of finance less progressive and, judging by the results presented in this volume for Switzerland and the US, where private insurance provides a much larger proportion of finance, it is likely that eventually it would become regressive.

EQUITY IN THE DELIVERY OF HEALTH CARE IN THE UK

Data and variable definitions

The data employed in our analysis of the delivery of health care are taken from the 1985 *General Household Survey* (GHS). The GHS is a national

Table 14.4. Estimated progressivity of UK health care finance (1985)

	Income tax	NI	Indirect tax	CSO unallocated tax	Prescriptions + OTC payments	Private health insurance[2]	Total
Kakwani index	0.195	0.069	−0.069	−0.019	−0.19	0.20	0.032
Suits index	0.213	0.051	−0.079	−0.025	−0.21	0.25	0.031
Weight[1]	0.268	0.119	0.253	0.224	0.087	0.048	

Notes: [1] Weights are based on data from National Income Accounts. Denominator is total health care expenditure and equals £20 627 million.
[2] The average Kakwani index from Table 14.3 is used as it is likely that health insurance premiums do vary with the number of persons covered by a policy, but less than proportionately.
Sources: FES (1985), columns 1–3, and 5; FES (1971), column 4; GHS (1987), column 6.

cross-sectional survey of over 10 000 households and 25 000 individuals which includes microdata on individuals' health care utilization, self-reported morbidity, and income. The survey was used in earlier research in this field (Le Grand 1978; Collins and Klein 1980; Hurst 1985).

Our income measure is gross equivalent family income, adjusted using the equivalence scale derived by McClements (1978). The 1985 GHS provides information on the utilization of GP, outpatient, accident and emergency, and inpatient care. No information on individuals' length of stay (LOS) as inpatients is provided, so we have assumed that average LOS is constant across income groups.[7] The GHS does not survey the institutionalized population, so—as with the other country reports—the distribution of institutional care is omitted from our analysis.

Both NHS and private care have been costed using the NHS unit costs.[8] There was a pragmatic reason for this: there are no reliable data on the costs of private hospitals. However, there is also a theoretical justification for using the same costs for both sectors. The aim of this study is to examine the distribution of the benefits from health care. If differences in costs between sectors reflect merely differences in 'hotel' services, rather than quality differences which have implications for the health of patients, then the estimated distribution of health care should not reflect such variations in cost. In the UK, the private sector concentrates on the provision of elective surgery and treatment is usually provided by the same doctors who carry out such operations on NHS patients and often in NHS hospitals. In these circumstances, little or no differences are expected in the quality of NHS and private care and so the use of the same costs for care in the two sectors would seem justified. The use of the same NHS costs for all income groups embodies the assumption of no systematic variation in the quality of NHS care across incomes. There is some evidence that this may be an incorrect assumption, at least with respect to GP consultations (Buchan and Richardson 1973; Cartwright *et al.* 1974; Metcalfe *et al.* 1983), but given the available data, could not be investigated in the present analysis.[9]

General Household Survey respondents are asked whether they have any long-standing illness, disability or infirmity. Those responding positively are asked whether they experience limited functioning due to this illness. Three measures, any chronic (ANYCHRON), non-limiting chronic (CHRONIC), and limiting chronic (LTDCHRON), are constructed from responses to these questions. The first was positive if the respondent answered 'yes' to the first question, the second was positive if they answered 'yes' to the first question but 'no' to the second, and the third was positive if they answered 'yes' to both. (As the measures are non-exclusive they obviously were not all used in any one analysis.)[10] In the GHS, adult respondents are also asked to rate their general health as:

'good', 'fairly good' or 'not good'. This subjective indicator of morbidity (Blaxter 1989) was also used in the present analysis, the variable HEALTH taking value 1 if the respondent recorded her health as 'not good'.

The GHS provides data on the morbidity (with the exception of the 'not good' health variable) and health care utilization of all household members, whether adults or children. For purposes of comparability with other country analyses, we defined two samples in our data: (1) a full sample containing data on adults and children; and (2) an adult-only sample. The analyses for the adult-only sample are presented first in the text.

Unstandardized distribution of morbidity and health care

Table 14.5, which presents the number of individuals in each income quintile who report each type of morbidity as a percentage of all individuals reporting that type of morbidity, indicates a negative association between income and self-reported morbidity for all measures of morbidity except non-limiting long-standing illness and in both the adult-only and the full sample. This is confirmed by the negative sign C_{ill} values (except for non-limiting chronic). Chi-squared tests indicate this association is statistically significant at the 0.001 level. However, although all but one of the self-reported morbidity indicators show the poor are less healthy than rich, there is some variation in the degree of inequality across morbidity measures. The measure of self-assessed health (available for adults only) shows most inequality. Limiting long-standing illness is more unequally distributed than non-limiting illness. This pattern appears in both the adult-only and the full sample. The absolute magnitude of the concentration indices are consistently slightly larger for the adult only sample than for the full sample, indicating that health inequalities are slightly less pronounced among children.[11]

Table 14.5 also indicates that the distribution of unstandardized expenditure—both NHS and total (public and private)—is pro-poor, but NHS expenditure is more pro-poor. Given the positive association in the UK between private insurance coverage and income and hence between income and private sector utilization, this difference in the distributions of NHS and total expenditure is in the expected direction.

Both morbidity and unstandardized expenditure are thus pro-poor. However, the positive HI_{LG} indices (calculated as $C_{exp} - C_{ill}$) signify that the *net* distribution of unstandardized expenditure and morbidity is pro-rich. That is, the degree of pro-poor inequality in the distribution of morbidity is greater than the pro-poor inequality in the distribution of health care. This is the case for both NHS and total health care expenditure, for all measures of self-assessed morbidity other than non-limiting long-standing illness and for both the adult-only and the full sample. As expected from the distribution of expenditure, total expenditure relative to morbidity shows more pro-rich bias than NHS expenditure. The indices show the most pro-rich bias to be in the distribution of expenditure relative to self-assessed health status. The distribution across adults appears to be slightly more unequal than for the full sample. However, it should be noted that standard errors have not been calculated for the indices,[12] and so it cannot be established whether these differences are statistically significant.

Standardized expenditure distribution

In view of the pro-rich bias inherent to the Le Grand (1978) methodology, as argued in Chapter 4 of this volume and elsewhere (O'Donnell and Propper 1991 *a*), we examine next the distribution across income groups of health care resources standardized for differences in morbidity, age, and sex. Standardization is carried out using the regression method described in Chapter 4. This methodology avoids the bias inherent in simple comparisons of the distribution of health care with that of morbidity. As a large proportion of the sample report zero utilization of health care, final standardized expenditure was calculated as the product of predicted expenditure conditional on it being positive and the standardized probability of expenditure being positive. Although this is not an explanatory model, merely a device for undertaking standardization, it is important to test the distributional assumptions embodied in the model, as incorrect distributional assumptions could result in biased estimates of the distribution of health care. We therefore undertook tests of two independence assumptions of the two-part model against alternative specifications. Tests for non-normality, ommitted variables and heteroscedesticity in the health care participation equation were also carried out. The tests and results are described in the Appendix and are more fully reported in O'Donnell *et al.* (1991 *a*). The results indicate that the two-part standardization with independence[13] is, at least in the British case, probably as appropriate as any other method of standardization and also gives very similar results to the direct standardization procedure used widely by epidemiologists (e.g., in the construction of standardized mortality ratios—SMRs).

The distribution of standardized health care for the adult-only sample is given in Table 14.6(a). Standardization was undertaken using several sets of morbidity measures; the variables used in each standardization are indicated at the top of the relevant column of the table. The morbidity

Table 14.5. Distribution of unstandardized morbidity and expenditure (percentage)

(a) Adults only ($n = 13\ 204$)

Income quintile	NHS expendit.	Total expendit.	All with limiting long-standing illness	All with non-limiting illness	All with any long-standing illness	All with health not good
Bottom	25.32	24.17	32.88	19.18	27.32	37.01
2nd	24.69	23.66	27.67	20.32	24.69	29.23
3rd	18.57	18.27	16.42	20.69	18.15	15.43
4th	17.25	17.48	12.34	18.56	14.86	11.03
Top	14.17	16.43	10.68	21.26	14.97	7.29
Conc. index	−0.121	−0.088	−0.243	0.0096	−0.140	−0.316
$C_{NHSexp} - C_{ill}$			0.122	−0.1306	0.019*	0.195
$C_{exp} - C_{ill}$			0.155	−0.0976	0.052	0.228

(b) Adults and children ($n = 17729$)

Income quintile	NHS expendit.	Total expendit.	All with limiting long-standing illness	All with non-limiting illness	All with any long-standing illness
Bottom	25.15	24.24	31.74	19.44	26.49
2nd	23.36	22.55	26.90	20.82	24.31
3rd	18.53	18.21	16.22	19.78	17.74
4th	17.83	17.96	12.98	18.06	15.15
Top	15.13	17.05	12.15	21.90	16.31
Conc. index	−0.106	−0.078	−0.215	0.0086	−0.119
$C_{NHSexp} - C_{ill}$			0.109	−0.1146	0.013*
$C_{exp} - C_{ill}$			0.137	−0.0866	0.041

Note: * Concentration curves cross.

Table 14.6. Distribution of standardized expenditure (percentage)

(a) Adults ($n = 13\,204$)

Income quintile	Standardizing variables							
	Age, sex, ANYCHRON [1]		Age, sex, HEALTH [2]		Age, sex, ANYCHRON, HEALTH [3]		Age, sex, LTDCHRON, CHRONIC, HEALTH [4]	
	NHS	Total	NHS	Total	NHS	Total	NHS	Total
Bottom	23.44	22.05	21.35	19.99	20.94	19.56	20.74	19.35
2nd	23.91	22.57	22.50	21.13	22.40	20.98	22.26	20.82
3rd	19.09	18.47	19.21	18.46	19.24	18.45	19.34	18.51
4th	18.23	19.03	18.95	19.62	19.34	20.03	19.45	20.16
Top	15.33	17.88	17.98	20.80	18.08	20.98	18.21	21.16
HI_{wvp}	−0.089	−0.048	−0.041	0.002*	−0.035	0.009*	−0.031	0.013*

(b) Adults and children ($n = 17\,729$)

Income quintile	Standardizing variables					
	Age, sex, ANYCHRON			Age, sex, LTDCHRON, CHRONIC		
	NHS	Total		NHS	Total	
	[1]			[2]		
Bottom	23.63	22.58		23.00	21.94	
2nd	22.59	21.59		22.19	21.17	
3rd	19.17	18.65		19.36	18.80	
4th	18.62	18.95		18.93	19.26	
Top	15.99	18.22		16.52	18.83	
HI_{wvp} indices	−0.080	−0.047		−0.067	−0.033	

Note: * Concentration curves cross the 45° line.

variables in column [(4)] is our preferred set of standardizing measures; the other sets are included for purposes of comparability with the results from other countries.

It is clear that all the standardized data display a more pro-poor distribution than the non-standardized, in other words, HL_{VWP} is more pro-poor than HI_{LG}. This result is in accord with the discussion in Chapter 4, and O'Donnell and Propper (1991 *a*).

Looking first at NHS expenditure, the negative HI_{WVP} values signify that this expenditure is weakly pro-poor.[14] Moving across the columns in Table 14.6, it is clear the effect of adding more, and more finely categorized, morbidity measures is to reduce the absolute size of the concentration index. This indicates that using more detailed measures of ill health reduces the apparently pro-poor bias in the distribution of NHS expenditure. The picture is a little different for total (public and private) standardized expenditure. If 'any chronic illness' is used as the morbidity indicator, the distribution is pro-poor, but less pro-poor than NHS expenditure as the absolute size of the index is almost 50 per cent lower than that for NHS expenditure. For all the other morbidity measures, the standardized distributions of total expenditure indicate little evidence of either pro-poor or pro-rich bias. All of the indices are positive, but small in magnitude. In general, the top and second bottom quintiles get more than their fair share of expenditure at the expense, in the main, of the middle quintile. All three concentration curves cross the 45° line. Calculating the HI_{WVP} index in this situation embodies the judgement that inequity favouring a lower quintile (in this case the second bottom) can be offset by inequity favouring a higher quintile (in this case the top) (Chapter 4, this volume). This assumption is adopted as our intention is to determine whether there is net inequity in favour of the rich or poor rather than to measure the gross level of inequity in the health care system.

The results for the full sample are presented in Table 14.6(b). The indices show a weakly pro-poor distribution for all the morbidity measures. Comparison of the indices across different morbidity measures indicates a similar pattern to the adult-only subsample: disaggregation of morbidity reduces the extent of measured pro-poor inequity. Total standardized expenditure is again less pro-poor than NHS standardized expenditure, the absolute values of the concentration indices being almost 50 per cent less for total expenditure than for NHS expenditure. It appears that, although small in aggregate, the use of the private sector seems to have a substantial effect on the distribution of health care in Britain.

The lack of a self-assessed health variable for children means that direct comparison of the standardized results across the two samples can only be made for the case of standardization by the 'any chronic illness' indicator of morbidity. For this measure the distribution of standardized expenditures in the two samples are very similar. The concentration indices for total expenditure for the adult-only and the full sample are −0.048 and −0.047, respectively. For NHS expenditure, the respective figures are −0.089 and −0.080.

In the absence of standard errors we cannot say whether the concentration indices presented in Table 14.6(a) and (b) indicate that the distributions are significantly different from an equal distribution. Nor can summary measures indicate the possible sources of income-related inequality. However, examination of the estimated probit and Ordinary Least Squares (OLS) equations from which the standardized results were derived can provide some guide to the significance and source of any income-related inequity.[15] The estimates and test statistics for adults only are shown in Table 14.A3 (for the full sample see O'Donnell *et al.* 1991). Log likelihood ratio tests, using the full sample, indicate that there are no significant differences across the quintiles in the level of total (public and private) health care expenditure. The likelihood ratio (LR) test statistics for the hypothesis of no income-related inequity, was 67, with 64 degrees of freedom (df) (1 per cent cv = 93.2), indicating that the null hypothesis of no inequity cannot be rejected. Neither the direct effect of income nor the indirect effect (through its interaction with morbidity, gender or age) appears to differ significantly across the five quintiles. We can thus perhaps conclude that the weakly pro-poor distribution indicated by the concentration indices in Table 14.6(b) does not appear to be significantly different from an equal distribution.

For the adult-only sample, income appears to affect levels of expenditure in two opposing directions. The 'autonomous' level of expenditure— that which is unrelated to any of the standardizing variables—is not the same in each quintile. In fact, this level is lower the higher the income group and tests (weakly) reject the hypothesis that these differences are due to chance variation. The level of treatment which is related to the standardizing variables also differs significantly across income quintiles. However, the difference across income groups is in the opposite direction; there is positive interaction between both age and morbidity and income; the lower income groups get less expenditure for a given level of age and morbidity. The LR test statistic for the total effect of income on expenditure has a value of 111.2 with 64 df (1 per cent critical value = 93.2), indicating that the hypothesis of no income-related inequity can be rejected. This result may seem surprising given that the figures in the column [4] of the Table 14.6(a) show no clear bias in favour of the rich or the poor. The explanation lies in the fact that the direct and indirect effects of income on health care consumption work in opposite directions, consequently the net effect of income is small.

Discussion

There is, then, little evidence of any major systematic bias in favour of either the rich or poor in the distribution of total health care expenditure in Britain. The results show some evidence of a slightly pro-poor distribution of NHS care, standardizing for differences in age, sex, and self-reported morbidity. One interpretation of these findings is that the rich substitute private for NHS care and consequently make less of a claim on NHS resources for a given level of need. Another (not mutually exclusive) interpretation is that, for a given level of self-reported morbidity, individuals in the lower income groups are, on average, in greater need of health care. If this is the case, then the slightly unequal distribution of NHS resources is not necessarily indicative of unequal treatment for equal need.

Approximately 30 per cent of the GHS sample reported long-standing illness in 1985. Substantial variation in the conditions suffered by these individuals would be expected. Unfortunately, data are not available in the 1985 GHS to determine whether there is systematic variation across income groups in the type and severity of conditions suffered. However, some light can be shed on this issue through examination of another large scale dataset. The *Health and Lifestyle Survey* (HLS) (Cox *et al.* 1989) carried out in 1984–5, is a large sample survey ($n = 9000$) of the adult population and includes information on income and self-reported morbidity, as well as physiological and psychological measures of health status. The more detailed health data available in the HLS allow examination of whether poorer individuals were more ill for a given level of self-reported morbidity. Details of our analysis are shown in O'Donnell and Propper (1991 *a*). The results suggest that the assumption that among individuals categorized by self-reported morbidity, health status is on average equal across income groups may be incorrect. For a given level of self-reported morbidity, the HLS data indicate that, individuals in the lower income groups are more likely to suffer multiple and more serious conditions and their health status, as measured by blood pressure and respiratory and cognitive functioning, is likely to be lower. We can thus perhaps conclude that the weakly pro-poor distribution of NHS care identified in Table 14.6 may actually reflect allocation according to need, rather than unequal treatment for equal health status.

CONCLUSIONS

In this Chapter we have adopted the distinction between equity in the delivery and in the finance of health care, as the equity goals advanced for these two sides of the health care sector differ. The tax-financed nature of the NHS suggests that the equity goals here are those that apply to the whole tax system—goals of progressivity or at least proportionality. On the delivery side, the often stated policy goal was and appears to remain 'equal treatment for equal need'.

The UK tax system, from which the vast majority of health care is financed, is slightly progressive. Over-the-counter charges for NHS prescriptions and other medicines are regressive. At present, private health insurance payments in Britain are progressive. Overall, our best estimate is that health care payments in the UK are close to being proportional to income.

It is well established that the distribution of health in Britain is unequal. Individuals in lower income groups report and have lower health status than those in higher income groups. The data used in the present study—self-reported morbidity measures from the GHS—confirm this pattern. However, the distribution of resources is also unequal—the GHS data indicating that individuals in lower income groups receive more NHS resources than those in higher income quintiles. A simple comparison of the distribution of resources with the distribution of reported morbidity, of the type pursued by Le Grand (1978), indicates a slight overall pro-rich distribution. However, this methodology is not appropriate for assessing whether the allocation of resources is consistent with the objective, 'equal treatment for equal need'. After appropriate standardization for differences in the distribution across income groups in age, gender, and the incidence of types of reported morbidity, there is little evidence of substantial inequity in the distribution of health care in Britain. For the full sample income was found to have no significant effect on the distribution of total health care resources. The significant impact of income in the case of the adult sample consisted of direct and indirect effects which worked in opposite directions and appeared to cancel each other out.

There are some systematic variations in the results. Total health care resources (i.e., private and NHS care) are distributed more in favour of the higher income groups than NHS resources, a result wholly consistent with the nature of the UK private health care system. The results are sensitive to the self-reported morbidity measures used to define 'need'; the addition of more measures and more finely defined measures reduces an apparently pro-poor bias in the standardized distribution.

The pro-poor bias in the standardized distribution of NHS resources is small. But there is evidence to suggest that even this may be an overstatement of the extent of pro-poor bias in the distribution of health care resources. The methodology used relies upon the assumption that health status within each morbidity category does not differ with income. Analysis of data from the *Health and Lifestyles Survey* undertaken elsewhere suggests this may be an incorrect assumption: within each morbidity group the poorer in fact appear to be sicker. Thus, we conclude that on these grounds the GHS data over-states the degree of any pro-poor bias in the distribution of health care resources.

Our conclusions are that the predominantly publicly financed and publicly provided health care system in Britain appears close to allocating health care resources on the basis of 'equal treatment for equal need' and extracting payments in proportion to incomes. This conclusion must be qualified with a reminder that the data available for analysis are incomplete and often crude, but these are the best data currently available for the UK.

NOTES

1. Total expenditure on health care includes: public expenditure on the NHS; payments for NHS issued prescriptions; purchases of private health care; and over-the-counter payments for pharmaceuticals and other medical goods.
2. In theory, those who bear the cost of a publicly funded service, such as the British NHS, are those who would benefit if it were to cease to exist and the resources released were put to some alternative use. The problem is to identify the most plausible counter-factual hypothesis. We make no attempt to identify the distribution of the economic cost of the NHS. The less ambitious objective is to describe the distribution of the total tax bill, from which the NHS is financed.
3. Income taxes and employees' National Insurance contributions are assumed to be incident upon the tax payer directly. Employers' National Insurance contributions are assumed to be incident upon consumers, as are indirect taxes on both final and intermediate goods and services.
4. Positive and negative indices represent progressive and regressive taxes respectively. Indices were calculated using the non-linear approximation method.
5. O'Higgins and Ruggles (1981) make the following incidence assumptions. Corporation taxes are assumed to fall half on capital incomes and half on consumption. Capital taxes are assumed to be incident on the recipient of capital incomes. Any indirect taxes (or employers NI contributions) assumed in national accounts to fall on gross domestic capital formation are assumed half incident on capital incomes and half on consumption. Taxes falling on general government final consumptions are allocated in proportion to total taxes.
6. The FES does provide data on payments for private health insurance made by individuals. However, individual purchase of private health insurance accounts for only 40 per cent of all purchases. Analysis of GHS data revealed that among the population covered by private health insurance the proportion of purchases made by employers increased with income group. Assuming the incidence of employer-provided health insurance is shifted on to salaries, analysis of the FES data would give a biased indication of the distribution of payments for private health insurance.

7. In the early 1970s, the GHS had information on LOS. Le Grand (1978) exploited this multiplying the number of inpatient days by the average cost per day, to get the total cost of inpatient care consumed by each individual. This procedure will not necessarily improve the accuracy of the estimated distribution of health care resources, as the marginal cost of an additional inpatient day is likely to be much less than the average cost. Thus the resource cost of longer than average lengths of stay will be overestimated using this methodology. Using 1974 data, which contains length of stay information, we found the distribution of health care to be more pro-poor when LOS was included.

8. The cost figures used for GP visits were estimated by the DHSS (Tinker 1984) and have been inflated to 1985–6 price levels using the hospital and community health services pay and prices deflator. *The Health service costing returns*, 1985–6 (DHSS and Welsh Office 1987) were used to calculate the average cost of an outpatient or accident and emergency department visit and the average cost of an inpatient stay in a non-long stay hospital in England and Wales.

9. In the figures presented, the same unit cost for a GP visit is used whether or not a prescription was issued. Analyses using a higher cost for consultations resulting in a prescription give similar results.

10. For analyses using additional indicators see O'Donnell and Propper (1991 *a*).

11. Analysis was also carried out by decile group. The results were not statistically different and in many cases were identical to the third decimal place.

12. A possible method of calculating standard errors for the indices has been proposed by Elleman-Jensen (1989).

13. The results indicate independence of the decision to consult and the level of expenditure conditional on consultation. This may reflect the nature of health care consumption. The decision to consult a doctor is made by the individual. Once the individual has initiated care, the level of care she receives is largely determined by the doctor. A degree of independence between the probability of consulting and the level of health care received by those who do consult may therefore be expected. Given that we have not estimated an explanatory model, we do not claim confirmation of such a hypothesis from our results but offer it as a possible rationalization of the results.

14. The concentration indices were calculated by the non-linear approximation method. For the adult plus children sample, they were also calculated by the method suggested by Jenkins (1988). The two methods gave very similar results.

15. The tests of significance of income effects are described in the Appendix.

Appendix

Tests of standardization procedure

A probit and OLS specification was adopted for the standardization procedure. This procedure implicitly assumes that the first equation is independent of the second. If this assumption is incorrect, the parameter estimates derived under the hypothesis of independence will be biased and the standardized results biased. Possible alternative hypotheses are a tobit model or a sample selection model (SSM). The tobit model embodies the hypothesis that the effect of the standardization variables on the probit equation are the same as in censored OLS. The SSM hypothesizes that the error term of the probit equation is not independent of the error term of the censored OLS. Likelihood ratio (LR) tests were undertaken of both these models, the tobit specification tested against a truncated OLS and a probit model (Godfrey 1988), the SSM against an independent probit and OLS.

The results are shown in Tables 14.A1 and 14.A2. The tobit specification was rejected in all cases for both samples; the sample selection model could be rejected for all but quintiles 1 and 4 in the adult sample. As the estimated correlation between the error terms in the two equations was insignificant even for these two quintiles, the two-part probit and OLS approach to standardization was adopted.

In probit models non-normality, heteroscedasticity or omitted variables may result in inconsistent parameter estimates (Godfrey 1988). Tests for non-normality and a general mis-specification test (Orme 1988) were undertaken. The Orme tests indicate some mis-specification (e.g., omitted variables) for quintiles 1–4 (adult only) and 2–4 for the full sample. As the form of the equations was chosen for the purpose of standardization and not as an explanatory model, it is not surprising that there may be some mis-specification. Thus, we should note that the parameter estimates used in the standardization procedure may be biased for quintiles 1–4, but the extent or effect of the bias has not been established and may be small. It is worth noting that for this data the direct standardization method gave very similar results to the standardization by regression.

Table 14.A1. Total sample ($n = 17\,729$)

	Income quintile				
	1	2	3	4	5
Tobit InL[1]	−10875.0	−9971.6	−9030.7	−8915.5	−8546.6
Trunc OLS InL[2]	−8643.2	−7820.0	−6995.6	−6853.5	−6530.4
Probit InL[2]	−2121.5	−2064.5	−1986.7	−1995.6	−1949.0
Heckman InL[2]	−9270.7	−8385.9	−7435.2	−7347.6	−7014.3
OLS InL	−9270.9	−8385.9	−7435.16	−7347.9	−7014.6
OLS R^2	0.019	0.038	0.037	0.031	0.033
Tests on probit, χ^2 (14 df)[3]	24.7	61.2	65.7	61.3	21.9
Normality (2 df)[4]	1.97	2.52	13.86	1.77	4.44
Skewness (1 df)	0.40	2.31	2.02	1.72	3.10
Kurtosis (1 df)	0.02	1.16	0.33	1.49	2.06
n	3545	3548	3546	3547	3543

Table 14.A2. Adults only ($n = 13\,204$)

	Income quintile				
	1	2	3	4	5
Tobit InL[1]	−8330.3	−7785.9	−6834.0	−6475.2	−6326.4
Trunc OLS InL[2]	−6735.0	−6187.7	−5359.8	−5014.1	−4855.0
Probit InL[2]	−1539.4	−1522.2	−1441.7	−1415.7	−1421.8
Heckman InL[2]	−7163.3	−6632.0	−5669.3	−5364.6	−5207.9
OLS InL	−7166.0	−6632.1	−5669.7	−5368.6	−5207.9
OLS R^2	0.047	0.082	0.049	0.095	0.144
Tests on probit, χ^2 (14 df)[3]	41.65	44.59	38.89	40.72	21.106
Normality (2 df)[4]	4.01	1.18	1.59	2.59	1.36
Skewness (1 df)	1.83	0.46	0.55	1.44	0.67
Kurtosis (1 df)	0.03	0.01	0.00	0.02	0.00
n	2642	2640	2639	2642	2641

Notes: [1] Log likelihood.
[2] Test for probit and OLS versus probit and Heckman two stage estimates = 2(Ln OLS − Ln Heckman)~χ^2 (1).
[3] χ^2 test is that of Orme (1988); degrees fo freedom in parentheses.
[4] Normality, shewness, and kurtosis tests from Bera, Jarque and Lee (1982); degrees of freedom in parentheses.

Table 14.A3. Probit and OLS estimates for all income groups together (adults only)

Variable	Probit estimate on pr (exp > 0)			OLS estimate on E (exp|exp > 0)		
	Coefficient	Standard error	Mean of X	Coefficient	Standard error	Mean of X
ONE	−0.62	0.06	1.00	540.34	43.67	1.00
AGE 44	−0.31	0.10	0.18	−211.62	64.31	0.16
AGE 64	−0.59	0.08	0.28	−166.52	52.56	0.26
AGEOLD	−0.42	0.07	0.21	−148.92	43.46	0.24
FEMALE	0.21	0.06	0.53	9.59	35.62	0.60
LTDCHRON	0.58	0.07	0.21	−23.87	43.50	0.36
CHRONIC	0.39	0.08	0.15	−77.89	52.63	0.17
HEALTH	0.70	0.07	0.13	212.30	37.90	0.27
EQINC2	−0.08	0.09	0.20	32.13	63.05	0.22
EQINC3	−0.18	0.08	0.20	−92.05	59.89	0.19
EQINC4	−0.18	0.08	0.20	−96.74	59.37	0.18
EQINC5	−0.22	0.08	0.20	−139.50	58.50	0.17
CHRONQ2	−0.15	0.11	0.03	42.46	75.47	0.03
CHRONQ3	0.08	0.11	0.03	61.33	72.28	0.04
CHRONQ4	0.02	0.11	0.03	41.24	74.30	0.03
CHRONQ5	−0.05	0.11	0.03	38.91	72.91	0.03
LCHRONQ2	−0.02	0.10	0.06	53.73	63.55	0.10
LCHRONQ3	−0.06	0.11	0.04	61.00	67.48	0.06
LCHRONQ4	−0.11	0.11	0.03	75.87	68.96	0.04
LCHRONQ5	−0.03	0.11	0.02	6.68	69.12	0.04
HEALTHQ2	−0.02	0.10	0.04	101.35	57.33	0.08
HEALTHQ3	0.15	0.12	0.02	−2.41	64.59	0.04
HEALTHQ4	0.36	0.13	0.01	168.20	67.06	0.03
HEALTHQ5	0.31	0.15	0.01	350.23	72.91	0.02
AGE44Q2	0.17	0.13	0.03	28.01	88.41	0.03
AGE44Q3	0.08	0.12	0.04	143.33	82.34	0.04
AGE44Q4	0.14	0.12	0.05	124.17	82.40	0.04
AGE44Q5	0.24	0.12	0.04	219.53	82.29	0.04
AGE64Q2	0.28	0.11	0.05	−47.29	74.35	0.05
AGE64Q3	0.25	0.11	0.06	52.96	71.35	0.05
AGE64Q4	0.32	0.11	0.06	58.99	71.16	0.05
AGE64Q5	0.42	0.10	0.06	69.05	70.23	0.05
AGEOLDQ2	0.19	0.10	0.07	−4.16	64.58	0.09
AGEOLDQ3	0.05	0.11	0.03	−1.14	75.10	0.03
AGEOLDQ4	0.17	0.14	0.01	−0.48	90.43	0.01
AGEOLDQ5	0.23	0.14	0.01	−47.44	95.43	0.01
FEMALEQ2	−0.07	0.08	0.11	−63.55	50.45	0.13
FEMALEQ3	0.07	0.08	0.10	27.18	52.12	0.12

Table 14.A3. (*cont.*)

Variable	Probit estimate on pr (exp > 0)			OLS estimate on E (exp|exp > 0)		
	Coefficient	Standard error	Mean of X	Coefficient	Standard error	Mean of X
FEMALEQ4	−0.01	0.08	0.10	14.42	52.66	0.10
FEMALEQ5	0.01	0.08	0.09	51.34	52.58	0.09
Sample size		13 204			3938	

(a) *Log likelihoods for probit regression*
Unrestricted log-likelihood	−7340.8
Restricted (no income cross-products) log-likelihood	−7363.9
Restricted (no income only terms) log-likelihood	−7345.5
Restricted (no income terms) log-likelihood	−7364.0

(b) *Log-likelihoods for OLS regression*
Unrestricted log likelihood	−30 068.0
Restricted (no income cross-products) log-likelihood	30 096.0
Restricted (no income only terms) log-likelihood	−30 073.8
Restricted (no income terms) log-likelihood	−30 100.4

Tests for income effects

To test for income effects in this specification, an LR approach was used. The probit and OLS models were estimated using the full sample, allowing interactions between four of the income groups and the age, sex, and morbidity dummies plus four income group dummies (the autonomous terms). The test statistic for no income effects is twice the difference between the log likelihood of this model and that with no income terms included. This test statistic is distributed X^2_r under the null, where r is the number of income parameters. The restrictions that the autonomous terms equal zero and the interaction terms equal zero can also be tested separately. The relevant log likelihood statistics for the adult only sample are presented at the bottom of Table 14.A3.

15

United States

Peter Gottschalk and Barbara Wolfe

INTRODUCTION

This chapter aims to identify the distributional burdens of paying for health care in the US and the distribution of the beneficiaries of that system. Our focus on who pays and who benefits is motivated by two issues that have dominated discussions in the US in recent years: (1) the lack of universal insurance cover; and (2) the rapid increase in medical care costs that have led to medical expenditures accounting for more than 12 per cent of GNP. The thrust of much of this discussion is that high costs may have led to limited access for those who are not covered by public or private insurance. If it is the (non-elderly) lower-middle class that are caught between having incomes too high for public insurance but too low to afford private insurance then their access is limited by income. Added to this are those with low income not insured by public coverage, who are also likely to be caught. Furthermore, if public insurance is largely financed by the middle class, then they are the ones paying for the services they are the least likely to utilize.

The objective of this chapter is to determine whether the financing and utilization of the health care system in the US is distributed equitably. The US system is a combined public–private system with extensive use of private insurance and out-of-pocket payments relative to most European countries. We seek to determine whether this form of financing is associated with lower expenditures on the poor.

THE US HEALTH CARE SYSTEM

The US has experienced rapid growth in health care expenditures in the last three decades. In 1970, 7.4 per cent of GNP went to health care; in 1980, 9.1 per cent; and in 1990, 12.1 per cent. The rate of price increases has outpaced that of the overall price index continuously over this time period. A considerable number of people (perhaps 31 to 33 million) are without any health insurance. About half of these are not covered for

We are grateful to Alpay Fitzliken for providing outstanding computer assistance.

more than eight months and must, therefore, rely on general assistance, charity, and their own resources to pay for their care.

The US has a private–public system of financing medical care. The public share accounts for approximately 40 per cent of medical expenditures. The majority of the remaining 60 per cent is private insurance which is dominated by employer-based insurance cover. The largest public programme is Medicare, which accounts for approximately 17 per cent of all expenditures, or 42 per cent of public expenditures. This programme covers groups older than 64, some disabled, and those in the end-stage of renal disease. The hospital component of this programme is financed largely through payroll tax contributions. Cover of physician care is financed through premiums and general revenues. The premium is based on projected outlays. Nearly 60 per cent of Medicare's payments go to hospitals; 28 per cent to physicians, but very little to long-term care. Since 1983–4, hospitals have been reimbursed for treating Medicare patients by a prospective payment scheme (diagnostic-related groups). As of 1992, a new system of fees for providers compensates them according to a relative value scale.

Medicaid is the other large public programme for medical care. This covers certain low-income groups including those eligible for other welfare programmes, such as single parents and low-income elderly. It now also covers pregnant women and children under 6 years old with incomes under 155 per cent of the poverty line, whether or not they are eligible for welfare. Children born after 1982 are covered if their family income is less than the poverty line. Medicaid is a joint federal–state matching entitlement programme. Eligibility for single parents and children is determined by each state. For the disabled and elderly, eligibility is determined by federal standards. Medicaid pays for about 10 per cent of all medical care expenditures in the US. Other public programmes, including veterans' insurance and health care for the military, cover some 14 per cent of the financing of medical care.

Because Medicare is available primarily to the elderly and Medicaid is largely focused on certain low-income groups, the non-elderly middle class, as well as some low-income people, are not well covered by public programmes, and must buy private health insurance, take the risk they will have to pay directly for health care services, or forgo access to the medical system.

In 1987, 81 per cent of private insurance was provided as a fringe benefit through employers. These benefits are subsidized by the tax system as they are not considered part of an individual's taxable income for payroll or income tax purposes. Insurance can be bought directly on the market, although at substantially higher premium than when it is provided by an employer.[1] Private insurance finances somewhat more than 30 per cent of all health care costs, and direct patient payments cover about 25 per cent of medical care costs. Thus, private payments cover a little more than half the health care costs in the US.

To view public and private programmes separately is, however, misleading as public programmes must be financed out of tax revenues and direct payments.[2] The Medicare programme is financed by: (1) payroll taxes on earnings up to a ceiling; (2) premiums paid by the insured; and (3) general revenues. Medicare also requires sizeable direct payments from patients for a share of physicians' bills, the first day of hospitalization, and hospitalization beyond 60 days. Medicaid is financed by a combination of federal and state general revenues with minimal direct payments by those covered by the programme.[3]

Gottschalk *et al.* (1989), proposed four goals for financing a system of medical care. These are: (1) induce a socially efficient level of health care utilization; (2) spread risk across people; (3) spread risk across a person's life; and (4) distribute resources according to need, where need reflects both health status and income. The four primary sources of revenue to finance medical care: income taxes; payroll taxes; direct payments; and insurance premiums, can be ranked according to their ability to achieve these goals. Direct payments rate highest in achieving efficiency in utilization. The income tax generally rates highest in achieving equity in terms of the distribution of health status and income although this depends on the tax structure. Payroll taxes are quite good at achieving risk-sharing as is the income tax.

PROGRESSIVITY OF HEALTH CARE FINANCE IN THE US

Table 15.1 shows the distribution of each source of revenue used to finance medical care in the US, as well as the distribution of overall financing.[4] In order to have a point of comparison, we compare the distribution of who pays for health care to the pre-tax distribution of income.[5]

Our allocation of income tax and payroll taxes by decile is derived from Pechman (1986). The incidence of the payroll tax is assigned to the employee. The premiums and direct payments are calculated from the US *National Medical Care Utilization and Expenditure Survey*. Direct payments are self-reported out-of-pocket payments for medical care. Premiums include out-of-pocket (direct premium) payments plus employer payments on behalf ot the employees. The full premium is allocated to the employee, consistent with the allocation of payroll taxes.

Comparing the distribution of total expenditures on medical care (across all sources) to pre-tax income, we find that the financing system

Table 15.1. Distribution of health care financing (percentage, 1981)

Income decile	Pre-tax income [1]	Income tax [2]	Indirect tax [3]	Payroll tax [4]	Direct payments [5]	Private premiums [6]	Total payments [7]
Bottom	1.3	0.4	2.8	0.5	8.9	2.6	3.7
2nd	2.8	1.0	5.0	1.5	10.3	4.1	4.9
3rd	4.2	2.0	6.3	3.5	8.8	6.0	5.6
4th	5.5	3.0	7.7	6.1	9.6	8.0	7.0
5th	7.0	4.6	9.1	8.9	9.5	10.3	8.5
6th	8.4	6.0	10.5	10.8	9.2	12.2	9.6
7th	9.9	8.1	11.6	12.6	9.3	13.4	10.7
8th	12.0	11.1	13.8	14.8	10.8	14.9	12.7
9th	15.1	15.7	15.0	18.1	11.7	14.9	14.6
Top	33.8	48.1	18.1	23.0	11.9	13.6	22.7
	100.0	100.0	100.0	100.0	100.0	100.0	100.0
Total revenue (%)		23.1	6.6	14.4	29.6	26.3	100.0
Linear approximations							
Index							
Gini/Conc.	0.4322	0.5942	0.2585	0.3974	0.0456	0.2372	0.2874
Kakwani		0.1620	−0.1737	−0.0348	−0.3866	−0.1950	−0.1448
Suits		0.1946	−0.2069	−0.0806	−0.3863	−0.2490	−0.1601

Notes:
[1] taken from Pechman (1986) tables 4–6, var 1c.
[2] = sum of personal income tax and corporate income tax taken from corrected Pechman, tables 4–10, var 1c, and applying effective rates.
[3] sales and excise taxes, corrected for tables 4–10, Pechman (1986).
[4] payroll taxes, corrected tables 4–10, var 1c, Pechman.
[5] and [6] from Gottschalk et al. (1989).
[7] macroweighted average of sources.

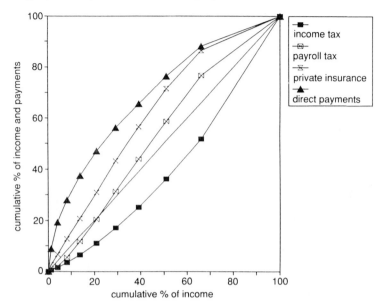

Fig. 15.1.   Progressivity of health care finance, US.

in the US is regressive. The proportion of health care costs paid by the lowest decile is substantially higher than the proportion of post-tax income it receives (3.7 per cent versus 1.3 per cent). At the other extreme, the highest decile pays 22.7 per cent of health care expenditures but receives 33.8 per cent of pre-tax income. Although these are the largest discrepancies between contributions to the health care system and income received, the pattern is regressive throughout the distribution—the proportion of expenditures paid by each of the lowest eight deciles is larger than the proportion of pre-tax income each receives.

Is the middle class the hardest hit by the financing mechanism in the US? The evidence in Table 15.1 suggests that, in fact, the poor bear the largest proportionate share of the costs. Although the lowest two deciles receive only 4.1 per cent of the pre-tax income, they bear 8.8 per cent of the cost. No other decile faces this 2:1 ratio.

Disaggregating the regressive pattern (see Fig. 15.1), we find that the substantial use of premiums and direct payments is responsible for much of the regressivity in the US—direct payments are distributed nearly equally across deciles, whereas income is not at all equally distributed. Income tax is the most progressive source of funding but accounts for only 23 per cent of health care revenues. Payroll tax is the next most progressive source of revenues, although the highest income decile pays only 23 per cent of the payroll tax, but receives nearly 34 per cent of income.

Progressivity index values confirm that income taxes are the most progressive source of funding, followed by payroll taxes, with direct payments being the least progressive. Private premiums and indirect taxes are intermediate, although they show a somewhat different pattern across deciles. Direct payments stand out in terms of having the largest (negative) Kakwani and Suits indices. If the share of direct payments was reduced or changed to an income-conditioned payment scheme, the progressivity of the US financing system would be increased.

EQUITY IN THE DELIVERY OF HEALTH CARE IN THE US

The previous section has shown who pays for health care in the US. In this section we focus on who uses the health care system. Again, we are interested in differences across the income distribution. Our underlying normative premise is that access for people with equal need should not depend on their incomes—two people with the same medical condition should have equal access to medical care, regardless of their financial status.[6]

Two measurement issues arise immediately in operationalizing this concept. First, it is necessary to define utilization in a way that takes account of the quality of care as well as its quantity—to know that low-income groups see medical personnel as often as those with high incomes is not very informative if low-income groups are seen by nurses aids but high-income groups have access to highly trained specialists. Secondly, one must define what is meant by equal need. Do high-income groups suffering from anxiety and low income groups suffering from malnutrition have equal needs? As we will show, neither measurement issue can be resolved completely with the available data.

As different conditions require utilization of different services, no single measure will completely describe utilization for people suffering from different conditions. The issue is, therefore, to identify the best available measure.

Data, variable definitions, and methodology

We measure the distribution of health care services from the *National Medical Care Utilization and Expenditure Survey* (NMCUES), conducted in 1980–1 by the National Center for Health Statistics. It is based on a sample of 6000 randomly selected households in the US. People were interviewed five times at approximately 3 monthly intervals over a 14 month period in 1980–1. Data were collected on health, health care service utilized, health care charges, sources of payment, and insurance cover. The primary sample we use is limited to persons 18 years and older. As NMCUES is a stratified random sample we use the sample weights in all of our calculations of summary statistics. The reported results are, therefore, representative of the US population aged 18 and over, as of 1980–1.

We measure utilization by the total charges for the services provided. As this measure captures the price as well as the amount of the service received, it has the advantaged of capturing quality as well as quantity. Alternatively, we could have used the number of visits to a provider or the number of nights hospitalized as measures of utilization. The disadvantage of these quantity measures is that they cannot be easily combined into a single index and that they do not take into account differences in intensity of usage—a visit to a provider may be a 5-minute return visit to check an injury or a complete 2 hour physical examination.

Although total charges have advantages, they also have drawbacks. Foremost, is the well known practice of physicians of prescribing procedures that have limited value to the patient. Inasmuch as these practices vary across income groups or by type of insurance, our measure will tend to over-state the services provided to groups more likely to be given services with low value (compared to their prices.) Less important are differences in charges across geographical areas. This is a problem if persons' locations differ systematically by income class. We assume they do not.[7]

We use two alternative measures of health status. The first measure is based on the answer to a question concerning health limitations. This measure has the advantage of being based on an objective condition—the health problem must have a direct impact on a person's activities. It is, therefore, less subjective than self-reported health status.[8] However, it does not distinguish between limitations—both a bad headache and a broken back may limit activities.

Our second measure of need is self-reported health. Interviewees are asked whether they would describe their health as excellent, good, poor, or fair. We use categories for poor health as well as for fair health. The drawback of this measure is that, inasmuch as people in different income categories are more likely to exaggerate their maladies, the bias in this measure of need will be correlated with income. The results in this chapter are, however, not sensitive to the choice between the use of health limitations or self-reported health status.

Unstandardized distribution of morbidity and health care

In order to gain a perspective on the distribution of utilization, we first turn to analyse the distribution of health limitations and morbidity or fair

Table 15.2. Unstandardized distribution of morbidity and expenditure (1980–1)

Income decile	Health limitations	Poor or fair health	Health care expenditures
	[1]	[2]	[3]
Bottom	0.214	0.244	0.15
2nd	0.162	0.183	0.15
3rd	0.125	0.125	0.10
4th	0.103	0.096	0.09
5th	0.086	0.085	0.10
6th	0.068	0.078	0.08
7th	0.064	0.058	0.08
8th	0.053	0.048	0.07
9th	0.057	0.046	0.09
Top	0.066	0.043	0.08
Conc. index	−0.244	−0.316	−0.115
HI_{LG}	0.129	0.202	

health. As would be expected, morbidity is concentrated most heavily in the lowest income groups.[9] (see Table 15.2). Using our primary definition of morbidity—the presence of a health condition that leads to a limitation —more than 20 per cent of those with such a condition are in the lowest income decile; more than 15 per cent of these are in the second decile; and more than 12 per cent are in the third income decile. By contrast, less than 7 per cent of those with limitations are in each of deciles 6 to 10. Using the alternative definition (those persons self-reporting poor or fair health on a scale of excellent, good, fair, or poor), those with poor or fair health are even more concentrated in the lower deciles of the income distribution. More than 24 per cent are in the lowest decile and 18 per cent in the second lowest decile. Less than 5 per cent are in each of the top four income deciles.[10] Thus, if expenditures were allocated only to those with poor or fair health, we would expect to see them heavily concentrated in the lower half of the income distribution. Medical utilization would be pro-poor in order to be directed toward those with poor health. The indices for these distributions (Table 15.2) suggest that poor or fair health is distributed more unequally than health limitations. The concentration index for morbidity or fair health is –0.316, that for health limitations is –0.244.

We next present data on the distribution of total medical expenses, which include outpatient visits, inpatient visits, and hospital stays. We do not include other types of care, such as dental treatment or prescribed

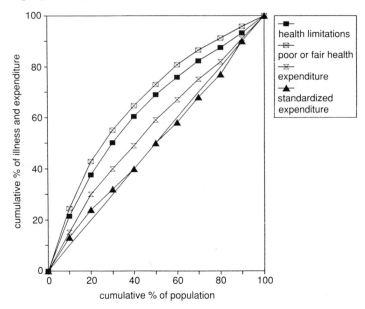

Fig. 15.2.   Inequity in the delivery of health care, US.

medicines. Including all types of care for all conditions has the advantage of being inclusive. However, such a comprehensive measure of utilization mixes people with very different needs who receive very different services. Therefore, in the following section we focus more narrowly on the distribution of expenditures on outpatient and inpatient care.

Table 15.2 and Fig. 15.2 show the results of our analysis of utilization across deciles. The distribution of unadjusted expenditures in column [3] or Table 15.2 shows that persons in the poorest deciles, particularly the first and second deciles, receive substantially more medical care (as measured by expenditures) than those in the other deciles. Expenditures in the third, fourth, fifth, and ninth deciles are approximately equal to their share of the adult population. The other deciles receive somewhat less medical care.

The pattern of greater relative use by those in the lowest two deciles is consistent with several interpretations. First, the US health care system may indeed be pro-poor. Alternatively, the lowest deciles may contain a disproportionate number of elderly persons, who tend to be higher users of medical care, or poor health and low income may be correlated even among the non-elderly. If the observed pattern in column [3] or Table 15.2 reflects greater needs among those in the lowest deciles, then one should not conclude that the US health care system provides greater services to the poor than to the non-poor with equal needs.

Table 15.3. Distribution of expenditures (percentage, adults only)

Income decile	Adult population[1]	Expenditures	
		Adjustment for age and gender[2]	Adjustment for age, gender, and health limitations
	[1]	[2]	[3]
Bottom	10.9	15	13
2nd	10.3	13	11
3rd	10.1	9	8
4th	9.9	8	8
5th	9.6	10	10
6th	9.4	8	8
7th	9.6	9	10
8th	9.4	8	9
9th	10.4	12	13
Top	10.4	8	9
Conc. index		−0.067	−0.005

Notes: [1] Deciles defined in terms of all persons, including persons less than 18.
[2] The four age groups are: 18–34, 35–44, 45–64, and 65+.

We turn to these issues below. As we have already documented that poor health is not equally distributed, we now wish to control for health (and age) in analysing the distribution of medical expenditures. We also include gender, because utilization frequently differs by gender, especially for women during child-bearing years. We do this in two ways. First, we use a standardized distribution of age and gender and then age, gender, and health status by decile. We then control for health, gender, and age by using regression analysis.

Standardized expenditure distributions

In Table 15.3 we calculate the distribution of expenditures across deciles for a group of people of similar age, gender, and health status (as defined by health limitations). Column [1] serves as the benchmark. It shows the distribution of adults across deciles.[11]

In column [2] we adjust for age and gender in order to hold the demographic composition of the population constant in each decile. We standardize for eight demographic groups—males and females in each of four age groups.[12] The average expenditures in each decile for each of these eight demographic groups are aggregated by using a common set of weights that reflect the demographic composition across all deciles. In essence, we calculate the average expenditures which would have been observed if all deciles had had the same age-gender composition.

As expected, taking the differences in the age and gender composition of the deciles into account reduces the pro-poor patterns found in Table 15.2, column [3]—the standardization reduces the relative use of medical care of those in the second decile and increases the relative use of those in three of the five highest income deciles, particularly the ninth decile. The net result is that the ninth as well as the first and second deciles now receive 12–15 per cent of expenditures, although containing only marginally more than 10 per cent of the adult population.

This standardization adjusts for differences in utilization across demographic groups but not within groups. In order to adjust further for differences in needs within demographic groups, we standardize the utilization patterns of the deciles by modifying the composition of each decile to reflect the overall composition of the population in terms of age, gender, and health status. The adjustment for differences in health-related limitations does cause substantial changes in the distribution of utilization. The first decile still receives marginally more than its share of expenditures but the second decile is now nearly in line with other deciles. The largest outlier is the ninth decile, which receives 13 per cent of all expenditures while containing 10.4 per cent of the adult population. These calculations imply that adults with health problems severe enough to limit their activities are indeed concentrated in the two lowest deciles. Therefore, much of the additional expenditures on health problems of the poor do not reflect greater access for equal need but rather greater need among low-income groups.

Adjusting for age and gender reduces inequality in the utilization of medical resources by more than half. The adjustment for age, gender, and health goes further and essentially shows an equal distribution of medical care finding across the income distribution (see the standardized expenditure concentration curve of Fig. 15.2).

In summary, these results suggest that: (1) the observed expenditures on medical care are highest among the lowest deciles; (2) adjusting for age and gender substantially equalizes utilization but still leaves a pro-poor pattern; (3) adjusting for health-related limitations or self-reported poor health within demographic groups substantially reduces any pro-poor bias. Thus, the poor do receive more services,but this reflects the disproportionate number of elderly persons who are poor and the disproportionate number of persons within a demographic group who experience health-related limitations.

Regression approaches

In this section, we present two alternative regression approaches to determining whether utilization is approximately equally distributed among the non-elderly population after taking 'need' into account. Our focus on people aged 18 to 65 is motivated by the general availability of public insurance (Medicare) for the elderly, which tends to equalize utilization across the income distribution. As we will show, medical expenditures are fairly equally distributed in the US even when this group is excluded. For comparability with other country studies we also present results for all persons (including the elderly) in the Appendix.

The two regression approaches differ in their methods of controlling for income. The first focuses on persons classified by quintile. It is provided for comparability with other country studies in this volume. The second method uses a continuous income variable and controls for insurance coverage, which is particularly important for the US.

The first method divides the adult population of the US into five groups or quintiles—determined on the basis of equivalent income going from lowest incomes to highest. For each quintile, we run a two-part regression model consisting of a logit and an ordinary least squares (OLS) equation. The variables included in the two-part model are two dummy variables for age groups (18–34 and 35–44), with those aged 45–64 as the excluded group; a dummy variable for gender (female); and three measures of health status (dummy variables for health poor, health fair, and health limitations).

The regression results for the entire sample and for each of the quintiles are reported in Table 15.4.[13] Below the set of coefficients is the expected expenditure on medical care for persons with positive expenditures in each quintile, the estimated probability of positive medical expenditure, and the expected expenditures for all persons, whether they had expenditures or not.[14] These are standardized values per quintile, calculated using the quintile-specific coefficients and the total sample means. The standardized expenditures, shown in Table 15.5 column [3], can be contrasted with the unstandardized expenditures, shown in column [4].[15] Columns [5] and [6] show the resulting distribution of standardized and unstandardized expenditures.

Once the standardization is carried out, income makes less of a difference in determining medical care use. The U-shaped profile is still apparent because the two highest average expenditures are the top and bottom income quintiles (U$840 and U$796, respectively.) The bottom income quintile accounts for nearly 23 per cent of expenditures; the top grows to nearly 24 per cent, whereas the intervening deciles account for 16, 18, and nearly 19 per cent, respectively. If there is any inequity due to income, it

Table 15.4. Calculation of mean standardized expenditure per quintile using the two-part regression model (Adults 18–64 only)

Regression coefficient	Whole sample		Quintile 1		Quintile 2		Quintile 3		Quintile 4		Quintile 5	
	Logit	OLS	Logit	OLS	Logit	OLS	Logit	OLS	Logit	OLS	Logit	OLS
Constant	1.3825	493.72	0.9127	822.73	1.3739	265.58	1.5418	403.66	1.4659	447.46	1.3955	636.72
Age 18–34	0.0151	−29.74	−0.3003	−136.20	0.1688	228.89	−0.1015	43.83	−0.0838	−77.06	−0.0862	−239.07
Age 35–44	−0.0592	−91.22	−0.5024	263.35	−0.0030	195.46	0.0243	−22.57	−0.3506	−120.48	−0.0772	−467.30
Female	0.6724	82.20	−0.9077	−113.88	0.6288	47.02	0.6637	222.67	0.7542	114.30	0.5448	90.94
Health poor	0.7340	1530.82	0.7915	458.64	1.7238	1910.94	0.4847	1064.57	0.8423	3080.16	0.2139	3950.09
Health fair	0.4354	434.60	0.4822	178.52	0.2739	452.80	0.4078	524.99	0.6801	229.71	0.8866	956.62
Health limitations	0.6229	571.04	0.5627	708.74	0.4045	374.55	0.8420	351.88	0.4015	592.95	1.2351	833.58
Exp. cond. expendit.		745.76		923.70		642.64		725.62		748.19		957.77
Pred. prob. pos. expendit.	0.8742		0.8614		0.8781		0.8890		0.8764		0.8774	
Expected expendit.		651.97		795.63		569.89		645.09		655.68		840.33
Log likelihood	−3390.9	−69 688.4	−491.1	−11 487.4	−601.3	−13 047.5	−656.2	−14 008.8	−759.9	−14 153.1	−866.5	−16 413.9
Sample means												
No. of observations	8813	7618	1379	1208	1648	1443	1793	1568	1896	1621	2097	1778
Constant	1.0000	1.0000	1.0000	1.0000	1.0000	1.0000	1.0000	1.0000	1.0000	1.0000	1.0000	1.0000
Age 18–34	0.4634	0.4604	0.4989	0.4934	0.5243	0.5232	0.4902	0.4821	0.4525	0.4534	0.3791	0.3740
Age 35–44	0.1784	0.1768	0.1066	0.1109	0.1305	0.1289	0.1701	0.1716	0.2268	0.2190	0.2265	0.2267
Female	0.5475	0.5698	0.6490	0.6738	0.5892	0.6071	0.5265	0.5466	0.5216	0.5484	0.4893	0.5090
Health poor	0.0443	0.0487	0.1197	0.1283	0.0540	0.0603	0.0351	0.0383	0.0185	0.0204	0.0181	0.0202
Health fair	0.1027	0.1095	0.2118	0.2210	0.1220	0.1261	0.0943	0.1001	0.0728	0.0796	0.0501	0.0557
Health limitations	0.1842	0.1977	0.3401	0.3576	0.2197	0.2308	0.1601	0.1728	0.1287	0.1370	0.1245	0.1395

Table 15.5. Distribution of unstandardized and standardized expenditure using the two-part regression model (Adults 18–64 only)

Income quintile	No. in quintile	Population (%)	Standardized expendit. per pers.	Unstandardized expendit. per pers.	Standardized expendit. (%)	Unstandardized expendit. (%)
	[1]	[2]	[3]	[4]	[5]	[6]
Bottom	1379	15.65	795.63	943.47	22.69	28.25
2nd	1648	18.70	569.89	618.10	16.25	18.50
3rd	1793	20.34	645.09	616.27	18.40	18.45
4th	1896	21.51	655.68	528.60	18.70	15.82
Top	2097	23.79	840.33	633.85	23.96	18.98
Whole sample	8813		651.97	651.97	100.00	100.00

appears to be the lower use of those in the lower-middle class. However, the difference is small. This group that receives 16.2 per cent of expenditures comprises 18.7 per cent of the population.[16]

Finally, we test explicitly for differences in expenditures across income groups by comparing the results of the regression models reported above to a more restricted model that imposes equality of coefficients across income groups. This is equivalent to comparing a two-part model using all variables in the model interacted with four quintile dummy variables to one that does not include any measure of income (or where the coefficients on the income terms are restricted to be zero). The test applied is a likelihood ratio test.'[17] The resulting test value, which is distributed asymptotically as a chi-squared random variable, is 1187.42, which is much larger than 43.2, the critical value of the chi-square distribution with 56 degrees of freedom. This suggests that the roughly U-shaped profile did not occur by chance.

Additional analyses

The logit and OLS specifications used are general in the sense that they impose no specific functional form on the income variable across quintiles. For example, it could have resulted that the lowest quintile and third quintile received the highest expenditures, whereas the second and fifth received the lowest expenditures. This type of saw-tooth pattern would be difficult to capture with a specific functional form. The specification is, however, restrictive because it assumes that all people within a decile receive the same expenditures. There are discrete jumps in expenditures between the person at the top of one decile and the lowest person in the next decile. Similarly the use of age categories implies constancy in expenditures within an age group, followed by discrete jumps when a person enters a new age group.

An alternative specification that avoids these discrete jumps is a polynomial in income needs and age. The results in Table 15.4 suggest that a quadratic will be sufficient to capture the shape of the expenditure profile. Columns [1] and [2] of Table 15.7 present the logit and OLS coefficients for a specification with quadratics in income/needs and age. Again, the significant coefficients on the income terms suggest that the profile is U-shaped, with the lowest expenditures occurring for a person in a family with income roughly five times the poverty level, which puts them in the top quintile.

The analysis above excludes the role of insurance, a factor thought to be important in creating inequity in medical care use. For example, Karen Davis (Chapter 18) suggests that among low-income groups, those with insurance consume medical care at a rate equal to that of higher income

Table 15.6. Likelihood ratio test of model restrictions
(Adults 18–64 only)

Model	LLLogit	LLOLS	LLSum	LR	r	χ^2 (P = 0.05)
1	−3374.9	−69110.7	−72485.6			
2	−3390.9	−69688.4	−73079.3	1187.42	56	43.2

Table 15.7. Regression specification with continuous variables and insurance cover

	Logit	OLS	Logit	OLS
	[1]	[2]	[3]	[4]
Constant	2.163	913.178	2.359	1032.510
	(7.06)	(3.64)	(7.60)	(4.10)
Age	−0.048	−15.259	−0.050	−16.244
	(3.03)	(1.19)	(3.13)	(1.26)
Age^2	0.001	0.240	0.001	0.246
	(3.03)	(1.53)	(3.08)	(1.57)
Female	0.692	85.281	0.685	79.655
	(10.80)	(1.60)	(10.67)	(1.49)
Income/Needs	0.032	−122.554	−0.014	−150.155
	(0.60)	(2.76)	(0.25)	(3.35)
(Income/Needs)^2	−0.002	12.695	0.002	15.017
	(0.29)	(2.66)	(0.38)	(0.00)
Health limitations	0.841	944.613	0.836	943.464
	(7.97)	(13.56)	(7.93)	(13.56)
No insurance			−0.562	−463.988
			(5.03)	(−4.20)
No. of obs.	8813	7618	8813	7618˙
Log likelihood	−3395.2	−69748.3	−3383.5	−69739.5

Notes: *t*-statistics in parentheses.

groups, but that uninsured low-income groups consume far less medical care.

One of the unique characteristics of the US health care system is that a significant percentage of the population (perhaps 33 million) is uninsured. About half of these persons are without insurance for a period of a few months. About 7 per cent of the adult population aged less than 65 are likely to be uninsured for an entire year or more.[18] Those with extended periods without insurance may be the most likely to have low medical care utilization.

Columns [3] and [4] of Table 15.7 show estimates for the continuous income model with a dummy variable added which is equal to 1 if the person was not covered by public or private insurance at any point in the year. The logit results provide evidence that those without insurance coverage are less likely to have used any medical care over a one year period and the OLS results show that the uninsured who do receive treatment have lower expenditures.

Overall, then, these results suggest that persons without health insurance are less likely to use medical care and tend to have lower medical expenditures when they do use medical care. (These results also control for age and health status.) The results for income are robust to these two alternative specifications.

CONCLUSIONS

This chapter has discussed the distribution of financing and of utilization of medical care by the US population. We found that the financing is regressive. This primarily reflects the heavy reliance on two sources of revenue: direct payments and premiums for private cover. The inequity we found is not focused on the middle class but rather on the poor—it is the lowest deciles that pay the highest proportion of their income on medical services.

The results of our standardizing procedure provide evidence that after controlling for age, gender, and health status, income makes a difference in determining expenditures on medical care. The bottom and top quintiles have the highest expected expenditures, suggesting the role of income is non-linear.

In terms of utilization, we found that medical care is fairly equal across the income distribution once we adjust for the differences in age and gender. Perhaps more surprising is that after adjusting for health status, the poor do not receive less than their share of health care funding. Our regression results for the adult population aged between 18 and 65 suggest that those with low incomes have greater expenditures than those with higher incomes, and that those with incomes around five times the poverty line have the lowest expenditures on medical care. Our regressions on this population also suggest that those with health limitations or poor or fair health have significantly larger expenditures.

Given the very regressive nature of direct or out-of-pocket payments in the US, we also explored the role of insurance cover in determining medical care expenditures. In these estimates, we find that among adults, the lack of insurance is an important determinant of both the probability of any use of medical care as well as the amount of use. The relationship between income and the probability of use and amount of use is unchanged with the inclusion of insurance cover in the model. This is the case even though those without any cover tend to be in the lower part of the income distribution and to pay a disproportionately large share of direct payments relative to their income.

We conclude then that the two factors important in determining medical care expenditures in the US are health status and insurance cover. That these are important is not at all surprising. However, the finding that income is not a major determinant of these expenditures is somewhat surprising.

NOTES

1. By setting up a risk pool of all employees, employers can avoid the adverse selection of a disproportionate number of persons with high expected health care costs who would have greater incentive to join an insurance plan.
2. Furthermore, private insurance policies are subsidized by the tax system.
3. Medicaid tends to reimburse providers at lower rates than Medicare, which itself, in general, reimburses at lower rates than private insurance coverage. This differential payment schedule is also believed to influence access to medical care. The elderly fear that the new payment schedule (RVRVS) will also decrease their access to medical care.
4. The total expenditures for medical care and the basic categories of expenditures (direct payments, private insurance, social insurance, and total taxes) are from the Health Care Financing Review. The breakdown for taxes is based on Pechman's unpublished Table 1, entitled 'Effective rates of federal, state, and local taxes', combined with information on expenditures by category from the Health Care Financing Administration. The distributions are based on Pechman's table 1 and tabulations of the *National Medical Care Utilization and Expenditure Survey*. The weighted composition of indirect taxes is from Pechman (1985, table 2–3). The distribution of these indirect taxes are again from Pechman's unpublished Table 1. These allocations are approximate, as indirect taxes vary across states that have very different income distributions.
5. In this analysis, we use family income in order to be consistent with the distribution used by Pechman (1985) for taxes. If we used instead family income adjusted for needs (by the official poverty lines), inequality as measured by the Gini coefficient would differ by only 0.008.
6. This normative criterion is less ambitious than the goal of achieving equal health, but more ambitious than achieving a minimum level of health for those with the same condition.
7. Charges also have the disadvantage of possibly reflecting a pricing strategy that leads to higher prices in the future. This is only a problem if these pricing strategies differ systematically with the patient's income. Again, we assume they do not.

8. This measure is defined as having a condition other than pregnancy, dislocation, sprain or strain that causes a limitation.

9. This expectation stems from the observation that those with poor health or limitations tend to have reduced earnings compared to their able-bodied peers.

10. If we include only those with poor health, they are even more concentrated in the lower income deciles. In this case, the concentration ratio is –0.411.

11. If the persons less than 18 years old had been uniformly distributed across deciles, all entries in column [1] would be 0.1. Entries less than 0.1 indicate that excluding persons less than 18 years old withdrew a disproportionate number of people from that decile.

12. The age groups are: 18–34, 35–44, 45–64, and over 64.

13. The sample includes persons aged 18 to 64.

14. Expected expenditures (the unconditional mean) is the product of of the probability of expenditures and the conditional mean.

15. As the average expenditures received by persons in the highest quintile is an average across all persons in that quintile, expenditures could continue to fall in the bottom of the fifth quintile (the average would be raised by persons higher in the quintile). The results in the model with continuous measures of income (presented in the next section) indicate that the bottom of the U-shaped profile does occur in the top quintile.

16. The reason there is not exactly 20 per cent of the population in each quintile is that persons of all ages were used to construct quintiles. If persons younger than 18 years and older than 64 years were included in the analysis, there would be exactly 20 per cent in each quintile.

17. This test is $-2(\ln L_1 - \ln L_2)$, where the log likelihood function of the two-part model is the sum of the log likelihoods of the logit and OLS regressions. L_1 (the log likelihood of the unrestricted model with the quintile interactions) is then simply the sum of these log likelihoods for each of the five quintiles. It is model 1 in Table 15.6. L_2 is the log likelihood function of the restricted model or model 2.

18. In our adult sample, 7 per cent reported that they were not insured for an entire year.

Appendix

Table 15.A1. Calculation of mean standardized expenditures per quintile using two-part regression model (All adults)

Regression coefficient	Whole sample		Quintile 1		Quintile 2		Quintile 3		Quintile 4		Quintile 5	
	Logit	OLS	Logit	OLS	Logit	OLS	Logit	OLS	Logit	OLS	Logit	OLS
Constant	1.6764	1133.67	1.6662	1469.63	1.8502	908.80	1.6494	1307.41	1.3277	1435.52	1.6006	1102.86
Age 18–34	−0.2576	−622.80	−0.3392	−661.99	−0.2893	−394.34	−0.1971	−885.78	0.0525	−1021.61	−0.2819	−666.46
Age 35–44	−0.3310	−686.11	−0.1019	−267.95	−0.4693	−423.64	−0.0648	−970.20	−0.2165	−1072.81	−0.2704	−887.08
Age 45–64	−0.2682	−592.73	−0.6427	−504.19	−0.4751	−636.45	−0.0627	−988.93	0.1670	−979.08	−0.1939	−420.59
Female	0.6190	−3.74	0.6992	−258.09	0.5339	4.99	0.6509	207.51	0.7380	12.31	0.5318	19.97
Health poor	0.6433	1521.74	0.7844	890.83	1.4177	1895.31	0.0626	820.82	0.9037	2748.41	0.4986	3913.33
Health fair	0.4431	335.58	0.5112	63.18	0.3627	352.13	0.3170	670.55	0.6477	−94.23	0.7147	1034.20
Health limitations	0.6539	657.93	0.4434	568.31	0.6665	470.47	0.7932	703.55	0.5483	982.77	1.1516	764.65
Exp. cond. expendit.		1090.64		1022.37		792.56		965.97		1003.72		1174.66
Pred. prob. pos. expendit.	0.8842		0.8732		0.8912		0.8937		0.8841		0.8879	

Table 15.A1. (*cont.*)

Regression coefficient	Whole sample		Quintile 1		Quintile 2		Quintile 3		Quintile 4		Quintile 5	
	Logit	OLS	Logit	OLS	Logit	OLS	Logit	OLS	Logit	OLS	Logit	OLS
Expected expendit.		964.33		945.13		706.33		863.32		887.43		1042.94
Log likelihood	−3818.3	−84 685.4	−692.4	−18 383.5	−701.7	−16 712.6	−717.2	−16 219.3	−796.3	−15 623.1	−894.5	−17 310.3
Sample means												
No. of observations	10 396	9077	2137	1909	2058	1824	1994	1751	2013	1726	2194	1867
Constant	1.0000	1.0000	1.0000	1.0000	1.0000	1.0000	1.0000	1.0000	1.0000	1.0000	1.0000	1.0000
Age 18–34	0.3928	0.3864	0.3220	0.3122	0.4198	0.4139	0.4408	0.4318	0.4262	0.4258	0.3624	0.3562
Age 35–44	0.1512	0.1484	0.0688	0.0702	0.1045	0.1020	0.1530	0.1536	0.2136	0.2057	0.2165	0.2159
Age 45–64	0.2904	0.2912	0.2330	0.2279	0.2575	0.2566	0.2919	0.2964	0.2956	0.3024	0.3710	0.3744
Female	0.5547	0.5742	0.6537	0.6700	0.5753	0.5883	0.5226	0.5414	0.5251	0.5510	0.4954	0.5147
Health poor	0.0576	0.0629	0.1315	0.1393	0.0671	0.740	0.0446	0.0474	0.0209	0.0232	0.0223	0.0252
Health fair	0.1263	0.1345	0.2405	0.2499	0.1419	0.1486	0.1093	0.1154	0.0800	0.0875	0.0583	0.0643
Health limitations	0.2279	0.2442	0.4057	0.4222	0.2643	0.2813	0.1896	0.2027	0.1396	0.1501	0.1363	0.1521

Table 15.A2. Distribution of unstandardized and standardized expenditure using two-part regression model (All adults)

Income quintile	No. in quintile	Population (%)	Standardized expendit. per pers.	Unstandardized expendit. per pers.	Standardized expendit. (%)	Unstandardized expendit. (%)
	[1]	[2]	[3]	[4]	[5]	[6]
Bottom	2137	20.56	945.13	1331.84	20.04	26.72
2nd	2058	19.80	706.33	937.15	16.27	18.80
3rd	1994	19.18	863.32	1019.83	20.92	20.46
4th	2013	19.36	887.43	853.75	21.27	17.13
Top	2194	21.10	1042.94	841.39	21.50	16.88
Whole sample	10396			964.33	100.00	100.00

Table 15.A3.   Likelihood ratio test of model restrictions
(All adults)

Model	LLlogit	LLOLS	LLsum	LR	r	χ^2 ($P = 0.05$)
1	−3802.2	−84 248.8	−88 051.0			
2	−3818.3	−84 685.4	−88 503.7	905.34	64	93.9

Part III

Reflections on equity in health care

16

Equity in health care: the role of ideology

Alan Williams

INTRODUCTION

According to my dictionary an ideology is 'a body of ideas, usually political and/or economic, forming the basis of a national or sectarian policy'. It usually also has a visionary characteristic, i.e., it is about the nature of a 'good' society, and it defines something to strive for, even though we do not expect ever to see it fully attained.

The notion of a good society that economists seem to be striving for is one that is both efficient and equitable. Being *efficient* means: (1) that no activity is undertaken unless the benefits gained outweigh the benefits foregone; (2) that the benefits foregone through the pursuit of any activity are kept to a minimum; and (3) that the mix of activities pursued is the one that maximizes the excess of benefits gained over benefits foregone. Being *equitable* means that the distribution of benefits gained and benefits foregone should be a just one, and should be reached by a method that is held to be fair (which usually means a method characterized by the impartial application of mutually agreed principles, although I do not intend to pursue this issue further here, important though it undoubtedly is).

Economists typically recognize that at the margin, society will face a trade-off between efficiency and equity, i.e., it will have reached a point where it has exhausted the possibilities open to it for improving both simultaneously. It will then have to judge whether, in the particular situation in which it finds itself, some equity should be sacrificed for the sake of efficiency, or vice versa.

There is a big difference of opinion amongst economists from here on, however, about what their proper professional role is. Some believe that we have no special expertise that is relevant to equity issues, and that we should therefore limit ourselves to the efficiency calculus and let others deal with equity issues and the equity–efficiency trade-off (if it exists). At the other extreme are those who would absorb equity issues into the efficiency calculus by eliciting equity weights, to be applied to benefits gained or benefits foregone according to who gains or loses them. In the middle are those who see their role as exploring the empirical implications of various concepts of equity, and estimating their respective efficiency costs in the particular situation under study.

Although I always advise my students to take up the latter position, I myself pursue the more adventurous second one. This is partly because the economists' notion of efficiency already contains within it a frequently unacknowledged equity principle, namely (in the strictest version, seldom applied in practice), that so long as there are no net losers and at least one net gainer from any change, that change is efficient *because it does not matter who the gainers are*. (In the less strict version, gainers have only hypothetically to be able to compensate losers for the change to be efficient, so the accompanying equity principle has to become correspondingly stronger, for it now has to say that *it does not matter who the gainers or losers are*). If you see 'efficiency' as already containing one particular notion of equity, then the efficiency–equity trade-off is better seen as a choice between one equity principle (the Paretian one) and some other equity principle (for which competitive role the candidates are legion!). So if what we are seeking is an alternative principle to displace the Paretian equity principle, it had better do so right where the Paretian equity principle already is, namely *inside* the efficiency calculus. Hence, I am a 'grand efficiency' person myself.

This COMAC-HSR project, on the other hand, is clearly motivated by a desire to contribute to what I called the middle position on the equity–efficiency trade-off, namely, to explore the implications of a particular (non-Paretian) equity principle. This could be a useful counterweight to the common preoccupation with efficiency issues when health care reforms are being discussed, but by itself it is nevertheless incomplete. To obtain a balanced picture both need to be appraised.

Against this background, my plan of campaign in this Chapter is, first of all, to explore alternative ideological positions and the kind of equity principles they generate, and to locate this particular project in that intellectual space. Then I shall characterize the kind of health care systems that would be consistent with two particular ideological stances, and suggest some tests that might be used to classify actual systems accordingly. Finally, I will offer a few suggestions about how the very impressive empirical data generated by this project might be used in ways that go beyond its present central concern.

IDEOLOGY AND EQUITY

It is clear that in the context in which this project is operating 'equity' means 'distributive justice'. As such, it draws upon Aristotle's formal principle of justice, namely, that equals should be treated equally, and unequals unequally in proportion to the relevant inequalities. The problem with this proposition as it stands is that it lacks substance until such time as: (1) the relevant inequalities have been defined; (2) an appropriate measurement method agreed; and (3) the exact proportionality rule established. So by itself it does not carry us very far.

Of the possible ideological stances which could generate substantive content for Aristotle's framework, the following candidates seem worth considering and here I am drawing heavily upon Gillon (1986):

Libertarian—emphasizes respect for individual liberty (including the right to life and to personal property).

Utilitarian—emphasizes total welfare (with a just aggregation rule, such as that everyone should count for one and nobody for more than one).

Marxist—emphasizes the meeting of needs, and, when allied with 'from each according to his ability', is held to be a strong egalitarian position.

Rawlsian—emphasizes the position of the least well-off, and holds that inequalities are unjust unless they work to the advantage of the least well-off.

Desert—emphasizes the reward of merit (those that do the most good, or have behaved in the most meritorious manner, should get the most).

It is obviously possible to blend these different stances together in various interesting ways. For instance, the reward-of-merit stance plus a libertarian position would lead one to hold as just the rich hanging on to their well-gotten gains. A more interesting blend in the present context is that of the utilitarian and Marxist positions. If the Marxist notion of 'need' for health care were to be determined through a social judgement about each person's capacity to benefit from health care, and the unit in which benefit is measured is common to all beneficiaries (e.g., years of life-expectancy), then a combination of the Utilitarian and Marxist positions would lead us to the view that equity simply requires us to maximize the benefits from (=satisfy the need for) health care. In other words, if we are efficient we are automatically equitable. From this ideological position, therefore, the equity–efficiency trade-off disappears.

However, to pursue the above argument it was necessary both to assign a particular meaning to need and to require the use of a common unit of benefit (be it life-years, quality-adjusted-life-years, or units of value cast in ECUs or some 'sovereign' currency!) which did not vary with the identity of the person getting it. It is not clear to me whether this could properly be held to reflect the utilitarian stance on equity, which postulates 'everyone counting for one and nobody for more than one'. Does this postulate mean that a life-year is a life-year, no matter who gets it, or does it mean that it is the rest of a person's life which is to count as one, no matter how long or short or how humane or brutish the rest of a person's life may be?

The characteristic stance of Paretian welfare economics, with its focus on valuations derived from willingness-and-ability-to-pay and expressed in money terms, is that it is not the *people* who count equally, but what they get. The system is neutral between people. In this context, if an equity–efficiency trade-off is being postulated, it could be that what is being asserted is that equity requires benefit valuations to vary according to who gets or loses the benefits, and to do this some other ideology than the utilitarian must be appealed to as a source of guidance about distributive justice.

It is clear to me that in the COMAC-HSR project it is the Marxist ideology which provides that source, but not in the particular interpretation I gave to it earlier. The principle to which appeal is made is still 'from each according to his ability, to each according to his need'. Ability is associated with income, and need with illness. Note that this latter association is different from need being associated with capacity to benefit. The assumption is that the more ill a person is, the more resources should be devoted to that person (irrespective of the effect of those resources on that person's health . . . i.e., ignoring considerations of efficiency). This is defensible if the purpose is to go on and discuss equity–efficiency trade-offs, or if efficiency objectives are held to be of no significance, but it leaves me rather uneasy.

I would be happier if the egalitarian impulses were to be directed either at the distribution of the *benefits* of health care (measured in *health* terms such as quality-adjusted-life-years gained), or at the distribution of the 'stock' of health within the community (e.g., at quality-adjusted-life-expectancy, or even at age-at-death). I am sure that these distinctions are appreciated by the COMAC-HSR group, but there is a tendency to apply the term 'inequitable' to any situation in which the distribution of health care resources between income groups is correlated in any way with income, once age, sex, and illness have been controlled for. Incidentally, controlling for age, sex, and illness before declaring a distribution of resources to be 'inequitable' implies that it is *not* inequitable to discriminate by age, sex, or illness when allocating health care resources.

A more specific reservation flows from the squeezing out of a rather important possibility, which has its origins more in a Rawlsian than in a Marxist ideology, namely that equity is satisfied if the worst-off in society are provided with a decent basic minimum level of health care. Those who hold such a view would argue that we do not really need to worry about who gets what across the entire spectrum, because there is no *general* aversion to inequality, all we need concern ourselves with is the extent of *deprivation* at one extreme of the distribution. This was mentioned early on in the project protocol as a possibility that might be worth exploring in some countries, but it now seems to have disappeared without trace.

The justification for the concentration on the single issue of whether income makes a difference to how much health care people get (after controlling for certain selected other things) is essentially that that is a commonly expressed objective, both in the statutes that ostensibly control public health care systems, and in the political rhetoric which dominates debates about health service policy. Clearly, this precise rhetoric has stronger appeal in some countries than in others, and one way of looking at the project would be to say that its prime objective is *not* (as I have been assuming) to assist in identifying the efficiency–equity trade-off, but rather to test the extent to which the political rhetoric is matched by the actual achievement. If so, I am not sure precisely what the hypothesis is. Is it that the stronger the rhetoric the greater should be the achieved equity, or is it rather that the greater is the actual inequity on the ground the stronger the rhetoric about equity is likely to be in public debate? The statement in the project protocol ducks this issue, and simply says: 'Establishing the extent of . . . *income-related inequity* is thus accepted as one of the principal objectives of empirical research in this area'. But the decent basic minimum approach (from Rawls) is also addressing a possible income-related inequity, and should not be excluded from the agenda, especially when the purposes of the project are cast in purely exploratory terms.

IDEOLOGY AND HEALTH CARE SYSTEMS

In order to simplify the exposition from here on I am going to concentrate on just two broad ideological positions. The first, viewpoint A, is a combination of the libertarian and desert ideologies, and despite the risk of generating avoidable confusion, will simply be called the libertarian viewpoint. The second, viewpoint B, is mostly Marxist (with some Rawls [?]), and will be called the egalitarian viewpoint. The third member of the famous trio of *Liberté, Egalité, Fraternité* seems to have got lost somewhere along the way! In the analysis which follows I have once more drawn heavily on Donabedian (1971), as well upon my own earlier writings with and without my immediate colleagues Culyer and Maynard (Culyer *et al.* 1981; Maynard and Williams 1984; and Williams 1988).

In the libertarian view, access to health care is part of the society's reward system, and, at the margin at least, people should be able to use their income and wealth to get more or better health care than their fellow citizens should they so wish. In the egalitarian view, access to health care is every citizen's right (like access to the ballot box or to the courts of justice), and this ought not to be influenced by income or wealth. Each of these broad viewpoints is typically associated with a distinctive configuration of views on personal responsibility, social concern (*fraternité* [?]), freedom, and equality. These are set out in Table 16.1.

Each of these broad viewpoints would generate a distinctive health care system whose characteristics would be very different from each other. In the libertarian system, willingness and ability to pay would be the determinant of access, and this would best be accomplished in a market-orientated 'private' system (provided such markets can be kept competitive). Equal opportunity of access for those in equal need would be the determining rule in the egalitarian system, and because this requires the establishment of a social hierarchy of need which is independent of who is paying for the care, it would be best accomplished in a publicly provided system (provided it can be kept responsive to social values and changing economic circumstances). The essential characteristics of such idealized system are set out in Table 16.2. Note that the success criterion to be applied to the egalitarian system is the level and distribution of *health* in the community, although some might argue that the process of gaining access as well as the outcome has to be egalitarian, and, going still further, that the financing of health care has also to be egalitarian. This wider view seems to be the one underlying the work of the COMAC-HSR project.

Needless to say, neither system lives up to its ideals, and most of the problems stem from the peculiar role of doctors in health care systems, and the problems associated with market deficiencies on the supply side, and information problems on the demand side. The full catalogue of 'horrors' is laid out in Table 16.3.

In most countries, health care is provided by a mixture of systems, with no common ideology. This may simply reflect the fact that we all live in pluralist societies which try to accommodate subgroups with incompatible ideologies (except, perhaps, that we all support tolerance for views we do not share, limited only by the sacrifices we have to make in the pursuit of our own vision of the good society in order to allow other people to pursue theirs). So it might be argued that we are not only trading-off efficiency against equity, but also one equity principle against another.

A hypothesis suggested by this analysis is that the structure of the health care system in each country is likely to be systematically related to the nature of the equity concerns that have been dominant in the (recent?) past, and is also likely to reflect the ideology which generated those concerns. An obvious instance is the balance between public and private provision, which differs markedly between countries. Another is the respective roles of national and regional governments in determining the geographical distribution of health and health care (which seems to override concerns relating to personal or family income in some systems). In other words, should we not look at the structure of the systems, as well as the rhetoric which surrounds them, to get some clues as to how important particular equity concerns seem to be?

Table 16.1. Attitudes typically associated with viewpoints A and B

	Viewpoint A (Libertarian)	Viewpoint B (Egalitarian)
Personal responsibility	Personal responsibility for achievement is very important, and this is weakened if people are offered unearned rewards. Moreover, such unearned rewards weaken the motive force that assures economic well-being, and in so doing they also undermine moral well-being, because of the intimate connection between moral well-being and the personal effort to achieve.	Personal incentives to achieve are desirable, but economic failure is not equated with moral depravity or social worthlessness.
Social concern	Social Darwinism dictates a seemingly cruel indifference to the fate of those who cannot make the grade. A less extreme position is that charity, expressed and effected preferably under private auspices, is the proper vehicle, but it needs to be exercised under carefully prescribed conditions, for example, such that the potential recipient must first mobilize all his or her own resources and, when helped, must not be in as favourable a position as those who are self-supporting (the principle of 'lesser eligibility').	Private charitable action is not rejected but is seen as potentially dangerous morally (because it is often demeaning to the recipient and corrupting to the donor) and usually inequitable. It seems preferable to establish social mechanisms that create and sustain self-sufficiency and that are accessible according to precise rules concerning entitlement that are applied equitably and explicitly sanctioned by society at large.
Freedom	Freedom is to be sought as a supreme good in itself. Compulsion attenuates both personal responsibility and individualistic and voluntary expressions of social concern. Centralized health planning and a large governmental role in health care financing are seen as an unwarranted abridgement of the freedom of clients as well as of health professionals, and private medicine is thereby viewed as a bulwark against totalitarianism.	Freedom is seen as the presence of real opportunities of choice; although economic constraints are less openly coercive than political constraints, they are none the less real, and often the effective limits on choice. Freedom is not indivisible but may be sacrificed in one respect in order to obtain greater freedom in some other. Government is not an external threat to individuals in the society but is the means by which individuals achieve greater scope for action (that is, greater real freedom).
Equality	Equality before the law is the key concept, with clear precedence being given to freedom over equality wherever the two conflict.	Because the only moral justification for using personal achievement as the basis for distributing rewards is that everyone has equal opportunities for such achievement, then the main emphasis is on equality of opportunity; where this cannot be assured the moral worth of achievement is thereby undermined. Equality is seen as an extension to the many of the freedom actually enjoyed by only the few.

Table 16.2. Idealized health care systems

	Private	Public
Demand	1. Individuals are the best judges of their own welfare. 2. Priorities determined by own willingness and ability to pay. 3. Erratic and potentially catastrophic nature of demand mediated by private insurance. 4. Matters of equity to be dealt with elsewhere (e.g., in the tax and social security systems).	1. When ill, individuals are frequently imperfect judges of their own welfare. 2. Priorities determined by social judgements about need. 3. Erratic and potentially catastrophic nature of demand made irrelevant by provision of free services. 4. Because the distribution of income and wealth unlikely to be equitable in relation to the need for health care, the system must be insulated from its influence.
Supply	1. Profit is the proper and effective way to motivate suppliers to respond to the needs of demanders. 2. Priorities determined by people's willingness and ability to pay and by the costs of meeting their wishes at the margin. 3. Suppliers have strong incentive to adopt least-cost methods of provision.	1. Professional ethics and dedication to public service are the appropriate motivation, focusing on success in curing or caring. 2. Priorities determined by where the greatest improvements in caring or curing can be effected at the margin. 3. Predetermined limit on available resources generates a strong incentive for suppliers to adopt least-cost methods of provision.

Adjustment mechanism	1. Many competing suppliers ensure that offer prices are kept low, and reflect costs. 2. Well-informed consumers are able to seek out the most cost-effective form of treatment for themselves. 3. If, at the price that clears the market medical practice is profitable, more people will go into medicine, and hence supply will be demand-responsive. 4. If, conversely, medical practice is unremunerative, people will leave it, or stop entering it, until the system returns to equilibrium.	1. Central review of activities generates efficiency adult of service provision and management pressures keep the system cost-effective. 2. Well-informed clinicians are able to prescribe the most cost-effective form of treatment for each patient. 3. If there is resulting pressure on some facilities or specialties, resources will be directed towards extending them. 4. Facilities or specialties on which pressure is slack will be slimmed down to release resources for other uses.
Success criteria	1. Consumers will judge the system by their ability to get someone to do what they demand, when, where and how they want it. 2. Producers will judge the system by how good a living they can make out of it.	1. Electorate judges the system by the extent to which it improves the health status of the population at large in relation to the resources allocated to it. 2. Producers judge the system by its ability to enable them to provide the treatments they believe to be cost-effective.

Table 16.3. Actual health care systems

	Private	Public
Demand	1. Doctors act as agents, mediating demand on behalf of consumers.	1. Doctors acts as agents, identifying need on behalf of patients.
	2. Priorities determined by the reimbursement rules of insurance funds.	2. Priorities determined by the doctor's own professional situation, by his assessment of the patient's condition, and the expected trouble-making proclivities of the patient.
	3. Because private insurance cover is itself a profit-seeking activity, some risk-rating is inevitable, hence coverage is incomplete and uneven, distorting personal willingness and ability to pay.	3. Freedom from direct financial contributions at the point of service, and absence of risk-rating, enables patients to seek treatment for trivial or inappropriate conditions.
	4. Attempts to change the distribution of income and wealth independently, are resisted as destroying incentives (one of which is the ability to buy better or more medical care if you are rich).	4. Attempts to correct inequities in the social and economic system by differential compensatory access to health services leads to recourse to health care in circumstances where it is unlikely to be a cost-effective solution to the problem.
Supply	1. What is most profitable to suppliers may not be what is most in the interests of consumers, and as neither consumers not suppliers may be very clear about what is in the former's interests, this gives suppliers a range of discretion.	1. Personal professional dedication and public-spirited motivation likely to be corroded and be degenerated into cynicism if others, who do not share those feelings, are seen to be doing very well for themselves through blatantly self-seeking behaviour.
	2. Priorities determined by the extent to which consumers can be induced to part with their money, and by the costs of satisfying the pattern of 'demand'.	2. Priorities determined by what gives the greatest professional satisfaction.
	3. Profit motive generates a strong incentive towards market segmentation and price discrimination, and tie-in agreements with other professionals.	3. Because cost-effectiveness is not accepted as a proper medical responsibility, such pressures merely generate tension between the 'professionals' and the 'managers'.

Adjustment mechanism	1. Professional ethical rules are used to make overt competition difficult. 2. Consumers denied information about quality and competence, and, because insured, may collude with doctors (against the insurance carriers) in inflating costs. 3. Entry into the profession made difficult and numbers restricted to maintain profitability. 4. If demand for services falls, doctors extend range of activities and push out neighbouring disciplines.	1. Because it does not need elaborate cost data for billing purposes, it does not routinely generate much useful information on costs. 2. Clinicians know little about costs, and have no direct incentive to act on such information as they have, and sometimes even quite perverse incentives (i.e., cutting costs may make life more difficult, or less rewarding for them). 3. Very little is known about the relative cost-effectiveness of different treatment, and even where it is, doctors are wary of acting on such information until a general professional consensus emerges. 4. The phasing out of facilities which have become redundant is difficult because it often threatens the livelihood of some concentrated specialized group and has identifiable people dependent on it, whereas the beneficiaries are dispersed and can only be identified as 'statistics'.
Success criteria	1. Consumers will judge the system by their ability to get someone to do what they need done without making them 'medically indigent' and/or changing their risk-rating too adversely. 2. Producers will judge the system by how good a living they can make out of it.	1. Because the easiest aspect of health status to measure is life-expectancy, the discussion is dominated by mortality data and mortality risks to the detriment of treatments concerned with non-life-threatening situations. 2. In the absence of accurate data on cost-effectiveness, producers judge the system by the extent to which it enables them to carry out the treatments which they find the most exciting and satisfying.

EPILOGUE

I have taken my remit to be to set the work of the COMAC-HSR project in a wider ideological frame of reference. But I am no philosopher, so my capacity to carry out this task is somewhat limited. Moreover, such an enterprise has the inevitable effect of directing attention to things that have not been done, or might have been done differently, which at the end of several years hard work is hardly what people want to hear, as it seems to diminish their achievements.

I would be very sorry if that were the impression that emerged from my observations, for I think that both what has been done (with such admirable clear-headedness and ingenuity) and the manner of doing it (on the basis of close personal co-operation between committed people) sets a model for subsequent work on the many other equity issues in health care. I hope that the group will go on and tackle some of these itself, for with this experience behind them they should be well placed to do so!

17

Health, health expenditures, and equity

A.J. Culyer

WHY HEALTH?

What motivates studies dealing with the interpersonal (or interfamily, interhousehold, interclass) distribution of income, wealth, health, and so on? They seem usually to have been undertaken so as to enable judgements to be made (by either their authors or their readers) of the 'fairness', 'justice', or 'equity' of such distributions with respect to some benchmark distribution (which need not, of course, be an equal distribution). It seems reasonable to ask two fundamental questions to do with their motivation. The first is: 'What is the ethical theory that underlies the study?' This issue is examined elsewhere in the present volume by Alan Williams (Chapter 16) and I shall not examine it further here other than to note that, because there is more than one 'ideology' serving as justification (e.g., utilitarian, desert-based, Rawlsian) it would be in general helpful (although no doubt rather complicated) if studies were to be so conducted as to enable equity judgements to be made from a variety of viewpoints or ideologies (rather than that only of the authors—if they have one). When one is confident of there being a consensus amongst the trageted readership, this desideratum is less compelling, of course. The second question is: 'Why study the distribution of whatever entity it is that has been studied?' In the case of the present volume, there are two entities—health care expenditures on the one hand, and health care payments on the other. In this section I shall explore some reasons why it may be interesting to examine the distribution of health expenditures. That of payments will be discussed subsequently.

An initial answer to the first question may be because the entity in question is itself of direct ethical interest. This view seems implicit in some of the early economic literature on externalities in health care (e.g.,

This chapter was written when the author was on leave from the Department of Economics and Related Studies at the University of York, England, as a visiting professor at the Medis Institut in Munich, Germany, and Scholar in Residence at the Department of Health Administration, University of Toronto, Canada. The Author gratefully acknowledges the detailed comments of Peter Coyte, Merton Finkler, Andreas Mielck, Owen O'Donnell, Adam Wagstaff, and Alan Williams on drafts of this chapter, and for the comments also of other participants at the Bellagio conference. The usual disclaimer applies, of course.

Culyer 1971 *a*, *b*; Pauly 1971) in which it was postulated that the health care consumption of one may be a source of utility to another; that there were, so to speak, two demands for health care: that of the individual in question (for preventive care when well and for cure, prevention of deterioration, or reduction in the speed of deterioration of health when sick) and that of 'the rest of society' who could be conceived of as 'caring' in some sense, being 'sympathetic' to, or 'solid' with, the individual (or group of individuals of a particular type, such as those falling within a particular social class). This gave rise to a variety of recommendations for subsidy of access (e.g., by subsidized insurance premiums) or of consumption (for example, by lower, or zero, user-charges). These had the apparent *character* of equity justifications. However, their justification was actually other than that. It was, in fact, an *efficiency* justification, to do with the quasi-utilitarian maximization of a (usually Paretian) social welfare function in which interpersonal distributional considerations were actually explicitly ruled out.

This approach is not strictly to do with any distributional concern of the usual sort (other than such concerns which may—or may not—arise from the *preferences* of individuals). It is also vulnerable to challenge on the grounds of 'What's special about health care?', or 'What makes health care different from, say, bicycles?' The presumption is, of course, that there is no general concern with the equitable distribution of bicycles, nor is there any obvious reason to suppose that the consumption of bicycles by one produces any direct effect on the utility of others. The vulnerability arises because the natural way to respond to the challenge just posed is to answer in terms of some more ultimate entity, in whose distribution one *is* ethically interested, and which there are grounds for believing is either *affected by* the distribution of health care (or bicycles) or is *correlated with* the distribution of health care (or bicycles), so the latter become useful indicators or tracer elements of the more ultimate entity that is of substantive interest.

In our case, a natural contender for this more ultimate entity is 'health'. It is widely believed that there are some entities, of which health is but one,[1] whose distribution is regarded as more important than the distribution of other entities—which may also be personal characteristics (like attractive hair) or consumption of goods (like bicycles). Such arguments have been put by economists of rather different political ideologies (e.g., Buchanan 1968; Tobin 1970). One reason for such beliefs may be to do with the important role these entities have in enabling people to fulfil their potential as persons: if it is possible for such entities not to be distributed in such a fashion as accords with perceived (or received) notions of what is equitable, then it is natural—and indeed necessary—to enquire about their actual distribution.[2] Philosophers such as Wiggins

(1987) commonly refer to 'potential' as having a 'flourishing' life, which seems to be the accepted translation of Aristotle's *eudaimonia.*

There may be other justifications for a focus on health care than this essentially instrumental view. One such, for example, may be a concern for the distribution of *overall* consumption, in which the distribution of health care (or, indeed, even bicycles) would be a part of some greater whole, which may itself be instrumental towards some more ultimate end. A utilitarian, for example, might take such a view: the more ultimate end being, of course, a concern with the distribution of utilities. I conjecture, however, that the most commonly held reason for having a concern for the distribution of health care is of the former kind—its instrumentality as an agent for the improvement of health (or the minimization of ill health). Indeed, other elements in the common language in which public concern for health care is couched lend support to this conjecture, one such being —as will be discussed later—use of the word 'need').

If this conjecture is correct, it has an important immediate implication: if the real (if implicit) distributional concern is with health then, because health care is *only one* of the instrumental variables which affect it, one is logically driven to examine the distribution of those of these other variables that are deemed most significant (such as housing, nutrition, public sanitation, social services, family support, health education, etc.) and for the self-same reasons as one is examining the distribution of health care, whose marginal impact may often be less than that of some of the others (see, e.g., McKeown 1976, for a historical review of the relative contribution of medicine to the reductions in mortality in the UK from infectious diseases). From this perspective, then, the results presented in Parts I and II of this volume, although amply justified in terms of the question with which this section began, can only be *partial*. They may provide important information for those with the distributional concerns described but they do not provide *all* the information required.

WHY PAYMENTS?

An ethical interest in the distribution of payments for health care may be motivated by (at least) four equity concerns.

The first is immediately implied by having an ethical concern (whether substantive or instrumental) about the distribution of health care: if the mechanisms of payment may possibly be such as to generate an inequitable distribution of health care, then one had better examine them to see whether there seems good reason to suppose they *actually* do so. As it is presumably the structural features of payment mechanisms which create this cause-and-effect link (such as eligibility under particular schemes of insurance, premium rates, out-of-pocket payments, and deductibles), the focus ought properly to be upon such important details that may affect the demand for care. However, it may also be the case that a more aggregated approach which lumped together the various contributions for relevant social groups could yield useful insights. This is particularly likely to be the case when the possibly inequitable effect of the mechanism(s) in question were itself associated with, say, employment or income status. For example, if health care insurance were available only for the employed and their families, then employment status could be used as a tracer indicator of inequity in the mechanism (inequitable by virtue of its causing inequity in the substantive variable, health, or the proximate variable, health care consumption). Employment is, of course, usually associated with a higher income.

A second reason for concern with the distribution of payments arises because disposable income after tax and health care payments may increase inequity in the distribution of other entities having similar 'ultimate' characteristics to health or, more specifically, in the distribution of consumption of goods that enhance these characteristics (for example, housing, education). As these goods generally have the feature that brands them as 'normal' goods in economists' terminology, having a positive income-elasticity of demand (so that their consumption rises as income rises), any reduction in disposable income will reduce these characteristics and any increase in the inequity of the distribution of disposable income will increase the other inequities: a regressive payments structure, for example, will worsen the distribution of these other characteristics.

A third reason for concern with the distribution of payments may arise from a concern to assess the overall effect of a sector, such as the health care sector, on the general distribution of income in cash and kind in an economy. If such is the case, an analysis of the 'net' contribution of one sector (and indeed of each) will be of interest, in order that a view may be formed about those sectors that contribute most to inequity in an overall sense and so that a view may also be formed about which inequities it might be most important to remove. This approach requires that inequities of some kinds may be 'traded-off' against others; they are not lexical or absolute ethical requirements.

A fourth reason for concern with the distribution of payments is of a similarly global type. Even if one has empirically examined and evaluated the equity of the distribution of ultimate characteristics or the utilization of resources that affect them, there may remain a residual equitable concern with the distribution of disposable income (net of taxes and all payments for ultimate goods and services). A commonly adduced reason for such a concern is because disposable income and economic or political power are thought to be positively associated and because one has a concern with the distribution of power, which may be inequitable even though the distribution of—other—ultimate goods is equitable. One may, alternatively, be concerned with the extent to which the activity of the state redistributes real income between units such as individuals or households (is it on balance regressive or progressive?) in which case a focus on payments as well as (the market value of) health care as influenced directly or indirectly by the activity of the state (but not otherwise) is appropriate. Or one may simply have an old-fashioned utilitarian interest in the distribution of net income in order to identify ways of shifting it in favour of those groups with high marginal utilities. As is well known, such an interest need by no means also be an egalitarian one.

MINIMUM STANDARDS?

If this discussion of the ultimate entities underlying distributional concerns is (at least partly) correct, the question arises as to whether one is concerned with the whole range of the distribution or only part of it. If, for example, 'protection from the elements' is an ultimate entity, and is met (at least partly) by being housed, then it seems unlikely that the concern will extend beyond that range of adequacy within which there is some likelihood that someone will not be protected. What the upper limit of this range will be is doubtless contentious, requiring substantive content to be put into the notion of 'protection'. However, that issue is resolved, it seems unlikely that it would require the inclusion of the entire range of quality and quantity of housing which income units may enjoy.

Is there such a limit in health care? There are plausible reasons for supposing not. It may be plausible to suppose that impairments of health that are both relatively minor and relatively infrequent impairments of health would be of small distributive concern. It may also be plausible to suppose that the distribution of health care which is *ineffective* in its impact on health is also of small distributive concern (this is in principle an important implication of the difference between taking health care or health as the distributions of substantive concern).[3] It is much less plausible to suppose, however, that the distribution of care that has an effective impact on life expectation, disability, pain or other distress, is of small concern. It follows that the accessibility and use of such care are also of distributive concern and that one should get as much of health care as one 'needs' rather than merely some minimum amount. The quotation marks here alert us to the presence of a dangerous—and much abused—word to which we shall have to return shortly (when the seemingly strong implication just noted will be qualified).

If concern about the distribution of the consumption of health care is essentially a matter of externality, then it is an empirical matter (although no easy one) to determine the 'list' of services deemed suitable for inclusion in a set of 'basic' services. One needs to form a judgement about what the external (as well as internal) willingness to pay for additional services is, as a matter of fact. As equity is not the same as externality, however, the idea of what a minimum (or, come to that, a maximum) set of services ought to include has to be informed both by empirical information, in this case about the effectiveness of health care in promoting health (assuming that equity ultimately depends on there being an equitable concern with the distribution of health itself), and by an ethical theory. The latter would supply both the *criterion* for inclusion in or exclusion from the 'list' and imply a fair *procedure* for determining basic services (Daniels 1985, p. 74). I conjecture that such a theory would require universal initial *access* to all diagnostic (and possibly preventive) services, and further access to therapeutic (etc.) care according to judgements about general effectiveness and, at the individual level, according to judgements about the strength of an individual's 'need' or, possibly, the 'distance' an individual's current health was from whatever health were required to enable that individual to 'flourish'. These conjectures require, however, much further thought.

WHAT IS HEALTH CARE?

The argument so far suggests that not all health care ought to be counted in studies of distributions when the ultimate concern relates to the health of individuals and groups (e.g., they should exclude any identifiable ineffective care, of which epidemiologists tell us there is a good deal) even though it has opportunity cost and may be unequally distributed. Much of the expenditure identified in the accounts as health care expenditure is not, however, even in principle addressed to the improvement of people's health. Capital spending on the lavish atriums found in some hospitals is an example. Recurrent expenditure on the hotel services of hospitals is another. If one is not concerned substantively with the distribution of expenditure on hotels then, unless there is something special about being sick in a hotel called a hospital, which makes its hotel services of distributional consequence (here perhaps a minimum standard *is* called for), such expenditures ought to be excluded. No doubt this is a formidable empirical task, but it is none the less an appropriate one if the ethical justification for taking an empirical interest in the distribution of health care expenditures is indeed (as I have conjectured) provided and motivated by an interest in the distribution of health.

TYPES OF EQUITY: HORIZONTAL AND VERTICAL

The distinction between horizontal and vertical equity is as old as Aristotle's *Nicomachean Ethics*. *Horizontal equity* requires the equal treatment of equals; *vertical equity* requires the unequal treatment of unequals (in proportion, according to Aristotle, to their inequality). One needs, of course, to identify the relevant *respects* in which individuals or groups are unequal, and the meaning to be attached to *treatment*.

There are several ways in which the issue of respects can be addressed. A broad distinction can be made between those aspects of persons that relate to health and those that relate to wealth. Candidates here considered in relation to health are:

(a) the initial or presenting state of health;
(b) the need for health care; and
(c) the final health state: the state of health after receiving health care.

These are not always carefully distinguished and the relationships between them are taken up in some detail later in the chapter. The relation that each has to horizontal or vertical equity can be shown by the following assertions (or ethical principles):

H1   Persons having the same presenting state of health ought to be treated equally.
V1   Persons having a worse presenting state of health ought to be treated relatively favourably (a weaker requirement than Aristotle's proportionality rule).
H2   Persons having the same need for health ought to be treated equally.
V2   Persons having a greater need for health ought to be treated relatively favourably.
H3   Persons having the same expected final health state ought to be treated equally.
V3   Persons having a worse expected final health state ought to be treated relatively favourably.

But what does equal or unequal *treatment* mean? It might be taken to mean 'the same, or more/less, value of health care resources', but this seems pretty arbitrary because it takes no account of the *effect* that the consumption of health care (or, come to that, of any other health-affecting resources) may have on health. Nor does it take account of the fact that some highly effective health care procedures may be cheap (small expenditure per case) and other less effective procedures may be dear (large expenditure per case). The use of expenditures as the relevant measure of 'treatment' will be discussed further below. At this stage it is more convenient (as well as being consistent with my own prejudices about the appropriate meaning of 'treatment') to reject this 'input' focus in favour of an 'outcome' focus, which seems *prima facie* more attuned with the idea that equity in health care is at root concerned with equity in health. I shall therefore, for the moment, interpret 'treatment' in terms of the effect that that health care has on health. Thus we have, rather more explicitly:

H1'   Persons having the same presenting state of health ought to be treated so that each receives the same expected increment of health.

Or

V2'   Persons having a greater need for health care ought to receive greater expected increases in health, etc.

The implications of these interpretations of horizontal and vertical equity for efficiency in resource allocation, and the consistency between the various concepts of horizontal equity, will be discussed in some detail below. A fuller discussion of vertical equity and the conflicts that may arise between the various versions of it and the various versions of horizontal equity, and the difficulties that arise when persons are equal in some relevant respects but unequal in other relevant respects, are taken up elsewhere (Culyer 1991).

As far as wealth is concerned, or its corresponding flow concept, permanent income (Friedman 1957), there are well-known practical difficulties of measurement (see, e.g., Simons 1938). A more pressing issue, however, relates to the extent to which one is concerned with equity in the payments for health care rather than with equity in the distribution of permanent income and the way the tax/benefit system of the fisc 'treats' those having equal or unequal permanent incomes. The distinction is important if, in the context of equity in finance, the relevant 'respects' in which equity or inequity are to be judged are defined in terms of health. For example:

Persons having the same initial health state ought to pay the same.
Or
Persons having a greater increase in health ought to pay more.

It seems unlikely, however, that many would be inclined to describe the relevant respects in which to judge equity in finance in such a fashion. A notable and important exception to this would be the so-called 'benefit principle' which would urge the equity of payment being proportionate to benefit and which leads rather directly to the view that an efficient allocation (in which those who value health care most at the margin get the most) is also an equitable distribution. I shall set this aside here on the grounds that readers of a volume such as this probably need no further convincing that there is something inherently inequitable about an allocation of health care that depends solely on willingness to pay, if only because willingness to pay and ability to pay are positively correlated, and ability to pay and health are also positively correlated.

Propositions more likely to command assent would be (for example):

Persons having the same initial permanent income ought to pay the same regardless of their health.

And

Persons having a greater initial permanent income ought to pay more regardless of their health.

These propositions sever, of course, any link between receipt of care, or health, and health care payments. Further, the payments notionally made under social security and/or general taxation financing of health care are impossible to apportion in any sensible way between health care itself and the other purposes for which the revenues are used (is the marginal tax dollar a contribution to health care, or unemployment insurance, or national defence, or . . .?). Therefore, as pro-rating them according to the shares of each expenditure programme in total expenditure is as arbitrary as distributing them in any other way, one is really dealing here with the general equity of the tax/premium system. It makes sense to to look at the 'contribution' to overall income equity made by the health care sector only when there is an earmarked tax/premium and/or specific out-of-pocket payments and, moreover, a balanced health care budget.

The rest of this chapter will focus on equity in health and health care rather than in payments, not least because equity in health and health care has received much less attention (the case here is not itself an equity case but based on my conjectures about the marginal payoff to analysis here rather than there!).

WHAT IS NEED?

The second interpretation of horizontal and vertical equity in health (or health care) related to 'need'. Despite its frequent use in an ill-defined way—often barely cloaking special pleading (see Culyer *et al.* 1971)—the term seems irremovable from public, political, and philosophical discussion and, consequently, on the 'if you can't beat 'em, join 'em' principle (but only on *my* terms!), it becomes necessary—stick though it may in the gullets of many economists so to do—to provide the word with suitable content. For consistency with the 'output' orientation described above, I shall initially draw on the tradition at York which defines need as 'ability to benefit' (Culyer 1976, 1978; Williams 1974, 1978). More health (somehow defined) is taken as a general ethical desideratum in much the same way, although less comprehensively, as more 'welfare' is a commonly accepted ethical criterion in normative economics, and need is a kind of social (as distinct from private) demand for health, from which there may be a derived demand (or need) for health *care*. The question of who the arbiters of the social 'demand' ought to be, and the extent to which consumer values are embodied in social judgements, is a major political question to which I, as an economist, cannot provide an author-itative answer. The matter is plainly an ideological one, to be determined by suitable political decisions, which may vary according to the tier of decision-making one is considering. For example, the answer at the tier of decision-making to do with determining the general resource constraints under which microdecisions at the hospital or clinical level are to be made may differ from the answers at these more microlevels. Distinctions between different individuals' or groups' needs thus become couched in terms of their ability to benefit from the consumption of health care, with benefit being measured in terms of expected health outcomes relative to what otherwise would have been the case. (The temptation to see benefit as a before-and-after comparison should be avoided.)

Need, in the outcome approach, is both a supply and a demand notion. It is a supply notion in that it embodies the productivity of health care resources (their potential for improving health) and a demand notion in that health (as will be seen) embodies value judgements about what it is that characterizes 'health', whose ultimate source, most will probably agree, ought whenever feasible to be actual or prospective patients, and about the relative value to be attached to a 'unit' of the health of different individuals or groups, whose source must be some over-arching social value-judgement. It is, in fact, analogous at the level of individual need to the microeconomic concept of a general equilibrium demand curve, in which the demand function is derived from an indifference map subject to the constraint, not of the individual's income, but of the economy's production possibilities curve, and with social decision-makers' prefer-ences replacing consumers'.

Later, the input approach to need will be considered, as this is plainly relevant in the context of the present volume, where the empirical work has been largely conceived (so far as I can tell) in this way.

WHAT IS HEALTH?

For the sake of convenience in what is to follow, I shall take health to be measured (on a ratio scale) by some appropriate empirical measure such as the quality-adjusted-life-year (QALY) (Torrance 1986; Williams 1985) or the healthy-years-equivalent (HYE) (Mehrez and Gafni 1989) without taking sides as to which approach, or which experimental method for deriving the empirical measure, is most appropriate (and skating over the difficulty that a common characteristic of these measures is that they use interval rather than ratio scales). It is sufficient for present purposes to suppose that there exists *some* acceptable measure, embodying acceptable and consistent value assumptions, which can be used to give substantive content to the word 'health'. (For further discussion of both 'health' and 'need', see Culyer 1990.)

The notion of 'health' clearly involves value judgements (see Culyer 1978) relating, amongst other things, to the relevant characteristics in terms of which health is to be reckoned (such as ability to perform activities of daily living, freedom from pain) and the trade-offs between these characteristics. Judgements about these elements have to be made at a variety of different tiers of decision-making (e.g., the amount of public expenditure to be devoted to health care, size and departmental composition of a hospital, clinical decisions about individual patients), each of which embodies an 'agency relationship' between the decision-maker or supplier of service and the ultimate beneficiary (the 'patient').[4] It is certainly not the case that the idea of health-as-QALYs necessarily involves the wholesale imposition of external values on individuals, or 'paternalism' (although those who wish to impose, reject consumers' values, or to be paternalist may certainly do all these three things via QALYs!). However, the necessity for establishing an interpersonal trade-off between the health of different individuals or groups is inescapable, whether one uses willingnesses to pay or some other basis for weighting individual benefits. This can be done only by making (preferably explicit) distributional value judgements.[5]

Health may be seen as both a stock and a flow: the stock being the sum of expected QALYs for an individual or group (I shall henceforth use QALYs as a suitable shorthand for 'health') and the flow being any change in the stock brought about by 'depreciation' of, 'investment' in, or external 'shocks' on, the stock (the language of capital and investment seems compelling).

EQUITY AND EQUALITY

With the above as a preparation, it is now possible to compare the ideas of horizontal and vertical equity in health and to relate them in a context that enables them to be considered at the same time as efficiency in health production. Before doing so, however, it is necessary to be explicit about how interpersonal comparisons of health are to be made. I shall assert, as an egalitarian principle which I term 'QALY egalitarianism', that *a QALY is of equal social value to whomsoever it accrues.* QALY egalitarianism is asserted in order to test its consistency with other equity objectives rather than because it is particularly compelling on ethical grounds (it is easy to imagine individuals whose QALYs ought possibly to command a relatively high weight, such as mothers with several dependent children; and it is not particularly compelling to treat as equally socially valuable 10 QALYs received by one person or one QALY received by each of 10 different, but equally meritorious, individuals). None the less, QALY egalitarianism is the value judgement with which we shall work and, as will be seen, the method of analysis enables alternative assumptions to be inserted at will.

The two kinds of equality or inequality of treatment to be considered are:

Horizontal
H1 Equal treatment of those with equal initial health.
H2 Equal treatment for equal need.
H3 Equal treatment of those with with equal expected final health.

Vertical
V1 More favourable treatment of those with worse initial health.
V2 More favourable treatment of those with greater need.
V3 More favourable treatment of those with a worse expected final health.

It will be noted that vertical equity principles adopted are rather weaker than Aristotle's (who recommended proportionality). The detailed consideration of these principles is, moreover, a matter for another chapter, and here we shall concentrate on horizontal equity.

EQUAL TREATMENT AS EQUAL ADDITIONAL HEALTH

Figure 17.1 shows a special situation in which, in a world of only two individuals of equal age,[6] there is equal initial health, equal need, and an equal expected final health outcome. The figure is based on one developed in Wagstaff (1991). The axes of the figure measure the stock of prospective health, H, in QALYs for each individual A and B. The 45° line is a locus of equality of health for A and B. Point S represents the initial stock of health of the two individuals ($h_B = h_A$). The dashed lines within the H-space represent additional H. Northerly movements from S

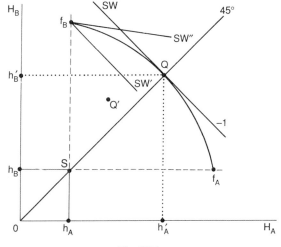

Fig. 17.1.

represent increasing H for B, and easterly movements represent increasing H for A. North-easterly movements represent increases in the stock of H for both individuals. The convex (from above) locus $f_B f_A$ represents the technically possible increases in H that are possible, given an overall amount of resources (inputs) available to this two-person economy. These increases are to be imagined as computed in a fashion developed by Williams (e.g., Williams 1981). Its slope implies that increasing H for one individual can be obtained only by increasing sacrifices of additional H for the other. This may arise either under diminishing returns in the health care production functions for A and B, or under constant returns in each 'technology' but with different input intensities in each. $f_B f_A$ is the 'health frontier'. It corresponds to, and can be derived from, the contract curve in an Edgeworth production box which is the locus of tangency points for isoQALY contours in the production functions for A's and B's health (see below). Given resource constraints, the maximum amount of additional H for B that is possible is Sf_B and the maximum amount for A is Sf_A. I take these limits as defining the 'abilities to benefit' of A and B. Any productively efficient combination must lie on $f_B f_A$. Any point on the frontier represents a cost-effective distribution of H between A and B in the sense that additional H for one can be procured only at the (opportunity) cost of less H for the other. All points below $f_B f_A$ indicate productive inefficiency and all points above it are unattainable. The $f_B f_A$ frontier is symmetrical about the 45° line, indicating that the capacity of each to benefit from health care is the same in QALYs (their needs are the same). The SW line with slope –1 is a social welfare contour embodying QALY egalitarianism and indicating that increments of H to either A or B are equally valued socially, independently of the amount of H that each has initially and that each receives additionally: any movement along a given SW contour represents a socially equal value of QALYs, although, of course, the distribution between A and B varies (if H were deemed to have a diminishing marginal social value as each individual had more, the SW contours would take on a shape that would be concave from above).

The figure captures the elements of horizontal equity previously discussed. Equal initial health is indicated by point S ($Oh_B = Oh_A$). If health care is efficient in its impact on H, the horizontal equity requirement H1 of equal treatment for equal initial health (in terms of outcome) requires equal receipt of additional health. The only point in the figure satisfying both this equity criterion and productive efficiency is point Q, at which A receives $h_A h_A'$ equal to B's receipt of $h_B h_B'$.

Equal expected final health is also shown by point Q, as it lies on the 45° line through the origin and is on the health frontier. Again, therefore, equal treatment in the form of equal additional health outcomes requires location at Q.

The *needs* of A and B are represented in Fig. 17.1 by Sf_A and Sf_B, corresponding to their respective abilities to benefit. These abilities depend crucially on the productivity of health care (the shape of the frontier). In Fig. 17.1, A and B have equal needs ($Sf_B = Sf_A$) and each ought therefore to receive equal amounts of additional QALYs according to the horizontal equity principle of equal treatment for equal need (output approach). This requires locating on the 45° line through S and, if productive efficiency is also to be realized, locating also on the health frontier. The point of intersection of the 45° line through S and the frontier is Q, indicating that this point is again that which satisfies the second horizontal equity requirement (*H2*).

Efficiency in meeting needs is interpreted here as selecting those needs that are to be met, or determining what may be termed 'entitlements to health', by prioritizing the more 'urgent' and so distributing health between A and B that, at the margin, the cost of A's and B's additional health is equal to the social value attached to the health of each. The relative social value (in QALYs) is given by QALY egalitarianism, expressed in Fig. 17.1 by the social welfare contours having constant slopes of −1. Full allocative efficiency requires attainment of the highest SW contour, which occurs at Q, where the frontier is tangential to an SW contour. Efficient meeting of needs is thus consistent with the existence of some unmet need (cf. Wiggins and Dermen 1987): the optimal unmet need is $n_B f_B$ and $n_A f_A$. The selection of any other point of $f_B f_A$ involves a lower social value of met need than that attainable at Q. For example, the selection of point f_B, at which B receives all the additional health, is efficient in cost-effective terms (A can have more only if B has less: it is still a point on the frontier) but it is not fully efficient. At f_B the social welfare contour SW' (also with slope −1) lies below the contour at Q and so does not maximize the social value of additional QALYs. This allocation of additional health between A and B would maximize the social value of additional health only if QALY egalitarianism were sufficiently relaxed, specifically requiring B's QALYs to receive a sufficiently higher social weight than A's to produce a tangency (or corner solution) on $f_B f_A$ with the much flatter contour SW''.

Figure 17.1 represents, of course, a specially constructed case in which there is no conflict between any of the various horizontal equity requirements, nor with any of them and efficiency. Details of the conflicts that do emerge when individuals are equal in some, but not all, respects, are explored elsewhere (Culyer 1991).

EQUAL TREATMENT AS EQUAL EXPENDITURE

The alternative way of considering 'treatment' is to regard it in input rather than output terms. The use of expenditures on health care is common in the literature (e.g., the pioneering work of Le Grand 1978) and is the approach selected by the author in the present volume. Under this approach, the horizontal equity principles become 'equal receipt of health care resources in value terms for equal initial health, need, or final health', and the question arises as to whether this introduces conflicts between equity and efficiency and whether the use of this approach implies different equitable distributions from those implied under the 'output' approach.

The version of the problem can be explicated with the help of Fig. 17.2. This is an Edgeworth Box in which the axes measure the available resources (two inputs, the services of capital and labour). The two production technologies for A's and B's health utilizing these two inputs are represented by the two expansion paths $O_A A$ and $O_B B$, which trace out the the optimal input combinations at the equilibrium input price ration P_E as each activity expands, assuming constant returns in each but differing factor intensities (A's health-improving technology is assumed to be relatively labour-intensive). Output is measured in QALYs and each isoQALY controur is analogous to an isoquant. The contract curve $O_A O_B$ is the usual locus of tangencies of the isoQALY curves. It is from this contract curve that the health frontier in Fig. 17.1 is derived, and productive efficiency requires the economy to be located on this locus.

Equal treatment in the sense of health care expenditures requires each technology (viz., that for A's health and that for B's) to share a common

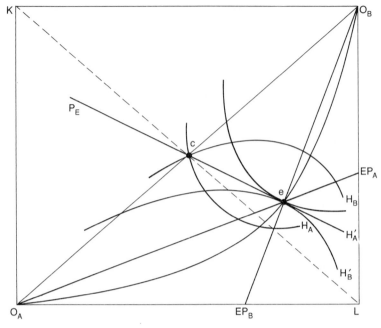

Fig. 17.2.

isocost line. Such an isocost line must pass through the centre of the Box, c, because the cost of A's and B'a health care must be equal when they use identical inputs and the the input prices are the same for each technology. The relevant isocost line must also, for efficiency, be tangential to two isoQALY curves on the contract curve. One may conceive of some Walrasian process in which the relevant input prices are established to ensure optimality at the efficiency point e. All points along ce therefore indicate equal expenditure on A and B. It is immediately clear that equal expenditure on inputs is consistent with productive efficiency, so long as input prices can adjust appropriately, and that equal expenditure is thus consistent with being on the health frontier in Fig. 17.1.[7]

There is in general, however, no reason to expect that this equal allocation of expenditure between the two individuals corresponds to an equal share in additional health. The two isoQALY curves through c (H_A and H_B) must represent equal additional QALYs for each on the assumption of constant returns and given equal needs. In Fig. 17.2, equal needs (capacities to benefit) imply that B's isoQALY curve at O_A and A's at O_B have the same value. As c represents half of the input flow at the origins, it must also represent half the output of QALYs, given constant returns. However, this point cannot be an equilibrium if factor intensities differ.

The output of QALYs is higher for both individuals at e than at c but is even higher for B than A ($H_A' < H_B'$). In general, additional health will not be the same at e, even though expenditure is the same (they are on the same) isocost line ce).

There is thus an inconsistency between the two versions of 'equal treatment', which makes the distinction between them of substantive importance, and requires an explicit choice, presumably by appeal to some underlying theory of horizontal equity. Equal treatment in the sense of equal expenditure is consistent with productive efficiency and may be equitable when needs are the same, but equal treatment in the sense of equal receipt of additional health, which may also be equitable when needs are the same, requires selection of a different point on the contract curve, where the *two isoQALY curves* have an equal value. This will also involve a different configuration of inputs in the health care system and different input prices. Because, at e, A receives less additional health (given the production functions as drawn in Fig. 17.2), equal treatment in the sense of equal additional health requires the selection of a point on the contract curve northeast of e and a relatively higher equilibrium price of input L.

The equity requirement of equal treatment in the sense of equal expenditure for equal need is also in general inconsistent with full allocative efficiency (under QALY egalitarianism) as this requires equal additional health for each. Relaxing QALY egalitarianism might produce a tangency in Fig. 17.1 that corresponds to the QALY distribution implied by equal expenditure, but because the factors determining the social trade-offs between A's and B's health are not the same as those determining their shares under equal expenditure, such an outcome can only be coincidental.

Thus, equal treatment in the sense of equal expenditure on health care implies different health outcomes and conflicts with both allocative efficiency and final health equality. Equal treatment in the sense of equal additional health is consistent with allocative efficiency and also with final health equality, but will involve different expenditures for equal needs. Both forms of 'treatment' are consistent with productive efficiency if input prices are free to adjust optimally.

The inconsistency between the two versions of 'equal treatment' arises out of the different productivities of health care for A and B (even under constant returns). Retaining this assumption, so that equal proportionate increases in inputs produce the same proportionate increase in QALYs within each activity, but assuming production homogeneity in the sense of identical input-intensities in each activity,[8] produces a special case where the conflict vanishes. Under these conditions, the contract curve coincides with the diagonal in Fig. 17.2 and a given increase in QALYs for one is

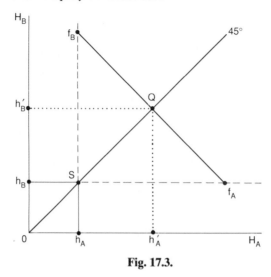

Fig. 17.3.

exactly compensated by the QALY loss for the other as one moves along the diagonal. The health frontier becomes linear, as shown in Fig. 17.3 and, for the case of equal need (equal capacity to benefit), is symmetrical about the 45° line through the origin. Given QALY egalitarianism, society is indifferent between points on the new health frontier.[9] Under these conditions, the equitable point Q is not only equitable under all the horizontal equity principles (provided that A and B are equal in all relevant respects) but the system is efficient in both productive and allocative senses, and expenditure on A and B is equal.[10]

In this special case,[11] provided that one can be confident about the production homogeneity of the As and Bs taken as a whole, equal expenditure for equal health, equal need, or equal final health, are all consistent and, moreover, consistent with QALY egalitarianism and productive and allocative efficiency. A relevant inequality of persons justifying a possibly equitable unequal treatment will, of course, arise where the homogeneity assumption does not hold. But, in horizontal equity, like expenditure for like cases becomes a principle consistent with the outcome approach.

TRADING-OFF HEALTH AGAINST OTHER GOODS

The entire discussion so far has treated equity and efficiency in health care and health within a given resource availability to the health sector. It will be apparent that the optimal size of the health care sector cannot be considered independently of, first, the productivity of other elements amongst those determining the health of individuals and groups relative to that of health care itself and, secondly, the value of health relative to the value of other produced goods and services. Although I have treated health as the efficiency maximand in this paper, and as the central matter of distributional concern, it is not synonymous with 'welfare' (notwithstanding a classic WHO early definition) and health is not the only moral pursuit or candidate for specific egalitarianism. One therefore needs also to consider the optimal size of the health care sector in terms of the valuation of health relative to the other good things of life and to evaluate the overall equity of a particular society by taking account of the equity of distributions of entities other than health care and health. It may be that relatively inequitable distributions of some entities may be compensated in such overall judgements by more equitable distributions of other entities. The question of the 'separability' and 'additivity' of degrees of inequality in specific entities of concern is, however, a difficult question— unresearched so far as I know—not considered further here.

SUMMARY

I have tried to provide some reasons why it may be interesting to examine the distribution of health, health care, and health care payments, the most important of which hinge on the notion of the existence of 'ultimate' entities that are of specific distributional concern which implies that other, less ultimate entities, are of less (or even no) distributional concern. I have argued that the ultimate entity of concern here is 'health', for which health care and health care expenditures are only instrumental. It is argued that the nature of health implies that it is an ultimate entity whose distribution across the whole range is of concern (unlike some others, where equity may be satisfied by the meeting of some minimum standard). A concept of need for health care was developed, analogous to the general equilibrium individual demand curve in that the constraint is taken as the economy's production possibilities but differing from that construct in that social values replace (at least in part) consumer values. Horizontal equity in health was considered in terms of three alternative principles, whose consistency with one another and with the efficient production of health was explored. It was shown that equality of treatment in the sense of either improved health (outcome view) or amount of health care expenditure (input view) were mutually consistent given appropriate patient classifications and also consistent with economic efficiency. A diagrammatic technique was introduced that enables the simultaneous consideration of these various equity principles, efficiency, and the interpersonal comparison of health. This technique can also be used to explore the consistencies and inconsistencies of vertical equity principles with one another and with efficiency, and to explore the difficulties that arise when individuals are like in some relevant respects but unlike in other relevant respects, although these issues are not pursued here. The comparisons made do not depend upon there being an explicit trade-off between health and other arguments of the social welfare function, although the optimal size of the health care sector will depend on such trade-offs, as well as the relative productivity of the health sector and other environmental influences in the promotion of health.

Postscript

Between writing this contribution and its final preparation for publication, sufficient time has elapsed for me to have had some changes of mind, particularly as the result of some ongoing joint research with Adam Wagstaff. In particular, I now think it more helpful in studies of distribution to focus on the need for health care than on the need for health (though it remains my view that the former has its entire ethical dependence hanging on the latter, and there are doubtless problems for which it would be more helpful to focus on the need for health, for example, as a necessary condition for 'flourishing'). Both for the sake of concreteness and because this sense seems to chime well with whatever sense we have been able to make of the use of 'need' by people who have thought carefully about how they use the word (especially philosophers), Wagstaff and I have also come to a stipulative definition of need as 'the minimum resources required to exhaust an individual's capacity to benefit from health care'. The ramifications of this idea have been worked out in a series of papers (Culyer and Wagstaff 1991 *a*, *b*, *c*).

NOTES

1. Others might include protection from the elements, opportunities to enter careers suited to talents, having one's legal rights protected—to which the corresponding less ultimate entities might be housing, schooling, and access to the courts.
2. Assuming that there is likely to exist some means by which the actual distribution, if found inequitable, can be altered for the better, or compensated by relatively favourable distributions of other entities, and that the means adopted for making changes in distributions satisfy any criteria relating to procedural equity.
3. It has been pointed out to me by Peter Coyte that inequality in the distribution of publicly financed ineffective care may be seen as unfair by those who are denied access to it by virtue of, say, geography, particularly when

ethnic minorities are more concentrated in a deprived region (such as native peoples in northern Ontario). However, it is quite consistent with my argument that inefficiency (in the production of community health) might cause or exacerbate inequity, even though, as in the case of an unequal distribution of ineffective care, the inequality may not itself be inequitable. This arises because the public finance of ineffective care to some groups constrains needlessly the system's ability to provide more *effective* care for other, deprived, groups. Inefficiency is not only unethical in its own right (because it fails to reduce mortality and morbidity as much as the available resources permit); it can be additionally unethical by virtue of the debilitating effect it may have on public policy's ability to tackle inequity.

4. For further discussion of these tiers see Culyer (1990).

5. It is worth emphasizing that the value judgements do not have to be those of the analyst. As far as possible, scholarly analysis should be used to explore the consequences of making value judgements rather than itself be intrinsically ideological.

6. It is assumed that A and B are of the same age but not that they have an equal expectation of life. Age standardization is required in order to avoid arbitrary (and inequitable) bias in favour of the young who, *ceteris paribus*, have a greater life expectancy at all ages in developed countries. Age is therefore another respect in which individuals are to be reckoned equal or unequal for equity purposes. In efficiency analysis, this assumption is not required, and if it is not made an inconsistency may arise between the demands of efficiency and those of equity. In this paper allocative efficiency is considered only with respect to persons of like age.

7. If input prices cannot adjust optimally there will be an excess demand for one input and an excess supply of the other, producing an interior solution in Fig. 17.1. Note also that, although expenditure includes all input costs, it does not include 'fixed' costs (if any).

8. This may be more likely to apply when A and B (or the groups of patients for whom A and B are representative individuals) belong to the same diagnostic group—suggesting another 'respect' in which to consider equality or inequality. However, this standardization may not always, or even usually, imply homogeneity on the production side; for example, duodenal ulcers may be treated either medically or surgically, with different input combinations and different costs per case.

9. For any other constant weighting of QALYs, the social optimum is a corner solution.

10. I assume no inter-regional variation in input prices.

11. 'Special' in the sense of requiring particular empirical conditions to apply for its valid application. Whether in practice they do commonly hold is another (empirical) matter.

18

Equity and health care policy: the American experience

Karen Davis

INTRODUCTION

The US is the only major industrialized nation without a national health plan that assures universal access to health care services. Rather, it has a mixed public–private approach to the financing of health care services. Public programmes finance health care for elderly, disabled, and some groups of poor people. Employers voluntarily provide private health insurance to the majority of workers and their dependents.

Delivery of health services is largely through private providers of health are services, who are free to set prices for their services in the market-place. However, in the larger cities and some rural areas, state and local governments support a public delivery system including public community hospitals and clinics for the indigent.

This mixed public–private system of health care financing and delivery fails to assure access to health care for the entire population. About 15 per cent of the US population has no health insurance cover from a public or private plan. Many low-income communities are not served by a public health care delivery system, and public facilities that do exist are often overcrowded and understaffed. As a result of these barriers to health care, the distribution of health services is very unequal and differs markedly by income, race, and geographical location. At least in part because of this inequality in access to health services, health outcomes and measures of health status also differ markedly on these characteristics.

Improving equity in access to health services was a major objective of US health policy in the 1960s and 1970s. The 1980s, however, were marked by a retrenchment in governmental commitment to universal access to health care. The widening disparity in access to services has led to renewed interest in public policy proposals that would assure universal health insurance cover for the entire population.

Increasing awareness of the poor comparative performance of the US health system relative to other industrialized nations has added to this movement. Many have come to feel that the US fails to achieve either an efficient or an equitable health care system—leaving millions of Americans without health insurance cover yet spending far more than any other industrialized nation on health care.

As the nation enters a new decade and nears the beginning of a new century, it is an important time of reassessment for national health policy. Several efforts are currently underway in the US to develop major health care reform proposals. This chapter summarises the experience to date with assuring access to health care in the US and describes the Pepper Commission comprehensive health financing reform proposal which has led to several legislative proposals currently before the US Congress. It concludes with an analysis of major proposals for reform and their merits for shaping the future of US health financing policy.

THE GREAT SOCIETY AND EXPANDED HEALTH INSURANCE COVER

Commitment to ensuring access to health care has never been complete in the US. Beginning in the early 1950s, employers have voluntarily provided private health insurance to workers and their dependants. Today, most of those who work receive some private health insurance cover through their employment (Davis 1975; Congressional Budget Office 1979; Congressional Research Service 1988). However, not all firms provide such cover. Many small businesses, and businesses in the agriculture, construction, retail trade, and service sectors of the economy do not provide cover for their workers.

In 1965, the federal government enacted Medicare and Medicaid to provide coverage under public programmes for many of those without access to employer health benefits—the aged and certain groups of poor (Davis and Schoen 1978). Medicare is a federal health financing programme that covers those who are permanently and totally disabled as well as nearly all individuals of age 65 and above. Medicaid is a federal–state government programme that covers low-income women, children, elderly, and disabled individuals. Many poor people are excluded, however, because of strict limits on income and assets to qualify for eligibility and because of exclusion of most working-age men and adults without children.

Other federal programmes enacted in the mid-1960s and early 1970s expanded the availability of health resources in rural and high poverty inner-city areas. State and local governments have traditionally sponsored public community hospitals and clinics to provide services as a last resort to those unable to pay. Some private, voluntary hospitals and most teaching hospitals have been a major source of charity care (Feder *et al.* 1984).

The accumulated evidence suggests that these governmental health

Table 18.1.   Life expectancy, by race and sex (1960–87)

	1960	1970	1975	1980	1987	Change (%) (1960–87)
Life expectancy at birth						
Total	*69.7*	*70.9*	*72.6*	*73.7*	*74.9*	*7.5*
White men	67.4	68.0	69.5	70.7	72.1	7.0
White women	74.1	75.6	77.3	78.1	78.8	6.3
Black men	60.7	60.0	62.4	63.7	65.4	7.7
Black women	65.9	68.3	71.3	72.3	73.8	12.0
Life expectancy at age 65						
Total	*14.3*	*15.2*	*16.1*	*16.4*	*16.9*	*18.2*
White men	12.9	13.1	13.8	14.2	14.9	15.5
White women	15.9	17.1	18.2	18.5	18.7	17.6
Black men	12.7	12.5	13.1	12.9	13.6	7.1
Black women	15.1	15.7	16.7	16.5	17.2	13.9

Source: Health U.S. (1988, p. 53).

programmes have been an important contributing factor to major gains in health in the past 25 years (Davis 1973, 1976; Rogers and Blendon 1977; Davis and Schoen 1978; Rogers *et al.* 1982). These gains have been especially noteworthy for the aged and for minorities. As shown in Table 18.1 and Fig. 18.1, life expectancy at birth in the US has jumped a total of five years from 1960 to 1987—from 69.7 years to 74.9 years. Blacks experienced greater gains in life expectancy at birth than whites, with especially marked improvements for black women (an increase of eight years in life expectancy at birth).

Longer life expectancy at birth reflects lower infant mortality and lower death rates in middle age. However, a substantial portion of the improvement in life-expectancy is accounted for by improvements in health of the aged. As shown in Table 18.1 and Fig. 18.2, life expectancy at age 65 increased 2.6 years between 1960 and 1987. Leading the gains in improved life expectancy among the aged were white women, who upon reaching the age of 65 in 1987 live an average of 18.7 more years, three years longer than in 1960. Medicare deserves at least a portion of the credit for the increased life expectancy experienced by those 65 and above.

Gains in health status have been especially rapid for those causes of death amenable to medical care intervention and which historically have been higher among the poor. As shown in Table 18.2 and Fig. 18.3, age-adjusted death rates for the entire population declined 29 per cent from 1960 to 1986. Deaths from strokes dropped by 61 per cent over this period —reflecting both the lower rate of uncontrolled hypertension in the popu-

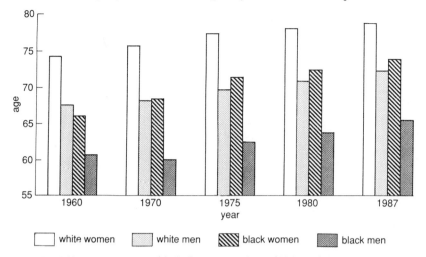

Fig. 18.1. Life expectancy at birth, by race and sex (1960–87). From *Health U.S.* (1988).

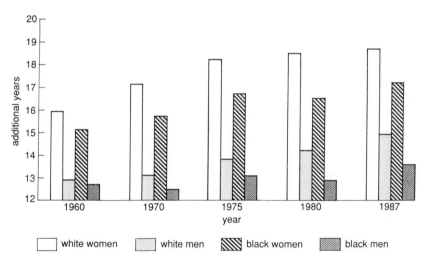

Fig. 18.2. Life expectancy at age 65, by race and sex (1960–87). From *Health U.S.* (1988).

lation and improved health services. Deaths from pneumonia and influenza were cut in half between 1960 and 1986; historically, the poor have died from these causes at a greater rate than higher income individuals. Heart disease death rates fell by 39 per cent; although the exact reasons for this decline are uncertain better availability of sophisticated health services and emergency medical care may be an important factor. Death

Table 18.2. Age-adjusted death rates, by cause, deaths per 100 000 population (1960–86)

	1960	1970	1980	1986	Change (%) (1960–86)
All causes	*760.9*	*714.3*	*585.8*	*541.7*	*−28.8*
Heart disease	286.2	253.6	202.0	175.0	−38.9
Cerebrovascular disease	79.7	66.3	40.8	31.0	−61.1
All cancers	125.8	129.9	132.8	133.2	5.9
Respiratory	19.2	28.4	36.4	39.0	103.1
Colorectal	17.7	16.8	15.5	14.4	−18.6
Breast	22.3	23.1	22.7	23.1	3.6
Pneumonia and influenza	28.0	22.1	12.9	13.5	−51.8
Cirrhosis and liver disease	10.5	14.7	12.2	9.2	−12.4
Diabetes mellitus	13.6	14.1	10.1	9.6	−29.4
Accidents	49.9	53.7	42.3	35.2	−29.5
Suicide	10.6	11.8	11.4	11.9	12.3
Homicide	5.2	9.1	10.8	9.0	73.1

Source: Health U.S. (1988, p. 62).

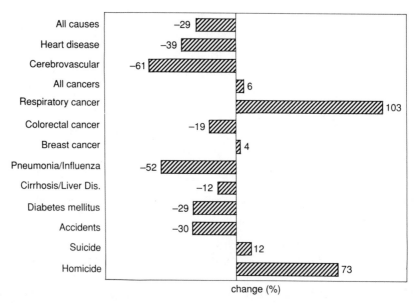

Fig. 18.3. Percentage change in age-adjusted death rates, by cause (1960–86). From *Health U.S.* (1988).

Table 18.3. Infant health (1960–81)

	1960	1970	1975	1980	1986	Change (%) (1960–86)
Infant deaths per 1000 live births						
Total	*26.0*	*20.0*	*16.1*	*12.6*	*10.0*[1]	*−61.5*[2]
White	22.9	17.8	14.2	11.0	8.9	−61.1
Black	44.3	32.6	26.2	21.4	18.0	−59.4
Live births with birth weight of 2500 grams or less (%)						
Total	n.a.	*7.94*	*7.39*	*6.84*	*6.81*	*−14.2*[3]
White	n.a.	6.84	6.26	5.70	5.64	−17.5[3]
Black	n.a.	13.86	13.09	12.49	12.53	−9.6[3]
Live births with prenatal care beginning in first trimester (%)						
Total	n.a.	*68.0*	*72.4*	*76.3*	*75.9*	*11.6*[3]
White	n.a.	72.4	75.9	79.3	79.2	9.4[3]
Black	n.a.	44.4	55.8	62.7	61.6	38.7[3]

[1] 1987. [2] Change (%), 1960–87. [3] Change, 1970–86. n.a. = not applicable.
Source: Health U.S. (1988, p. 47, 54).

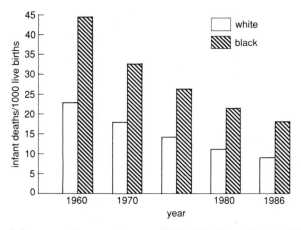

Fig. 18.4. Infant mortality rate, by race (1970–86). From *Health U.S.* (1988).

from diabetes declined moderately over the period, as did accidental death. Upward trends were evident in deaths from cancer, especially respiratory cancer, suicide, and homicide. These increases are more related to smoking, stress, and crime levels and could not be expected to be especially sensitive to the availability of improved health services.

Infant health has also improved over the last 25 years. Infant mortality, as shown in Table 18.3 and Fig. 18.4, has dropped by 62 per cent between

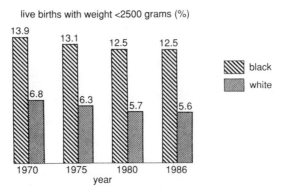

Fig. 18.5.   Rates of low birth weight weight, by race (1970–86). From *Health U.S.* (1988).

1960 and 1987, dropping from 26 deaths per 1000 live births in 1960 to 10.0 deaths per 1000 live births in 1987. This is especially significant in the light of the fact that infant mortality rates were virtually unchanged in the 10 years preceding passage of Medicaid and other Great Society health programmes for the poor. Rates for both whites and blacks have declined at similar rates—with black infant mortality rates continuing to be about twice as high as those of whites throughout the period. Some progress has also been made in reducing the proportion of low birth weight (LBW) infants. The percentage of infants weighing less than 2500 grams has declined from 7.9 per cent in 1970 to 6.8 per cent in 1986 (see Table 18.3 and Fig. 18.5).

More women are getting care early in pregnancy. Studies have shown that receiving prenatal care in the first trimester is important in reducing infant mortality and LBW infants—by identifying high risk mothers and getting chronic health problems that can have an adverse effect on birth outcomes under control (e.g., diabetes, anaemia) (Institute of Medicine 1985). The proportion of white women receiving prenatal care in the first trimester increased from 72.4 per cent in 1970 to 79.2 per cent in 1986. For black women the gains were even more striking. The proportion of black women receiving prenatal care in the first trimester increased from 44.4 per cent in 1970 to 61.6 per cent in 1986 (see Fig. 18.6).

Perhaps the most compelling evidence on the success of the Great Society programmes for the poor has been the improved access to physician services. The poor, now as in the past, are much more likely than high-income groups to have fair or poor health and to suffer from chronic health conditions (Davis and Schoen 1978). Despite their poorer health status, low-income groups in 1964 were twice as likely not to have seen a physician in the previous two years as high-income groups (Table 18.4 and

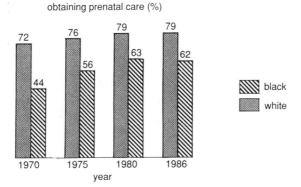

obtaining prenatal care (%)

black
white

year

Fig. 18.6. Obtaining prenatal care in the first trimester, by race (1970–86). From *Health U.S.* (1988).

Table 18.4. Percentage of the population with an interval of 2 years or more since last physician contact, by family income (1964, 1982, 1987)

	1964	1982	1987	Change (%) (1964–87)
Percentage not seeing a physician in previous 2 years				
All family income*	*19.1*	*13.2*	*12.8*	*–33.0*
Under US$10 000	28.2	12.5	12.8	–54.6
US$10 000–US$14 999	23.3	13.9	14.9	–36.0
US$15 000–US$19 999	18.7	14.9	14.9	–20.3
US$20 000–US$34 999	15.7	13.7	12.9	–17.8
US$35 000 and over	13.5	11.8	10.8	–20.0

* Family income categories for 1987. Income categories in 1964 are: less than US$2000–US$3999; US$4000–US$6999; US$7000–US$9999; US$10 000 or more. In 1982 are: less than US$7000; US$7000–US$9999; US$10 000–US$14 999; US$15 000–US$24 999; US$25 000 or more.
Source: Health U.S. (1988, p. 107).

Fig. 18.7). By 1987 the proportion of the low-income population not seeing a physician in the last two years was only 20 per cent greater than that of the high-income population.

The introduction of Medicaid and other Great Society health programmes had a major impact in assisting those covered with gaining access to physician services at levels comparable to those of higher income persons with similar health problems. This is particularly evident when the rate of physician visits of poor people with and without Medicaid are compared. As shown in Table 18.5 and Fig. 18.8, in 1982, poor people on Medicaid saw physicians an average of 5.7 times per year, compared to 5.3

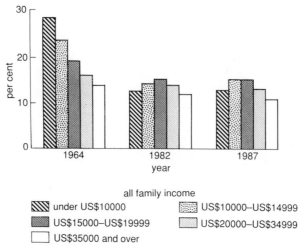

Fig. 18.7. Percentage of the population not seeing a physician in the previous 2 years, by family income (1964, 1982, 1987). From *Health U.S.* (1988).

Table 18.5. Adjusted mean annual physician contacts according to poverty and Medicaid status (1982)

	Above poverty	Below poverty	
		With Medicaid	Without Medicaid
All ages	5.3	5.7[1]	3.9[3]
Under 17 years	4.4	4.2[1]	3.3[3]
17–44 years	4.8	6.3[2]	3.9[3]
45–64 years	6.5	4.0[1]	1.6[3]
65+ years	7.9	9.2[1]	7.1[1]

[1] Not significant ($P \geq 0.05$). [2] $P < 0.05$. [3] $P < 0.01$.
Source: Newacheck (1988, p. 411).

times for non-poor persons—adjusting for differences in health status. Poor people not covered by Medicaid, however, lagged well behind in use of physician services—averaging 3.9 physician visits per person annually.

Hospital utilization among the general population has declined over the period since the introduction of the Great Society. In 1964, hospital discharges per 1000 population averaged 109.1; by 1987 this had dropped to 96.5 (see Table 18.6). With shortening hospital stays over this period, days of hospital care dropped even more rapidly. Important increases in hospital utilization did occur, however, for the poor and for the aged. As

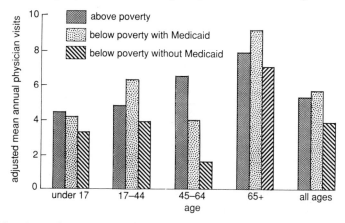

Fig. 18.8. Annual number of physician visits, by poverty and Medicaid status (1982). From Newacheck (1988).

Table 18.6. Hospital discharges per 1000 population, by age and family income (1964, 1981, 1987)

	1964	1981	1987	Change (%) (1964–87)
Total	*109.1*	*121.7*	*96.5*	*−9.6*
By age				
< 15 yrs	67.6	64.3	48.6	−28.1
15–44	100.6	97.0	69.2	−31.2
45–64	146.2	175.1	143.3	−2.1
65 yrs and over	190.0	283.6	255.6	34.5
By family income[1,2]				
Under US$10 000	102.4	165.1	143.7	40.3
US$10 000–US$14 999	116.4	137.5	132.6	13.9
US$15 000–US$19 999	110.7	124.5	102.4	−7.5
US$20 000–US$34 999	109.2	119.8	87.9	−19.5
US$35 000 or more	110.7	104.6	77.1	−30.4

[1] Age adjusted.
[2] Family income categories for 1987. Income categories in 1964 are: less than US$2000; US$2000–US$3999; US$4000–US$6999; US$7000–US$9999; US$10 000 or more. In 1981 are: less than US$7000; US$7000–9999; US$10 000–US$14 999; US$15 000–US$24 999; US$25 000 or more.
Source: *Health U.S.* (1988, p. 111).

shown in Table 18.6, hospital discharges for the aged increased from 190 per 1000 in 1964 to 256 per 1000 in 1987. Studies have demonstrated that much of this gain in hospital use reflects an improved quality of life for the elderly—with major increases in cataract surgery and hip replacements (Davis and Schoen 1978). Medicare has made this use of modern medical technology affordable for the old and their families.

RETRENCHMENT IN THE REAGAN ERA

The US health financing system came under considerable strain in the 1980s. Federal and state government budgetary restraint has curbed the growth in outlays under Medicaid (Rowland *et al.* 1988). The changing nature of employment and pressure from international competition have contributed to cutbacks in employee health benefits (Davis *et al.* 1991). Competition among health care providers has reduced the availability of charity care (Rowland 1987).

These changes began in 1981 as the Reagan administration ushered in a major shift in health policy. Unlike previous administrations, it did not propose expanded cover through a national health insurance plan. Rather, it called for major cutbacks in Medicare and Medicaid, and governmental funding for direct primary care delivery programmes (Davis 1981).

The US Congress responded by attempting to protect the poor and elderly from harmful cuts in health programmes. Medicare deductibles for hospital and physician services were increased, but Reagan budget proposals to institute a 10 per cent hospital copayment and to increase the Medicare premium paid by beneficiaries to cover a greater share of outlays for physician services were not enacted. Similarly, cover of the working poor under Medicaid was restricted in 1981, but the Congress subsequently expanded cover for poor pregnant women, children, elderly, and disabled. Reagan administration proposals for New Federalism to set a cap on federal payments for Medicaid or to turn the programme over to state governments were defeated. Reagan administration proposals to reduce funding for primary care delivery programmes by 25 per cent and fold into state block grants were similarly rejected. Instead, Congress increased funding moderately for primary care centres and explicitly exempted them from Gramm–Rudman automatic budget cuts. However, the need to find budgetary savings to counter Reagan administration proposals led to a number of legislative changes to tighten hospital and physician payment rates under Medicare and to give states greater flexibility to set payment limits under Medicaid.

The state of Oregon has requested a waiver that would permit it to establish an explicit rationing system for care for low-income women and children covered under the state Medicaid plan. Under federal law, states are prohibited from limiting health care services on the basis of diagnosis or procedure. Although states set limits on number of hospital days or physician visits covered per year, they may not decline to cover care for patients with specific diagnoses or health conditions or specific services or procedures other than those in an experimental, developmental stage. The Oregon proposal would request a waiver of this prohibition to limit coverage of specific services on a demonstration basis. Low-income elderly and disabled would not be affected by this change. A state commission composed of lay people would rank all services and procedures from those that provide the greatest value per dollar to those providing the least value per dollar. State fiscal resources would determine a line below which services would not be covered. This waiver has been extremely controversial and has yet not been approved by the US Department of Health and Human Services. If approved, it could be subject to legislative action to repeal the waiver. Proponents believe that the waiver would give states flexibility to allocate resources more rationally. Opponents point to the fact that it would ration care only for poor women and children, not higher income persons, and that there is no scientific basis for the method of ranking services. They further note that the state of Oregon already has an extremely limited programme, and fails to cover many groups, such as the medically needy that are covered by other states.

The preoccupation with cutting Medicare, Medicaid, and primary care budgetary outlays and the absence of any presidential leadership in support of national health insurance, however, have stymied serious efforts to make further progress in improving access to health care. The result has been a marked slowdown in further improvements in improving health of the poor, and mounting evidence of a deterioration in access to health care services.

The number of uninsured has increased steadily throughout the 1980s (see Fig. 18.9). As shown in Table 18.7, the proportion of the population under age 65 without health insurance coverage from either a private plan or a public programme increased from 12.5 per cent in 1980 to 15.3 per cent in 1986—or from about 29 million people in 1980 to 37 million people in 1986.

The majority of non-elderly Americans receive health insurance coverage through their employers. Consequently, the common impression is that the uninsured are outside the work force—mostly young adults who have not yet found jobs. This is not the case. Surprisingly, over half of the uninsured, 19.6 million people, are in families where at least one member has a full-time job working 35 or more hours per week. Two-thirds of the uninsured are in families where at least one member works at least 17.5 or more hours per week (Congressional Research Service (CRS) 1988).

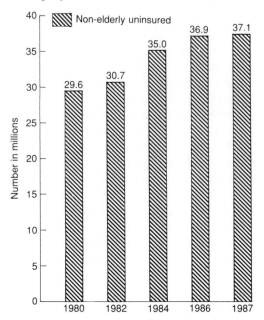

Fig. 18.9. The number of non-elderly uninsured (1980–7). Congressional budget tabulations based on Current Population Survey 3/80–3/86. Estimates by Karen Davis, John Hopkins University, based on Current Population Survey 3/87.

Table 18.7. Percentage of the population under age 65 without health insurance cover, by family income (1980 and 1986)

	1980	1986	Change (%) (1980–6)
*Total, all family incomes**	*12.5*	*15.3*	*22.4*
Less than US$10 000	31.0	37.0	19.4
US$10 000–US$14 999	25.9	31.3	20.8
US$15 000–US$19 999	15.0	21.2	41.3
US$20 000–US$34 999	6.2	8.4	35.5
US$35 000 or more	3.9	3.9	0.0

* Family income categories for 1980 are: less than US$7000; US$7000–US$9999; US$10 000–US$14 999; US$15 000–US$24 999; US$25 000 or more.
Source: *Health U.S.* (1988, p. 171).

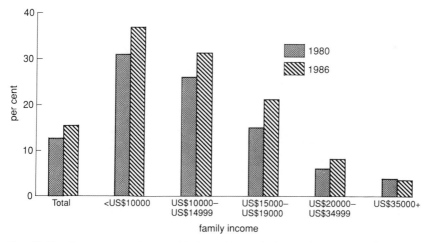

Fig. 18.10. Percentage of non-elderly uninsured, by family income (1980 and 1986). From *Health U.S.* (1988).

Gaps in employer-provided health insurance coverage occur because such cover is optional for employers. About half of all employed uninsured persons work in companies with fewer than 25 employees. Employer-provided health insurance coverage is particularly low in certain industries—including agriculture, construction, retail trade, and services. Cover of workers is lower in the south and west than in the north and central regions of the country.

About one-third of the uninsured are children under age 18. Half of the uninsured are parents or other adults between the ages of 17 and 45. The remaining 16 per cent of the uninsured are split equally between older adults between the ages of 45 and 54 and between the ages of 55 and 64. Many of these older adults are widows or spouses of retired persons who do not yet qualify for Medicare.

Nearly all of the uninsured have modest incomes (see Fig. 18.10). About one-third have incomes below the poverty level. Only 20 per cent have incomes greater than three times the poverty level. Individual purchase of private health insurance is not economically feasible for most of the uninsured. Individual plans typically have inadequate benefits and charge premiums well in excess of actual benefit outlays (Congressional Research Service, CRS 1988).

Although Medicaid provides a safety net for many low-income families, it covers only about half of the nation's poor (Holahan and Zedlewski 1991). Absence of Medicaid coverage among the poor occurs because states set income eligibility levels well below the federal poverty level and because categorical restrictions limit cover largely to one-parent families

—excluding two-parent poor families, childless couples, and single individuals (Schoen 1984; CRS 1988).

To a considerable extent health insurance cover in the US is a matter of luck. Those fortunate enough to be employed by large, unionized, manufacturing firms are also likely to be fortunate enough to have good health insurance cover. Those who have modest incomes, live in the south and west, or in rural areas, and those who are black or minority group members are more likely to bear the personal and economic effects of lack of insurance and the consequent financial barriers to health care.

Several factors account for deterioration in health insurance coverage in the 1980s:

- The growth of jobs in the service sector which tend not to have health insurance cover.
- The growth of jobs in smaller firms.
  The increasing tendency for employers to require employee contributions to health insurance premiums, including paying the full cost of dependant cover.
- The growth in one-parent families, who are less likely to have health insurance cover than two-parent families.
- The growth in the number of adults between the ages of 17 and 45 who are less likely to have health insurance cover.
- Financial pressures on government and employers that have led to a reduction in coverage.

Although considerable further analysis and research will be required to sort out the independent contribution of these and other factors, it is clear that gaps in employer-provided health insurance are responsible for a large portion of the uninsured population.

The reversal of trends in health insurance cover have important implications for trends in improving health of the disadvantaged and in access to health care services. A close examination of the trends in health status shown in Tables 18.1–18.3 reveals that most of the gains in improved health occurred in the period from 1960 to 1980, with relatively little further progress during the 1980s. Life expectancy at birth and at the age of 65 have increased only moderately since 1980. Age-adjusted deaths from pneumonia and influenza are up slightly in the 1980s, although further improvements have occurred in death rates from diseases of the heart and cerebrovascular diseases. Infant mortality rates have declined slowly in the 1980s (Griffith and Cislowski 1986). However, the percentage of black babies weighing less than 2500 grams is up slightly, and the percentage of black women receiving care in the first trimester of pregnancy is down somewhat. These data suggest that progress in improving

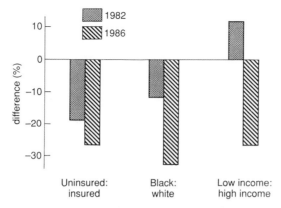

Fig. 18.11. Percentage difference in number of physician visits, by insurance cover, race, and income (1982–6). From Freeman *et al.* (1987).

health of poor and minority population groups has certainly slowed or halted, if not actually reversed.

A 1986 report supported by the Robert Wood Johnson Foundation contained evidence on the deterioration in access to health care in the 1980s (see Fig. 18.11) (Freeman *et al.* 1987). According to the survey, the years 1982 through 1986 witnessed a reversal in the trends over several prior decades of improving access to health services for low-income groups. For example, the rate of physician visits by low-income and black individuals in fair or poor health decreased between 1982 and 1986 (Table 18.8). On the other hand, physician visits by non-poor and white individuals with similar health status increased over the same period, widening a gap that had virtually disappeared prior to the last decade.

The uninsured are one-third more likely to be in fair or poor health than the non-elderly insured. Yet despite their poorer health status, in 1986 the uninsured received 27 per cent fewer physician services (Table 18.8) and were hospitalized 19 per cent less frequently than the insured. Further, one-fifth of the uninsured with chronic illnesses did not see a physician during the year. Fully two-thirds of the uninsured with serious symptoms (e.g., bleeding, loss of consciousness, chest pain, shortness of breath, weight loss unrelated to diet) did not see or contact a physician. One-fifth of uninsured pregnant women did not receive care in the first trimester of pregnancy. Twenty-two per cent of the uninsured with hypertension did not receive a blood pressure check in the year (Freeman *et al.* 1987).

Use of preventive services is particularly a problem for those without insurance. A study of the use of preventive screening services by women between the ages of 45 and 64 found that absence of insurance was the

Table 18.8. Mean number of physician visits, by insurance cover, race, and income (1982 and 1986)

	1982	1986	Change (%)
Uninsured	3.8	3.2	−16.8
Insured	4.7	4.4	−6.4
Difference (%)	−19.0	−27.0	
Black*	7.6	6.8	−10.5
White*	8.6	10.1	17.4
Difference (%)	−12.0	−33.0	
Poor and near-poor*	9.1	8.4	−7.7
Non-poor[1]	8.1	11.5	42.0
Difference (%)	+12.0	−27.0	

* Includes only individuals reporting their health as fair or poor.
Source: Freeman *et al.* (1987, pp. 10–13).

Table 18.9. Predictors of inadequate screening: logistic regression models

Predictor variable	β coefficient[1]				
	2 Hypertension screening	4 Pap. smear	2 Clinical breast examination	3 Glaucoma test	Any test
Lack of insurance	0.38^2	0.33^2	0.34^2	0.26^2	0.31^2
< 12 yrs educations	0.09^2	0.20^2	0.23^2	0.18^2	0.23^2
Black race	-0.25^2	-0.27^2	-0.20^2	0.002	0.19^2
Poverty	−0.05	0.10	0.11	0.15^3	0.12^3
Healthy	-0.50^2	0.003	0.003	0.02	0.07
Rural residence	−0.002	0.08	0.10	0.11^3	0.10^3
Intercept	2.22	0.79	0.26	0.44	−0.61

[1] β coefficient is for logistic model predicting inadequate receipt of recommended screening tests.
[2] $P < 0.01$.
[3] $P < 0.05$.
Source: Woolhandler and Himmelstein (1988).

single greatest barrier to obtain preventive care (see Table 18.9, Woolhandler and Himmelstein 1988).

Clearly, lack of health insurance coverage presents a significant threat to maintaining health and economic security. In all, 13.5 million people reported not receiving medical care for financial reasons in 1986. An estimated one million individuals actually tried to obtain needed care but

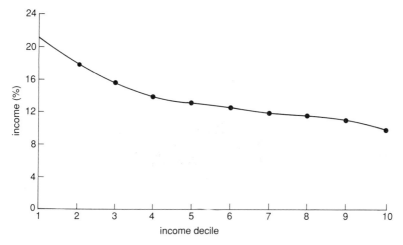

Fig. 18.12. Percentage of household income spent on health care, by income decile (1977). From Cantor (1988).

were turned away. Millions of Americans are at risk of death and disability because of an inability to pay for needed health care (Freeman *et al.* 1987).

The patchwork system of insurance cover leads to an inequitable distribution of the financial burden of health care. Cantor (1988), for example, finds that households in the lowest decile of money income spend 21 per cent of their incomes on health care—including direct outlays for health care and insurance as well as indirect outlays through taxes or costs shifted by employers (see Fig. 18.12). This contrasts with less than 10 per cent of income going for health care by households in the top income decile.

LOOKING FORWARD TO THE 21ST CENTURY

The US moves toward the 21st century with several major problems in its system of financing health care for its citizens. Over 35 million Americans have no health insurance cover—and evidence of the failure to get needed medical care as a result is a national embarrassment. The private health insurance market is becoming increasingly selective—with insurers declining to cover or restricting benefits for individuals viewed to be poor health risks. AIDS and biomedical advances in genetic screening that make it possible to identify individuals at risk for a wide range of health conditions will exacerbate this trend.

In addition, as the US population ages markedly in the next several decades the inadequacy of financing long-term care will become more serious. Over 30 per cent of the nation's elderly live alone—many without a child nearby to provide assistance when their ability to care for themselves becomes impaired (Commonwealth Fund Commission 1987). Substitutes for family care in the form of formal personal care are not widely available, not covered by Medicare or private health insurance, and of very uneven reliability and quality where they exist.

At the same time the US spends 11 per cent of its GNP on health care —more than 40 per cent more than the next closest country (Schieber and Poullier 1989 *a*). Further, health as a per cent of GNP has been increasing steadily throughout the 1980s, whereas it has stabilized at about 7 to 8 per cent of GNP in most other industrialized nations. Medicare and Medicaid represent the most rapidly increasing segments of federal and state government budgets.

To further complicate matters, Medicare will enter the next century on the brink of insolvency. The hospital portion of Medicare is financed by a payroll tax set at 2.9 per cent of earnings (including both the employer and employee share). By 1995 outlays under the hospital portion of Medicare will exceed payroll tax revenues flowing into the Hospital Insurance Trust Fund—beginning the depletion of accumulated reserves US Congress Committee on Ways and Means 1989). By the year 2006 under the most realistic economic assumptions, the Trust Fund will be bankrupt. This is just before the impact of the post-World War II baby boom bulge begins to affect retirement and growth in Medicare enrolment.

OPTIONS FOR REFORM

The magnitude of the problem the US faces is beginning to be reflected in calls for a fundamental reform of its health care financing system. In March 1990, a Bipartisan Commission on Health Care Reform—called the Pepper Commission in honour of the late Senator Claude Pepper who proposed legislation establishing the Commission—issued a report calling for universal health insurance cover and long-term care financing for all Americans (Pepper Commission 1990; Rockefeller 1991). Although the recommendations of this Commission are controversial and by no means certain of adoption, they have spawned several legislative proposals by leading members of Congress.

Proposals that have been advanced range from giving individuals publicly financed vouchers to purchase private catastrophic health insurance (advocated by the Heritage Foundation—a conservative think-tank) to those who advocate a Canadian-style system with comprehensive public financing of health services (Blendon and Edwards 1991; Butler 1991; Davis 1991; Enthoven and Kronick 1991; Grumbach *et al.* 1991; Rockefeller 1991). These approaches vary in their emphasis on efficiency versus equity. The Heritage plan, for example, places considerable reliance on patient out-of-pocket costs as a means of containing health care costs (Butler 1991). This approach, however, leads to considerable inequity. Low-income families pay a higher proportion of incomes than higher income families. It also leads to considerable horizontal inequity in that at any given income level those with more serious illnesses pay more.

Approaches such as the Pepper plan or a Canadian-type plan are primarily concerned with equity and removing financial barriers to care for those with low income. Some have argued, however, that by abandoning private market approaches to containing costs, a system modelled on the Canadian plan could lead to inefficiencies and lack of innovation in the long-run. Below, the Pepper plan is described in more detail.

THE PEPPER COMMISSION

Universal health insurance

The Pepper Commission proposal for assuring universal health insurance coverage has the following elements:

- All businesses with more than 100 employees would be required to provide all employees and non-working dependants with private health insurance with specified minimum benefits or make a payroll tax contribution to a public plan. Employers would have to pay at least 80 per cent of the private insurance premium. The minimum benefit plan includes hospital and physician services subject to a US$500 family deductible and a 20 per cent co-insurance with a maximum US$3000 annual ceiling on out-of-pocket spending. Preventive services, such as prenatal care, well-child care, mammograms, and Pap smears, are covered with no cost-sharing.

- Businesses with less than 100 employees would receive incentives to provide cover voluntarily to employees and dependants. This includes a tax credit/subsidy of 40 per cent of private health insurance premiums, reforms to make such insurance more affordable, and the option of purchasing coverage for employees under a public plan by making a payroll tax contribution. If, after five years, at least 80 per cent of small businesses did not provide cover to workers voluntarily, such coverage would be mandatory.

- The Pepper plan calls for replacing Medicaid with a new public plan with provider payment rates set at Medicare levels. It would eliminate all premiums and co-insurance for persons with incomes below the poverty level and provide subsidies for those with incomes between 100 per cent and 200 per cent of the federal poverty income level.

- Finally, the Pepper plan would permit any individual not covered by an employer plan to purchase such coverage from a public plan. Premiums would be eliminated for those with incomes below the poverty level, and subsidized for those with incomes between 100 and 200 per cent of the poverty income level.

- The plan is phased in gradually over seven years, beginning with cover of larger firms and public plan cover for poor pregnant women and children.

Long-term care financing

The Pepper Commission also contains major recommendations to improve financing for long-term care services for disabled individuals of all ages. These recommendations include:

- Providing up to 400 hours of home care for disabled individuals annually. Adult day care services may be substituted on a two-for-one basis with hours of home care coverage.
- Cover of the first three months of nursing home care.
- Cover of nursing home expenses after an individual has contributed all except US$30 000 of assets excluding the home and 30 per cent of income.

Health system reform

The Pepper Commission also set forth recommendations for major reforms in the health system:

- Private health insurance sold to small businesses would be regulated to guarantee community rating, prohibit refusing cover to high-risk groups or individuals, or excluding cover for pre-existing health conditions.

- Managed care options, such as health maintenance organizations and preferred provider organizations, would be made available to all persons covered by private or public plans.

- Private plans would be encouraged to pay physicians and hospitals according to Medicare payment rules which provide for compensation to physicians on the basis of a resource-based relative value fee schedule tied to a target on total outlays and to hospitals on the basis of

Diagnosis-Related Group prospective per patient payment rates. The new public plan for employment groups and individuals would also follow Medicare provider payment rules.

- The two Congressional Commissions charged with developing recommendations for the Congress on payment of hospitals (Prospective Payment Assessment Commission) and physicians (Physician Payment Review Commission) under Medicare would be asked to develop recommendations with regard to provider payment under private health insurance plans.

- Primary care services in underserved rural and inner-city poverty communities would be expanded.

- Funding for health promotion, disease prevention, risk reduction, and health education programme would be expanded by US$1 billion.

- Development of national practice guidelines and standards of care, expanded funding of effectiveness and health outcomes research, development of more effective methods of quality assessment and assurance, and a uniform health care data system would be facilitated.

Cost

The Pepper Commission estimated that the total cost of the plan when fully implemented would be US$66.2 billion in net new annual federal expenditures. This includes US$23.4 billion for universal health insurance cover and US$42.8 billion for long-term care financing. Some of these costs represent the replacement of federal government expenditures for services that are now financed privately—typically directly by patients who would be subsidized under the plan. The net new spending in the health system for acute health care services is estimated at US$15 billion.

These costs, although while modest compared to the US$600 billion the US spends on health care, have proved to be the most controversial features of the plan. The plan did not make recommendations about specific new taxes to finance the public cost of the plan, but rather stipulated that any financing source should be progressive, adequate to cover expenditures both initially and over time, and applied to persons of all ages—rather than financed by only the working population or the elderly population, for example.

Evaluation

The Pepper plan has several key characteristics that are particularly designed for the US economic and political system. It builds on the

American tradition of employer-provided health insurance cover for workers and their families and public plan cover for those falling outside the workplace. Building on this structure, it proposes a fundamental strengthening and integration of our mixed private–public system of health insurance cover to guarantee cover to all Americans. There are many innovative features of this plan which deserve special attention.

Insurance market reform

The private health insurance market is becoming increasingly selective— with insurers declining to cover individuals viewed to be poor health risks or instituting restrictions or waiting periods for pre-existing conditions. Small businesses, in particular, risk having their cover dropped if a worker or family member gets ill, or have certain individuals excluded from cover, or find premiums raised to exorbitant levels.

One of the most important features of the Pepper plan is the reform of the insurance market. It would prohibit excluding individuals or pre-existing conditions in small group plans. It would require that the same cover be offered to all firms on the same terms. A voluntary re-insurance mechanism for high-risk individuals would be established. These changes would go far to curb the worst abuses in the small employer insurance market, and forestall even greater trends toward denying cover to high-risk individuals.

Option of purchasing Medicare-type public cover

Another extremely innovative feature of the Pepper plan is the option it gives all employers and all non-working individuals to purchase coverage from a Medicare-type public plan. Employers could make a payroll tax contribution to cover all workers, or part-time workers only. This would eliminate the necessity for small businesses to provide and administer an adequate private insurance plan. It would provide subsidies for low-wage firms who found the private health insurance premium excessive. It would provide a stable source of insurance coverage for part-time, temporary, and seasonal workers who are in and out of the workplace. Unemployed workers could continue their cover by picking up the premiums based on their ability to pay.

Most importantly, retired individuals or other non-working adults under the age of 65 would have the opportunity of buying-in to a Medicare-type plan before 65. Employers would have the option of purchasing this cover for retirees rather than attempting to purchase such cover from very expensive private plans. In other cases, retirees do not receive any employer-provided health insurance. For these older adults the option of purchasing Medicare-type cover would be particularly attractive. Even disabled individuals must wait at least two years for Medicare cover. Spouses or widows of Medicare beneficiaries who are under 65 do not quality for Medicare. Such individuals could purchase cover with subsidies for those with incomes below 200 per cent of the poverty level.

MEDICAID REFORM

The Pepper plan would replace the current Medicaid programme with a universal low-income entitlement programme that is not tied to the welfare system—either in terms of eligibility or in terms of administration. All poor groups would receive cover without charge under this new federal public plan. Near-poor persons would contribute up to 3 per cent of income.

This new low-income plan would reverse some of the deterioration in the Medicaid programme that has occurred as the result of budgetary cutbacks in the 1980s. Physicians and hospitals would be paid at Medicare payment rates. Currently, Medicaid pays physicians at 64 per cent of the Medicare rate on average, but it varies widely from state to state. As a result, in many states physician participation rates in the Medicaid programme are quite low. Paying physicians at the Medicare rate should encourage greater provider participation and reverse the trend toward refusing care to Medicaid beneficiaries.

Cost containment and health system reform

The Pepper plan also contains a number of innovative features to encourage efficiency in the health care system. The most important in my view is extending Medicare's provider payment principles to a broader beneficiary base. The recently enacted Medicare physician payment reform represents a fundamental reform of physician payment in this country. It would reverse the bias toward high-cost speciality care and provide greater rewards for primary care. It would limit the financial burden to beneficiaries through limits on the actual amounts that a physician may charge a Medicare patient. Currently, physicians are free to set their own fees for Medicare patients. The difference between what the programme allows and what the physician charges is called 'balance billing' and is the financial responsibility of the patient. Under the new system balance billing could not exceed 15 per cent of the Medicare fee. It would establish targets on total Medicare physician outlays, known as Volume Performance Standards, to curb rising expenditures.

The Pepper plan would extend this system of payment as well as the

Medicare hospital prospective payment system to all beneficiaries covered under the public plan including employment groups and non-working individuals electing to purchase such public plan cover. This would greatly expand the scope and effectiveness of Medicare's cost containment measures. It would also strongly encourage private plans to adopt similar provider payment methods.

The one lesson from the experience of other industrialized nations that is most compelling is the effectiveness of cost containment in those systems with a strong government role in setting or negotiating provider payment rates. The Pepper plan is a significant step toward such an approach. Expanding the mandate of the Prospective Payment Assessment Commission and the Physician Payment Review Commission to develop recommendations on effective cost containment measures for both the public and private sectors is especially laudable.

Other recommendations that include support for effectiveness research, data systems including physician profiling and practice patterns for care of all patients not just Medicare beneficiaries, choices of managed care systems, funding of prevention, health education, outreach, and primary care, and quality assurance mechanisms are also extremely important.

Phasing

The Pepper plan would begin by insuring all the US nation's children followed by phased implementation of insurance cover for adults. This phasing places top priority on investing in the health of future generations by immediately assuring universal cover of pregnant women and young children, with complete cover of prenatal, well-baby, and other preventive services, such as Pap smears and mammography. All uninsured pregnant women, and children under the age of 6 would be eligible for public plan cover, with full subsidies for those in families with incomes below 185 per cent of the federal poverty level.

Cover of working families and adults outside the workforce would be phased in beginning with incentives for smaller firms to offer cover voluntarily, and following with mandatory cover for larger firms and then smaller firms if cover targets are not met voluntarily. In the final phases non-working adults would be permitted to purchase public plan coverage, with subsidies for poor and near-poor adults.

This phasing enhances both the economic and administrative feasibility of the plan. It gives employers opportunities to plan for workers' cover, and subsidizes the start-up of cover by firms. It would give employers time to make adjustments in total compensation packages to minimize unemployment and economic disruption effects.

Another advantage of the phasing approach is that it permits mid-course corrections to be made if economic conditions change or if the demands on the federal budget or health system should prove different than anticipated. Subsequent phase can be delayed or accelerated, for example, if initial cost estimates prove high or low. Experience with the cost-containment provisions can indicate whether more stringent measures are required, or whether private and public plans are building on the best elements of managed care and provider payment currently incorporated in Medicare and employer plans. Cover of an initial set of preventive services will provide evidence of the desirability of a broader preventive care benefit package.

Summary

The Pepper plan both as a comprehensive package and as innovative improvements in existing programs has much to commend it. It represents an equitable sharing of the burden of the cost of financing health care among large and small employers, among workers, those able to afford to contribute individually to their own cover, and federal and state governments. It builds on the administrative expertise in the private health insurance industry, while eliminating practices that have made health insurance unaffordable for many businesses. It institutes many much needed health system reform measures to curtail rising health care costs, and shifts the emphasis in the US health system toward prevention and primary care. It moves immediately to address our under-investment in the health of our children.

The Pepper Commission estimates that expanded health services for the uninsured would lead to a total increase in health spending of US$15 billion annually—about 2.5 per cent of current national health expenditures. With the expanding supply of physicians and hospital occupancy rates at record low levels, this new demand for health services should be easily accommodated without inflationary pressures.

Although the cost and economic impact would be small relative to our nation's economic resources, the improved access to health care services would have a major impact on solving one of the US nation's most pressing social problems. It would contribute to improved health of the population by removing financial barriers to medical care and increasing funding for prevention and primary care. Maternity and infant care services would be covered without cost-sharing for those covered by both employer plans and the new public plan that replaces Medicaid. Improved access to acute care for the uninsured will improved health and give children a better chance at productive lives.

The proposal would lead to a more equitable distribution of the financial burden of health care expenses. Maximum out-of-pocket ceilings on health care expenses would be instituted in all plans. Incentives to control costs and improve efficiency would be provided through numerous provider payment and system reform provisions. Quality standards would be developed and monitored through the public plan, private health insurance plans, and health maintenance organizations. Provider payment rates would be set to ensure continued room for technological progress and development.

Although the fate of the Pepper Commission recommendations remains in doubt, it has stimulated serious debate in the US about alternative directions for the health system. It is becomingly increasingly clear that the US cannot afford to continue on its present course—with a costly health system that lets many of its most vulnerable citizens fall through the safety net.

The Pepper Commission approach at this point seems to be receiving the greatest legislative attention. Its central feature of giving employers a choice of purchasing private health insurance for workers and dependants or paying a payroll tax to the government to provide cover under a public plan is at the core of legislative proposals by several leading members of Congress. These proposals differ on the extent of cost controls, and whether the governmental plan would be a uniform federal programme or a federal–state programme, but they share most of the key features of the Pepper Commission recommendations.

IMPLICATIONS OF COMAC-HSR FOR THE AMERICAN HEALTH POLICY DEBATE

The COMAC-HSR study has important implications for the American health policy debate. Perhaps the most important is that by documenting the degree of inequality of the financing of health care and in the receipt of health care services in contrast to that of European countries it can help to motivate change in the American political system. Americans are only recently becoming familiar with the fact that the US pays far more than any other nation for health care. It is also beginning to be aware that the US ranks relatively low on measures of health outcome, such as infant mortality or life expectancy.

However, virtually nothing is known to date about how the US compares in terms of the progressivity or regressivity of its health financing and delivery structure relative to that of other countries. The extreme inequality in the financing of health care services in the US relative to other countries is striking. It demonstrates that the patchwork system of health insurance cover and the heavy reliance upon out-of-pocket payment as well as flat insurance premiums imposes a far greater burden on lower income and modest income families. The US health financing system is not only regressive, but has an extreme degree of horizontal inequity. Out-of-pocket expenses, in particular, put heavy burdens on the sickest individuals at any income level.

The COMAC-HSR results, however, indicate that the programmes that the US has instituted since the mid-1960s, such as Medicare and Medicaid, have helped achieve greater equality in the utilization of health care services. With the exception of low-income individuals who are not covered by public programmes such as Medicaid, use of health services is relatively uniform across income classes. Basic health insurance cover for the elderly has helped bring their utilization in line with their need for health care.

The COMAC-HSR study also is useful in establishing a baseline by which to evaluate changes over time and against which to analyse the impact of alternative policy reforms in the US. It will be extremely important to learn whether the emphasis upon a competitive market approach in the 1980s has led to a further deterioration in the equity of financing and delivery of services in the US relative to European countries. As the US and other nations modify their systems, a follow-up study to discern the impact of such changes on trends in the equitable distribution of financing and delivery of services should be a high priority.

19

Equity in the distribution of health care: the British debate

Julian Le Grand

INTRODUCTION

In 1978, I published an article in *Economica* on the distribution of public expenditure on health care in England and Wales (Le Grand 1978). The article compared the distribution of illness with the distribution of public expenditure and arrived at the conclusion that, once the distribution of illness was taken into account, the distribution of public spending favoured the higher social groups. In other words, contrary to its stated intentions, the British National Health Service (NHS) was not providing equity in at least one interpretation of that term, equal treatment for equal need. Rather, it was providing more treatment per person ill for the better-off.

The research received a good deal of attention at the time, both from academics and from the national media. This was partly because it challenged popular preconceptions about the NHS in particular and about the welfare state in general. It appeared to show that, instead of being an instrument for helping the less well-off, a key part of the welfare state actually favoured the already comfortably off. Subsequently, this argument was elaborated, both within and outside the health care context, by a variety of authors in a number of books and articles (see, e.g., Le Grand 1982; George and Wilding 1984; Goodin and Le Grand, 1987; Ringen 1987; Pampel and Williamson 1989, Bramley *et al.* 1989).

Not surprisingly, there has also been research that has challenged both the original study and the others that gave a similar picture. The methodology has been criticized, different data have been marshalled and new, and sometimes conflicting, results obtained.

The issues involved in this debate are of great significance for policy, not only in the UK, but in all countries where the distribution of health care is an issue (which probably means all countries). Many of the questions raised are also of considerable methodological interest. Hence the aim of this chapter is to give a brief review of the debate, to assess

This work was funded under ESRC Research Grant No. R 000231635.

where we are now and give some suggestions for the direction that work in the area might take in the future.

THE DEBATE

The Le Grand study used data from the 1972 *General Household Survey* (GHS) on morbidity and on NHS utilization as reported by members of the households sampled.[1] Reported morbidity was of two kinds: acute sickness and chronic sickness.[2] People were allocated to a socio-economic group (SEG) on the basis of the occupation of the head of the household in which they lived. The numbers of people in a SEG who reported either acute or chronic or both were taken as an indicator of the group's need for health care. The GHS utilization data consisted of the number of GP consultations, outpatient attendances, and stays as a hospital inpatient undertaken by each member of each household. These data together with official estimates of the cost to the NHS of each unit of utilization (the cost per GP consultation, the cost per outpatient consultation, and the cost per inpatient day) were used to calculate the total cost of the health service resources used by each SEG. The estimates were divided by the numbers of people reporting illness to obtain the NHS expenditure per person in 'need'.

As mentioned above, the results showed a distribution that favoured the higher income groups. Expenditure per person ill on the highest SEG (professionals, employers, and managers, and their families) was over 40 per cent more than that for the bottom group (semi-skilled and unskilled manual workers and their families). This result remained even when the results were standardized for differences in the age and sex distribution of the groups.

Although, to judge from the reaction, both these results and similar ones concerning the extent of middle class use of other parts of the welfare state came as a surprise to many people unfamiliar with its detailed workings, they were consistent with the views of more experienced analysts of social policy. Twenty years earlier, Brian Abel-Smith (1958, pp. 56–7) noted that 'the working classes could... get... free health services before the war. The contributor to National Health Insurance had the services of a panel doctor and anyone who was poor could go to a voluntary or local authority hospital without any payment'. 'The main consequence of the development of the welfare state', he went on, 'has been to provide free social services to the middle classes'. Ten years later, Richard Titmuss (1968, p. 671) pointed to the welfare state's failure 'to close many gaps in differential access to, and effective utilisation of particular branches of our social services'. Peter Townsend's major study of poverty in the UK (1979, p. 222) found that, 'contrary to common belief, fewer individuals in households with low than with high incomes received social services in kind of substantial value'.

Moreover, the results were consistent with the findings of other studies that were specifically related to the NHS. Alderson (1970) concluded that, with respect to mass radiography, cervical screening, pregnancy and infant care, dental treatment, breast operations, and hospital referrals, use in relation to need was highest among social classes I and II and lowest among social classes IV and V. The *National Child Development Study* found that children up to the age of 7 in social class I, when compared with those in social class V, were twice as likely to have visited a dentist and 5, 10, and 11 times as likely to have been vaccinated against small-pox, polio, and diphtheria, respectively (Central Statistical Office, 1975).[3] Forster (1976) used GHS data on doctor consultations and reported morbidity to calculate use/need ratios for different SEGs. He found that these increased with SEG: that is, the higher groups used GPs more relative to their need than the lower ones. Hurst (1985) took 1976 GHS data on self-reported morbidity and utilization (GP and outpatient consultations, and inpatient nights) to calculate expenditure by income group. He concluded that there was extra use of the health services by the poor, but this fell 'somewhat short of their extra morbidity'.[4] A more qualitative study of GPs and their elderly patients (Cartwright and O'Brien 1976) found that GPs not only spent longer on average per consultation with their middle class patients than with their working class ones, but also discussed more problems with them and knew more about their health and domestic situations.

However, a number of studies appeared in the 1980s which appeared to yield rather different conclusions. First among these was a study by Collins and Klein (1980) that disaggregated 1974 GHS data on NHS utilization between genders and between the sick and the not-sick (as defined by self-reported morbidity). They found that the only consistent class gradient that favoured the top SEGs was for males in the not-sick category. The gradients for not-sick females and for sick males and females were either not smooth or favoured the lower SEGs. These results were confirmed by a subsequent analysis, using discriminant analysis (Collins and Klein 1985). Puffer (1986, 1987) undertook an econometric analysis of the determinants of GP use, again using GHS data. He found that, for a given level of morbidity, low income men may consult their GPs more, but low income women consult less, than the rest of the population. He also found only weak assocations between utilization and SEG.

A more disaggregated study of GP utilization by Evandrou *et al.* (1990), using 1980 and 1985 GHS data, yielded different conclusions for different age groups. Higher income/class respondents among males aged 41–64 and among females aged 16–40 and over 59 tended to under-consult relative to need, whereas higher income/class respondents among men 65 and over tended to over-consult. Only for males under 41 and for females aged between 41–59 was self-reported morbidity the sole determinant of utilization.

One difference between these studies and some of the earlier ones is that the later studies refer to GP utilization, whereas some of the others (including my own) incorporated hospital utilization (as outpatient and inpatient) as well. However, a study by O'Donnell and Propper (1991 *a*; see also chapter 14), applied the Le Grand methodology to 1985 GHS data on all three forms of utilization. They found that the distribution relative to need favoured the three higher SEGs, although the gradient was not smooth, with the skilled manual and own-account non-professionals having a greater expenditure per person reporting illness than the other two groups (professionals, employers, and managers, and intermediate and junior non-manual). However, this gradient disappeared when the results were standardized for age and sex differences between the groups, with the results showing no systematic bias in either direction.

So we have a puzzle. Several studies, mostly relying on data from the early 1970s, indicate that the distribution of NHS utilization relative to need favours the better-off and therefore is inequitable. On the other hand, there is another set of studies, mostly relying on somewhat later data, indicating that there is no systematic bias, except perhaps in a few age and sex groups, and hence conclude that the distribution of NHS utilization is broadly equitable.

How can the differences between these two sets of studies—the 'inequitable' and the 'equitable'—be explained? There are three kinds of possible explanation. One is that there were sampling or some other form of statistical errors in either (or both) sets of studies. A second is methodological; several of the studies used different methodologies and it is perhaps hardly surprising if, on occasion, this has led to different conclusions. The third possible explanation is that there were actually significant changes between the different data points in the factors determining the distribution. Given the number of studies in each set that give broadly similar pictures, the first explanation seems unlikely. The other two, however, deserve more consideration.

METHODOLOGY

Some of the 'equity' studies make a number of methodological criticisms of the 'inequity' studies, mostly arguing that the methodology used by the latter biases the results in favour of the better-off. For instance, the Le Grand study did not distinguish between users of the NHS who were sick and those that were not sick. Collins and Klein (1980, 1985) argued that, at least for the sick, their results showed there was no evidence of class bias in utilization; the inclusion of the not-sick (where there was a class bias) therefore simply distorted the picture. Wagstaff *et al.* (Chapter 4 and 1991 *a*) developed the argument. They showed that, if the not-sick were regarded as in need of some form of medical care (presumably rather less than the sick, but still positive), then, even if both sick and not-sick received the treatment that they needed, the 'inequity' methodology would yield results that were pro-rich, so long as there was a greater proportion of not-sick among the rich. O'Donnell and Propper (1991 *a*) make a similar point.

However, this argument does depend on the assumption that the not-sick can be properly described as in 'need' of medical care. As I argued elsewhere (Le Grand 1991), if that assumption does not hold, then the pro-rich 'bias' in the methodology no longer appears. Essentially, the difference between the two positions is whether the use of reported illness as an indicator of need (as in most of the studies on both sides) implies that those who do not report illness are not in need; one accepting that implication, the other rejecting it.

This argument raises questions concerning the nature of need that will not be resolved here. However, the explanation for the difference in the results cannot be laid simply at the door of methodology. For the differences occur even when the same methodology is applied (as in the case of O'Donnell and Propper, Hurst and Le Grand). Sampling errors aside, this suggests that there must have been some change in the underlying phenomena being explored.

EMPIRICAL CHANGES

There are a number of possible empirical explanations for the apparent change. The first of these is the possibility that they are due to various equalizing measures undertaken as acts of deliberate government policy. Most notable of these was the so-called RAWP policy to equalize hospital resources between regions in England.[5] This was instituted in 1976 and continued until the present (it is currently being abolished). It was quite successful with the relatively deprived regions experiencing a steady growth in their resources, while the better-provided regions have seen expenditures stay constant or fall. Overall, the variance in regional expenditures fell in every year, except two, since the inception of RAWP (Le Grand *et al.* 1990, p. 116).

However, RAWP only referred to hospitals; there was no equivalent equalizing policy for other aspects of care. In consequence, there was little change in these areas; the variance in GPs per capita across the regions, for example, remained constant throughout the period (Le Grand *et al.* 1990, p. 120). This is significant for, when O'Donnell and Propper disaggregated their figures between primary care and hospital care, they found the equalizing trend applied to both. This suggests that, whatever the consequences of RAWP, there must have been some other equalizing factors at work as well.

Another possible explanation concerns private care. The numbers of people covered by private health insurance in England and Wales more than doubled between 1976 and 1986, as did the number of beds available in private hospitals and nursing homes (Le Grand *et al.* 1990, p. 106). Because it is likely that most of the increase in the users of private medical care came from the better-off, it is possible that this depressed middle class use of the NHS relative to that of the less well-off and therefore that this contributed to the equalization. However, again this is not likely to be the totality of the explanation. Even after the growth in private medical care, the sector remained small relative to the NHS as a whole; in 1987, benefit payments by private health insurers amounted to less than 3 per cent of NHS expenditures in total (Le Grand *et al.* 1990, p. 108). Moreover, to test this explanation, O'Donnell and Propper added in estimates of private expenditures to public expenditures and found it made very little difference to the overall results.

The most plausible explanation is also discussed by O'Donnell and Propper. This concerns an increase in the proportion of individuals reporting illness over the period. Although, somewhat surprisingly, all groups showed such as increase, it was significantly larger among the higher income groups. Thus, the percentage of professionals reporting illness nearly doubled from 1972 to 1985, whereas that for employers and managers increased by well over a third. In contrast, the percentage for semi-skilled manual workers increased by under a third and that for unskilled manual workers by only one-ninth (O'Donnell and Propper 1991 *a*, Table 6). Overall, it would appear that middle class health, at least as reported to the GHS, has declined relative to working class health; but this has not been matched by an increase in middle class utilization of the NHS.

This apparent equalization of morbidity over the period is in contrast to some of the analysis of mortality differentials between the social classes carried out in the tradition of the report by Black (1980). This suggests a widening of the gap, at least between 1970 and 1980. However, the methodology of studies that rely on the mortality experiences of different classes is suspect, not least because most deaths now occur outside the age ranges to which social class classifications can be confidently applied. Moreover, the SEG equalization in morbidity is at least consistent with the reduction in inequality in *population* mortality detected in other work (see, for example, Illsley and LeGrand 1987).[6]

What is rather more worrying is the secular growth for all groups in self-reported morbidity—at least from the point of view of those using this as an indicator of need (as virtually all the distribution of health care studies do). For it is hard to believe that there has 'really' been a decline in the average health of the population over the period. Moreover, it conflicts with the well-attested continuous decline in age-specific mortality rates.

Le Grand, Winter, and Woolley discuss some of the possible reasons for the apparent growth in morbidity. First, the population as a whole is ageing, which in so far as increasing age is correlated with increasing ill health should lead to a rise in the latter, even if age-specific mortality rates were declining. However, Winter (1991) in an analysis of the changes in self-reported morbidity rates for different cohorts of males found that the rate was increasing even for males of the same age. Secondly, there may be an increased willingness to report illness but the illness may be less serious; a proposition for which there is some support from the GHS. Finally, Winter found some evidence that the increase in self-reported morbidity was linked to unemployment, the impact on mortality of which is yet to appear.

Overall, this discussion casts doubt on the use of GHS-type reported morbidity questions as an indicator of need. An important task for the future is to refine these indicators.

WHERE DO WE GO FROM HERE?

As I have said elsewhere (Le Grand 1991), it seems to me the jury is still out as to whether the British NHS provides equal treatment for equal need. But that does not mean the debate has been a waste of time. It has led (and continues to lead) to some interesting and important debates concerning the methodology of these kind of studies. More importantly, as we have seen, it has cast some doubt on GHS-type of self-reported morbidity as an indicator of 'need'. For reasons given elsewhere (Le Grand 1982, pp. 35–6) I am convinced that self-reported morbidity is the best (or, rather, the least worse) indicator of need. However, an urgent task for this kind of work in the future is to undertake these kinds of studies with more sophisticated indicators of self-reported morbidity.

Another gap in the literature concerns the groups with whose use relative to need we are concerned. All of the studies discussed here have concentrated on income or occupational groups. However, there are other ways of 'slicing' a society. A distribution by different regions would be interesting, as might be a distribution comparing urban and rural areas. A distribution by ethnic origin might be revealing. But perhaps even more interesting (and relatively easy to do with available data) would be a distribution by gender. This would not only be of importance in its own right, but it might have implications for the policy conclusions to be drawn from the socio-economic studies. For instance, if it was established that there was a middle class bias in utilization relative to need, the policy conclusions might be different if it arose from middle class women using maternity services rather than middle class men with stress-induced ulcers. There are important issues here which a narrow focus on socio-economic categories neglects.

NOTES

1. The *General Household Survey* is a continuous survey of some 32 000 people that has been carried out annually by the Office of Population Censuses and Surveys (OPCS) every year since 1971. The most recent at the time of writing is reported in OPCS (1990).
2. The relevant GHS questions were: (acute) During the last two weeks, did you have to cut down on any of the things you usually do ... because of illness or injury?; (chronic) Do you have any long-standing illness, disability or infirmity ... that limits your activities in any way?
3. Social class, like socio-economic group, is a classification system based on the occupation of the head of the household. However, it is slightly different; see OPCS (1980).
4. He was obviously not very happy with this conclusion for he goes on: 'However, more sophisticated analysis of the GHS may give a different answer' (Hurst 1985).
5. It was called RAWP after the initials of the working group that set it up: the Resource Allocation Working Party. For the report of this working party, see Department of Health and Social Security (1976).
6. As some readers will be aware, this paragraph does less than justice to a ferocious debate concerning the existence or otherwise of a class gap in mortality in England and Wales that is widening over time. As well as the references in the text, the flavour of the debate is illustrated by the contributions of Townsend (1990) and Klein (1991); these also contain references to most of the other relevant contributions. An interesting attempt to reconcile some of the differences between the protagonists can be found in Wagstaff *et al.* (1991 *b*).

Equity in health care and health care financing: evidence from five developing countries

Judy L. Baker and Jacques van der Gaag

INTRODUCTION

Health care as a measure of development

It is often argued that a country's per capita income is a poor indicator of the welfare of its population. One objection to this average measure is that it ignores distributional aspects. For example, a country with a relatively high per capita income can still have large numbers of poor people due to a highly skewed income distribution.[1] Average per capita income says nothing about the living conditions of these people.

Another objection is that income is just one aspect of welfare. Security, freedom, longevity, health status, literacy, and nutrition are all relevant to a person's overall well-being. The arguments to incorporate these aspects in the assessment of a country's level of development have recently been put forward forcefully in the *World Development Report* (World Bank 1990). Some of these other dimensions of well-being are hard to measure (e.g., freedom), but others have long been documented for many developing countries. In this chapter we will focus on those aspects of well-being that are directly related to health: health status indicators, health care utilization patterns and health care financing.

Health status is one of the most prominent 'non-monetary' indicators of a country's development performance. Indicated by such measures as life expectancy at birth or infant mortality,[2] it shows a country's success or failure in providing the most basic necessities to its population. These necessities go well beyond medical care. They include adequate food supply, access to clean drinking water, safe sewerage, sanitary housing conditions, as well as knowledge regarding nutrition practices, family planning, and preventive health measures. They also include, of course, access to and utilization of pre- and postnatal health care services, preventive care, primary health care, and immunization services.

In Fig. 20.1 we present life expectancy at birth and infant mortality rates, as a function of GNP per capita, for 34 countries. The countries

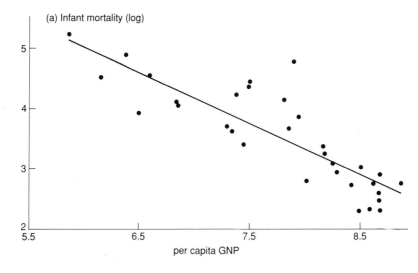

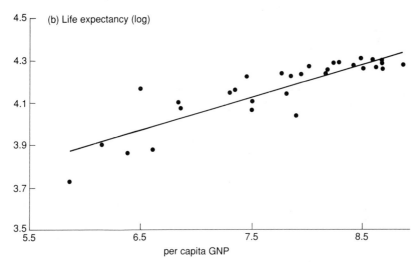

Fig. 20.1. Health indicators and GNP for 34 countries (listed in Table 20.1). From Gertler and van der Gaag (1990).

chosen are the same as those included in Kravis *et al.* (1982) and represent all stages of development. The countries are listed in Table 20.1 in ascending order of per capita GNP. The lines drawn through the scatter diagrams in Fig. 20.1 represent double logarithmic regressions (see Gertler and van der Gaag 1990, for a detailed explanation). Two results stand out. First, there is a strong correlation between these health status indicators and GNP per capita. Health status is, on average, considerably

Table 20.1.   GNP per capita, selected countries (1975, US$)

Country	US$	Country	US$
Malawi	351	Iran	2704
Kenya	470	Uruguay	2844
India	470	Ireland	3048
Pakistan	590	Hungary	3558
Sri Lanka	667	Poland	3597
Zambia	737	Italy	3861
Thailand	936	Spain	4010
Philippines	996	UK	4587
Korea	1484	Japan	4906
Malaysia	1540	Austria	4994
Colombia	1608	Netherlands	5397
Jamaica	1722	Belgium	5574
Syria	1794	France	5876
Brazil	1811	Luxembourg	5883
Romania	2386	Denmark	5910
Mexico	2487	Germany	5952
Yugoslavia	2591	US	7176

Source: Kravis (1982).

higher in the richer countries than in the poor ones, and the difference is large. Life expectancy ranges from 43 in Guinea to 76 in the US, and the infant mortality rate ranges from 168 in Mali to 5 in Japan.

Secondly, even at given levels of development as measured by GNP per capita—some countries perform much better than others. For instance, Chile with a GNP of US$1510 in 1988 had a life expectancy rate of 72 and infant mortality of 20. In Sri Lanka, GNP was much lower, US$420, but life expectancy (71) and infant mortality (21) are very similar to rates in Chile.

These examples show that there is not a simple relationship between income growth and improved health status. Much depends on policies that directly or indirectly effect the population's health. This makes health status interesting as an indicator of a country's level of development.

The role of the government

Given the importance of health status as one measure of success or failure in development,[3] it is perhaps not surprising that the government plays a large role in providing health care services, health care financing, or in both. Indeed, in developing and developed countries alike, the government is often the largest actor in the health care sector.

Governments in developing countries typically attempt to provide a health care system that enables equal access for everyone. Through a variety of mechanisms the government supplies free or low-cost curative care, administers social security systems that cover curative services for insured workers, supports medical personnel training, and finances control programmes for vector-borne diseases, water and sanitation projects, and other public health activities. Public funding for health care is supported almost exclusively by general tax revenues, and redistributed through the ministry of health.

A government's level of commitment to improving health status is extremely important in affecting progress. In Costa Rica for example, the government implemented several high-cost health and nutrition initiatives in the 1960s and 1970s. By 1985, Costa Rica was spending 23 per cent of its government budget on health.[4] As a result of this long-term effort infant mortality rates have decreased from 114 per 1000 live births in 1965 to 18 in 1988. Life expectancy, now 75, is the same as in industrialized countries, such as the UK, Germany, and New Zealand.

Although this level of commitment is lacking in many countries, the overall improvements in health care over the last three decades indicate that as a whole, governments in the developing world have made significant efforts to provide access to medical services for all segments of the population.[5] Still, as shown above, between country inequalities in health outcomes are large. In the next section we will take a closer look at some within-country inequalities.

Evidence of within-country inequalities

Despite efforts to provide equal access to health care for everyone, there are great disparities in the care received among the population in developing countries. Limited financial resources have meant that it is impossible to provide an adequate level of care for everyone. Through government policies regarding the dispersion of resources and the existing distribution of welfare among the populations, patterns of inequality have emerged which favour urban-based curative care over basic preventive measures that could greatly benefit the large numbers of poor people that reside mainly in rural areas (see Akin *et al.* 1987).

In most developing countries 70 per cent or more of government spending on health goes to urban hospital-based care. Even in China, a country that has promoted equity in all major aspects of well-being as an official government objective, rural households account for 79 per cent of the total population, but receive only 29 percent of expenditures for health care (Akin *et al.* 1987).

Hospitals, which are very expensive to operate, are primarily located in the cities in part because they need a large enough catchment area to operate on full capacity. Although hospitals do play an important role in the health care system, they absorb a disproportionate amount of resources thus impeding sufficient funding for basic curative and pre- ventative services. The most common cause of hospitalization in the developing world is infectious diseases. If public resources were funnelled to basic services, many of these diseases could be treated at an earlier stage or prevented altogether.

The portion of the budget allocated to rural care is insufficient; many rural facilities operate with deteriorating buildings, no electricity, a non- working water supply, and shortages of drugs and equipment. Low salaries and poor working conditions contribute to a loss of trained personnel. India, for example, which is widely regarded as having a surplus of physicians, had vacancy rates of 30–90 per cent in the early 1980s for professional health positions in rural states (Akin *et al.* 1987).

The inequity in spending is further exacerbated by the unequal distri- bution of income in developing countries. Private costs, rationing, and higher family incomes in the cities cause the wealthy to benefit more from public services than the poor. Individuals must incur the costs of trans- portation to the hospitals or clinics (which are often far away), and then must spend time waiting in lines. Studies from Uganda, Nigeria, and Côte d'Ivoire report that patients spent between 2 to 8 hours for a few minutes of attention. These costs may be greater for the poor in relation to their income and even in absolute terms. The poorest groups tend to live in the rural areas where the transportation costs to hospitals and clinics are greater than for urban dwellers. In some cases, people have to pay for lodging and meals as well (see de Ferranti 1985; Jimenez 1986).

The differential access is largely responsible for the wide differences in medical consumption between urban and rural sectors. The disparities are also reflected in large urban–rural differentials in health status. In Côte d'Ivoire, life expectancy was approximately 56 years in the capital city Abidjan, compared with only 39 years in the rural Savanna regions (1979). In Peru, the infant mortality was 53 in Lima and as high as 127 in the Huancavelica district (1989).

The evidence shows overwhelmingly that many countries have failed to obtain equity in health status and in access to medical care. Given the importance of the issue, it is surprising that there are only a few studies that look at equity in health and medical care in a systematic way for developing countries. The few available studies are reviewed in Selden and Wasylenko (1990). Those which are based on household level data include Meerman (1979) for Malaysia, Selowsky (1979) for Colombia, and Foxley *et al.* (1979) for Chile.

The Selowsky study (1979) finds significant variation in health services among urban areas of different sizes in Colombia. Urban households receive a subsidy at least twice as large as that received by their rural counterparts, and almost three times as large in the poorest quintile. Meerman (1979) finds differences in mortality rates in Malaysia for the various racial groups (which he uses as a proxy for different income groups). The Malays (characterized as poor and rural) had above average mortality rate, although consumption levels of medical care in rural areas are above average for the country and far ahead of those for the metropolitan areas. This suggests that the poor rural population receives care of a quality below that of the care received by the urban and better off. Foxley *et al.* (1979) determines that all national health service programmes in Chile are distributed in a strong progressive pattern. Health benefits are equivalent to 16 per cent of a poor family's income, but only 0.7 per cent of a well-off family's income.

In the remaining sections of this chapter we will look at detailed, household level data for five developing countries. We will examine to what extent equity has been achieved in health status and health care utilization. We will also try to complete the picture by looking at equity in health care financing.

In the next section we will present brief descriptions of the health care delivery and financing systems in the five developing countries. In the third section (p. 379) we will show how health status and health care utilization differs between urban and rural areas and, within these areas, by level of income. The final section of this chapter draws conclusions.

HEALTH AND DELIVERY SYSTEMS AND EQUITY IN FINANCING

In this section we will briefly describe the health care delivery systems in Côte d'Ivoire, Ghana, Jamaica, Peru, and Bolivia. These countries were chosen for the sole reason that for each of them *Living Standard Measurement Study* (LSMS) data are available. These data include individual and household level information that allows for the precise measurement of health care utilization by income group and by urban and rural regions. The LSMS project and the data used are discussed briefly in the next subsection.

The countries represent various levels of development, with Jamaica being the richest in terms of GNP per capita, US$1260, and Ghana the poorest, US$390 (see Table 20.2). They also show a wide range in life expectancy, from 53 years in Côte d'Ivoire to 73 in Jamaica, and in infant mortality rates from 16 in Jamaica to 106 in Bolivia.

Figure 20.2 shows that Jamaica in terms of health outcomes, given its GNP per capita, out-performs the other countries. The regression line in

Table 20.2. Socio-economic indicators for 5 developing countries

Country	GNP per capita (US$)	Life exp. at birth	Infant mort. per 1000	Pop. per doctor	Pop. per nurse	Total expendit. on health (%)	Per capita expendit. on health (US$)*
	1989	1989	1989	1984	1984	1988	
Côte d'Ivoire	790	53	92	16 320	4240	8.0	6.00
Ghana	390	55	86	14 890	640	9.0	4.00
Jamaica	1260	73	16	2040	490	6.5	35.75
Peru	1010	62	79	1040	–	5.8	7.50
Bolivia	620	54	106	1540	2480	1.9	5.70

* Per capita expenditures are for the years 1987 in Jamaica, 1988 in Côte d'Ivoire and Bolivia, and 1990 in Ghana and Peru.
Source: World Bank (1991).

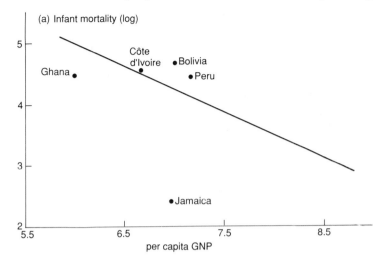

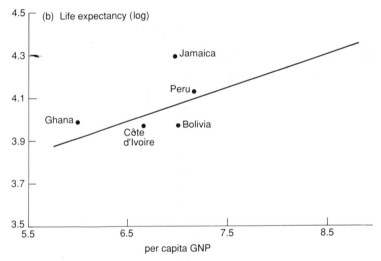

Fig. 20.2. Health indicators and GNP for 5 developing countries, 1988 (listed in Table 20.2).

each figure is the same as in Fig. 20.1. Bolivia and Côte d'Ivoire, on the other hand show below average health status indicators.

The descriptions of health care systems on pp. 364–79, will also provide the information on health care financing. Unfortunately, due to data limitations, the analyses of the equity of *public* financing (that is, of the tax revenues or public insurance system) can only be impressionistic. Reliable data on tax incidence are not available.

Living standard measurement studies

The data used in this study are from the *Living Standards Measurement Study* (LSMS) in the above-mentioned countries. The LSMS programme at the World Bank was instigated in 1980 based on the need to improve data collection efforts in developing countries in order to understand better the extent of poverty and the determinants of living standards (see Glewwe 1990, for a more detailed description of the LSMS). The survey is designed to provide household level data for evaluating the effect of various government policies on the living conditions of the population. Surveys have thus far been carried out in six countries; Côte d'Ivoire (1985, 1986, 1987, 1988), Ghana (1987–8, 1988–9), Peru (1985–6, 1990), Bolivia (1988, 1989), Jamaica (1988, 1989), and Mauritania (1987–8). Field work and preparatory activities are currently underway in Laos, Morocco, Pakistan, Venezuela, and Poland.

The data collected by the LSMS surveys relate to all aspects of household decision-making and well-being including income, consumption, savings, employment and unemployment, health, education, fertility and contraceptive prevalence, nutrition, housing, and migration.

For the purposes of this study, LSMS data on consumption, health status, and health care from the five countries listed above (excluding Mauritania) were analysed. Each country has been divided into rural and urban groups, and then into income quintiles based on *per capita* consumption. Separate rural and urban quintiles were created because of the large regional disparities in welfare.

The questions in each survey were almost identical, with the exception of a few country-specific variations. The questions relating to health status are whether a household member had been ill or injured during the last four weeks, and how many days that illness or injury had prevented that person from their usual activity. Questions concerning health care include whether or not care was sought for that illness or injury, who was consulted, where the consultation took place, if the patient was hospitalized, and for how many days the hospitalization lasted. For those who have received care, expenditures for the medical consultation, hospital care, and medication are recorded. Finally, there are questions related to the incidence of preventive care such as whether or not a household member had been vaccinated in the past year.

Health care delivery and financing systems in five countries

Côte d'Ivoire

Delivery   Health-related indicators for Côte d'Ivoire are low and below what would be expected for a country of its level of income (Table 20.2).

Life expectancy is only 53 years and the infant mortality rate of 92 per 1000 live births is well above the average of 57 for other lower-middle income economies. The causes of mortality and morbidity are similar to those in other West African countries, with measles, tetanus, lower respiratory infections, malaria, and whooping cough, and meningitis, compounded by malnutrition as the primary causes of death.

The public health care delivery system is run by the Ministry of Public Health and Population (Ministère de la Santé et de la Population, MSSP) which operates three university hospitals (located in the capital, Abidjan), seven regional hospitals in the cities of Bouake, Man Daloa, Abengourou, and Korogho, and a network of small local hospitals, health centres, dispensaries, and maternities. Other public sector units that provide health care include the armed services and the Caisse Nationale de Prévoyance Sociale (a social security system for civil servants and professional classes). Medical care in these facilities is free although some efforts are currently underway to introduce user-fees for hospital care.

In 1983, the public health system employed approximately 600 doctors, 2200 nurses, 1000 midwives, and 7000 non-civil services support staff (of which a vast majority are unskilled workers). The hospital sector employs 70 per cent of all doctors, 45 per cent of all midwives, and over 50 per cent of all nurses (Dor and van der Gaag 1987). The overall ratios of population per physician (16 323) and population per nurse (4245) are low (see Table 20.2).

Private health care in Côte d'Ivoire is available through 40 clinics (with 550 hospital beds) which are primarily located in Abidjan and Bouake. In 1987, these clinics employed 63 full-time and 122 part-time physicians, and 237 full-time and 48 part-time paramedics. The Polyclinic Saint Anne-Marie in Abidjan is the largest clinic, which alone has over 40 per cent of all private beds and employs 75 part-time doctors. There are a number of doctors and dentists with private practices, however, no official count of them has been made. The quality of care available in the private sector appears to be quite high, as are the costs. Only those who are very wealthy or have private medical insurance can afford to seek private health care.

The manufacturing and distribution of pharmaceuticals is primarily done in the private sector. In 1988, the company CIPHARM produced 250 million pills (aspirin, chloroquine, etc.) which were dispersed through 200 private pharmacies and 250 warehouses (mainly concentrated in Abidjan).

The distribution of the available resources in the health care system appears to be unequal, favouring curative, urban-based care. Although only 45 per cent of the population lives in urban areas, all major hospital facilities are located in the cities. The number of hospital beds per 10 000 population is 6.7 in the South Region which includes the capital, Abidjan, but only 1.8 in the West. There is also a great disparity in the staffing patterns between urban and rural posts. In rural areas, there were only 0.6 physicians and 10 nurses per 100 000 population. The three teaching hospitals in Abidjan alone employ a disproportionate 36 per cent of all physicians, and 22 per cent of all nurses.

Finance   The majority of the health budget comes from the government, with only a small portion generated from local government, international agencies, and direct payments from consumers. Government spending on health care in 1988 was about 1.3 per cent of GDP, or 8 per cent of the total recurrent budget. This translated to US$6 per capita which is relatively high by West African standards.

Personnel costs account for over 70 per cent of the health budget with the remainder being spent on materials, equipment and maintenance (21 per cent), and medicines (7 per cent). Large budget allocations on urban, hospital-based care partially explain some of the shortage in resources for materials, pharmaceuticals, and nursing staff. In 1985, only 11 per cent of the recurrent budget went to rural operations, whereas 51 per cent went directly to hospitals.

Tax revenues are the main source of overall government financing (70 per cent in 1984), with the remaining 30 per cent from property income, government fees and charges, and grants (see Table 20.3). The tax structure in Côte d'Ivoire is mildly progressive with revenue generated from four principle sources; direct taxes (6 per cent of GDP), indirect taxes on domestic goods and services (6.6 per cent of GDP), agricultural export taxes (6.9 per cent of GDP), and import duties (7.3 per cent of GDP).

Direct taxes, which are derived from taxing personal and corporate income, are progressive. Rates on personal income rise incrementaly, from 26 per cent for the lowest income level to 32 per cent for the wealthiest individuals. Note that only 12 per cent of the population participating in the labour force is a wage earner (Newman 1987) and that, in general, wage earners are in the middle and upper-middle part of the income distribution.

Government revenue from indirect taxes on domestic goods and services are also progressive, generated primarily from value-added tax (VAT) and excise taxes. VAT is levied at varying rates; 5 per cent on palm oil, 9.5 per cent on non-exempt foodstuffs, fertilizers, and equipment goods, 19 per cent on general manufactured items, and a higher rate of 25 per cent on jewellery, cosmetics, and firearms. Many basic items are exempt from VAT including: (1) imports and local sales of most basic foodstuffs, books, and fertilizers, minerals, metals and pharmaceuticals; (2) agriculture, fishing, and forestry; (3) most agro-processing activities;

Table 20.3. Côte d'Ivoire: structure of government revenue (1984)

Source	Total revenue (%)
Individual tax	5.9
Corporate tax	4.5
Total income tax	*11.4*
Sales tax and VAT	7.8
Excises	4.5
Services	3.3
Total indirect tax	*15.7*
Import Duties	19.1
Export Duties	7.6
Total international tax	*26.7*
Social security	4.4
Employers payroll	3.6
Property	2.7
Other taxes	5.9
Total tax revenue	*70.4*
Non-tax revenue	*29.6*

Source: *Government Finance Statistics Yearbook* (1987).

and (4) transportation of goods produced in Côte d'Ivoire. The excise on petroleum is substantial, accounting for 4 per cent of revenue of which 40 per cent are paid by goods transport, 10 per cent by industry, and 50 per cent on gasoline paid by consumers who drive private automobiles. This too is considered a progressive tax because petroleum is consumed at higher levels by urban dwellers, which on average have higher per capita income. In the rural villages, 1.22 per cent of household consumption goes towards the purchase of petrol compared with 2.45 per cent in Abidjan and 2.92 per cent in other urban areas.

Government revenues from export taxes on cocoa and coffee could, if passed on from the exporters to producers, be considered a proportional tax. Coffee and cocoa producers in Côte d'Ivoire are distributed most heavily in the middle income deciles (and are underrepresented in the top three deciles) (see Benjamin and Deaton 1988).

Import duties which account for the most substantial portion of revenue are structured progressively, with tariffs ranging from 10 per cent on food items to 215 per cent on imported beverages. Many of the tariffs on more basic food items and pharmaceuticals are exempted from collection.

Financing for health care is also supplied by The National Fund for Social Security which provides insurance payments for pensions, worker accidents, and curative, and preventive care for its members. Eligible workers pay a percentage from their salaries, which is sometimes matched by the employer, to the system. Cover is limited to the small proportion of the labour force who are wage earners and excludes the vast majority of the population who are self-employed.

In sum, the public health care financing system in Côte d'Ivoire is likely to be mildly progressive due to the facts that virtually all resources come from the central government, taxes are progressive, and the small part of social security payments that is used to cover health care cost is only levied on wage earners.

Ghana

Delivery   Ghana's health indicators, although slightly better than in neighbouring Côte d'Ivoire, despite it's lower per capita GNP, still show that the population suffers from a relatively poor health status (see Table 20.2). Preventable infectious and parasitic diseases account for the majority of morbidity, with malaria alone responsible for 43 per cent of those illnesses. Life expectancy in 1989 was 55 years and infant mortality 86 per 1000 live births.

Delivery of health services is carried out through the Ministry of Health (MOH), a large representation of Non-Government Organizations (NGOs), and a significant private sector. Most hospitals (70 per cent) are run by the Ministry of Health with 49 general hospitals, 12 specialized hospitals, 12 hospitals run by 'parastatals', and another 10 hospitals run by the armed forces and police. The remaining 30 per cent of the hospitals in the country are mission facilities. Clinics, health centres, and maternity homes are primarily operated by the private sector (400 clinics and 300 maternity homes) and the MOH (310 health centres and 170 maternity centres).

Of the estimated 965 doctors practising in Ghana, 65 per cent work in the public sector, and 35 per cent in the private sector (which includes the 9 per cent working in missions). Approximately half of the registered nurses in the country are professional and the other half are auxiliary nurses. The MOH employed 50 per cent of all nursing staff, the private sector 40 per cent, and the missions 10 per cent.

Health coverage is skewed; only about 50 per cent of rural dwellers have access to local services, whereas 100 per cent of those in urban areas do. In rural areas that cover varies greatly, from 10 per cent in the least-served regions to 100 per cent in the most widely covered. Seventy-two per cent of MOH hospitals are located in urban areas where only 33 per cent of the population live. Population per physician ratios indicate that the distribution of personnel is also very uneven. For the country, the population per physician ratio is 14 890, and population per nurse 640. In Greater Accra that ratio was 5764 persons per physician and in the

Table 20.4. Ghana: structure of government revenue (1988)

Source	Total revenue (%)
Individual tax	9.3
Corporate tax	19.4
Total income tax	*28.7*
Sales tax and VAT	8.0
Excises	17.6
Services	0.5
Total indirect tax	*26.1*
Import duties	16.6
Export duties	15.9
Total international tax	*32.5*
Other taxes	4.9
Total tax revenue	*92.2*
Non-tax revenue	*7.8*

Source: *Government Finance Statistics Yearbook* (1987).

northern region 63 095. A major problem with Ghana's health care system is the under-utilization of facilities which is attributed to a past declining quality of services and greatly increased fees and drug charges.

Finance Expenditures on health services in Ghana consist of MOH, NGO, and private expenditures. An estimated breakdown of those expenditures indicates that 37 per cent came from the MOH (including the recurrent budget and user-fees), 51 per cent from private-for-profit expenditures, and 12 per cent from NGOs. Government spending on health in 1990 was about 2 per cent of GDP, and 11 per cent of the total recurrent budget. This is equivalent to US$4 per capita.

The most significant portions of the MOH budget are allocated to personnel costs (46 per cent) and supplies (equipment, drugs, dressings, etc.). Transport and maintenance received 2 and 4 per cent, respectively, and subventions (mainly for staff admission hospitals) accounted for 8 per cent. Primary health care comprised 25 per cent of the total budget.

The majority of MOH financing comes from the recurrent government budget, which in turn receives over 90 per cent of its revenues from taxes. Cost recovery (particularly for drugs), accounted for approximately 7 per cent of MOH expenditures in 1989. The largest shares of tax receipts in Ghana are generated from taxes on domestic production and consumption and international transactions which together account for 58 per cent of government revenue (see Table 20.4).

The sales tax (which is currently undergoing reform) is a progressive tax applicable on selected domestically produced goods at a rate of 25 per cent on soft drinks, cigarettes, beer, and wine in 1988. Luxury goods were taxed at a higher rate and items, such as drugs, basic raw materials, and agricultural machinery and equipment, are exempt from the tax. The import sales tax levied on these items is a flat rate of 20 per cent.

In addition to the sales taxes there is an excise tax whch collects about three-quarters of its revenue from the sale of cigarettes and beer. The rates are 87 per cent on beer an 205 per cent on tobacco. The share of taxes from cigarettes and beer is borne disproportionately by the low-income groups making the excise regressive. At the same time, Ghana's share of taxes on vehicles and fuels, which are borne primarily by the rich, is among the lowest in the world.

The only export duty is on cocoa exports which generated 16 per cent of tax revenue in 1988. Recent tax reforms have decreased taxes on cocoa exports to stimulate production. Most cocoa producers are found in the middle-to-lower part of the income distribution (Glewwe and Twum-Baah 1991).

Income taxes in Ghana account for 28.7 per cent of revenue and are collected most intensively from corporations. Individual income tax includes salaries (as well as pensions) and earnings of the self-employed at progressive rates ranging from zero per cent for the poor to 55 per cent for the wealthy. The company income tax is levied at differing rates across sectors. These taxes, such as the 45–55 per cent rate on management fees, interest, and royalties are high by international standards. In Ghana, it is unclear how these company taxes are passed on to the consumer. As discussed in Shah and Whalley (1990) the shifting assumption commonly used in developing country incidence work for the corporate tax is that 50 per cent of the tax is shifted forward to consumers and 50 per cent is borne by owners of capital in the economy. Under these assumptions, incidence is found to be regressive for the lowest income brackets, and progressive for the higher income groups. Overall, the public financing scheme looks slightly progressive at best.

The other significant form of financing health care is private expenditures (Vogel 1988). Out-of-pocket expenditures on private care, both modern and traditional, accounted for 51 per cent of total health expenditures. Private doctors, midwives, and pharmacists work on a fee-for-service basis. Drugs are customarily sold with a 50 per cent mark-up. Detailed information on per capita expenditures are given pp. 000–000.

Jamaica

Delivery   Jamaica's health care delivery system is well developed, particularly in relation to other countries with a similar per capita income

(Table 20.2). Life expectancy is 73 years and infant mortality 16 per 1000, rates which are comparable to industrialized countries. The leading causes of death are chronic and degenerative diseases (cerebrovascular diseases, heart disease, cancer, hypertension, and diabetes). Infectious and parasitic diseases are no longer the significant causes of morbidity and mortality.

The Ministry of Health provides free health care for all Jamaicans through a network of 24 hospitals and 361 primary health care centres. Each of the 14 parishes has at least one public hospital and a number of health centres. There are 2.7 beds per 1000 population which are sufficient to meet the inpatient needs. Ninety per cent of Jamaicans live within 10 miles of a health centre. However, the health centres and hospitals are dilapidated and in need of modernization and rehabilitation.

There are approximately 12 000 trained personnel working in the public health sector, with 65 per cent in hospitals, 25 per cent in primary health centers, and the remaining 10 per cent in administration. The population per physician ratio is 2040 and population per nurse 490. Deteriorating conditions in public hospitals and health centres have led many physicians and nurses to seek employment in the private health sector and overseas.

The private sector plays a major role in the Jamaican health care system, primarily in providing ambulatory services. Fifty-four per cent of the country's physicians are in private practice, and about 60 per cent of those employed by the MOH have private afternoon practices. There are 280 private hospital beds accounting for 6 per cent of all beds.

Finance Approximately two-thirds of all expenditures on health care in Jamaica come from the Ministry of Health with the remaining third from the private sector. Public expenditures on health were about 3.0 per cent of GDP in 1987 (or 6.5 per cent of the total government expenditures), this amounted to US$35.75 per capita.

The MOH budget includes expenditures for hospitals, clinics, primary health care, family planning, and other preventive care. The largest share of the budget in 1985 was allocated to salaries and wages (55 per cent), which is comparatively low. Conversely, the shares spent on drugs and supplies (17 per cent) were relatively high resulting from the high costs of imported pharmaceuticals. Travel and subsistence, utilities, and maintenance each accounted for 3 per cent of expenditures. The share allocated to maintenance is insufficient as evidenced by the declining conditions of the facilities.

More than 90 per cent of the MOH budget is financed from general government revenue, with the remaining 7–8 per cent coming from user-fees. Tax revenues comprised 86 per cent of general government revenue in 1987/88 (Table 20.5).

Thirty four per cent of the current revenue in the fiscal year 1987/88

Table 20.5. Jamaica: structure of government revenue (1987/88)

Source	Total revenue (%)
Total income tax	*34.2*
Total indirect tax	*33.3*
Total international tax	*17.1*
Bauxite levy	6.7
Property tax	1.3
Total tax revenue	*92.6*
Non-tax revenue	*7.4*

Source: *Central Government Statistics* (1988).

came from direct taxes. The personal income tax is applied on all income (including that received in kind) above J$8580 at a flat rate of 33.33 per cent. The very poor are relieved of any income tax burden. The corporate income tax is levied at 33.50 per cent with adjusted investment and depreciation allowances. These income taxes are slightly progressive for the very poor. However, when income surpasses the cut-off point, the flat rate is regressive for the lower-middle class.

The existing excise duty, sales tax, and consumption duty have recently undergone reforms and have been replaced with a general consumption tax (GCT) (Bahl 1989). This is a broad-based tax levied on importers, manufactures, and large distributors, and has a value-added feature of allowing credit for taxes paid on inputs. The rate structure has only two rates: (1) a general rate for most goods; and (2) a luxury rate for items, such as cigarettes, gasoline, and alcoholic beverages. Exemptions are to be limited to basic foodstuffs, prescription drugs, and certain agricultural inputs. These exemptions favour the progressivity of the GCT.

International taxes generated 17 per cent of total government revenue. The tariff system is also undergoing reform to convert to a more simplified system of four rates in the range of 5 to 30 per cent and the elimination of quantitative restrictions (which are mostly on food items) that are not necessary for health and security reasons. The stamp duties on capital goods are 20 per cent, and there are tax concessions on 148 critical raw materials imports, such as sewing machine needles and heat elements. The maximum stamp and tariff duty combined is limited to 60 per cent.

The bauxite levy has also recently been reformed and is now based on profitability which establishes a base levy at US$5/ton when the price of aluminum on the London Metal Exchange is 60 US cents/lb or below, equivalent to US$12/ton of aluminium produced. For prices above 60 cents, the levy is adjusted proportionally, by a factor equal to the ratio of the current price to 60 US cents. With this levy system, bauxite costs will compare favourably with most other sources of supply, and the tax burden on the company would decrease during periods of unfavourable prices.

Some financing of health care in Jamaica also comes from the private insurance industry which covers approximately 14 per cent of the population. Cover is available through employment-based insurance plans extended to employees and dependants. In some instances, the monthly premium is sponsored entirely by the employer, and in other cases the employee shares up to 50 per cent of the cost.

Overall, the Jamaican tax system appears to be progressive for the lower income groups, through a combination of income tax exemptions for the poor and low sales tax rates for necessities. The regressive nature of the income tax for the lower-middle class, however, seems not to be off-set by any of the other tax instruments.

Peru

Delivery Peru's health status is poor relative to other Latin American countries, with a low life expectancy rate, 62 years (lower than all other neighbouring countries except Bolivia) and an infant mortality rate of 79 per 1000 births. Acute respiratory infection is the leading cause of mortality and morbidity among all age groups accounting for 32.5 per cent of infant deaths and 17 per cent of adult deaths in 1988. Acute diarrhoeal disease, which is closely linked to poor water and sanitation problems, is the second most common cause of mortality for infants and morbidity for adults.

The Ministry of Health provides care to approximately 56 per cent of the population through a network of hospitals, health centres, and health posts. Usage of these services is generally free of charge, however, regional and space availability inhibit accessibility. Many of the MOH's clients live in remote areas without any access to MOH facilities. Only an estimated 30 per cent of Peruvians are effectively covered by MOH health services. The Peruvian Institute of Social Security (IPSS) provides pension and health benefits to approximately 27 per cent of the population including permanently employed wage earners in the formal sector, employees of the government, and those self-employed who wish to contribute to the fund. The private sector covers an additional 15 per cent through private insurance schemes and private voluntary organizations who deliver for-profit and non-profit health services for a fee. An estimated 25–30 per cent of the population receives no care at all due to a lack of access to health facilities. Most of this under-served population lives in rural areas.

There are a total of 368 hospitals, 1020 health centres, and 3173 health posts throughout the country. These facilities are most heavily concentrated in urban coastal areas (Ministry of Health Peru, 1990). Fifty-five per cent of all inpatient beds are located in Lima where only 28 per cent of the Peruvian population lives. The Amazonas, Tumbes, and Madre de Dios districts each have less than 0.3 per cent of all hospital beds in the country. Although there are a considerable number of private hospitals (191), they cover a relatively small percentage of the population.

The MOH employs over 26 000 medical and technical staff (1990) of which only 34 per cent are involved in the delivery of primary health care in the health centres and posts (Development Group 1991). The remaining 66 per cent work in hospitals or elsewhere. The distribution of physicians is also extremely uneven. In Lima, there is 1 physician per 436 inhabitants, whereas in some remote areas (such as Selva), there is only 1 physician per 47 500 population. The disparity in the distribution of human resources is similar for nurses. In an attempt to disperse human resources more equally, the government established a law in 1976 requiring a doctor to devote 1 year, and a nurse 6 months, of work in rural health facilities before being legally qualified for professional practice. Upon fulfilling this requirement, however most of the medical personnel move back to the large cities.

Finance   The health care system in Peru is primarily funded by the public sector. Of total expenditures in 1984, approximately 36.5 per cent comes from the MOH, 44 per cent from the IPSS, 8.5 per cent from other public sector providers, such as the armed forces and police, and 11 per cent from the private sector. MOH expenditures in 1990 were about 0.5 per cent of GDP, and 7.4 per cent of total government expenditures. This translated to US$7.50 per capita. The IPSS share spent only on medical care and maternity programmes was US$224 million in 1987, representing US$119 per beneficiary.

The MOH health budget in 1984 allocated approximately 70 per cent to wages and salaries, 17 per cent to supplies and materials, and 10 per cent to capital expenditures (Suarez–Berenguela 1987). The high proportion spent on personnel suggests that MOH primarily provides medical care. The cost of drugs and materials that are part of the treatment are borne by the patient.

The majority of MOH financing comes from government revenue (86 per cent), with the remaining amount from foreign loans (6.3 per cent), donations (1.3 per cent), and revenues (3.2 per cent). The social security system is financed from workers, employers, and the government. Workers' contributions represent 6 per cent of total payroll, the employers' share is 14 per cent, and the state (as an employer) contributes 2 per cent.

Tax revenue comprised 93 per cent of general government revenue in

Table 20.6. Peru: structure of government revenue (1987)

Source	Total revenue (%)
Individual	1.6
Corporate	17.7
Total income tax	*19.3*
Sales tax and VAT	8.0
Excises	38.0
Services	0.8
Total indirect tax	*46.8*
Import duties	21.2
Export duties	0.3
Total international tax	*21.5*
Employers payroll tax	0.2
Property tax	4.1
Other taxes	1.3
Total tax revenue	*93.2*
Non-tax revenue	*6.8*

Source: *Government Finance Statistics Yearbook* (1987).

1987 and is generated from a combination of sources (Table 20.6). Sales taxes comprise the most significant portion, accounting for over half of total government revenue. Most of this comes from the high excise on gasoline, and from VAT. VAT is constructed as a flat rate of 10 per cent levied on the sales of domestic produced and imported goods on a value-added basis. The most important items in the consumers' basket, such as food and medicines, are exempt, as well as agricultural implements, books, and newspapers. Peru also has a selective consumption excise levied on the production, consumption, and import of tobacco, alcoholic beverages, soft drinks, cosmetics, electrical appliances, and vehicles. Rates vary from 25 per cent on colour televisions to 250 per cent on whisky and brandy. The progressivity of the excise rates and exemptions to the VAT demonstrate that the sales taxes are designed to be progressive for the poor. However, the high excises on tobacco and alcoholic beverages are regressive in their impact on low-income consumers for whom the purchase of these goods represents a relatively large proportion of their income.

International taxes are primarily generated from customs duties applied on an *ad valorem* basis. The duties range from zero to 155 per cent for the whole economy with the highest exemptions for agriculture and manufacturing industries. Export taxes are applied on the FOB value of minerals, oil, coffee, sugar, fish, and cotton-derived products at varying rates from zero to 5 per cent. As discussed in Shah and Whalley (1990), most incidence studies assume that export taxes are paid by the producer–exporter groups (in the higher income ranges), and thus derive a progressive incidence pattern for the poor.

Direct taxes from personal and corporate income accounted for 19.6 per cent of government revenue. Corporate income taxes in Peru are set at a flat rate of 35 per cent, and personal income taxes are based on a progressive rate schedule. Those rates range from 8 per cent for the poorest group to 45 per cent for the wealthiest.

On the whole, the system in Peru is progressive. Tax rates on income are lower for the poor than for the rich. Consumer taxes could be regressive, but basic food items and medicines which are essential to the poor are exempt. Excises are high, although mainly on luxury items such as alcohol and electronics, which are consumed by the wealthy.

Bolivia

Delivery   The health indicators for Bolivia are poor, representing the least-developed medical care system of the countries in this study. Infant mortality is 106 per 1000, the crude death rate is 14 per 1000, and life expectancy 54 (see Table 20.2). The greatest causes of morbidity and mortality are infectious diseases exacerbated by poor housing and sanitation conditions. Only 69 per cent of the urban population and 10 per cent of the rural population have access to piped water, and 37 per cent of those in cities and 4 per cent in rural areas to sanitary facilities.

The Ministry of Social Welfare and Public Health (MPSSP), the Bolivian Institute for Social Security (IBSS), and approximately 300 Non-Government Organizations (NGOs) all provide various health care services in Bolivia. In 1987, the MPSSP covered 30 per cent of the population, IBBS approximately 25 per cent, and NGOs 10–25 per cent (in urban areas they reach about 10 per cent of the population, and in rural areas, 25 per cent.) An estimated 30 per cent of the population in Bolivia receives no cover at all.

The MPSSP operates approximately 55 per cent of available beds through 177 public hospitals, clinics, and health centres. IBSS runs 120 inpatient facilities which tend to be newer and better equipped than MPSSP hospitals. The private sector has 77 facilities which typically are small, short-stay clinics for the provision of acute care. Overall, the urban inpatient capacity averages 1 bed per 250 population and the rural ratio is 1 bed per 1300 population. Public services for ambulatory care are almost entirely located in the rural sector, where the MPSSP operates 971 facilities (141 health centres with beds and 923 health posts). NGOs operate approximately 150 facilities throughout the country with the majority in the capital city of La Paz.

Table 20.7. Bolivia: structure of government revenues (1989)

Source	Total revenue (%)
Total income Tax	*5.8*
VAT	23.4
Specific taxes	3.9
Transaction tax	3.6
Direct taxes (Bolivian Petroleum Corporation)	42.5
Total indirect tax	*73.4*
Import duties	11.0
Total international tax	*11.0*
Property	3.1
Other taxes	3.4
Total tax revenue	*96.7*
Non-tax revenue	*3.3*

Source: World Bank (1989).

The placement of staff is highly skewed. Of the approximately 4000 physicians in Bolivia, 70 per cent live in urban areas. The most critical personnel problem, however, is a shortage of nurses. The ratio of nurses to population is the lowest in South America, and in the public sector there is only one nurse to every two physicians.

Finance The Ministry of Social Welfare and Public Health (MPSSP) is the largest provider of finance to health care services in Bolivia. Government expenditures on health care in 1988 were approximately 0.9 per cent of GDP, and 7.9 per cent of the total recurrent budget (Grosti 1990). Per capita expenditures on health were US$5.70.

During the mid 1980s an average of 94 per cent of MPSSP's total expenditures have been attributed to operating expenses. Wages and salaries consume about 75 per cent of expenditures and supplies (including drugs) and equipment about 19 per cent. The investment share was approximately 5 per cent of total health expenditures.

The sources of public health financing vary from year to year, but typically comprise approximately 57 per cent from the national treasury, 30 per cent from external aid, and 13 per cent from user-fees (an estimated 80 per cent of user-fees come from abortions).

The national treasury gets the majority of its budget from tax revenues (1989), which is broken down by type of tax in Table 20.7. Taxes on goods and services are the primary source of revenue accounting for over 70 per cent in 1989. There is VAT (generating 23.4 per cent of revenue) which is levied at a flat rate of 10 per cent on all transactions (including foodstuffs and medicines) except for real estate, export activities, interest payments, and most capital market transactions. Taxes on specific consumption account for 3.9 per cent of revenue and are charged at the rates of 20 per cent on gaseous beverages, 30 per cent on perfumes, cosmetics, and alcoholic beverages, 45 per cent on beer, and 50 per cent on tobacco. The largest proportion of revenue (42.5 per cent) is generated through an excise on petroleum which is gained from direct taxation and a transfer system between the Bolivian Petroleum Corporation and the government.

Collection of import duties totalled 11 per cent of treasury revenues in 1989 and are levied at the rate of 10 per cent on capital goods and 17 per cent on consumer goods. The uniform tariff rates are a result of the difficulties involved in administrating a more complicated rate structure. Uniform rate structures tend to be regressive for the poor.

Income taxes only amounted to 5.8 per cent of total revenue in 1989, and are designed to capture income through measuring assets. The assets chosen for this purpose are urban real estate, vehicles, and rural real estate, all items owned by the wealthiest groups.

The heavy dependence on VAT and other consumption taxes, along with the uniform VAT rate, has raised complaints that the system is regressive. However, excise taxes are primarily imposed on luxury goods and the lowest income groups are exempt from some taxes and evade others by working in the 'informal' sector. On the whole, the tax system is likely to be slightly progressive.

Other sources for financing health care are external aid and the social security system. External aid from USAID (35 per cent), UNICEF (25 per cent), PAHO/WHO (19 per cent), and others are channelled directly through the MPSSP. Medical care provided by the social security system (comprised of 40 social security schemes) is financed by payroll deductions paid by employees and employers, covering about 24 per cent of the population. This cover provides care to workers primarily in the urban industrial areas in Potosi, Oruro, and La Paz. The majority of the population (54 per cent), however, live in rural areas and have no access to social security schemes.

Summary

With the exception of Ghana, the vast majority of health care services in the five countries we studied, is provided by the central government, and financed by a variety of taxes. Although the available information does not allow us to conduct a full tax incidence study, the tax instruments used suggest mildly progressive public financing systems in all countries.

In some countries, private health care facilities exist side-by-side with the public facilities. Indeed, in Ghana 60 per cent of total health expenditures are out-of-pocket. In other countries as well, some fees are charged for the use of public facilities or the consumption of drugs. We will give details on these out-of-pocket expenditures on pp. 386–8, after discussing health status differentials by income groups and corresponding health care consumption data.

EQUITY IN HEALTH STATUS AND HEALTH CARE UTILIZATION

In this section health status and health care consumption data are presented for each country, for urban and rural regions separately, and by per capita consumption quintiles. Tables 20.8 and 20.9 compare total per capita consumption expenditures and shares in each quintile, in local currency. Quintile 1 contains the poorest 20 per cent of the population and quintile 5 contains the wealthiest 20 per cent. The data indicate that there are wide disparities in the distribution of welfare—with the poorest 40 per cent accounting for approximately 16 per cent of total expenditures, whereas the wealthiest 20 per cent account for close to 50 per cent. Consumption levels in all of the countries are significantly higher in urban areas, as much as three times more in some cases. Bolivia (urban) shows a particularly skewed distribution, whereas income inequality is lowest in Ghana, as shown by the Gini coefficients for per capita consumption presented in Table 20.10.

Health status

In measuring the health status of the population, household members were asked if they had been ill or injured during the past four weeks. From Table 20.11, it is evident that the occurrence of illness or injury within the past four weeks does not follow any distinctive pattern between countries, income quintiles, and rural and urban areas. With the exception of Côta d'Ivoire, the prevalence of illness or injury seems to be higher in the fourth and fifth quintiles. Peru has the highest incidence of self-reported illness or injury with an average of 40 to 45 per cent being ill during any four week period.

One would expect, with the high association of GNP to health indicators as discussed in the beginning of the Chapter, that there would also be a close association between GNP and health status, and health indicators and health status. This does not hold to be true for this self-reported health measure. Peru, which has the highest GNP and about

Table 20.8.   Average per capita consumption

Country	Rural quintiles					
	1	2	3	4	5	All
Côte d'Ivoire (CFA)	42 711	70 311	95 755	130 269	223 768	112 395
Ghana (cedi)	15 501	25 514	35 886	51 766	101 413	45 990
Jamaica (J$)	1360	2367	3517	5244	11 844	4873
Peru (inti)	73	131	187	275	607	255

Country	Urban quintiles					
	1	2	3	4	5	All
Côte d'Ivoire (CFA)	85 795	139 235	191 220	282 217	661 137	271 208
Ghana (cedi)	22 635	37 358	49 698	67 616	141 742	63 777
Jamaica (J$)	2528	4475	6494	9657	19 568	8542
Peru (inti)	155	262	379	565	1357	543
Bolivia (Boliviano)	54	69	102	152	375	148

Notes: All amounts are shown in local currency. The currency unit is given in parentheses. No data are available for rural Bolivia.

average life expectancy and infant mortality rates, had the highest occurrence of illness or injury. Bolivia, whose health indicators are very poor (life expectancy was only 54 and infant mortality 106) reported relatively low frequency of illness. One might also expect that Ghana and Côte d'Ivoire would report similar levels of health status. Both countries are located in West Africa, depend heavily on cocoa and coffee exports for income, have relatively similar levels of GNP, infant mortality, and life expectancy. However, the percentage of the population reporting illness is substantially higher in Ghana, especially in urban areas. In contrast,

Table 20.9. Percentage of total consumption by quintile

Country	Rural quintiles				
	1	2	3	4	5
Côte d'Ivoire	8	12	17	23	40
Ghana	7	11	16	22	44
Jamaica	6	10	14	21	49
Peru	6	10	15	21	48
	Urban quintiles				
	1	2	3	4	5
Côte d'Ivoire	6	10	14	21	49
Ghana	7	12	16	21	44
Jamaica	6	11	15	22	46
Peru	6	9	14	21	50
Bolivia	7	9	14	20	50

Note: No data are available for rural Bolivia.

Table 20.10. Gini coefficients on per capita consumption

Country	Total	Rural	Urban
Côte d'Ivoire	0.436	0.321	0.416
Ghana	0.377	0.372	0.365
Jamaica	0.438	0.425	0.398
Peru	0.437	0.415	0.436
Bolivia	–	–	0.507

objective measures of health status (such as life expectancy) show Ghana to be much better off than Côte d'Ivoire.

The second question relating to health status measures the severity of the illness by the average number of days inactive (for those who reported illness or injury, see Table 20.12). Activity here refers not only to income-earning activities, but also going to school, being a housewife, or whatever the person's profession is. Overall, this average is slightly higher in rural areas. Thus, although the incidence of self-reported health problems appears to be higher in the cities, health problems are more severe in rural areas. Apparently, many minor health problems by rural dwellers are not

Table 20.11.   Percentage ill or injured during the past 4 weeks

Country	Rural quintiles					
	1	2	3	4	5	All
Côte d'Ivoire	29	20	18	19	19	21
Ghana	25	25	33	36	45	33
Jamaica	14	16	17	17	18	16
Peru	36	40	41	40	45	40
	Urban quintiles					
	1	2	3	4	5	All
Côte d'Ivoire	20	17	15	21	18	18
Ghana	35	37	38	40	46	39
Jamaica	13	14	13	14	17	14
Peru	41	46	46	46	45	45
Bolivia	16	16	18	19	19	18

Note: No data are available for rural Bolivia.

Table 20.12.   Average number of days inactive due to illness

Country	Rural quintiles					
	1	2	3	4	5	All
Côte d'Ivoire	7.2	6.9	8.1	7.0	7.0	7.2
Ghana	3.9	3.9	4.5	4.3	4.9	4.3
Jamaica	6.2	5.9	4.7	4.9	4.7	5.3
Peru	2.6	2.7	2.6	3.0	2.9	2.8
	Urban quintiles					
	1	2	3	4	5	All
Côte d'Ivoire	5.5	4.9	5.6	5.3	5.1	5.3
Ghana	3.0	3.5	3.3	3.4	3.6	3.4
Jamaica	6.8	5.3	4.5	4.0	3.5	4.8
Peru	2.0	1.8	1.8	1.7	1.8	1.8
Bolivia	4.2	5.8	5.9	6.2	6.8	5.8

Note: No data are available for rural Bolivia.

recognized as such, if only—perhaps—because many have no easy access to medical care to alleviate the problem.

This interpretation of the somewhat surprising results on self-reported health status is strengthened by the results for Peru, where the occurrence of illness or injury is extremely high, but the severity appears to be relatively low. Conversely, the frequency of illness in Côte d'Ivoire is relatively low, but the number of days of resulting inactivity is relatively high.

The data on health status do illustrate the significance of health problems in developing countries. During any given four week period, between approximately 20 and 40 per cent of the population is ill, and on average, those that are ill lose a fifth or a quarter of their time due to sickness.

Given the difficulty of interpreting these self-reported health data, we will not adjust the health care consumption data presented in the remainder of this study for health care 'need' differences. Chances are that this will result in an underestimation of the existing inequalities in consumption because objective measures of health, where available, indicate poorer health status in rural areas and at lower income levels.

Health care consumption

Of those that have been ill or injured in the past four weeks, we asked what percentage has sought some form of medical care. Overall, the percentages seeking care are substantially higher in urban areas largely due to the easier access to care. Travel distances are much shorter and medical facilities are much more abundant than in rural areas. The likelihood of an individual to seek medical care is, in some instances, twice as high in urban areas (Table 20.13 and Fig. 20.3). Income differences are also significant, with the rich consuming up to twice as much as the poor.

The wide disparity between the percentages of poor and rich seeking care is particularly striking in view of the public health systems in each country. Health care is made available free of charge or at a very low cost expressly so that it is accessible to all income groups.

In addition to comparing the consumption of medical care, measuring the quality of that care is equally as important. The two measures of quality examined were: (1) the type of health worker consulted; and (2) the type of facility visited.

Personnel involved in the delivery of health care in developing countries includes physicians, nurse practitioners, nurses, health officers, pharmacists, midwives, and traditional healers. Based on the assumption that physicians have had the most extensive medical training and therefore can supply the highest quality of care, the percentages of people

Table 20.13.   Percentage seeking care for illness or injury

Country	Rural quintiles					
	1	2	3	4	5	All
Côte d'Ivoire	23	35	49	39	44	36
Ghana	26	39	41	46	46	41
Jamaica	44	41	47	46	56	47
Peru	20	20	30	34	39	29
	Urban quintiles					
	1	2	3	4	5	All
Côte d'Ivoire	49	58	63	65	64	60
Ghana	40	46	55	58	59	52
Jamaica	43	52	57	58	60	54
Peru	35	44	48	53	57	48
Bolivia	61	45	55	61	69	58

Note: No data are available for rural Bolivia.

consulting a doctor were used for comparison. Again these percentages were consistently higher in urban areas, and increased substantially with income level (see Table 20.14).

As was discussed in the country-by-country review of health care delivery systems, the distribution of personnel is highly skewed. The ratio of population per doctor is considerably lower in urban areas which concurs with the findings below. The unequal distribution across quintiles may be a function of the increasing ability to pay for private care as income levels rise.

The disparities exist for every country except Jamaica, where the distribution of those seeing a doctor was fairly equal. In comparing the poorest 20 per cent of the population with the wealthiest 20 per cent in the rural areas of Ghana, twice as many of the wealthy group received care from a doctor. In Côte d'Ivoire, over five times as many people in the wealthiest urban quintile saw a doctor.

As would be expected, the overall number of those seeing a doctor was lowest in Ghana and Côte d'Ivoire, where the population per physician ratios are highest.

The second measure of quality refers to the place where care was received. Available health care facilities include a hospital, clinic, health centre, sanitation booth, dispensary, pharmacy, consultant's home, or

(a) Rural areas

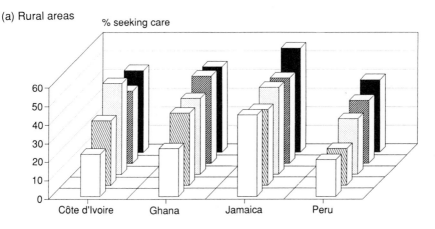

(b) Urban areas

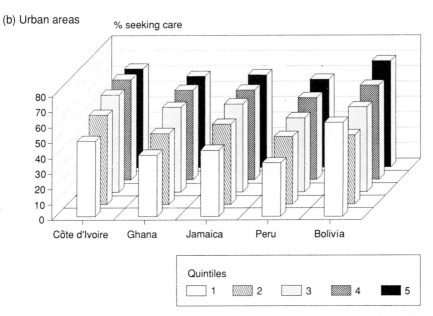

Fig. 20.3. Percentage seeking medical care, by quintile. (No data are available for rural Bolivia.)

patient's home. Because hospitals in developing countries tend to receive most resources in terms of equipment, staff and supplies, it is assumed that the quality of care received there is highest.

As indicated in the tables below, the percentages of those ill persons who have sought care in a hosptial ranges from about 20 to 40 per cent with the highest proportion in the urban areas. In all rural areas except

Table 20.14.   Percentage consulting a doctor

Country	Rural quintiles					
	1	2	3	4	5	All
Côte d'Ivoire	10	21	16	14	24	17
Ghana	24	41	41	40	47	41
Jamaica	71	84	88	85	88	84
Peru	39	34	40	51	58	47

	Urban quintiles					
	1	2	3	4	5	All
Côte d'Ivoire	11	38	39	50	59	41
Ghana	55	51	57	60	76	62
Jamaica	87	98	91	94	90	92
Peru	78	83	82	88	90	85
Bolivia	90	91	94	94	95	93

Note: No data are available for rural Bolivia.

Jamaica, this also increased with consumption levels. The frequency of visiting a hospital may be associated with the wealthier individuals' ability to pay for travel to the cities where the majority of hospitals are located.

The quality of health care as measured by the type of health worker and facility is, on the whole, distributed inequitably. The higher quality care is being consumed in some cases two to three times more often by wealthy urban individuals. Explanations for this inequity include the bias in public health spending toward urban, hospital-based care, the difficulties for the rural poor to incur the cost of travel to a hospital or facility staffed with physicians which often is far away, and the ability for wealthy individuals to pay for private medical care if deemed necessary.

Health expenditures

Out-of-pocket expenditures on health care also vary among income groups and between urban and rural regions, displaying a resemblance to the distribution of per capita consumption. Two types of expenditures have been examined: (1) outlays on medication; and (2) fees for health care services. Overall, expenditures for both are substantially higher in urban areas and increase by consumption level.

Medication accounts for the largest health expenditure in the majority of countries, with the percentage of people purchasing drugs for their

Table 20.15.   Percentage seeking care in a hospital

Country	Rural quintiles					
	1	2	3	4	5	All
Côte d'Ivoire	15	31	31	33	38	30
Ghana	15	28	32	35	44	35
Jamaica	25	18	18	19	19	19
Peru	17	9	17	20	28	20
	Urban quintiles					
	1	2	3	4	5	All
Côte d'Ivoire	39	53	39	41	35	41
Ghana	43	41	48	42	48	45
Jamaica	30	36	28	22	12	28
Peru	28	27	32	30	27	29
Bolivia	32	37	36	32	28	33

Note: No data are available for rural Bolivia.

illness quite different among income levels and urban and rural areas. In Côte d'Ivoire for example, three times as many people in the wealthiest urban quintile purchased medication for their illness than those in the poorest rural quintile. Much of the disparity between rural and urban areas is due to the fact that drugs, if available at all, are more readily found in the cities. Furthermore, charges for drugs and medication in private pharmacies are often so high that the poor cannot afford them (Tables 20.16 and 20.17).

Expenditures on care are strongly dependent on per capita consumption, resulting in a similar distributional pattern as for drugs (Table 20.18 and Fig. 20.4). Most fees in public institutions are low, only accounting for a small percentage of cost recovery. The majority of out-of-pocket expenditures are for fee-for-service to private physicians, traditional healers, and midwives.

The role of preventive care in developing countries is a small one, accounting for only 10 to 20 per cent of government spending (de Ferranti 1985). Roughly one-third of the population in the five countries studied received some form of patient-related preventive care in the past year (Table 20.19). This care includes services to well patients, particularly infants, mothers and pregnant women, and hypertension control. Preventive services are generally provided free of charge.

The proportion of those seeking preventive care varied from country to

Table 20.16.   Percentage purchasing medication

Country	Rural quintiles					
	1	2	3	4	5	All
Côte d'Ivoire	27	42	58	53	54	45
Ghana	25	25	33	36	45	33
Jamaica	37	40	47	54	51	46
Peru	51	62	70	75	77	67

	Urban quintiles					
	1	2	3	4	5	All
Côte d'Ivoire	52	65	66	69	74	65
Ghana	35	37	38	40	47	39
Jamaica	49	60	58	66	69	61
Peru	77	79	82	80	81	80
Bolivia	62	63	73	66	68	67

Note: No data are available for rural Bolivia.

country, but was distributed relatively equitably between urban and rural regions. Across income groups, the distribution patterns showed less equity. With the exception of Ghana, there was a gradual increase in the percentages receiving preventive care as consumption levels rose. Ghana had the highest incidence, with 43 per cent in rural areas and 41 per cent in urban areas receiving some form of preventive care within the past 12 months.

CONCLUSION

In this chapter we presented evidence on equity—or, rather, lack of equity—in health, health care, and health care financing in developing countries. The cross-country comparisons reiterated the well-documented fact that large discrepancies exist in health outcomes. Variations in health outcomes show a close correlation with the countries' per capita income levels. Despite this, some countries have been considerably more successful than others, at *given* income levels, in providing the infrastructure, and goods, and services to the population that produce good health. This latter observation makes health an interesting indicator of a country's level of development.

In the five case studies we tried to assess the equity of health care

Table 20.17. Average expenditure on medication

Country	Rural quintiles					
	1	2	3	4	5	All
Côte d'Ivoire (CFA)	3667	4388	6788	4793	5739	5075
Ghana (cedi)	368	445	520	530	562	485
Jamaica (J$)	32	37	40	53	71	47
Peru (inti)	24	27	28	60	85	45

Country	Urban quintiles					
	1	2	3	4	5	All
Côte d'Ivoire (CFA)	3391	4917	5204	5032	6296	4968
Ghana (cedi)	394	445	511	511	750	522
Jamaica (J$)	32	52	56	66	78	57
Peru (inti)	43	52	70	88	132	77
Bolivia (Boliviano)	12	19	26	45	71	35

Notes: All amounts are shown in local currency. The currency unit is given in parentheses.
No data are available for rural Bolivia.

financing and health care utilization along the same lines as presented in the other chapters of this volume. In that we were only partly successful. As we showed, the vast majority of health care expenditures in these countries is financed from general revenues of the central government. A proper treatment of the 'equity in financing' issue would involve a full fledged tax incidence study for which the necessary data are simply not available. Still, we were able to put together an overall picture that shows the following.

Public funding is the most prevalent source of financing health care services. Funds are principally provided by general tax revenue, and

Table 20.18.   Average per capita expenditure on care

Country	Rural quintiles					
	1	2	3	4	5	All
Côte d'Ivoire (CFA)	26	279	94	478	205	216
Ghana (cedi)	131	256	208	248	204	209
Jamaica (J$)	41	27	34	38	93	47
Peru (inti)	8	8	9	14	29	14
	Urban quintiles					
	1	2	3	4	5	All
Côte d'Ivoire (CFA)	59	339	2354	538	2431	1144
Ghana (cedi)	132	185	178	209	419	225
Jamaica (J$)	19	23	37	39	59	35
Peru (inti)	12	21	24	30	43	26
Bolivia (Boliviano)	5	6	11	15	86	25

Notes: All amounts are shown in local currency. The currency unit is given in parentheses. No data are available for rural Bolivia.

account for between 2 and 9 per cent of total government expenditures. Tax revenue is generated through a variety of direct and indirect taxes, which are on the whole likely to be mildly progressive. Social security institutions, which are most prevalent in Latin America (in this study, particularly in Peru) are generally financed through both employer and employee payroll deductions. The allocation of funds by health ministries tends to favour urban, hospital-based care. This results in an overall inequitable distribution of resources which under-serves the rural population.

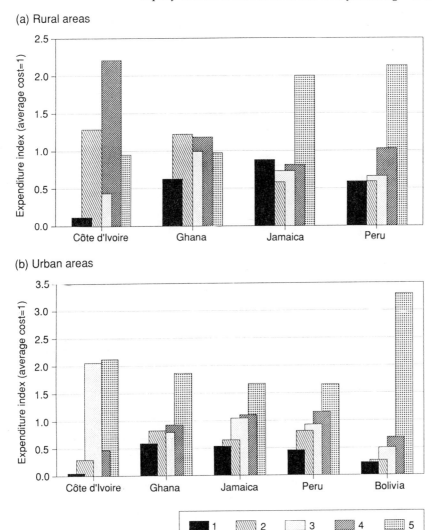

Fig. 20.4. Average per capita expenditure on health care, by quintile. (No data are available for rural Bolivia.)

Private expenditures account for a small proportion of financing and generally are comprised of user-fees in public facilities, fees-for-service in the private sector to physicians, pharmacists, traditional healers, and traditional midwives, and fees for medication. Consumer spending on health care varies substantially between income groups and rural and urban areas. Individuals who live in urban areas and are in the higher

Table 20.19.   Percentage receiving preventive care in the past 12 months

Country	Rural quintiles					
	1	2	3	4	5	All
Côte d'Ivoire	28	23	25	30	33	28
Ghana	45	44	41	41	42	43
Jamaica	10	14	17	18	25	17
Peru	11	10	13	12	15	12
	Urban quintiles					
	1	2	3	4	5	All
Côte d'Ivoire[1]	26	36	35	37	32	33
Ghana	43	44	42	40	38	41
Jamaica[2]	11	14	18	18	27	18
Peru	17	20	24	26	32	24
Bolivia[3]	29	35	37	40	46	39

Notes:
[1] Data for Côte d'Ivoire refer to the percentage of the population vaccinated in the past 12 months.
[2] Data for Jamaica refer to the percentage of the population receiving preventive care within the past 6 months.
[3] Data for Bolivia refer to the percentage of the population receiving a yellow fever vaccination within the past 5 years.
No data are available for rural Bolivia.

income groups spend many times more on medical services than low-income households in rural areas. At the same time, however, average income levels between these groups range from a factor 9 in Ghana to 18 in Peru (Table 20.8).

Our analyses of health care utilization patterns fall short of a true 'benefit' study because—ideally—we would like to measure benefit as an improvement in health status. We were able, however, to present the empirical evidence on differentials in health care *utilization* patterns between urban and rural areas, and within these areas, among income groups. The results here are very striking. The general distributional pattern (to which Jamaica forms an exemption) indicates that individuals in urban areas and at higher income levels seek care much more often than the poor living in rural areas. In terms of quality, the pattern is simi-lar. Patients treated by physicians and in hospitals tend to be urban dwellers, and are in the higher income groups.

Perhaps the biggest surprise is not the existence of these large dif-ferences *per se*. In fact, most of the results confirm our priors and are consistent with those reported in the literature. Rather, the fact that these differences exist, *despite* the explicit objective of government policies to provide equal access to medical care for all in need, is both surprising and cause for concern.

The results are also in stark contrast with those found for industrialized countries. Even in the US, a country that relies more heavily on the private provision of health services and on private financing than any other developed country, medical care use is fairly equally distributed across the income distribution (Gottschalk and Wolfe 1990).

Many of the government interventions in the health care sector in developing countries are motivated by concern regarding equity. This objective is being pursued through the direct provision of medical care and/or pricing policies that provide the services at well below marginal costs. As our data clearly show, this strategy has failed to generate an equal distribution of health care utilization. As overall resources are limited, and price rationing is ruled out, other rationing mechanisms take over. These mechanisms appear to produce the same result as if prices had been charged: with health care being a normal good, having positive income and negative price elasticities, those in the upper half of the income distribution consume much more than the poor.

Some countries clearly spend much too little on health care. At an annual per capita expenditure level of US$4, as in Ghana, one can hardly expect that the available care is equally distributed according to need. Additonal resources are required, including private payments of user-fees. However, the distributional consequences of introducing user-fees need to be carefully monitored (see Gertler and van der Gaag 1990), the current practice of providing care free of charge can hardly be maintained on the basis of equity. A shift of public resources from tertiary care to primary care and from urban to rural areas is also necessary (see Akin *et al.* 1987). If 80 per cent or more of the total health budget is spent on urban hospitals, one should, again, not expect an equal distribution of health care consumption.

In very poor countries, it is perhaps futile to strive for equality *per se.* However, current situation could be greatly improved if public resources were used to increase access for the (mostly rural) poor to preventive and basic curative care. Greater cost recovery for tertiary care would make such improvement possible. It would also make the financing of care more progressive. Equity can only be achieved if over time, more resources for health care become available through the further development of the country.

NOTES

1. Brazil, for instance, has a per capita income of US$1390. It has been estimated that in 1985, 33.2 million people lived below a poverty line of US$200 per year (Fox and Morley 1990). The Gini coefficient of Brazil's income distribution is 0.61 (CEPAL 1986).
2. The number of children that die before the age of one, per 1000 live births.
3. Health is also an *input* in the economic development process. We will not discuss this issue here (see, e.g., World Bank 1990, Chapter 5).
4. The high level of health care spending came at the expense of the military budget which received only 3.2 per cent of government expenditures between 1975 and 1985.
5. Infant mortality in all developing countries has dropped from an average of 153 per 1000 births in 1960, to 67 in 1988. Life expectancy has risen from 44 to 62 years during the same period.

References

Abel-Smith, B. (1958). Whose welfare state? In *Conviction* (ed. N. Mckenzie). McGibbon, London.

Acton, J.P. (1985). Non-monetary factors in the demand for medical services: some empirical evidence. *Journal of Political Economy*, **83**, 595–614.

Aday, L.A. and Andersen, R. (1980). *Health care in the US: equitable for whom?* Sage, Beverly Hills, USA.

Akin, J., Birdsall, N., and Ferranti, D. de (1987). *Financing health services in developing countries: an agenda for reform*. World Bank Policy Study, Washington, D.C.

Alderson, M. (1970). Social class and the health service. *Medical Officer*, **124**, 51–9.

Alvarez González, L.J., Bermejo Muñoz, L., and Hevia Payá, J. de (1988). *La incidencia de la imposición indirecta en España en el año 1980*. Instituto Universitario José Ortega y Gasset Papeles de Trabajo, Economía, Universidad Complutense de Madrid.

Andersen, R. (1975). Health service distribution and equity. In *Equity in health services* (ed. R. Andersen, J. Kravits, and O. Anderson). Ballinger, Cambridge Mass.

Andersen, T.F. and Mooney, G. (ed.) (1990). *The challenge of medical practice variations*, Macmillan, London.

Argimón, I. and González Páramo, J.M. (1987). *Traslación e incidencia de las cotizaciones sociales por niveles de renta en España, 1980–1984*. Fundación Fondo para la Investigación Económica y Social, Documentos de Trabajo 01/1987. Obra Social de la Confederación Española de Cajas de Ahorro, Madrid.

Assembleia da República (1979). *Servico nacional de saúde*. Direcção dos Serviços de Documentação e Informacão Bibliográfica, Lisbon.

Atkinson, A.B. and Stiglitz, J.E. (1987). *Lectures on public economics*. McGraw-Hill, London.

Bahl, R. (1989). *Tax reform in Jamaica*. Oelgeschlager, Gunn & Hann, Cambridge, Mass.

Bariletti, A., Gabriele, S., Marè, M., and Piacentino, D. (1986). *Indagine sui consuimi sanitari delle famiglie. Primi risultati*. Research Report, Centro Europa Ricerche, Rome.

Bariletti, A., Gabirele, S., Marè, M., and Pacentino, D. (1990). Aspetti distributivi del consumo dei servizi sanitari in Italia. *Economia Pubblica*, **4–5**, 193–200.

Barry, B. (1989). *Theories of social justice. Vol. 1. A treatise on social justice*. Harvester–Wheatsheaf, London.

Béland, F. (1990). *Episodes of care and long term trends in individuals' pattern of utilisation of medical care*. Conference of the Association for Health Services Research, Washington, D.C.

Benham, L. and Benham, A. (1975). Utilization of physician services across income groups 1963–1970. In *Equity in health services* (ed. R. Andersen *et al.*), Ballinger, pp. 97–103. Cambridge Mass.

Benjamin, D. and Deaton, A. (1988). *The living standards survey and price policy reform. A study of cocoa and coffee production in Côte d'Ivoire*. Living Standard Measurement Study Working Paper, No. 44. World Bank, Washington, D.C.

Bentzen, N., Christiansen, T., and Pedersen, K.M. (1988). *The Danish Health Study 1982–83*. Department of Economics, Odense University, Odense.

Bera, A.K., Jarque, C.M., and Lee, L.S. (1982). Testing normality assumptions in limited dependent variable models. *International Review of Economics*, **25**, 563–78.

Bernardi, L., Marenzi, A., and Pozzi, F. (1990). *Un modello di microsimulazione delle imposte dirette e dei contributi sociali a carico delle famiglie*. Paper presented to ISPE's conference Bilancio Pubblico e Redistribuzione, 12–13 March 1990, Rome.

Black, A.D. (1986). *An anthology of false antitheses*. Rock Carling 1984 Fellowship, Nuffield Provincial Hospitals Trust, London.

Black, D. (1980). *Inequalities in health*. Report of a research working group chaired by Sir Douglas Black, Department of Health and Social Security, London.

Blaxter, M. (1989). A comparison of measures of inequality in morbidity. In *Health inequalities in European countries* (ed. J. Fox). Gower, Aldershot and London.

Blendon, R.J. and Edwards, J.N. (1991). Caring for the uninsured: choices for reform. *Journal of the American Medical Association*, **265**(19), 2563–5.

Bramley, G., Le Grand, J., and Low, W. (1989). How far is the poll tax a 'community charge'. The implications of service usage evidence. *Policy and Politics*, **17**, 187–205.

Buchan, I.C. and Richardson, I.M. (1973). *Time study of consultations in general practice*. Scottish Health Studies, No. 27. Scottish Home and Health Department.

Buchanan, J.M. (1968). What kind of redistribution do we want? *Economica*, **35** 185–90.

Buglione, E. and France, G. (1984). Skewed fiscal federalism in Italy: implications for public expenditure control. In *Comparative international budgeting and finance* (ed. A. Premchand and J. Burkehad). Transaction Books, New Brunswick, USA.

Buhmann, B., Rainwater, L., Schmaus, G., and Smeeding, T.M. (1988). Equivalence scales, well-being, inequality, and poverty: sensitivity estimates across ten countries using the Luxemburg Income Study Database. *Review of Income and Wealth, June*, 115–42.

Buratti, C. (1990). Successi e fallimenti del Servizio Sanitario Nazionale: un bilancio dei primi 10 anni. *Economia Pubblica*, **3**, 145–54.

Butler, S. (1991). A tax reform strategy to deal with the uninsured. *Journal of the American Medical Association*, **265**(19), 2541–4.

Callan, T., Nolan, B., Whelan, B., Hannan, D., and Creighton, S. (1989). *Poverty, income and welfare in Ireland*. The Economic and Social Research Institute, General Research Series, Paper 146. Dublin.

Campos, A.C. de (ed.) (1987). *A combinação público-privada em saúde: privilégios, estigmas e ineficiências*. Escola Nacional de Saúde Pública, Lisbon.

Cantor, J. (1988). The burden of financing health care in the United States. Doctoral dissertation. The Johns Hopkins School of Hygiene and Public Health, Baltimore.

Carloni, D. (1988). Aspetti economici e sociali del finanziamento del servizio sanitario nazio nale. *Previdenza Sociale, May–June,* 683–717.

Cartwright, A. and O'Brien, M. (1976). Social class variations in health care and in the nature of general practitioner consultations. In *The sociology of the National Health Service* (ed. M. Stacey). Sociological Review Monograph, No. 22. Keele University Press, UK.

Cartwright, A., Lucas, S., and O'Brien, M. (1974). *Exploring communication in general practice.* Report to the Social Science Research Council.

Centraal Bureau voor de Statistiek (CBS) (1989). *Vademecum gezondheidsstatistiek Nederland 1989.* CBS, 's-Gravenhage, the Netherlands.

Centraal Plan Bureau (1988). *Centraal economisch plan.* Staatsuitgeverij, 's-Gravenhage, the Netherlands.

Central Statistical Office (1975). *Social trends.* HMSO, London.

Central Statistical Office (1983). *Redistributive effects of state taxes and benefits on household incomes in 1980.* Stationery Office, Dublin.

Central Statistical Office (1986). The effects of taxes and benefits on household income, 1985. *Economic Trends, November.*

Central Statistical Office (1989). *Household budget survey 1987,* 1. Stationery Office, Dublin.

Centro Europa Ricerche (1988) La spesa sanitaria. *Rapporto, 2,* 84–95.

Comision Economica Para America Latina y el Caribe (1986). *Antecedentes Estadisticos de la Distribucion del Ingresso: Brasil, 1960–1983.* United Nations, Santiago.

Charraud, A. (1988). Les enseignements des enquêtes sur la consommation medicale en France: Culture, argent, profession et recours aux Soins. In *La sociéte inquiète de la santé* (ed. G.S. Santé), Eres, Lyon, 33–48.

Christiansen, T. (1990). *Measurement of health status. Vol. III. Reliability and validity of scores in the Danish health study.* Department of Economics, Odense University.

Citoni, G. (1990). *La distribuzione dei benefici dei servizi sanitari.* Paper presented to ISPE's conference Bilancio Pubblico e Redistribuzione, 12–13 March 1990, Rome.

Cmd. 6502 (1944). *A National Health Service,* HMSO, London.

Cmd. 555 (1989). *Working for patients.* HMSO, London.

Cochrane, A.L. (1972). *Effectiveness and efficiency,* Nuffield Provincial Hospital Trust.

Coll, P. (1985). La financiación de los sistemas sanitarios, El caso de España. *JANO,* **656–H,** 47–9.

Collins, E. and Klein, K. (1980). Equity and the NHS: self reported morbidity, access and primary care. *British Medical Journal,* **281,** 1111–5.

Collins, E. and Klein, R. (1985). *Self-reported morbidity, socio-economic factors and general practitioner consultations.* Bath Social Policy Papers, No. 5. University of Bath.

Commissie Structuur en Financiering van de Gezondheidszorg (Commissie SFG) (1987). *Bereidheid tot Verandering,* Adviesrapport, Staatsuitgeverij, Den Haag.

Commonwealth Fund Commission on Elderly People Living Alone (1987). *Medicare's poor: filling the gaps in medical coverage for low-income elderly*

Americans (prepared by Diana Rowland and Barbara Lyons). The Commonwealth Fund Commission on Elderly People Living Alone, 20 November, Baltimore.

Congressional Budget Office (CBO) (1979). *A profile of the uninsured: The haves and have nots.* Washington, D.C.

Congressional Research Service (CRS) (1988). *Health insurance and the uninsured: background data and analysis.* A report prepared for the U.S. House of representatives, Energy and Commerce Committee, Subcommittee on Health and the Environment, Committee. Print Serial 100 X. U.S. Government Printing Office, Washington, D.C.

Cox, B.D. *et al.* (1987). *The health and lifestyle survey.* Health Promotion Research Trust, London.

Cullis, J.G. and West, P.A. (1979). *The economics of health: An introduction.* Martin Robertson, Oxford.

Culyer, A.J. (1971 *a*). The nature of the commodity 'health care' and its efficient allocation. *Oxford Economic Papers*, **23**, 189–211.

Culyer, A.J. (1971 *b*). Medical care and the economics of giving. *Economica*, **151**, 295–303.

Culyer, A.J. (1976). *Need and the National Health Service: economics and social choice.* Martin Robertson, London.

Culyer, A.J. (1978). Need, values and health status measurement. In *Economic aspects of health services* (ed. A.J. Culyer and K.G. Wright), pp. 9–31. Martin Robertson, London.

Culyer, A.J. (1980). *The political economy of social policy.* Martin Robertson, Oxford.

Culyer, A.J. (1989). Health care: the political economy of its finance and provision. *Oxford Review of Economic Policy*, **5**, 34–58.

Culyer, A.J. (1990). *Ethics and efficiency in health care: some plain economic truths.* Perey Lecture, McMaster University, Canada.

Culyer, A.J. (1991). Conflicts between equity concepts and efficiency in diagrammatic approach. *Osaka Economic Papers*, **40**, 141–54.

Culyer, A.J., Evans, R.G., van der Schulenburg, J.M., van der Ven W.P.M.M., and Weisbrod B.A. (1991). *International review of the Swedish health care system*, Occasional Paper no. 34, Center for Business and Policy Studies (SNS), Stockholm.

Culyer, A.J., Lavers, R.J., and Williams, A.H. (1971). Social indicators: health. *Social Trends*, **2**, 31–42.

Culyer, A.J., Maynard A., and Williams, A. (1981). Alternative systems of health care provision: an essay on motes and beams. In *A new approach to the economics of health care* (ed. M. Olson). American Enterprise Institute, Washington, D.C.

Culyer, A.J., Maynard, A., and Posnett, J. (1990). *Competition in health care: Reforming the NHS.* MacMillan, London.

Culyer, A.J. and Wagstaff, A. (1991 *a*). *Need, equality and social justice.* Discussion Paper 90, Centre for Health Economics, University of York.

Culyer, A.J. and Wagstaff, A. (1991 *b*). *QALYs, efficiency and distributive justice.* Discussion paper, Centre for Health Economics, University of York.

Culyer, A.J. and Wagstaff, A. (1991 *c*). *Need, Equity, and equality in health and health care.* Discussion paper 95, Centre for Health Economics, University of York.

Daniels, N. (1985). *Just health care*, Cambridge University Press.

Danmarks Statistik. (1987). *Statistisk 10 års oversigt 1987.*

Danmarks Statistik. (1985). *Statistiske Efterretninger: Indkomst, forbrug og priser 1985: 12.*

Danmarks Statistik. (1986) *Statistiske Efterretninger: Indkomst, forbrug og priser 1986: 9.*

Davis, K. (1973). *Lessons of Medicare and Medicaid for National Health Insurance.* Hearings on National Health Insurance, Subcommittee on Public Health and Environment, Committee on Interstate and Foreign Commerce. U.S. Congress, 12 December, Washington, D.C.

Davis, K. (1975). *National Health Insurance: Benefits, costs and consequences.* The Brookings Institution, Washington, D.C.

Davis, K. (1976). Achievements and problems of Medicaid. *Public Health Reports,* **912**(4), 309–16.

Davis, K. (1981). Reagan administration health policy. *Journal of Public Health Policy,* **2** (4), 312–22.

Davis, K. (1991). Expanding Medicare and employer plans to achieve universal health insurance. *Journal of the American Medical Association,* **265**(19), 2525–8.

Davis, K. and Schoen, C. (1978). *Health and the war on poverty: A ten year appraisal.* The Brookings Institution, Washington, D.C.

Davis, K. Anderson, G., Rowland, D., and Steinberg, E. (1990). *Health care cost containment.* The Johns Hopkins Press, Baltimore.

Department of Health (1986). *Health: The wider dimensions.* Department of Health, Dublin.

Department of Health (1988). *Health Statistics 1987*, Stationary Office, Dublin.

Department of Health (1989). *Health Statistics 1988*, Stationary Office, Dublin.

Department of Health and Social Security (1976). *Sharing resources for health in England: report of the resource allocation working party.* HMSO, London.

Department of Health and Social Security and Welsh Office (1987). *Health Service Costing Returns 1985/86.* HMSO, London.

Development Group (1991). *Peru health sector assessment.* Report submitted to USAID/Peru, Alexandria, VA.

Di Nicola, F. (1990). *Effetti redistributivi dell'IVA.* Paper presented to ISPE's conference Bilancio Pubblico e Redistribuzione, 12–13 March 1990, Rome.

Dirindin, N. (1991). Redistribuzione dei redditi e sistema sanitaria. In *Welfare state e redistribuzione: gli effetti della spesa sanitaria e pensionistica in Italia negli anni '80* (ed. R. Brunetta and L. Tronti), pp. 271–312. Franco Angeli, Milan.

Domingues, O., Estêves, R., Figueira, C., Martins, A., and Matias, A. (1984). Incidência por classe de rendimento do Imposto sobre o Valor Acrescentado. In *O Impacto do IVA na economia Portuguesa* (ed. Comissão do IVA/IACEP-GEBEI). Imprensa Nacional-Casa do Moeda, Lisbon.

Donabedian, A. (1971). Social responsibility for personal health services: an examination of basic values. *Inquiry,* **8**, 3–19.

Dor, A. and Gaag, J. van der (1987). *The demand for medical care in developing countries: quantity rationing in rural Côte d'Lvoire.* Living Standards Measurement Study Working Paper, No. 35. World Bank, Washington, D.C.

Elleman-Jensen, P. (1989). *Bootstrapping concentration indices.* COMAC Project on Distributive Aspects of Health Care, Research note, No. 1.

Elola Somoza, F.J. (1991). *Crisis y reforma de la asistencia sanitaria pública en Espana (1983–1990).* Fondo de Investigaciones Sanitarias de la Seguridad Social, Madrid.

Elola Somoza, F.J., Mengual García, E., and Velayos Florido, J. (1988). Asistencia sanitaria pública en España, Gasto y cobertura. In *Salud y equidad. VIII jornadas de economìa de la salud. Las Palmas de Gran Canaria, 25, 26, 27 de Mayo de 1988* (co-ordinated by J. Montserrat and C. Murillo), pp. 299–314. Ministerio de Sanidad y Consumo, Madrid.

Enthoven, A. (1979). *Health plan.* Addison Wesley, New York.

Enthoven, A. (1985). *Reflections on the management of the national health service.* Nuffield Provincial Hospitals Trust, Occasional Paper No. 5, London.

Enthoven, A.C. and Kronick, R. (1991). Universal health insurance through incentives reform. *Journal of the American Medical Association,* **265**(19), 2532–6.

EuroQol Group (1990). EuroQol—a new facility for the measurement of health—related quality of life. *Health Policy,* **16**, 199–208.

Evandrou, M., Falkingham, J., Le Grand, J., and Winter, D. (1990). Equity in health and social care. Welfare State Programme Discussion Paper No. WSP/52. London School of Economics, Suntory–Toyota International Centre for Economics and Related Discipline. *Journal of Social Policy.*

Feder, J., Hadley, J., and Mullner, R. (1984). Falling through the cracks: poverty, insurance coverage and hospital care for the poor, 1980 and 1982. *Milbank Memorial Fund Quarterly.*

Ferranti, D. de (1985). *Paying for health services in developing countries.* World Bank Staff Working Paper, No. 721. World Bank, Washington, D.C.

Ferrera, M. (1986). Assetti organizzativi e domanda sanitaria: il caso Italiano. In *La salute che noi pensiamo: Domanda sanitaria e politiche pubbliche in Italia* (ed. M. Ferrera and G. Zincone). Il Mulino, Bologna.

Folketinget præsidiet (1971). *Folketingets Forhandlinger 1970–1.* Copenhagen.

Folketingets Forhandlinger 1970–1 (1971). Folketinget, præsidiet, Copenhagen.

Folketingstidende (1970–1), Tillaeg A. (1971). Folketinget, præsidiet, Copenhagen.

Formby, J.P., Seaks, T.G., and Smith, W.J. (1981). A comparison of two new measures of tax progressivity. *Economic Journal,* **91**, 1015–9.

Forster, D.P. (1976). Social class differences in sickness and general practitioner consultations. *Health Trends,* **8**, 29–32.

Fox J. (ed.) (1989). *Health inequalities in European countries.* European Science Foundation. Gower, Aldershot.

Fox, J. and Morley, S. (1990). *Who paid the bill? Adjustment and poverty in Brazil, 1980–1995,* mimeo. World Bank, Washington, D.C.

Foxley, A. (1979). *Redistributive effects of government programs.* Pergamon Press, Oxford.

Freeman, H.W., Blendon, R., Aiken, L., Sudman, S., Millinix, C., and Corey, C. (1987). Americans report on their access to health care. *Health Affairs,* **6**(1), 6–18.

Freixinho, J.C. (1990). *Subsistemas de Saúde em Portugal: Estudo, características e evolução futura.* Dissertação ao XIX Curso de Administração Hospitalar, mimeo. ENSP.

Frey, R.L. and Leu, R.E. (1983). Umverteilung über den Staatshaushalt. Die personelle Budgetinzidenz der Schweiz 1977. *Zeitschrift für Volkswirtschaft und Statistik,* **119**, 1–21.

Friedman, M. (1957). *A theory of the consumption function,* Princeton University Press, Princeton.

Fuchs, V. (1984). Rationing health care. *New England Journal of Medicine,* 18 December.

Fuller, M.F. and Lury, D.A. (1977). *Statistics workbook for social science students.* Philip Allan, Oxford.

George, V. and Wilding, P. (1984). *The impact of social policy,* Routledge and Kegan Paul, London.

Gertler, P. and Gaag, J. van der (1990). *The willingness to pay for medical care.* World Bank, Washington, D.C.

Gillon, R. (1986). *Philosophical medical ethics.* John Wiley, Chichester.

Glewwe, P. (1990). *Improving data on poverty in the Third World. The World Bank's living standards measurement study.* World Bank Working Paper, No. 416. World Bank, Washington, D.C.

Glewwe, P. and Twun-Baah, K. (1991). *The distribution of welfare in Ghana, 1987–1988.* Living Standard Measurement Study Working Paper, No. 75. World Bank, Washington, D.C.

Godfrey, L. (1988). *Mis-specification tests in econometrics.* Cambridge University Press.

Goodin, R.E. and Le Grand, J. (1987). Introduction. In *Not only the poor: the middle classes and the welfare state* (ed. R.E. Goodin and J. Le Grand). Allen & Unwin, London.

Gottschalk, P. and Wolfe, B. (1990). *Equity in the finance and utilization of medical care in the United States,* Mimeo.

Gottschalk, P., Wolfe, B., and Haveman, R. (1989). Health care financing in the US, UK and Netherlands: distributional consequences. In *Changes in revenue structures,* pp. 351–73.

Government of Jamaica (1988). *Central Government Statistics,* Kingston, Government of Jamaica.

Griffith, J.E. and Cislowski, J.A. (1986). *Infant mortality: Are we making progress?.* Congressional Research Service Review, January.

Grosh, M. (1990). *Social spending in Latin America: the story of the 1980s,* World Bank Discussion Paper, No. 106. World Bank, Washington, D.C.

Grumback, K., Bodenheimer, T., Himmelstein, D.U., and Woolhandler, S. (1991). Liberal benefits, conservative spending: the physicians for a national health program proposal. *Journal of the American Medical Association,* **265**(19), 2549–54.

Gutzwiller, F., Leu, R.E., Schulz, H.R., and Zemp, E. (1985). *Gesundheit und medizinische Versorgung in der Schweiz. Ergebnisse der ersten repräsentativen Gesundheitsbefragung.* Mimeo, Basel.

Gygi, P. and Frei, A. (1985). *Das Schweizerische Gesundheitswesen.* Krebs, Basel.

Ham, C., Robinson, R., and Benzeval, M. (1990). *Health check; health reforms in an international context.* King's Fund Institute.

Hemming, R. and Keen, M.J. (1983). Single-crossing conditions in comparisons of tax progressivity, *Journal of Public Economics*, **20**, 373–80.

Hochman, H.M. and Rodgers, J.D. (1969). Pareto optimal redistribution. *American Economic Review*, **59**, 542–57.

Holahan, J. and Zedlewski, S. (1991). Expanding Medicaid to cover uninsured Americans. *Health Affairs*, **10**(1), 45–61.

Hooijmans, E.M. and Rutten, F.F.H. (1984). The impact of supply on the use of hospital facilities; differences between high and low income groups. *Acta Hospitalia*, **2**, 41–8.

Hurst, J.W. (1985). *Financing health services in the United States, Canada and Britain*. Nuffield/Leverhulme Fellowship Report, King Edward's Hospital Fund for London.

Hurst, J.W. (1991 *a*). The reform of health care: a comparative analysis of seven OECD countries. OECD, Paris.

Hurst, J.W. (1991 *b*). Reforming health care in seven European nations. *Health Affairs*, **10**(3), 7–21.

Iglehart, J.K. (ed.) (1991). Pursuit of health systems reform. *Health Affairs*, **10**(3), special issue.

Illsley, R. and Le Grand, J. (1987). The measurement of inequality in health. In *Health and economics* (ed. A. Williams). Macmillan, London.

IMF (International Monetary Fund) (1987). *Government Finance Statistics Yearbook* volume XI, Washington D.C., International Monetary Fund.

Indenrigsministeriet og Sundhedsstyrelsen (1985). *Det Danske Sundhedsvæsen: En Status med Perspektiver mod År 2000*, Copenhagen.

INSALUD (1990). *Informe económico-funcional de las instituciones sanitarias, 1988*. Ministerio de Sanidad y Consumo, Madrid.

Institute of Medicine, Committee to Study the Prevention of Low Birthweight (1985). *Preventing low birthweight*, National Academy Press, Washington, D.C.

Instituto Nacional de Estadistica (1977). *La renta nacional en 1976 y su distribución*. Ministerio de Sanidad y Consumo, Madrid.

Istat (Istituto Centrale di Statistica) (1986). *Indagine statistica sulle condizioni di salute della popolazione e sul ricorso ai servizi sanitari: November 1983*. Istat, Rome.

Istat (Istituto Centrale di Statistica) (1989). *I Consumi Delle Famiglie: anno 1987*. Istat, Rome.

Janssen, R.T.J.M. (1989). The effects of time-prices on medical consumption and health in Dutch. Doctoral dissertation, University of Limburg, Maastricht.

Jenkins, S. (1988). Calculating income distribution indices from microdata. *National Tax Journal*, **61**, 139–42.

Jiminez, E. (1986). The public subsidization of education and health in developing countries: A review of equity and efficiency. *The Research Observer*, **1**, 111–29.

Kahn, K.L. *et al.* (1990). The effects of the DRG based prospective payment system on quality of care. *Journal of the American Medical Association*, **264**(15), 1953–94.

Kakwani, N.C. (1977). Measurement of tax progressivity: an international comparison. *Economic Journal*, **87**, 71–80.

Kakwani, N.C. and Podder (1976). Efficient estimation of the Lorenz curve and associated inequality measures from grouped observations. *Econometrica*, **44**, 137–48.

Kaplan, R., Bush, J., and Berry, C.C. (1976). Health status: types of validity for an index of well being. *Health Services Research*, **11**, 478–507.

Klein, R. (1991). Making sense of inequalities: a response to Peter Townsend. *International Journal of Health Services*, **21**, 175–81.

Kravits, J. and Schneider, J. (1975). Health care need and actual use by age, race and income. In *Equity in health services: empirical analysis in social policy* (ed. R. Andersen, J. Kravits, and O. Anderson). Ballinger, Cambridge, Mass.

Kravis, I., Heston, A., and Summers, R. (1982). *World product and income*. Johns Hopkins University Press, Baltimore.

Lagares Calvo, M. (1989). *Evaluación del fraude en el impuesto sobre la renta de las personas físicas, ejercicio 1979 a 1986*. Instituto de Estudios Fiscales, Madrid.

Laing (1987). *Laing's review of private health care 1987*. Laing and Buisson, London.

Lambert, P.J. and Pfähler, W. (1988). On aggregate measures of the net redistributive impact of taxation and government expenditure. *Public Finance Quarterly*, **16**, 178–202.

Lambert, P.J. (1989). *The distribution and redistribution of income. A mathematical analysis*. Basil Blackwell, Oxford.

Langendonck, J. van (1991). The role of the social security systems in the completion of the European internal market, *Acta Hospitalia*, **31**, 35–57.

Leenen, H. (1984). Gelijkheid en ongelijkheid in gezondheidszorg. *Nederlands Tijdschrift voor Gezondheidsrecht*, **8**, 53–67.

Le Grand, J. (1978). The distribution of public expenditure: the case of health care. *Economica*, **45**, 125–42.

Le Grand, J. (1982). *The strategy of equality*, Allen & Unwin, London.

Le Grand, J. (1987). Equity, health and health care. *Social Justice Research*, **1**, 257–74.

Le Grand, J. (1991). The distribution of health care revisited: a commentary on Wagstaff, Van Doorslaer and Paci, and O'Donnell and Propper. *Journal of Health Economics*, **10**, 239–45.

Le Grand, J. and Rabin, M. (1986). Trends in British health inequality: 1931–83. In *Public and private health services* (ed. A.J. Culyer and B. Jönsson). Basil Blackwell, Oxford.

Le Grand, J., Winter, D., and Woolley, F. (1990). The National Health Service: safe in whose hands? In *The state of welfare: the welfare state in Britain since 1974* (ed. J. Hills). Oxford University Press.

Leu, R.E. and Frey, R.L. (1985). Budget incidence, demographic change and health policy in Switzerland. In *Public finance and social policy* (ed. A.J. Culyer and G. Terny). Wayne State University Press, Detroit.

Leu, R.E. and Gerfin, M. (1991). *Equity in the finance and delivery of health care in Switzerland*. Diskussionsbeiträge des Volkswirtschaftlichen Instituts der Universität Bern.

Leu, R.E., Buhmann, B., and Frey, R.L. (1988). Einkommens- und Vermögensverteilung: Die Begüterten und die weniger Begüterten. In *Der Sozialstaat unter der Lupe. Wohlstandsverteilung und Wohlstandsumverteilung in der Schweiz* (ed. R.L. Frey and R.E. Leu). Helbing & Lichtenhahn, Basel.

Lindsay, C.M. (1969). Medical care and the economics of sharing. *Economica*, **144**, 351–362.

Lugaresi, S. (1990). *L'impatto redistributivo dell'indicizzazione dell'IRPEF. Una microsimul azione con ltaxmod.* Paper presented to ISPE's conference Bilancio Pubblico e Redistribuzione. 12–13 March 1990, Rome.

McClements, L.D. (1978). *The economics of social security.* Heinemann, London.

McKeown, T. (1976). *The modern rise of population.* Arnold, London.

McLachlan, G. and Maynard, A. (1982). The public/private mix in health care: the emerging lessons. In *The public/private mix in health care: the relevance and effects of change* (ed. G. McLachlan and A. Maynard). Nuffield Provincial Hospitals Trust, London.

Mackenbach, J.P. (1991). *Socio-economic health differences in The Netherlands: a review of recent empirical findings.* Proceedings of the Symposium on Socio-economic Health Differences. 1 February 1991, Rotterdam.

Maher, J. *et al.* (1990). Who gets radiotherapy? *Health Trends*, **22**(2), 78–82.

Manning W.G. *et al.* (1981). A two-part model of the damand for medical care: preliminary results from the RAND health insurance study. In *Health, economics and health economics* (ed. J. van der Gaag and M. Perlman). North-Holland, Amsterdam.

Maynard, A. (1975). *Heath care in the European community.* Croom Helm, London.

Maynard, A. and Williams, A. (1984). Privatisation and the National Health Service. In *Privatisation and the welfare state* (ed. J. Le Grand and R. Robinson). Allen & Unwin, London.

Maxwell, R.J. (1981). *Health and wealth: An international study of health care spending.* Mass., Lexington.

Meerman, J. (1979). *Public expenditure in Malaysia: who benefits and why?*, Oxford University Press.

Mehrez, A. and Gafni, A. (1989). Quality-adjusted life years, utility theory, and healthy years equivalents. *Medical Decision Making*, **9**, 142–9.

Metcalfe, D. *et al.* (1983). *A study of process of care in urban general practice.* A report prepared for the Department of Health and Social Security, UK.

Miller, D. (1976). *Social justice.* Clarendon Press, Oxford.

MEFA (various years) *Tal og data. Medicin og sundhedsvæsen (1983, 1984, 1990).* Copenhagen.

Ministerie van Welzijn, Volksgezondheid en Cultuur (1988). *Grenzen van de Zorg*, Regeringsstandpunt inzake het advies van de Ziekenfondsraad, de Nationale Raad voor de Volksgezondheid, Tweede Kamer, vergaderjaar 1987–8, 20620, nrs 1–2.

Ministério da Saúde (1987). *Inquérito nacional de Saudé.* DEPS, Lisbon, Portugal.

Ministerio de Economía y Hacienda (1983). *Memoria de la Administración Tributaria*, Madrid.

Ministerio de Trabajo y Seguridad Social (1985). *Documento base para la reforma de la Seguridad Social para la Comisión Tripartita del Acuerdo Económico y Social (A.E.S.).* Colección Informes, Madrid.

Ministero del Tesoro (1988). *Relazione generale sulla sittuazione economica del paese*, Vol. III. Ministero del Tesoro, Rome.

Ministero della Sanità—Servizio Centrale della Programmazione Sanitaria (1986 *a*). *Attivita gestionali ed economiche delle USL—Anno 1985.* Minitero della Sanità, Rome.

Ministero della Sanità—Servizio Centrale della Programmazione Sanitaria (1986 *b*). *Rendiconti trimestrali delle USL: aggregazioni economiche.* Ministro della Sanità, Rome.

Ministero di Grazia e Giustizia (1978). Legge 833: Istitutizione del Servizio Sanitario, *Supplement to Gazzetta Ufficiale 28*, December 1978, Rome.

Ministry of Health, Peru (1990). *Direccion tecnica de desarrollo de recursos humanos*. Peru, Lima.

Mooney, G. (1983). Equity in health care: confronting the confusion. *Effective Health Care*, **1**, 179–85.

Mooney, G. (1986). *Economics, medicine and health care*. Wheatscheaf, Brighton.

Mooney, G. and McGuire, A. (1987). Distributive justice with special reference to geographical inequality in health care. *In* A. Williams (ed.) *Health and Economics*, Macmillan, London.

Murillo, C. and González-Valcárcel, B. (1990). *Salud, uso y consumo de servicios sanitarios*. Working paper, University of Barcelona, Barcelona.

Murphy, D. (1984). The impact of state taxes and benefits on Irish household incomes. *Journal of the Statistical and Social Inquiry Society of Ireland*, **XXV**, Part 1, 55–120.

Netherlands Central Bureau of Statistics (1988). *Netherlands Health Interview Survey 1981–1985*. Staatsuitgeverij. CBS publications, the Hague.

Newacheck, P.W. (1988). Access to ambulatory care for poor persons. *Health Services Research*, **12** (3), 401–19.

Newhouse, J.P., Manning, W.G., and Morris C.M. (1981). Some interim results from a controlled trial of cost sharing in health insurance. *New England Journal of Medicine*, **305**, 1501–5.

Newman, J.F. (1975). Health status and utilization of physician services. In *Equity in health services; empirical analysis in social policy* (ed. R. Andersen, J. Kravits, and O. Anderson). Ballinger, Cambridge, Mass.

Newman, J. (1987). *Labour market activity in Côte d'Ivoire and Peru*, Living Standards Measurement Study Working Paper, No. 36. World Bank, Washington, D.C.

Nicholl, J.P., Beeby, N.R., and Williams, B.T. (1989). Role of the private sector in elective surgery in England and Wales, 1986. *British Medical Journal*, **298**, 243–7.

Nolan, B. (1991). *The utilization and financing of health services in Ireland*. The Economic and Social Research Institute, General Research Series Paper No. 155 Dublin.

Nozick, R. (1974). *Anarchy, state and utopia*. Basil Blackwell, Oxford.

O'Donnell, O. and Propper, C. (1991 *a*). Equity and the distribution of UK National Health Service resources. *Journal of Health Economics*, **10**, 1–19.

O'Donnell, O. and Propper, C. (1991 *b*). Equity and the distribution of UK National Health Service resources: a reply. *Journal of Health Economics*, **10**, 247–250.

O'Donnell, O., Propper, C., and Upward, R. (1991 *b*). *An empirical study of equity in the finance and delivery of health care in Britain*. Discussion Paper 85. Centre for Health Economics, University of York.

OECD (1985). *Measuring health care 1960–1983. Expenditures, costs and performance*. OECD, Paris.

OECD (1987). *Financing and delivering health care*. OECD, Paris.

OECD (1989). Health care expenditure and other data: An international compendium. *Health Care Financing Review*, Annual Supplement, 111–94.

OECD (1990). *Health care systems in transition. The search for efficiency*. OECD, Paris.

Office of Population Censuses and Surveys (1980). *Classification of occupations*. HMSO, London.

Office of Population Censuses and Surveys (1990). *The General Household Survey, 1988*. HMSO, London.

Office of Health Economics (OHE) (1987). *OHE compendium of health statistics* (6th edn). London.

O'Higgins, M. and Ruggles, P. (1981). The distribution of public expenditures and taxes among households in the United Kingdom. *Review of Income and Wealth*, **27**(2), 298–326.

O'Higgins, M., Schmaus, G. and Stephenson, G. (1990). Income distribution and redistribution: a microdata analysis for seven countries. In *Poverty, inequality and income distribution in perspective: the Luxembourg income study* (ed. T. Smeeding, M. O'Higgins, and L. Rainwater). Harvester, London.

Ooijendijk, W.T.M., Brekel, E.J.G. van den, Stompedissel, I., Ginneken, J.K.S. van, and Schaapveld, K. (1991). *Sociaal-economische status, gezondheid en medische consumptie. Secundaire analyse van de CBS Gezondheidsenquête 1983–1988*. NIPG-TNO en CBS, Leiden.

Orme, C. (1988). The calculation of the information matrix test for binary data models. *The Manchester School*. **CVI**(4), 370–6.

Paci, P. and Wagstaff, A. (1991). *Equity in the finance and delivery of health care in Italy*. Discussion Paper 20. Applied Econometrics Research Unit, City University, London.

Pampel, F. and Williamson, J.B. (1989). *Age, class, politics and the welfare state*, Cambridge University Press.

Pamuk, E. (1985). Social class inequality in mortality from 1921–1972 in England and Wales. *Population Studies*, **39**, 17–31.

Pamuk, E. (1988). Social-class inequality in infant mortality in England and Wales from 1921 to 1980. *European Journal of Population*, **4**, 1–21.

Pauly, M.V. (1971). *Medical care at public expense*. Praeger, New York.

Pechman, J. (1985). *Who paid the taxes, 1966–85?* Brookings, Washington, D.C.

Pechman, J. (1986). Pechman's tax incidence study: a note on the data. *American Economic Review*, December.

Pedersen, K.M. (1989). *Danmark i Danmark. Om sygeforsikring i Danmark*. Vejle amtskommune.

Peet, J. (1991). Surgery needed: a survey of health care. *The Economist*, 6 July.

Pepper Commission (1990). *Report of the Bipartisan Commission on Comprehensive Health Care*, March. U.S. Government Printing Office, Washington, D.C.

Pereira, J. (1988). *Inequality in health care in Portugal. Evidence from the national health interview survey*, October. mimeo, University of York.

Pereira, J. (1990). Equity objectives in Portuguese health policy. *Social Science and Medicine*, **31**(1), 91–4.

Pereira, J. (1992). *Horizontal equity in the delivery of Portuguese health care*, Revista Portuguesa de Saúde Pública (forthcoming).

Pereira, J., and Pinto, C.G. (1990). *Regressivity in an NHS-type system. The financing of Portuguese health care*. Paper presented at the EC-COMAC Conference on Equity in the Finance and Delivery of Health Care, November. Bellagio, Italy.

Preston, S.H., Haines, M.R., and Pamuk, E. (1981). Effects of industrialization and urbanization on mortality in developed countries. In *Solicited papers*, Vol. 2. IUSSP 19th International Population Conference, Manila. IUSSP, Liege.

Priestman, T. *et al.* (1989). The Royal College of Radiologists fractionation study. *Clinical Oncology*, **1**, 63–6.

Propper, C. and Maynard, A. (1990). Whither the private health care sector? In *Competition in health care: reforming the NHS* (ed. A. Culyer, A. Maynard, and J. Posnett). Macmillan, London.

Puffer, F. (1986). Access to primary care: a comparison of the US and UK. *Journal of Social Policy*, **15**, 293–313.

Puffer, F. (1987). *The effect of regional and class difference in the U.K. on access to health care.* Paper presented to the Health Economists Study Group, January. University of Warwick.

Quirino, P. (1991). I problemi connessi con une più equilibrata ripartizione del Fondo Sanitario Nazionale. In *Welfare state e redistribuzione: gli effetti della spesa sanitaria e pensionistica in Italia negli anni '80* (ed. R. Brunetta and L. Tronti), pp. 313–32. Franco Angeli, Milan.

Rawls, J. (1971). *A theory of justice.* Harvard University Press, Cambridge, Mass.

Report of the Commission on Health Funding (1989). Stationery Office, Dublin.

Ringen, S. (1987). *The possibility of politics*, Oxford University Press.

Rockefeller, J.D. (1991). A call for action: The Pepper Commission's blueprint for health care reform. *Journal of the American Medical Association*, **265**(19), 2507–10.

Rodríguez, M. (1990). El gasto sanitario privado en España: su naturaleza y su efecto sobre la equidad del sistema. In *Salud y Equidad. VIII Jornadas de economía de la salud, Las Palmas de Gran Canaria, 25, 26 y 27 mayo de 1988* (eds. J. Montserrat and C. Murillo), pp. 285–97. Ministerio de Sanidad y Consumo, Madrid, 285–97.

Rogers, D.E. and Blendon, R.J. (1977). The changing American health scene: sometimes things get better. *Journal of the American Medical Association*, **237**, 1710–14.

Rogers, D.E., Blendon, R.J., and Moloney, T.W. (1982). Who needs Medicaid? *New England Journal of Medicine*, **307**, 13–8.

Rowland, D. (1987). Hospital care for the poor. Doctoral dissertation, The Johns Hopkins School of Hygiene and Public Health, Baltimore.

Rowland, D., Lyons, B., and Edwards, J. (1988). Medicaid: health care for the poor in the Reagan era. *Annual Review of Public Health*, **9**, 427–50.

Rutten, F. and Janssen, R. (1987). Een economische beschouwing over gelijkeid in de gezondheidszorg, in Wetenschappelijke Raad voor het Regeringsbeleid, *De Ongelijke Verdeling van Gezondheid*, Staatsuitgeverij, Den Haag.

Santos, J. (1984). Escalas de equivalência. *Estudos de Economia*, **5**(1), 43–65.

Schieber, G.J. and Poullier, J.P. (1989 *a*). International health care expenditure trends. *Health Affairs*, **8**(3), 169–77.

Schieber, G.J. and Poullier, J.P. (1989 *b*). Overview of international comparisons of health care expenditures. *Health Care Financing Review Annual Supplement*, 1–8.

Schieber, G.J. and Poullier, J.P. (1991). International health spending: issues and trends. *Health Affairs*, **10**(2), 106–16.

Schieber, G.J. and Poullier, J.P., and Greenwald, L.M. (1991). Health care systems in twenty-four countries. *Health Affairs*, **10**(3), 22–38.

Schiepers, J. (1988). Huishoudensequivalentiefactoren volgens de budgetverdelingsmethode, *Sociaal-economische Maandstatistiek*, Supplement 7, **2**, 28–37.

Schneeweiss, R. and Coll (1983). Diagnosis clusters: a new tool for analyzing the content of ambulatory medical care. *Medical Care*, **21**, 105–12.

Schoen, C. (1984). Medicaid and the poor: Medicaid myths and reality and the impact of recent legislative changes. *Bulletin of the New York Academy of Medicine*, **60**, 1.

Selden, T. and Wasylenko, M. (1990). *Benefit incidence analysis in developing countries*, mimeo. World Bank, Washington, D.C.

Selowsky, M. (1979). *Who benefits from government expenditure? A case study of Colombia*. Oxford University Press.

Shah, A. and Whalley, J. (1990). *An alternative view of tax incidence analysis for developing countries*, World Bank Working Paper, Series No. 462. World Bank, Washington, D.C.

Simons, H.C. (1938). *Personal income taxation*, University of Chicago Press, Chicago.

Sociaal en Cultureel Planbureau (1981). *Profijt van de overheid in 1977*. Staatsuitgeverij, 's-Gravenhage, the Netherlands.

Socialreformkommissionen (1969). Socialreformkommissionens r. betœnkning. *Betœnkning*, **543**.

Suarez-Berenguela, R. (1987). *Financing the health sector in Peru*. Living Standards Measurement Study Working Paper, No. 31. World Bank, Washington, D.C.

Sugden, R. (1983). *Who cares?* IEA Occasional Paper, No. 67. Institute for Economic Affairs, London.

Suits, D. (1977). Measurement of tax progressivity. *American Economic Review*, **67**, 747–52.

Tanzi, V., and Wulf, V. de. (1976). A distribuição de carga fiscal por grupos de rendimento em Portugal. In *I Conferência Internacional sobre Economia Portuguesa*. Fundação Calouste Gulbenkian, Lisbon.

Teekens, R. (1990). Inequality and poverty. Portugal compared with Greece, Ireland and Spain. *Estudos de Economia*, **10**, 111–42.

Tinker, A. (1984). *Staying at home*. Department of the Environment. HMSO, London.

Titmuss, R. (1968). *Commitment to welfare*. Allen & Urwin, London.

Tobin, J. (1970). On limiting the domain of inequality. *Journal of Law and Economics*, **13**, 263–78.

Torrance, G.W. (1986). Measurement of health state utilities for economic appraisal: a review. *Journal of Health Economics*, **5**, 1–30.

Townsend, P. (1979). *Poverty in the United Kingdom*. Penguin, Harmondsworth.

Townsend, P. (1990). Widening inequalities in health; a rejoinder to Rudolph Klein. *International Journal of Health Services*, **20**, 363–72.

Townsend. P. and Davidson N. (1982). *Inequalities in health: The Black Report*. Penguin, Harmondsworth.

Undritz, N. (1987). *Gesundheitswesen in der Schweiz*. Verlag Neue Zürcher Zeitung, Zürich.

United Nations Development Programme (1990). *Human Development Report*, Oxford University Press. New York.

U.S. Congress Committee on Ways and Means (1989). *1989 Green Book: Background Material and Data on Programs Within the Jurisdiction of the Committee on Ways and Means*, Washington D.C., Government Printing Office.

Van Doorslaer, E. (1987). *Health, knowledge and the demand for medical care:*

an econometric analysis. Wolfeboro, New Hampshire and Van Gorcum, Maastricht/Assen.

Van Doorslaer, E. and Wagstaff, A. (1989). *Inequity in the delivery of health care in the Netherlands: Preliminary empirical results and guidelines for participants in the EC study on cost containment*. EC Cost Containment Project Working Paper, No. 3, June. University of Limburg, Maastricht.

Van Doorslaer, E. Van, Janssen, R., Wagstaff, A., Emmerik, J. Van, and Rutten, F. (1991). Equity in the finance of health care: effects of the Dutch health insurance reform. In *Incentives in health systems* (ed. G. Lopez-Casasnovas), pp. 153–168. Springer, Berlin.

Ven W. van de (1990). From regulated cartel to regulated competition in the Dutch health care system. *European Economic Review*, **34**, 632–45.

Ven, W. van de (1991). Perestrojka in the Dutch health care system; a demonstration project for other European countries. *European Economic Review*, **35**, 430–40.

Vliet, R. van and Ven, W. van de (1985). *Differences in medical consumption between publicly and privately insured in the Netherlands: standardization by means of multiple regression*. Paper presented to International Meeting on Health Econometrics of the Applied Econometrics Association, 16–17 December, Rotterdam.

Vogel, R. (1988). *Cost recovery in the health care sector, selected country studies in West Africa*. World Bank Technical Paper, No. 82. World Bank, Washington, D.C.

Volatier, J.L. (1990). *Modes de protection sociale*. March 1984. Credes, France.

Wagstaff, A. (1991). QALYs and the equity-efficiency trade-off. *Journal of Health Economics*, **10**, 21–41.

Wagstaff. A. and Doorslaer, E. Van (1989). *Measuring the progressivity of the Dutch health care financing system: preliminary empirical results and guideliness for participants in the EC study on cost containment*. EC Project Working Paper No. 4. University of Maastricht, Limburg.

Wagstaff, A., Doorslaer, E., Van, and Paci, P. (1989). Equity in the finance and delivery of health care: some tentative cross-country comparisons. *Oxford Review of Economic Policy*, **5**, 89–112.

Wagstaff, A., Paci, P., and Van Doorslaer, E. Van (1991 *a*). On the measurement of inequalities in health. *Social Science and Medicine*, **33**, 545–57.

Wagstaff, A., Van Doorslaer, E., Van, and Paci, P. (1991 *b*). On the measurement of horizontal equity in the delivery of health care. *Journal of Health Economics* **10**, 169–206.

Wagstaff, A., Van Doorslaer, E., Van, and Paci, P. (1991 *c*). Horizontal equity in the delivery of health care: a reply. *Journal of Health Economics*, **10**, 251–6.

Whelan, C.T., Hannan, D.F., and Creighton, S. (1990). *Unemployment, poverty and psychological distress*. The Economic and Social Research Institute, General Research Series Paper No. 150, Dublin.

Wiggins, D. (1987). *Needs, values, truth*, Basil Blackwell, Oxford.

Wiggins, D. and Dermen, S. (1987). Needs, need, needing. *Journal of Medical Ethics*, **13**, 63–8.

Wilkinson, R. (ed.) (1986). *Class and health*. London, Tavistock.

Wilkinson, R. (1989). Class mortality differentials, income distribution and trends in poverty 1921–1981. *Journal of Social Policy*, **18**, 307–35.

Williams, A.H. (1974) 'Need' as a demand concept (with special reference to health). In *Economic policies and social goals: Aspects of public choice* (ed. A.J. Culyer). Martin Robertson, London.

Williams, A.H. (1978). 'Need'—an economic exegesis. In *Economic aspects of health Services* (eds. A.J. Culyer and K.G. Wright). Martin Robertson, London.

Williams, A.H. (1981). Welfare economics and health status measurement. In J. van der Gaag and M. Perlman (ed.) Health, Economics and Health Economics, North-Holland, Amsterdam.

Williams, A.H. (1985). Economics of coronary artery bypass grafting. *British Medical Journal*, **291**, 326–9.

Williams, A. (1988). Priority setting in public and private health care: a guide through the ideological jungle. *Journal of Health Economics*, **7**, 173–83.

Winter, D. (1991). *A cohort analysis of chronic morbidity and unemployment in the General Household Survey.* London School of Economics, Welfare State Programme Discussion Paper JWSP/59, London.

WHO Regional Office for Europe (1985). *Targets for health for all 2000.* Copenhagen.

Woolhandler, S. and Himmelstein, D.U. (1988). Reverse targeting of preventive care due to lack of health insurance. *Journal of the American Medical Association*, **256**, 2872–4.

World Bank (1989). *Bolivia Country Economic Memorandum*, mimeo. The World Bank, Washington D.C.

World Bank (1990). *World Development Report*, Oxford University Press, New York.

World Bank (1991). *World development report.* Oxford University Press.

Wu, A.W. *et al.* (1991). Health status questionnaire using 30 items from the Medical Outcomes Study. *Medical Care*, **29**, 786–98.

Zweifel, P. (1983). Inflation in the health care sector and the demand for insurance: a micro study. In *Social Insurance* (ed. L. Söderström). North Holland, Amsterdam.

Index